The Multilingual Apple

The Multilingual Apple

Languages in New York City

Second edition
with a new foreword

Edited by
Ofelia García
Joshua A. Fishman

Mouton de Gruyter
Berlin · New York 2002

Mouton de Gruyter (formerly Mouton, The Hague)
is a Division of Walter de Gruyter & Co., Berlin

First edition published in 1997.

⊗ Printed on acid-free paper which falls within the guidelines of the ANSI to ensure permanence and durability.

Library of Congress Cataloging-in-Publication Data

The multilingual Apple : languages in New York City / edited by Ofelia García, Joshua A. Fishman. – 2nd ed. / with a new foreword.
p. cm.
Includes bibliographical references and index.
ISBN 3-11-017281-X (pbk. : alk. paper)
1. Linguistic minorities – New York (State) – New York. 2. Sociolinguistics – New York (State) – New York. 3. New York (N. Y.) – Languages. I. García, Ofelia. II. Fishman, Joshua A.
P40.5.L562U556 2002
306.44′09747′1–dc21
2001047667

Die Deutsche Bibliothek – Cataloging-in-Publication Data

The multilingual apple : languages in New York City / ed. by Ofelia García ; Joshua A. Fishman. – 2. ed. with a new foreword. – Berlin ; New York : Mouton de Gruyter, 2002
ISBN 3-11-017281-X

Disk conversion and printing: Arthur Collignon GmbH, Berlin. – Binding: Werner Hildebrand, Berlin. – Printed in Germany.

To all the multilingual people of New York City
– immigrants and natives –
who struggle in many languages
to enrich the Big Apple.

And to our Spanish-speaking and Yiddish-speaking
spouses, children, and grandchildren
who enrich our lives
with their love.

¡Me espanta la ciudad! Toda está llena
De copas por vaciar, o huecas copas.

I'm terrified of the city! It is all filled
with glasses not yet drunk, or with empty glasses.

José Martí, "Amor de Ciudad Grande",
New York, April 1882. From *Versos Libres*, 1882.

אונדזער גאָרטן

אַזאַ גאָרטן, וווּ דער בוים
האָט זיך זיבן בלעטער קוים.
און עס דאַכט זיך, אַז ער טראַכט:
־ווער האָט מיך אַהער געבראַכט?
אַזאַ גאָרטן, אַזאַ גאָרטן,
וווּ מיט אַ פֿאַרגרעסער־גלאָז
קאָן מען זען אַ ביסל גראָז.
זאָל דאָס אונדזער גאָרטן זײַן,
אָט אַזאַ אין מאָרגנשײַן?
אַוודאי אונדזער גאָרטן.
וואָס דען, ניט אונדזער גאָרטן?

משה־לייב האַלפּערין, „אונדזער גאָרטן“.
פֿון אין ניו־יאָרק (1919)

undzer gortn

aza gortn, vu der boym
hot zikh zibn bleter koym.
un es dakht zikh, az er trakht:
– ver hot mikh aher gebrakht?
aza gortn, aza gortn,
vu mit a fargreser-gloz
kon men zen a bisl groz.
zol dos undzer gortn zayn,
ot aza in morgnshayn?
avade undzer gortn.
vos den, nit undzer gortn?

Our Garden

What a garden, where the tree is
Bare but for its seven leaves!
It appears to be amazed:
"Who has set me in this place?"
What a garden, what a garden –
It takes a magnifying glass
Just to see a little grass.
Can this be our garden, then,
Just as is, in the light of dawn?
Sure, it's our garden.
What else? It's not our garden?

From Moyshe-Leyb Halpern, "Our Garden". From *In New York* (1919).

Foreword

Ofelia García and Joshua A. Fishman

This anniversary edition continues to tell the story in English of how Languages Other than English (LOTEs) have contributed to making New York City one of the most culturally vibrant and linguistically diverse metropolis in the world today.

The U. S. 2000 census has confirmed that the United States will be increasingly multilingual in the 21st century. The number of adults in the United States who speak a LOTE at home increased by 41 % in one decade, and those who report some difficulty with English increased by 40 %. As the 21st century starts, approximately 18 % of U. S. households speak a LOTE at home. In states like California, New Mexico, Texas, New York, Hawaii, Arizona and New Jersey, well over 25 % of the population live in households where a LOTE is spoken.

New York City's multilingualism in 2000 has been spurred by a level of immigration unequal since 1910, with one million immigrants arriving in the last decade of the 20th century. In 2000, 40 % of New Yorkers were foreign born, compared to 28 % in 1990. The greater diversity of national origins of New Yorkers who speak the same LOTE makes New York not only a multilingual city, but a true laboratory of dialectal heterogeneity. The city's largest group of LOTE speakers is still Spanish-speaking. But Puerto Ricans, in 1990 half of New York Latinos, now make up 36 % of New Yorkers, with the island-born population declining sharply. In 1999, there were 744,000 Puerto Ricans, of whom 290,000 were born in the island. This represents a 12 % decrease in one decade. At the same time, the number of Mexicans increased by 203 %, making Mexicans the third biggest single group of Spanish speaking New Yorkers after those of Puerto Rican and Dominican ancestry.

The greater diversity in national origins of Spanish speakers is also evident among Asians. The number of New Yorkers of Chinese origin did not rise as sharply as the number of New Yorkers of Bangladeshi, Pakistani and Indian descent. Whereas New Yorkers of Chinese descent increased by 51 %, those of Asian descent increased by 81 %. Pakistani Urdu speakers rank among the fastest-growing groups of immigrants.

And immigration from the former Soviet Union continues to increase, with Russian spoken often in the city, especially in areas of Brooklyn.

This book's introduction, written by García, provides more comprehensive quantitative and qualitative data to show that standard American English is not today, and has never been, the daily vernacular of most New Yorkers. García shows that when one takes into account the number of New Yorkers who speak Spanish, Chinese, Italian and a host of other languages, and then adds those New Yorkers who speak different varieties of English, the linguistic profile of New York begins to look quite different from what many casual observers might imagine. García also analyzes how LOTEs, as well as other dialects of English, have been used as important tools in the economic, social and poltical life of New York.

The chapters in sections II, III and IV are sociolinguistic studies of the languages of a variety of different ethnolinguistic groups, encompassing those whose LOTE voices, because they arrived early, have been somewhat silenced (Nilsen on Irish, Costello on German, Kliger and Peltz on Yiddish), those whose voices are still loudly heard today (Haller on Italian, Costantakos and Spiridakis on Greek, Zentella on Spanish, Schiff on Hebrew) and newer groups whose LOTEs are acquiring an important voice in the city (Pan on Chinese, Sridhar on the languages of India, Joseph on Haitian Creole, and Winer and Jack on Caribbean English Creole).

All these chapters include an analysis of the LOTEs' linguistic and usage characteristics in the country of origin of the ethnolinguistic group. The chapters look at how factors such as age, gender, religion, education, occupation, as well as geographical region or social setting have an effect on linguistic items in the LOTE, often resulting in distinct varieties that are differently valued and used.

The chapters then study the evolution of those LOTEs in New York City, and how the different sociopolitical environment and the contact with English have affected the linguistic characteristics of, and the attitude of the group toward, the LOTE. In particular, the chapters study how the social factors just mentioned, in combination with those that are relevant for ethnolinguistic groups in a new context, such as birth place, generation, race, and intermarriage, affect how the group uses the LOTE as well as English, and whether the group is maintaining the LOTE or shifting to English. The individual chapters also look at how LOTEs are being used in the city at large, beyond the ethnic home and community, in such public settings as government agencies, hospitals, schools, as well as in private business.

Fishmans conclusion calls the LOTEs of New Yorkers "the overlooked elephant at the zoo". It asks the important question regarding the reasons why U. S. social scientists and sociolinguists have ignored the presence of the LOTEs in our midst.

The chapters in this book provide important information on the sociolinguistic landscape of New York. They can be read by lay readers who want more information about their ancestry language and its contribution to life in the city. They will also be useful to economic and social planners who need more information about the lives of those who speak LOTEs and their communication network, both throughout history and today. New Yorkers involved in the delivery of services or goods to LOTE speaking groups, whether educators, health and social services providers, or business persons will also find the information in these chapters extremely beneficial.

Students and scholars of sociology of language and urban multilingualism will also be challenged by the extensive and differing treatment of language in these chapters. All contribute to our better understanding of the various languages of New York, but do so taking different perspectives, sometimes focusing on qualitative aspects (as in Kliger and Peltz on Yiddish), other times on more quantitative data (as in Haller for Italian).

In documenting the linguistic diversity of New Yorkers, the book does not ignore the significant question of whether these LOTEs are being maintained or whether shift to English is occurring. The chapters in this book attest to the unequivocal shift to English among all ethnolinguistic minorities, while suggesting that the bilingual stage among some post-1965 groups in the urban context may be surviving the traditional shift by the third generation.

Two major societal changes may be responsible for this situation. One, the U. S. economy has shown signs of slowing down, giving immigrant LOTE speakers less opportunities than it has in the past. Two, the Immigration Act of 1965 increased the number of immigrant LOTE speakers who were racially distinct, and therefore experience more overt segregation and exclusion than pre-1965 immigrants.

The speed with which the inexorable shift to English of ethnolinguistic minorities occurs will continue to depend upon the economic, political and education access that they have. Ironically, access to these opportunities will depend upon the degree that we're willing to use their LOTEs for the sophisticated societal participation that is required of U. S. citizens.

The editors of this anniversary edition continue to hope that this book will bring solace and information to ethnic New Yorkers who have lost their ancestral language, and recognition to those who still speak it. But beyond our hopes for intra-ethnic comfort and self-knowledge, we hope that the book will be able to build an improved forum for *inter-ethnic* communication, where all of us, whether speakers of Standard American English, a different variety of English, or LOTEs, work to make the city a better place in the future.

Our children and grandchildren will surely be better speakers of English than of LOTEs, but in the city, and in our extended world, they will continue to live side by side with many multilingual others. It is the hope of the editors that this book alleviate some of the ignorance and contempt in which we have held U. S. urban ethnolinguistic minorities, so that our children can inherit a more inclusive and compassionate city. And beyond compassion, perhaps we will gain some understanding of the value of bilingualism and LOTEs for Americans as individuals and for U. S. society in general.

Contents

IV. THE LANGUAGES WITH THE NEWEST SOUNDS AND OF NEWEST FACES

V. CONCLUDING OBSERVATIONS TO THE MULTILINGUAL APPLE

I INTRODUCTION TO THE MULTILINGUAL APPLE

New York's multilingualism: World languages and their role in a U. S. city[1]

Ofelia García

"On the island of Manhate, and in its environs, there may well be four or five hundred men of different sects and nations: The Director General told me that there were men of eighteen different languages." (Father Jogues of the Society of Jesus, 1646, quoted in Federal Writers' Project 1938b: 81)

"The city of New York is composed of inhabitants from all the countries of Christendom." (James Fenimore Cooper, 1827–1828, quoted in Rosenwaike 1972)

"The city is like poetry: it compresses all life, all races and breeds, into a small island .... The collision and the intermingling of these millions of foreign born people representing so many races and creeds make New York a permanent exhibit of the phenomenom of one world." (E. B. White, 1949. *Here is New York.* New York: Curtis Publication Company, Quoted in Klein, ed. 1955: 8).

"I do not know of a single European country ready or able to conceive of, much less deal with, the multinational mosaic I daily encounter in New York." (Gross 1990: 9)

1. *Introduction*

The citations above attest to the great ethnolinguistic diversity that has characterized New York City since the seventeenth century and does still today. Yet, despite this great and long-standing linguistic diversity there are no studies of the multilingualism of New York City. Scholars have paid well-deserved attention to the city's immigrants, its foreign-born population, its multiethnic character.[2] Other scholars have studied the city's economy and trade.[3] Linguists and sociolinguists have studied English in New York.[4] But little has been said about the city's multilingualism and the way in which Languages Other than English (LOTEs from now on) have always been used in city life.[5]

This paper documents, describes and analyzes New York's multilingualism, today and in the past, claiming for New York its rightful title as the most multilingual city in the world. Through anecdotes, census data and historical evidence, the long-standing presence of many LOTEs in the city is made evident, demonstrating that standard English has never been, and cannot be considered today, New York's vernacular.[6] The paper also documents the public use of LOTEs by New Yorkers in businesses and institutions today, as well as in the past, and the benefits accrued to all New Yorkers as a result. In this regard, we will see that there is a lack of fit between the official non-recognition of New York's multilingualism, the linguistic practices of its LOTE-speaking citizens, and the official multilingual policies that New York City has adopted for use in its agencies with non-English speaking clients in the last decade.

The paper starts by describing in detail New York's multilingualism as the 20th century comes to a close, drawing on anecdotal evidence, as well as census data. It then questions whether the multilingual situation of today is an historical anomaly, first by comparing it with the rest of the 20th century and then with our more remote past. The history of multilingualism in New York is provided within an interpretative language policy framework, analyzing not only the presence of LOTEs in New York, but also the government's response to them in relation to the city's socioeconomic and sociopolitical context. Finally, the paper looks at how LOTEs are being used in the city today, both by business and government, thus making apparent the city's implicit language policy.

2. *New York's multilingualism at the end of the 20th Century*

2.1. Is New York really multilingual? Some anecdotal evidence

Multilingualism is such a natural part of the life of New Yorkers that it takes visitors and foreigners to recognize it and validate it. A *New York Times* reporter, studying the changing immigration to New York in the 1980s, interviewed a Nigerian woman whose words summarize well New York's surprising multilingualism: "I came to New York so that I could learn English. What I got in my life is something else. I do not know where I am. Spain? China?" (Kleiman 1982). The visitor to New York City is perplexed by the vast presence of LOTEs in the city, a multilingualism that they have never read about, and one that they do not hear in the many movies portraying New York. Yet, New York's multilingualism is so extensive that some European sociolinguists (Gross 1990; Campbell 1994) have studied New York's language use in preparation for the multilingualism of the European Union. Gross (1990: 7) summarizes

New York's multilingualism by saying: "In linguistic terms it [New York] is arguably the most sophisticated area on the face of the world .... Thirty-six TV channels plus a hundred or more radio stations offer me an assortment of languages and cultures quite beyond the imagination of most Europeans."

To acknowledge New York's multilingualism, it would be important to reflect on some of the ways in which LOTEs are used by New Yorkers:

- New Yorkers can get married in any of twenty-two languages, since the city's chief marriage-maker has memorized the ceremony in all those languages and uses them frequently (Clines 1994).
- New Yorkers can hear Catholic Mass in twenty-seven different languages. Mass is said in Spanish in two hundred and four Catholic churches in the Archdiocese of New York and the Diocese of Brooklyn and Queens. Besides Spanish, Catholic Mass is said in Italian in sixty-six churches, in French in eighteen, in Polish in sixteen, in Haitian Creole in nine, and in Korean in six. There are less than five churches in the city which say Mass in these other LOTEs, given here in descending order as they appear in the Parish Service Bulletins for 1995: Chinese, Sign Language, German, Lithuanian, Czech-Slovak, Portuguese, Croatian, Filipino, Latin, Old Slavonic, Albanian, Arabic, Armenian, Greek, Hungarian, Rumanian, Russian, Slovenian, Ukrainian and Vietnamese.
- New Yorkers can follow a mayoral campaign in at least four LOTEs. For example, the 1993 race for mayor used four different LOTEs in campaign buttons: Spanish, Chinese, Russian and Haitian Creole (Purdum 1993).
- New Yorkers can receive interpretation services in as many as sixty-four languages in government agencies. A Language Bank Directory of government employees able to provide interpretation is available to all city agencies (See Section 5.2, this paper).
- New Yorkers can read twenty-nine daily newspapers in ten different LOTEs published in the city (See Table 10, this paper). This does not include the many LOTE newspapers readily available in the city that are published in other U. S. cities and even other countries.
- New Yorkers can watch television programs in as many as sixteen different languages (See Table 9, this paper).
- New Yorkers can listen to radio programs in forty-seven different languages. One station, WNWK-FM broadcasts in over twelve different languages (Howe 1992).

- When New Yorkers get into a taxicab, they're most likely to have an Urdu speaking driver. This was the finding of a 1992 survey by the NYC Taxi and Limousine Commission (Kandel 1992). The Commission also concluded that New York taxi drivers speak over sixty different languages and sometimes English is not one of them.
- New Yorkers involved in Court proceedings can get interpretation in forty-four different languages. Spanish is the language most requested for interpretation, but Spanish is followed by Chinese, then Russian, Korean, Arabic, Polish and then surprisingly Wolof (See Table 11, this paper).
- New York's school children can speak fifty different languages in a single school. This is the case of Intermediate School 237 in Queens (Jones 1994).
- Spanish-speaking New Yorkers are more numerous than Spanish-speakers of thirteen Latin American capitals. In 1990, 1,486,815 New Yorkers claimed to speak Spanish at home. This represents more Spanish speakers than those who live in Asunción, Guatemala, La Paz, Lima, Managua, Montevideo, Panamá, Quito, San José, San Juan, San Salvador, Santiago de Chile and Tegucigalpa.
- New Yorkers often learn a second LOTE before learning English as a second language. For example, Margolis (1994: 243–4) recounts her experience with Brazilian New Yorkers:

> I was amazed at the number of Brazilians who spoke a minimal amount of English but who had no problem communicating in Spanish. When I was interviewing one Brazilian in her apartment, the doorbell rang, and the visitor turned out to be a Spanish-speaking woman handing out pamphlets for the Jehovah's Witnesses. They had a brief discussion in Spanish .... This woman speaks almost no English after more than two years in New York but handles Spanish with ease. Parenthetically, her Brazilian husband, who has also learned Spanish since coming to New York, prepared for and received his First Communion in Spanish at a local Hispanic church.

That LOTEs are a way of life in New York City is attested by all the anecdotal evidence above. But what is the sociolinguistic profile of New Yorkers? What languages do they speak at home and what is their English language ability? The answers to these questions, derived from the 1990 census, are extremely important, especially for institutions of higher education which might have to adapt their English language expectations and their curriculum to fit the sociolinguistic profile of New Yorkers.

2.2. *Are New Yorkers really multilingual? Some evidence from the 1990 census*

The limitation of all census data is that it is based on self-report. Thus, the sociolinguistic profile of New Yorkers given in this section reveals only what New Yorkers say they do, rather than give us objective measures of their language use. Another shortcoming of this data is that the 1990 census seriously undercounted the language minority population, in particular the undocumented. Yet a third problem with this data is that the U. S. census has little historical experience with LOTE use, making trend comparisons difficult. Up to 1970, the census asked for the respondents' *mother tongue*; specifically it asked about the language spoken in the respondents' home in childhood. Since 1980, the census seeks information only about the *language used* by the respondent in the home. A final limitation is that the U. S. census has little familiarity with the linguistic diversity of Asian and African countries from which many immigrants have recently come. Thus, linguistic categories for these languages are often inaccurate.[7] Nevertheless, as we will see, the census is a rich source to answer the following four questions that together reveal a sociolinguistic profile of New Yorkers:

a. What are the household languages in New York City?
b. What are the different languages spoken by New Yorkers at home?
c. What is the English language ability of New Yorkers who use LOTEs at home?
d. Are New Yorkers maintaining their LOTEs or are they shifting to English? And what is the differential rate of maintenance or shift for the different LOTEs?

a. What are the household languages in New York City?
As shown in Table 1, almost one-half (46%) of households in New York speak a LOTE, and the other half (54%) speak English. In understanding the English spoken by this 54% at home, it is important to bear in mind that 25% of New Yorkers in 1990 were black, and thus New York English certainly includes both African American varieties of English, as well as varieties of Caribbean English (See Winer and Jack, this volume).[8] Standard English is definitely not the vernacular of the majority of New Yorkers.

It is also important to point out that almost a fourth of households in New York speak Spanish (24%), making Spanish a very important language for New Yorkers. In fact, English is spoken only by twice the number of households as Spanish.

Table 1
Household languages in 1990, NYC*

English Only	54%	
LOTE	46%	
Spanish		24%
Other Indo-Eurpn		15%
Asian or Pacific		5%
Other		2%

*** Source: 1990 Census of Population and Housing. Public Use Micro Data Sample.**

b. What are the different languages spoken by New Yorkers at home?
Table 2 displays the languages spoken by New Yorkers older than five years of age. Clearly LOTEs are widely spoken by New Yorkers at home, since only 3 out of 5 New Yorkers (61.92%) claim to use English at home.

This table again confirms that Spanish is the most important LOTE in the city, with one out of five New Yorkers (20.42%) claiming to speak Spanish at home. In fact, over half of those who speak LOTEs at home (53.63%), speak Spanish.

But New York is not only a bilingual city. As shown in Table 2, there are more than 1,000 speakers of fifty-two different languages, clearly making New York the most multilingual city in the United States and in any other developed country. Almost half of those who speak LOTEs (46.4%), speak LOTEs other than Spanish. In fact, seven other LOTEs besides Spanish are spoken by more than 50,000 New Yorkers: Chinese, Italian, French, Yiddish, Russian, Korean and Greek.

But how bilingual are New Yorkers who speak LOTEs at home? And does LOTE use at home respond to a communicative need? A surprising finding shown in Table 2, last column, is that New Yorkers who speak LOTEs at home do so by choice, rather than out of necessity, since over 50% of the speakers of all LOTEs also claim to have good English-speaking ability. In fact, even in the case of the ethnolinguistic group with the least English ability, the Cambodians, more than half of the group claim to speak English very well or well.

The different ethnolinguistic groups can be broken down into three categories according to their degree of bilingualism, given here in order of decreasing bilingualism:

- *Those that are highly bilingual: 100% to 90% proficient in English*
  Speakers of Dutch, Finnish, Danish, Sindhi, Sinhalese (all 100% bilingual)

Table 2
Languages at home in NYC, 1990*

LANGUAGE	Total Spks[a]	% Total Pop Spks this Lang.	% LOTE-Spks Spks this LOTE	Total SpKs this LOTE NOT Eng-Spk[b]	% Spks this LOTE NOT Eng-Spk
English	4,507,520	61.92%			
LOTE (All)	2,772,586	38.08%			
	7,280,106	100.00%			
SpecificLOTEs					
Spanish	1,486,815	20.42%	53.63%	397,380	26.7%
Chinese[c]	211,447	2.91%	7.81%	92,123	43.6%
Italian	202,538	2.78%	7.31%	31,486	15.6%
French	105,756	1.45%	3.81%	11,925	11.3%
Yiddish	93,529	1.28%	3.37%	8,532	9.1%
Russian	65,895	.91%	2.38%	24,406	37.0%
Korean	62,671	.86%	2.26%	26,259	41.9%
Greek	55,461	.76%	2.00%	9,793	17.7%
German	49,271	.68%	1.78%	2,033	4.1%
Polish	47,575	.65%	1.72%	12,230	25.7%
FrenchCreole	43,660	.60%	1.57%	8,222	18.8%
Hebrew	40,044	.56%	1.44%	1.964	4.9%
Hindi-Urdu	37,123	.51%	1.34%	5,017	13.5%
Filipino-Tagalog	35,094	.48%	1.27%	1,554	4.4%
Arabic	31,460	.43%	1.13%	4,028	12.8%
Portuguese	14,649	.20%	.53%	3,286	22.5%
Hungarian	14,464	.20%	.52%	2,217	15.3%
Japanese	13,277	.18%	.48%	2,889	21.8%
SerboCroatian	11,967	.16%	.43%	2,495	20.9%
Kru-Ibo-Yoruba	10,508	.14%	.38%	174	1.7%
Rumanian	10,424	.14%	.38%	1,967	18.9%
Bengali	10,405	.14%	.38%	1,248	12.0%
PersianFarsiDari	9,187	.13%	.33%	1,803	19.6%
Ukranian	7,489	.10%	.27%	875	11.7%
Gujarati	7,331	.10%	.26%	1,176	16.1%
Malayalam	7,200	.10%	.26%	803	11.2%
Vietnamese	5,948	.08%	.21%	2,098	35.3%
Albanian	5,791	.08%	.21%	1,137	19.6%
Turkish	5,544	.08%	.20%	767	13.8%
Armenian	5,223	.07%	.19%	757	14.5%
ThaiLaotn	4,608	.06%	.17%	894	19.4%
JamaicanCreole	4,490	.06%	.16%	248	5.5%
Croatian	4,207	.06%	.15%	592	14.1%
Patois	3,902	.05%	.14%	203	5.2%
IrishGaelic	3,715	.05%	.13%	130	3.5%
Punjabi	3,709	.05%	.13%	668	18.0%
Dutch	3,288	.05%	.12%	0	0.0%

(Continued next page)

Table 2 *(Continued)*
Languages at home in NYC, 1990*

LANGUAGE	Total Spks[a]	% Total Pop Spks this Lang.	% LOTE-Spks Spks this LOTE	Total SpKs this LOTE NOT Eng-Spk[b]	% Spks this LOTE NOT Eng-Spk
Czech	3,069	.04%	.11%	270	8.8%
Slovak	2,500	.03%	.09%	279	11.2%
Norwegian	2,361	.03%	.09%	62	2.6%
Swedish	2,010	.03%	.07%	47	2.3%
Tamil	1,773	.02%	.06%	75	4.2%
Telugu	1,769	.02%	.06%	126	7.1%
Mon-Khmer-Cambd	1,693	.02%	.06%	826	48.8%
AfricanNtSpc	1,625	.02%	.06%	0	0.0%
Lithuanian	1,483	.02%	.05%	78	5.3%
PashtoAfghan	1,171	.02%	.04%	330	28.2%
AmrcnIndian	1,043	.01%	.04%	163	15.6%
Indonesian	1,035	.01%	.04%	86	8.3%
Amharic	1,022	.01%	.04%	17	1.7%
Finnish	964	.01%	.03%	0	0.0%
Fulani	945	.01%	.03%	253	26.8%
Swahili	904	.01%	.03%	11	1.2%
Bulgarian	817	.01%	.03%	118	14.4%
Estonian	765	.01%	.03%	65	8.5%
Lettish (Latvian)	744	.01%	.03%	20	2.7%
Danish	725	.01%	.03%	0	0.0%
Malay	724	.01%	.03%	162	22.4%
BurmseTonkin	711	.01%	.03%	246	34.6%
Serbian	642	.01%	.02%	185	28.8%
Ladino	590	.01%	.02%	182	30.9%
Marathi	543	.01%	.02%	59	16.1%
Sindhi	543	.01%	.02%	0	0.0%
Sinhalese	428	.01%	.02%	0	0.0%
Mande	411	.01%	.01%	106	25.8%
BantuXhosZulu	394	.01%	.01%	19	4.8%
Nepali	368	.01%	.01%	107	29.1%
OtherLOTEs[d]	3,149	.07%	.11%	131	4.2%
TOTAL	2,772,586	38.08%	100.00%	667,402	

* **Source: 1990 Census of Population and Housing. Public Use Micro Data Sample.**

[a] Only those 5 years old and above are included.

[b] Represents those who answered Not Well or Not at All in English language ability.

[c] For this table we have summed up results that the Census breaks up into three categories: Chinese (Cantonese,Yueh, Min) with 206,515 claimants and 90,220 non-English proficient; Formosan (Nan, Min) with 3,351 claimants and 1,194 non-English proficient; and Mandarin (Hanan, Hopei, Pei) with 1,581 claimants and 709 non-English proficient.

[d] This category includes all LOTEs that received less than .01%.

Speakers of Swahili, Amharic, Kru-Ibo-Yoruba, Swedish, Norwegian, Lettish (Latvian), Irish, German, Tamil, Filipino, Bantu languages, Hebrew, Patois, Lithuanian, Jamaican Creole, Telugu, Indonesian, Estonian, Czech, Yiddish

- *Those that are very bilingual: 90% to 70% proficient in English*
  Speakers of Slovak, Malayalam, French, Ukrainian, Bengali, Arabic, Hindi-Urdu, Turkish, Croatian, Bulgarian, Armenian, Hungarian, Italian, Gujarati, Marathi, Greek, Punjabi, French Creole, Rumanian, Thai, Albanian, Persian, Serbo-Croatian, Japanese, Malay, Portuguese, Polish, Mande, Spanish, Fulani, Pashto, Serbian, Nepali, Ladino
- *Those that are least bilingual: 71% to 50% proficient in English*
  Speakers of Burmese, Vietnamese, Russian, Korean, Chinese, Mon-Khmer.

As we saw before, Spanish is the language of the home for many New Yorkers. But it is instructive to realize that Spanish-speaking New Yorkers are *not* the least English proficient group, with approximately three-fourths in their group claiming to speak English well. In absolute numbers, however, it is Spanish speakers who make up the bulk of non-English speaking New Yorkers, with 397,380 claiming to have limited English speaking ability. That is, 59% of the non-English speaking population speaks Spanish. The Spanish-speaking limited-English-proficient group is followed by Chinese speakers (92,123) who make up 14% of the limited-English-proficient population, and then Italian speakers (31,486) making up 5% of those who do not speak English well. Determining which ethnolinguistic group has limited proficiency in English might be an important consideration for agencies and institutions that need to provide services to these groups. It seems then, that in absolute numbers, the ten languages most needed in interpretation and translation are, in order of need: Spanish, then Chinese and then Italian, followed by Korean (26,259 speakers with little English speaking ability), Russian (24,406 speakers), Polish (12,230 speakers), French (11,925 speakers), Greek (9,793 speakers), Yiddish (8,532 speakers) and then French Creole[9] (8,222 speakers). It is instructive to realize that the need for French Creole may be greater than that revealed by census data, since many Haitians claim French as the language of the home, when Haitian Creole is truly the language spoken (see Joseph, this volume).

c. *What is the English language ability of New Yorkers who use LOTEs at home?*

Table 3 displays the overall results for the question on English speaking ability asked of those who claimed to use LOTEs at home. Three-fourths

Table 3
Ability to speak English of LOTE claimants in NYC*

English ability	No. of claimants	%
Very well	1,422,936	51%
Well	682,248	25%
Not Well	483,559	17%
Not at All	183,843	7%
TOTAL	2,772,586	100%

* **Source: 1990 Census of Population and Housing. Public Use Micro Data Sample.**

(76%) of New Yorkers who speak LOTEs at home are bilingual, claiming to speak English either very well (51%) or well (25%). This is an important finding since it confirms that most New Yorkers who speak LOTEs at home choose to do so, even when English is an option, given their language proficiency. In fact, only 7% of those who speak LOTEs at home are LOTE monolinguals, indicating that LOTE-speaking New Yorkers are, for the most part, bilingual.

d. Are New Yorkers maintaining their LOTEs or are they shifting to English? And what is the differential rate of maintenance or shift for the different LOTEs?

The multilingualism of New Yorkers is obvious from the above census data. Yet, it is important to consider whether New Yorkers' multilingualism is a transitional phenomenom, as it is in other places in the United States, or whether New Yorkers' multilingualism is more stable. Table 4 attempts to answer this very important question by trying to determine the percentage of native born New Yorkers who still speak their LOTE at home, since intergenerational transmission depends upon LOTE use at home especially by the mother (Fishman 1966).

As shown in Table 4, the most important ancestry group of New Yorkers is the Latino one, with Puerto Ricans constituting 50% of the Latino ancestry. Latinos are followed by those of Italian ancestry, and then Irish, German, West Indian (not shown in Table), Russian-Ukrainian, Polish, Chinese, Asian Indian, Greek, Hungarian and Korean. Some groups are heavily foreign born, especially the Koreans (82% foreign born), followed by the Chinese (73% foreign born), Latinos (61% foreign born), Asian Indians (45% foreign born) and the Greeks (38% foreign born). Some groups are heavily native born, with the Irish having only 6% foreign born, followed by the Germans (only 9% foreign born), the Italians (12% foreign born), and the Hungarians (19% foreign born).

Table 4
Rate of language maintenance of ethnolinguistic groups in NYC*

Ancestry	TotalPop	FB	NB	%FB	LOTEUse	NBLOTE Use [a]	LOTEMnt %NB [b]
Latino[c]	1,724,812	1,055,271[d]	669,541	61%	1,486,815	431,544	64%
Italian	838,780	101,651	737,129	12%	202,538	100,887	14%
Irish	535,846	30,541	505,305	6%	3,715	−26,826	–
German	395,230	33,947	361,283	9%	49,271	−15,324	–
RussUkr[e]	330,797	80,333	250,462	24%	73,384	−6,949	–
Polish	296,809	61,634	235,175	21%	47,575	−14,059	–
Chinese	238,919	173,512	65,407	73%	211,447	37,935	58%
A. Indian	94,590	42,764	51,826	45%	69,447	26,683	51%
Greek	82,690	31,792	50,898	38%	55,461	23,669	47%
Hungarian	75,721	14,051	61,670	19%	14,464	413	1%
Korean	69,718	57,488	12,230	82%	62,671	5,183	42%

* **Source: Selected Social Characteristics. 1980 and 1990 Summary Tape Files 3 and 4. 1990 Census of Population and Housing. Public Use Micro Data Sample. From Department of City Planning 1993. *Socioeconomic Profiles. A Portrait of New York City's community Districts from the 1980 and 1990 Censuses of Population Housing.***

[a] NB LOTE Use has been calculated by subtracting the total foreign born population from the total LOTE Use. An assumption has been made that the foreign born population speaks LOTE at home.

[b] LOTE Maintenance has been calculated by dividing the number of the NB LOTE Use by the number of native born population.

[c] Latinos include the following categories, given here in order of frequency: Puerto Ricans 851,291; Dominicans 328,634; Colombians 85,975; Ecuadorians 76,144; Cubans 58,381; Mexicans 57,298; Salvadorans 25,030; Peruvians 23,798; Panamanians, 21,929; Spaniards 20,210; Hondurans 20,154; Guatemalans 15,765; Argentineans 13,934; Nicaraguans 9,660; Costa Ricans 6,920; Chileans 6,721; Venezuelans 4,172; Bolivians 3,465; Uruguayans 3,233; Paraguayans 1,380; other South Americans 912; other Central Americans 452; others 89,354.

[d] This figure includes Puerto Ricans born in the island.

[e] The fifth ancestry group in New York is West Indian. It is not included here because language maintenance of English Creole cannot be arrived at through census figures.

That foreign born New Yorkers, even if bilingual, should speak LOTEs at home is not surprising. But what are native born New Yorkers doing? Given the linguistic heterogeneity in the city, are native born New Yorkers of different ancestries using LOTEs at home or are they using English? The answer to this question is important in understanding New Yorkers' multilingualism, for it allows us to examine whether New York is different from other places in the United States where shift to English among immigrant populations is completed by the third generation (Fishman 1966, 1972). Paulston (1994: 9) has said that "[E]thnic groups within a modern nation-state, given opportunity and incentive, typically shift to the language of the dominant group." Do ethnic New Yorkers fit within this generalization? And do all ethnolinguistic groups behave similarly?

Table 4 shows that all groups are experiencing shift to English, but at differing rates. The rate of shift to English is proceeding at extremely rapid rates among Poles, Russians and Germans. Even first generation immigrants of these three groups are using English at home (as shown by the minus signs in the last column), revealing a faster rate of shift to English than what has been historically expected, since second generation Polish, Russian and German New Yorkers can then be expected to be English monolinguals. The historical pattern of English language shift by the third generation is also very evident in the case of Hungarians and Italians. Only 1% of native born Hungarians and 14% of native born Italians speak their LOTE at home, guaranteeing the shift to English of the entire group by the third generation.

Koreans and Greeks have a somewhat slower rate of English language shift than do Hungarians and Italians, with 42% of the native born Korean population and 47% of the US born Greeks claiming to speak their LOTE at home. Because less than half of native born Koreans and Greeks are able to transmit their LOTE to their children, it is likely that English language shift will occur by the third generation, although it is also possible that some will remain bilingual.

A slower rate of English language shift than that which has been historically expected is being experienced especially by Latinos, Chinese and Asian Indians. Over half of the native born second generation Latinos, Chinese and Asian Indians use their LOTE at home, making it more likely that their bilingualism will persist longer.

A word of caution is necessary so the reader does not interpret this to mean that the bilingualism of Latinos, Chinese and Asian Indians in New York is stable and not transitory (see chapters by Zentella, Pan and Sridhar, this volume). What these results imply is that despite the use of English at home of almost half the population of native born Latinos, Chinese and Asian Indians, the use of the LOTEs by the majority of the native born in these groups will guarantee a longer period of bilingualism spanning the second and third generation.

A number of social factors seem to support the slower shift to English of these three groups. On the one hand, these three groups are among the four with a larger foreign born population, allowing for the use of

LOTEs to communicate intraethnically with those who have recently arrived and who may not be English proficient. These three groups are also among the four that are racially distinct and thus may suffer social segregation and economic exploitation in the city. It is instructive to understand why the fourth group which shares with these three groups the social characteristics of having a large foreign born population and being racially distinct, the Koreans, does not fit the same pattern of language maintenance. Korean New Yorkers, many of middle-class socioeconomic status, have been able to form ethnic enclaves which support their economic activity (Kim 1981), enabling them to escape the social stigmatization to which Latinos and Chinese have been subjected.

Despite the more stable presence of Spanish and Chinese in New York, these LOTEs have received little recognition as mainstream resources, as we will see in the last section of this paper. For example, only in the ethnic markets of New York's segregated neighborhoods are Spanish and Chinese valuable economic resources of the ethnic community (García – Otheguy 1994). Spanish and Chinese remain important instruments of communication only in the ethnic community, with little value assigned to it in mainstream institutions, except to communicate with those who do not speak English.

In sum, the sociolinguistic profile of New Yorkers confirms their pervasive bilingualism, with LOTEs competing with English in the home. But all ethnolinguistic groups are experiencing shift to English by the third generation, with Latinos, Chinese and Asian Indians showing a more moderate rate of shift.

3. New York's multilingualism throughout the 20th century

3.1. Is the multilingualism of today different from that of the rest of the century?

An important question for language planners in New York City is to determine whether the multilingual situation of today is different from that of the rest of the 20th century. Should we be alarmed by New York's multilingualism today? How different is the sociolinguistic profile of New Yorkers today from that of the recent past?

Again we turn to census data to help us answer this question. Table 5 compares the results of the 1980 census for LOTE use at home with those of the 1990 census given previously as Table 2. As we said before, the 1980 census was the first to ask for LOTE use rather than Mother

Table 5
LOTES at home in NYC, 1990 and 1980*

	1990	1990	1980	1980
LANGUAGE	Total SpksLOTE	% Pop SpksLOTE	Total SpksLOTE	% Pop SpksLOTE
English	4,507,520	61.92%	4,667,960	65.8%
LOTE (All)	2,772,586	38.08%	2,424,240	34.2%
	7,280,106	100.00%	7,092,200	100.00%
SpecificLOTEs				
Spanish	1,486,815	20.4%	1,260,040	17.8%
Chinese[a]	211,447	2.9%	112,800	1.6%
Italian	202,538	2.8%	289,660	4.1%
French	105,756	1.5%	101,660	1.4%
Yiddish	93,529	1.3%	133,820	1.9%
Russian	65,895	.9%	40,800	.6%
Korean	62,671	.9%	21,340	.3%
Greek	55,461	.8%	70,980	1.0%
German	49,271	.7%	73,500	1.0%
Polish	47,575	.7%	43,860	.6%
FrenchCreole	43,660	.6%	6,160	.1%
Hebrew	40,044	.6%	30,980	.4%
Hindi-Urdu	37,123	.5%	15,500[b]	.2%
Filipino-Tagalog	35,094	.5%	18,860	.3%
Arabic	31,460	.4%	17,580	.2%
Portuguese	14,649	.2%	9,320	.1%
Hungarian	14,464	.2%	22,640	.3%
Japanese	13,277	.2%	11,300	.2%
SerboCroatian	11,967	.2%	15,900	.2%
Kru-Ibo-Yoruba	10,508	.1%	3,880	.1%
Rumanian	10,424	.1%	6,760	.1%
Bengali	10,405	.1%		
PersianFarsiDari	9,187	.1%	5,280	.1%
Ukranian	7,489	.1%	9,960	.1%
Gujarati	7,331	.1%		
Malayalam	7,200	.1%		
Vietnamese	5,948	.1%	1,800	.1%
Albanian	5,791	.1%	3,580	.1%
Turkish	5,544	.1%	4.980	.1%
Armenian	5,223	.1%	6,940	.1%
ThaiLaotn	4,608	.1%	3,080	.0%
JamaicanCreole	4,490	.1%	1,080	.0%
Croatian	4,207	.1%	3,440	.0%
Patois	3,902	.1%	660	.0%
IrishGaelic	3,715	.1%	2,920	.0%
Punjabi	3,709	.1%		
Czech	3,069	.04%	6,100	.1%
Norwegian	2,361	.03%	5,580	.1%

(For notes, see p. 17)

Tongue, and thus results prior to 1980 are not comparable. But even in a decade, we can discern some differences in the sociolinguistic profile of New Yorkers.

From 1980 to 1990 both our multilingualism and our linguistic heterogeneity have increased, although not remarkably. The number of New Yorkers who speak English at home today remains similar to that in 1980. What seems to be different is the origin and racial composition of those who are LOTE speakers today, and also the way in which language minorities view themselves. For example, whereas in 1980 all Hindi Related languages accounted for only .2%, in 1990 Hindi/Urdu alone accounted for .5%, with four more East Indian languages accounting for .1% each: Bengali, Gujarati, Malayalam and Punjabi. Because of greater linguistic consciousness, in 1990 claimants of Jamaican Creole and Patois grew by more than four times.

With the exception of Russian, Polish, Rumanian, Albanian and Irish, the languages of Europe (Italian, Yiddish, Greek, German, Hungarian, and Serbo-Croatian) show a decline in 1990. In 1980 Italian was the second most used LOTE at home, but in 1990 Italian moved to third place, with Chinese becoming the second most used LOTE. Although Spanish, French and Portuguese have experienced increases, the speakers of these languages have been, for the most part, Latin Americans, coming from South and Central America and the islands of the Caribbean, or Africans.

French Creole has experienced great growth, but this is a result of greater linguistic consciousness among Haitians, claiming now Haitian Creole rather than French, instead of an actual increase. Beyond Haitian Creole, the greatest increase has been experienced by Korean, Kru-Ibo-Yoruba and Vietnamese, tripling in use, followed by Hindi-Urdu, Chinese, Filipino, Arabic, Persian, all doubling in use.

The differences in the sociolinguistic profile of New Yorkers reflect the heterogeneity of the origin of the LOTE speaking population, increasingly from Asia and the Caribbean. Whereas in 1970, Asian and Pacific

---

*** Source: 1990 and 1980 Census of Population and Housing. Public Use Micro Data Sample. Only LOTEs that account for over .1% in 1990 or 1980 are here included.**

[a] For this table we have summed up results that the Census breaks up into three different categories: In 1990 Chinese (Cantonese, Yueh, Min) had 206,515 claimants, Formosan (Min Nan) 3,351 claimants, and Mandarin(Honan, Hopei, Pei) 1,581 claimants. In 1980 Chinese (Cantonese, Yue, Yueh, Min) had 111,980 claimants; Formosan (Ch'ao Shan, Min Nan, Taiwanese) 740 claimants, and Mandarin (Honan, Hopei, Pei) 80 claimants.

[b] Includes the category "Hindi Related Languages".

Origin New Yorkers accounted for only 1.0% of the population, in 1980 they represented 3.4%. By 1990 the Asian and Pacific population in New York represented 6.7% of the population. The Hispanic Origin population has also grown, representing 15% in 1970, 19% in 1980, and 24% in 1990.

Throughout the 20th century, bilingualism has been an important part of the sociolinguistic profile of New Yorkers. Although trend comparisons in LOTE Home use are impossible to make, an analysis of the foreign born population of New York throughout the 20th century, given here as Table 6, confirms New Yorkers' bilingualism.

Table 6
Foreign-born persons as percent of the total population of New York City, 1910–1990*

Year	Total pop	Foreignborn	% Foreignborn
1910	4,767,000	1,944,400	40.8%
1920	5,620,000	2,028,200	36.1%
1930	6,930,000	2,358,700	34.0%
1940	7,455,000	2,138,700	28.7%
1950	7,892,000	1,861,000	23.6%
1960	7,782,000	1,559,000	20.0%
1970	7,895,000	1,437,000	18.2%
1980	7,092,000	1,675,000	23.6%
1990	7,322,564	2,082,931	28.4%

* **Source: A composite of information taken from Bogen (1987) Table 3.1, Youssef (1992) Table 2.1.**

Although 28% of New Yorkers in 1990 were foreign born, this in itself is nothing new. Indeed, the proportion of foreign born New Yorkers in 1990 is less than that of the first four decades of the 20th century. Except for the 1970 census, foreign born New Yorkers have always represented more than one fifth of the population.

Puerto Ricans born in the island are not counted as foreign born since they're U. S. citizens. One can then argue that the proportion of non-native New Yorkers in 1950, 1960 and 1970 would have been higher if the Puerto Rican migration, prevalent during those three decades, would have been counted. There is thus nothing unusual about New Yorkers at the end of the 20th century. New York has always been, and continues to be, a city mostly populated by newly arrived immigrants and migrants, eager to benefit from the greater economic incentives of a huge metropolis.

Nevertheless, it is important to realize that New Yorkers who are in positions of influence today may remember a New York with less public linguistic heterogeneity than that of today. But these mature native New Yorkers must understand that the ethnolinguistic composition of the New York they remember in the 1960s and 1970s was highly unusual, and was not a reflection of the rest of the century.

3.2. What is the real difference between today and yesterday? And given the difference, are there any policy implications for institutions of higher education?

The big difference between today and the past is not the sociolinguistic profile of New Yorkers, but the socio-educational changes that have been brought about by a highly technological society. As recently as 1970, adult immigrants had few educational and social opportunities. For example, it was only the children of immigrants who were welcomed in the city's public colleges. But the social change brought about through the greater economic prosperity and the greater social and racial tolerance of the 1960s opened the doors of institutions of higher education to immigrants themselves.

Increased access to colleges and work places meant that the sociolinguistic profile of New Yorkers who were now included in institutions and businesses changed. Yet, institutions of higher education were unable to make the changes in curriculum, pedagogy, and assessment that would have been necessary. Students who failed to meet the sociolinguistic expectation of native English language proficiency were relegated to the remedial track that was created.

If New Yorkers were serious about educating immigrants, they would need to teach them in much the same way they educate foreigners in overseas programs, with native English language proficiency being one more by-product, and not a pre-requisite, of a college education. Challenging academic courses would be opened to all, with instructors willing to contextualize language and to scaffold their instruction to accommodate for different English language skills. New York institutions of higher education might have to model their curriculum, practices, and assessment in what is done in most countries in the world, where higher education, especially in the scientific and technological fields, is in English, a second language for students. Given New York's sociolinguistic profile, there is no other appropriate educational choice for institutions of higher education if all New Yorkers are to be educated.

4. *New York's multilingualism throughout history. Is the sociolinguistic profile of New Yorkers different today from that of the past?*

New York's multilingualism today is a result of the legacy of the Dutch of New Amsterdam whose interest in trade and their tradition of religious tolerance encouraged people from all over Europe to settle in what today is New York City. And so, even today, it is precisely the economic competitiveness of New York, together with the greater tolerance toward linguistic, cultural and racial differences that New Yorkers exhibit, which attracts citizens from all over the globe to become New Yorkers.

This section traces New York's multilingualism from its earliest history through quotes and anecdotal evidence contained in historical sources, and census data when available. The historical evidence of New York's multilingualism is here organized into four different historical periods, each representing a distinct government response to the presence of LOTEs, motivated mostly by socioeconomic and sociopolitical concerns. Organizing the historical evidence in this way leads us to identify four different language policies held in the city:

I.	A Policy of Promotion of LOTEs	17C–1880
II.	A Policy of Tolerance of LOTEs	1880–1920
III.	A Policy of Restriction of LOTEs	1920–1950
IV.	A Policy of Tolerance of LOTEs	1960–1990s

4.1. *A policy of LOTE Promotion: 17C – 1880. Encouragement of trade and of religious differences*

What evidence do we have of linguistic heterogeneity in New Amsterdam? As early as 1628, the Reverend Jonas Jansen Michielse had found Walloons and Frenchmen among the fifty communicants in the Dutch Reformed Church (Rosenwaike 1972: 4). And, as seen in the first quote which precedes this paper, by 1646 eighteen different languages had been identified in the island of Manhattan by Father Jogues. Describing these early New Yorkers, Charles M. Andrews writes in 1664: "Racially these people were of great variety, Dutch, Walloons, French, English, Portuguese, and after 1655, Swedes and Finns. There were a few Jews, and many Negroes from Brazil and elsewhere" (Federal Writers' Project, 1938b: 88).

Does multilingualism disappear with English rule in 1664? There's evidence that after 1664, the heterogeneity in language, ethnicity and religion actually increased. In 1692 Charles Lodwich complained of this heterogeneity: "Our chiefest unhappyness here is too great a mixture of Nations, and English ye least part" (Still 1956: 21).

The 18th century saw the decline of Dutch influence. By 1703 less than 50% of heads of family were Dutch (Hansen 1931: 364, quoted in Rosenwaike 1972: 10). A French visitor in 1765 described the Dutch language decline: "There are still two Churches in which religious worship is performed in the Dutch language but the number that talk it Diminishes Daily" (Still 1956: 22). Besides these two Dutch churches, there were three churches that had services in English: an Anglican Church, a Presbyterian and a Quaker one, two with services in German (a German Lutheran and a German Reformed Faith), one in French (a French Huguenot Church), and a Jewish Synagogue (Still 1956: 23). By 1790 only 1/6 of the white population of New York was Dutch, another 1/6 was Irish, and 1/10 was German.

How was multilingualism affected by the commercial expansion of New York during the late 18th and especially the early 19th century? New York was built as a major commercial center by powerful and wealthy people of different ethnicity and language backgrounds. For example, the charter members of the New York Chamber of Commerce in 1786 included a French Huguenot, a Scot, two Irishmen, an Englishman, as well as two native born New Yorkers of Dutch origin and four of English origin (Federal Writers' Project 1938b: 81). New York established itself as the center of international trade especially after the construction of the Erie Canal in 1825.

During this time, English gained mostly in economic power. Commenting on the great diversity of the people of New York, a visitor in 1794 said: "[S]ince the wealthier elements are English, the whole feeling and behavior of the town seems to be English" (Rosenwaike 1972: 19). Although the New Englanders and the Knickerbockers, New Yorkers whose ancestors had settled in the city in the colonial period, formed the governing classes in the early 19th century, there were more people of Irish and German than of English parentage in New York during this entire period (Rosenwaike 1972: 35).

Dwight, who prepared a list of New Yorkers on the eve of the War of 1812, could not describe a "typical" New Yorker: "Among so many sorts of persons, you will easily believe it must be difficult, if not impossible, to find a common character; since the various immigrants themselves, and to some extent their children, will retain the features derived from their origin and their education" (Quoted in Rosenwaike 1972: 23). Levasseur, secretary to General Lafayette during his travels in the United States declared in 1824: "Of all the cities in the United States, New York is certainly the one in which society has lost most of the national character. The great number of foreigners which incessantly flow into it, is a continually operating cause" (Levasseur 1829: 125. Quoted in Rosenwaike 1972: 35).

In a work of nonfiction, James Fenimore Cooper (1827–1828) describes New York's heterogeneity:

> The city of New York is composed of inhabitants from all the countries of Christendom. ... It is computed that one in three are natives of New England, or are descendants of those who have emigrated from that portion of the country. To these must be added the successors of the Dutch, the English, the French, the Scotch and the Irish, and not a few who came in their proper persons from the countries occupied by these several nations. In the midst of such a melange of customs and people, it is exceedingly difficult to extract anything like a definite general character (In *Notions of the Americans*, p. 135, quoted in Rosenwaike 1972: 34).

The 1830 census counted 108,000 foreign-born persons in the United States. New York City, with 17,773, had four times more foreign-born residents than Philadelphia (4,184 in the city and county) and five times more than Boston (3,468) (Rosenwaike 1972: 35). Francis Lieber in 1835 refers to: "English, German, French and Spanish, which, with the addition of Italian, you may hear almost any day, in Broadway at the hours when it is most frequented" (Ernst 1949: 23).

The foreign born were not only poor immigrants, but included many of the intellectual and political elite of other countries. For example, as early as 1830 three Spanish-language journals were published in New York for the benefit of Latin American revolutionaries and merchants who lived in the city: *El Redactor*, *El Mercurio de Nueva York* and *Mensajero Semanal* (Ernst 1949: 157). It was also intellectual elite who in 1827 started the French language paper now called *France Amérique* (Leeds 1991: 10).

Italian revolutionary leaders also came to New York City after the unsuccessful Italian uprisings of 1820, 1821, 1830 and 1848 against Austrian rule. Among these was Giuseppe Garibaldi, leader of Italy's revolutionary forces. Italian cultural activity in New York had started in 1806 with the arrival of Lorenzo Da Ponte, famous as librettist of Mozart's operas and first professor of Italian at Columbia University (Federal Writers' Project 1938a: 94). The leader of the 1848 Magyar revolution, Louis Kossuth, also spent his exile in New York, spreading the message of a free Hungary against the Hapsburg Empire (Leeds 1991: 56).

German intellectuals and freethinkers, including Franz Lieber, professor of international law at Columbia University, and Carl Schurz, editor of *The New York Evening Post*, lived in New York as political refugees after the defeat of the German revolution in 1848.

Most of the two million Irish who left their homeland after the Potato Famine of 1846–1847 came to New York (Federal Writers' Project 1938b: 102). During this period, more than 70% of immigrants to the United States settled in the city (Dinnerstein – Reimers 1988).

The 1845 U. S. Census, the first to ascertain birthplace, noted that 36% of New Yorkers were foreign born. The New York foreign born population was estimated to be approximately 52% from Ireland, 22% from other areas of British sovereignty, 19% from German states, 3% from France, 3% from other European countries and 1% from Mexico or South America (Derived from Rosenwaike 1972: 40).

The 1870 census, the first to ask parentage, determined that almost 83% of New Yorkers had at least one foreign born parent, and by 1900 this percentage remained almost the same (84%) (Rosenwaike 1972: 71, 91). In 1870 New York continued to be the U. S. city with the greatest concentration of Irish, Germans and English. This in itself distinguished New York from other United States cities, where those of third generation or later American stock predominated (Rosenwaike 1972: 110).

But was the New York of the mid-19th century simply multiethnic and not multilingual? To answer this question we must look at the sociolinguistic profile of both the Irish and the Germans during this important historical period.

The use of Irish Gaelic by Irish New Yorkers has been well documented by Nilsen (this volume). Suffice it here to say that approximately 28% of the Potato Famine immigration were Irish speakers and that there were as many speakers of Irish Gaelic in Brooklyn as there were in Cork City. A most important sociolinguistic role that New York has had includes being the promoter and protector of LOTEs that have been oppressed in the country of origin. This was indeed the role that New York played with regards to Irish Gaelic, with an Irish language column appearing in a New York Irish newspaper in 1857 before it was done in Ireland. It was also in New York where the first society for the preservation of the Irish language was founded in 1873, three years before the Dublin society was established (Nilsen, this volume).

During the same period, German was used broadly in the city. Speaking of the lives of Germans in the New York City of the 1850s in a way that is reminiscent of what many say of New York Latinos today, Karl

Theodore Griesinger, a German who was exiled in New York between 1852 and 1857 writes:

> Life in Kleindeutschland is almost the same as in the Old Country .... There is not a single business which is not run by Germans. Not only the shoemakers, tailors, barbers, physicians, grocers, and innkeepers are German, but the pastors and priests as well. There is even a German lending library where one can get all kinds of German books. The resident of Kleindeutschland *need not even know English in order to make a living* (Still 1956: 162. My emphasis).

Germans speakers complained of harassment in government agencies. Ernst (1949: 175) tells us: "As a result, the Germans demanded bilingual keepers of almshouses, hospitals, and dispensaries, German interpreters in the courts, and the publication of city ordinances in the German newspapers." Clearly, German was used not only in the ethnic community, but throughout the city to do business whether of an economic or social nature with German speakers.

It is clear from the above evidence that New York's multilingualism was promoted from its earliest history to the end of the 19th century, as a means to encourage trade. But a change of immigration starting in 1880, along with an increasingly shrinking economy, and the experience of the First World War, brought about changes in attitudes toward newcomers, played out many times, as objections to the use of LOTEs in society. In the midst of increasing multilingualism, our language policy changed from promotion to just plain tolerance.

4.2. A policy of LOTE tolerance: 1880–1920. Italians, Jews, and a shrinking economy

The New York of the late 19th century was extremely multilingual, as attested by Moss (1897) when describing the Lower East Side:

> Within these narrow limits we have people from every quarter of the globe – Americans, Irish, Germans, Italians, French, Hungarians, Englishmen, Chinamen, and a dozen other nationalities. ... On Greenwich Street we will see immigrants' boarding-houses which will bring us in touch with every nation of Europe. ... Signs in Syrian, Turkish and Arabian characters may be seen, and frequently the anglicized names of the store-keepers may be read on the sign-boards and window-panes in our own language (Moss 1897, Vol. III: 161, 269).

A taste of the restriction that was to come was felt in 1882 when the Chinese Exclusion Act was passed, legislation that had little effect in New York City, but that reflected the attitude of the country at large toward ethnolinguistic groups who were not only linguistically and culturally, but also racially, different.

The great influx of immigrants in the late 20th century was precisely of Italians and Eastern Europeans, mostly Jews, who were not only linguistically and culturally different, but who were seen as racially distinct. At first, tolerance was exhibited. Table 7 shows the 26 countries from which immigrants came between 1892 and 1924 and who were processed at the federally financed facility at Ellis Island. One third of the immigrants who passed through Ellis Island reported New York City as their final destination.

Table 7
Countries of origin of immigrants entering Ellis Island, 1892–1924*

Country	No. of Immigrants
Italy	2,502,310
Austria-Hungary	2,275,852
Russia	1,893,542
Germany	633,148
England	551,969
Ireland	520,904
Sweden	348,036
Greece	245,058
Norway	226,278
OttomanEmpire	212,825
Scotland	191,023
WestIndies	171,774
PolishRepublics	153,444
Portugal	120,725
France	109,687
Denmark	99,414
Roumania	79,092
Netherlands	78,602
Spain	72,636
Belgium	63,141
Czechslovakia	48,140
Bulgaria(1901–31)	42,085
Wales	27,113
Yugoslavia	25,017
Finland	7,833
Switzerland	1,103

* **Source:** ***Annual Reports of the Commissioner General of Immigration, 1892–1924.*** **Washington, D. C.**

A December 1912 Report by the Commissioner of Immigration at Ellis Island, William Williams, confirms the heavy reliance on LOTEs to work:

> Not one of the least difficult features of Ellis Island work is that *much of it must be done through a great number of foreign languages*. The service of interpreters are required who read, write and speak the following languages or dialects : Albanian, Armenian, Bohemian, Bulgarian, Croatian, Dalmatian, Danish, Dutch, Finnish, Flemish, French, German, Greek, Italian, Lithuanian, Magyar, Montenegrin, Norwegian, Persian, Polish, Portuguese, Rumanian, Russian, Ruthenian, Servian, Slovak, Slovenian, Spanish, Swedish, Syrian, Turkish, Yiddish (pp. 26–27) (My emphasis).

The same report quotes the following rule for the Registry Division:

> No inspector shall attempt to inspect an alien with whom he cannot converse either personally or through an interpreter (p. 2).

The Railroad room at Ellis has been described as a place in which "linguists worked the floors separating the aliens into groups ... and where [e]ach ticket seller had to have a number of languages at his command in order to ask an alien where he or she was going" (Corsi 1935, in Botkin 1956: 199). Missionaries at Ellis also served as interpreters and distributed Bibles and other literature in as many as twenty-eight LOTEs.

The linguistic diversity of the city during this time was considerable, since there were great linguistic differences among Italians and Jews. The great linguistic heterogeneity of Italians was captured by Fiorello La Guardia (1961: 65), mayor of New York from 1934 to 1946 and interpreter at Ellis Island, in this instance of miscommunication with a girl from northern Italy: "No one understood her particular dialect very well, and because of hesitancy in replying to questions she did not understand, she was sent to the hospital for observation. ..."

The linguistic heterogeneity of Jews is made evident in the following quote: "Jews of New York come from nearly every country under the sun, talk fluently in nearly every known tongue and dialect, and mentally reveal the imprint of an infinite variety of cultures" (Federal Writers' Project 1938b: 126). Of the Lower East Side, where many Jews settled, Roskolenko (1971) says: "The Lower East Side was a small nation unto itself .... The signs on the stores were mostly in Hebrew or Yiddish, with some occasional English lettering to help out the strangers from uptown or the Gentiles wandering about Orchard Street's bargains" (p. 83). Speaking of his mother, Roskolenko (1971) tells us: "My mother could talk Russian to Russians, Polish to Poles, and Yiddish to our own .... My mother, who arrived in 1895 speaking Russian, Polish, Yiddish, and

Hebrew, never learned to speak English. She picked up some simple phrases, all mispronounced with ease, but she continued to speak all the tongues of her childhood" (pp. 17, 131).

Not only were households such as that of Roskolenko multilingual, but the interaction with neighbors was also multilingual. And beyond the home and the immediate community, even the work domain functioned in LOTEs. Roskolenko describes his mother's work place: "They talked every language but English; and the foreman, when queried over some confusion in the work, *answered in every language* (Roskolenko 1971: 54. My emphasis).

During the period of massive immigration, public bilingual education, with transitional purposes such as the one common today, was available in New York City. Jacob A. Riis (1892), describes these bilingual efforts:

> To help them along, it [the Declaration of Independence] is printed in the school-books with a Hebrew translation and another in Jargon, a "Jewish-German," in parallel columns and the explanatory notes in Hebrew. The Constitution of the United States is treated in the same manner (p. 53).

On the eve of World War I, New York City had three times the number of foreign-born residents than the average city (Bogen 1987). And by the 1920s, one out of every four immigrants to the United States chose New York as their place of residency (Rosenwaike 1972: 92).

But the presence of the many Italians and Jews in the city, clearly seen as racially distinct, the city's changing economy, and the impending world crisis, paved the way for the change to the restrictive language policy of the 1920s. In what is reminiscent of the English Only Language Amendments of the 1980s and 1990s, in 1915 New York Republicans suggested an amendment to the New York State Constitution that would mandate literacy in English for all voters in New York (Fishman 1993). The aim of this legislation was to weaken the power in the polls of New York Jews who tended to vote Democratic and Socialist. Restriction of LOTEs began to be seen as a way to limit the participation of LOTE speakers in the city's political, social and economic life.

Despite the impending restriction, New York City published newspapers in the greatest number of languages in the world throughout this period. Park (1922: 7) describes the situation in New York City in the 1920s:

> The Albanians, Armenians, Bulgarians, Chin, Czechs, Croatians, Danes, Finns, French, Germans, Greeks, Italians, Japanese, Jews, Levantine Jews, Letts, Lithuanians, Magyars, Persians, Poles, Portuguese, Rumanians, Russians, Serbs, Slovaks, Slovenians, Spanish, the Swabians of Germany, the

> Swedes, Swiss, Syrians of New York City, all have a press. The Hindu and Turkish press have only gone out of existence since the war. There is the Hebrew press, which represents a class rather than a large group. There are also language colonies in New York like the Asyrrians, Belgians, Dutch, Esthonians, Flemish, Norwegians, the Spanish of Catalonia, Uhro-Russians, Welsh and Wends, which have a press outside the city.

Clearly New York was highly multilingual during this era, although the government's response to the use of LOTEs in the city for the greater social, political and economic participation of its citizens, was starting to change.

4.3. A policy of LOTE restriction: 1920s to 1950s. The 1930 economic depression

Restrictive legislation requiring English to participate in political life, requiring being white for equal participation as citizens, and finally restricting access to the United States of all but those belonging to the old ethnolinguistic groups, was quickly passed in the 1920s.

In 1921 the English Literacy Law was passed, requiring English Literacy for voting. In 1923 the U. S. Supreme Court ruled that East Asians were not eligible for citizenship because they were not white, according to a 1790 naturalization law that restricted citizenship only to free white people. Finally, in 1924 the Johnson-Reed Act[10] was passed, establishing a quota of 2% of the foreign born of each nationality that had been counted in the 1890 census.

The effects of the restrictive immigration policy and the decrease in immigration brought about by the Depression of the 1930s, brought about the gradual decline of the use of LOTEs in New York City. As fewer speakers of LOTEs came into the city, shift to English occurred. But despite the rapid language shift of Italians and Eastern Europeans, an important change in the linguistic landscape of the city occurred between the 1940s and the 1950s, with the great influx of African Americans and Puerto Ricans, both ethnolinguistic groups which were non-immigrant, and yet had been excluded from greater socioeconomic opportunities because of skin color and/or colonial status (For more on the Black migration to New York, see Rosenwaike 1972: 140).

In 1940 eighty-eight percent and in 1950 eighty-three percent of Puerto Ricans in the United States were living in New York City. The role that the Puerto Rican migration to New York has had on its multilingualism cannot be underestimated, for this migration consisted of a group of LOTE speakers who were U. S. citizens, and yet were subjected to greater segregation than earlier groups. New York's more enduring multilingualism today, especially with regard to Spanish, is a result of the greater exclusion which Puerto Ricans have suffered. At the same time, the linguistic demands that these U. S. citizens placed in the city were answered differently from when they came from immigrants with few rights. The more pervasive multilingualism of New York City today in comparison to other U. S. contexts can clearly be traced to the presence of a large Puerto Rican population in the city.

4.4. A Return to LOTE tolerance: 1960s to 1990s. Civil rights and economic expansion

The Immigration and Nationality Act of 1965 abolished the national origin system[11] and gave preference to those who had close relatives in the United States, those with occupational skills needed, and refugees. This led to a renewed and more diverse immigration, especially from Asian countries, as well as from all of Latin America, the Caribbean and African countries.

As in the 1960s, today New York continues to have the largest number of Puerto Ricans in the United States. But New York City is also the place in the United States with the greatest number of Dominicans, Jamaicans, Barbadians, Trinidadians, Guyanese, Haitians (Youssef 1992: 63), Chinese from the Mainland, from Hong Kong and Taiwan, (Youssef 1992: 65), Indians and Pakistanis (DeCamp 1991: 37), Colombians, Ecuadorians, Salvadorans, Peruvians, Soviet Jews, Poles, Rumanians, Italians and Greeks (DeCamp 1991: 50–51), Israelis (both Hebrew-speaking Jews and Arabic-speaking Palestinians) and Egyptians.

As we saw in section 2, the new immigrants are more different racially and linguistically than in the past. But many are better educated and occupationally prepared than earlier immigrants. Leeds (1991: 5) has said about these new immigrants: "Many were trained professionals who didn't have to assimilate culturally to enjoy the city's economic benefits." Many of the new immigrants were also already bilingual and speakers of English as a Second Language or a different variety of English upon arrival. It remains to be seen whether this greater familiarity with the English language and bilingualism might result in increased LOTE maintenance among this new wave of immigrants.

New York City still attracts most foreign firms who want to expand to the United States, as well as national businesses wanting to develop their operations abroad. It is precisely the multilingual ability of New

York that enhances the importance of New York City in the growing internationalization of business:

> Foreigners, whether immigrants or visitors, feel more at home in New York than in any other American city. Attracted by its cosmopolitan culture, its vibrant bustle, its creative tempo, they regard it as more hospitable and politically stable than metropolitan centers in Europe or Asia (Twentieth Century Fund 1980: 5).

The multilingualism of New York City gives voice and expression not only to the tired, the poor and the huddled masses, but also to the business executive, the diplomat, the politician, the artist and the intellectual. Power factors are often inverted in New York City, with wealthy LOTE speakers being sometimes more powerful than their English-speaking counterparts. As we saw in section 2, today, as in the past, New Yorkers are highly multilingual.

5. Do New York's businesses and government institutions have different language policies? What are those policies?

As we have seen, New York has done more than tolerated its multilingualism, it has actually promoted it for expediency.[12] From early times, except for a short restrictive period, New York has been conscious of its need to use LOTEs for its own benefit, sometimes to reap the *economic benefits* of selling more, both to the international community and to the large ethnolinguistic community, sometimes to obtain the *social and political benefits* of integrating the numerous newcomers as soon as possible and of participating in the international multilingual community.

Yet, there has always been a difference in the way that private businesses and public agencies view LOTE use. In private business, a policy of LOTE promotion is usually followed because doing so increases the number of potential buyers and participants, and thus profits. In government agencies, at best, only a policy of LOTE tolerance has been instituted. This section explores the city's language policy today, giving instances of LOTE promotion by business and LOTE tolerance by government agencies.

5.1. New York's business policy of LOTE promotion

That LOTEs have been instrumental in the *economic* development of New York is attested to by the linguistic and cultural flexibility shown by those who sell in the city. An example of this flexibility is given by Raquel Rivera, a Puerto Rican woman, who recollects how Spanish was used by Jewish merchants in East Harlem: "In the 20s and 30s the *Marqueta* was almost all Jewish. What happened was the Jews began to sell Puerto Rican products like *plátanos* and other items. Everyone communicated very well .... The Jewish vendors always knew a few words in Spanish ..." (Quoted in Sánchez-Korrol 1983: 56).

The use of LOTEs in order to sell in New York City has been a prevalent strategy throughout history in every single business domain. Speaking of the Bronx Hunts Point Market, a supplier of figs says:

> When I first came into this business and that was before the war – to do business here you had to know Jewish phrases. Then, some years later, you had to pick up a few Italian words to make it. Now I'm trying for all the Korean words I can (*New York Times*, February 18, 1976, quoted in Kim 1981: 3).

Today, *businesses in New York, whether international or domestic, have a policy of LOTE promotion*, with LOTEs being used to capture the pocketbooks, as well as the hearts, of those with purchasing and investment power. For example, the AT & T Language Line, a twenty-four hour toll-free telephone service that gives access to interpreters in one hundred and forty languages, is used not only by public New York City agencies, but also by many hotels, banks, airlines, law offices, utilities, and Fortune 500 businesses, as Table 8 indicates. LOTEs are used not only with clients or customers who speak little English, but in an effort to communicate better with and to sell more to those who may be bilingual.

Con Edison, New York's utility company, acknowledges LOTEs as tools to provide better services to their customers. Bills are printed in Spanish, and Spanish Call Centers have been created where customers can speak to a Spanish speaking representative. Con Edison field personnel now have access to a guide that provides translation into ten languages of customers: Chinese, French, Greek, Italian, Korean, Polish, Russian, Spanish, Vietnamese and Yiddish. Likewise, NYNEX, the telephone company, has established a Multilingual Center with approximately two hundred and twenty-five Spanish speaking and forty Chinese speaking representatives in order to remain competitive.

Today LOTEs are also widely used not only in the press, but also in TV and radio programming in New York City. This LOTE use benefits not only the LOTE speaking community, but New Yorkers in general. Information about the United States and the world is provided, allowing LOTE speakers to be knowledgeable participants in U. S. society. Also,

Table 8
NYC institutions/business regularly using the AT&T Language Line*

Social/Health Services
NYC Sheriff's Office, NYC Police Department, NYC Commission on Human Rights, NYC Health Department, NYC Poison Control, NYC Mayor's Office, NYC Transit Authority, NYC Department for the Aging, NYC Youth Line, NYC Department of Environment, NYC Housing Preserve and Development Agency, NYC Sanitation Department, NYC Emergency Medical Center, NYC 911, United Lifeline, Healthfirst, Hospitals & Health Services 61, NYC Health and Hospital Corporation
Legal Services
District Attorney: Queens, Bronx, Kings, New York County, Bureau of Prisons, NY Victim Services, Legal Referral Service, NYC Department of Probation, NYC Department of Juvenile Justice
Business(Consumer Service)
Northwest Airlines, Kraft General Foods, Pepsi Cola Co, Con Edison, LILCO, Brooklyn Union Gas, NYNEX, Vicon Fiber Optics Corp., Goldman Sachs & Co, Prudential Securities, Frey Realty, Chemical Investment Services, Nabanco, Thomas J. Lavin Law Offices, International Warranty, Riverside Memorial Chapel
Business(Tourism/Hotels)
Hilton Hotels, Marriott Hotels, Grand Hyatt New York, Loews New York, Helmsley Hotels, Palace Hotel, Sheraton New York
Business (Finance/Banks)
Bank of NY Mortagage Co, Four Seasons New York, Chase Manhattan, American Express Bank

*** Source: Mike Cuno, AT&T Language Line**

products are advertised in LOTEs, expanding the market and spurring economic activity.

LOTE radio programming abounds in New York City. For example, WNWK-FM, devotes many hours to Spanish, differentiating between various Latino groups, about thirty-five hours to Greek, twenty-three hours to Italian and one hour or less to Arabic, Armenian, Bengali, Bulgarian, Farsi, Macedonian, Serbian, Slovak, and Urdu (Moss – Ludwig 1991: 256). There are four full-time Spanish language AM radio stations: WSKQ, WKDM, WADO and WJIT. A new technological innovation, the Subsidiary Communications Carrier or SCA makes it possible for many ethnolinguistic groups to have access to the radio. There are several Chinese, three Haitian, one West Indian, and two Italian subcarriers in

New York. Customers buy a receiver for about $100. One Chinese language broadcasting company, transmitted through the SCA, has reported that it sold over ten thousand receivers in the city (Moss – Ludwig 1991: 257).

Five UHF television stations also broadcast programming in different languages: WNYC, Channel 31, WNYE, Channel 25, WNJU, Channel 47 (located in northern New Jersey), WXTV, Channel 41; and LPTV, Channel 44. WXTV, owned by Spanish International Television (SIN) provides twenty-four-hour-a-day Spanish language programming with Spanish language films and variety shows. Although WNJU has predominantly Spanish language television, it also transmits in seven other languages, including Tagalog, Chinese, Korean and Serbo-Croatian. WNYC, a public broadcasting station, offers 16 hours of TV programs in Italian, 12 hours in Japanese, 4 hours in Cantonese with Mandarin subtitles or vice-versa; it also broadcasts in Greek, Polish and Brazilian Portuguese (Leeds 1991: 11, Moss – Ludwig 1991: 258). LPTV provides public access at $120 per airtime hour. Programming includes Farsi, Bengali, Hebrew, Greek, Russian and English Creoles. Table 9 displays the hours devoted by UHF television and Cable Television to LOTE TV programming. As the Table shows, American Cablevision of Queens (ACQ) and Brooklyn-Queens Cable (BQ) have added five pay channels in LOTEs: the Korean Channel, Apple Television (Chinese), Indian TV, Greek Channel, and Galavisión (Spanish). Spanish is the language most used in television broadcasts, and if Cable TV is included, it is followed in descending order by Chinese, Korean and Greek (See Table 9).

At present, New York has twenty-nine daily newspapers in LOTEs, as shown in Table 10. Over half of these were established after 1970. The Chinese and Koreans have eight and seven dailies respectively and Latinos have two (See the section by Ramón Vargas in Diloné et al. 1995).

5.2. New York's institutional policy of LOTE tolerance

Spurred by the extensive LOTE use of many New Yorkers, city agencies have developed and adopted multilingual policies in the last decade. But although, as we have seen, businesses promote the use of LOTEs in the city, *governmental agencies only tolerate its use as a very transitional and temporary measure with those who do not speak English.* It is to these official multilingual policies for non-English speakers in city agencies and institutions that we now turn.

Table 9
LOTEs in UHF and Cable Television (Hours per week)*

LOTE	CH31 WNYC	CH25 WNYE	CH47 WNJU	CH41 WXTV	CH44 LPTV	MH[a] Cble	ACQ[b] Cble	BQ[c] Cble	TOTL HRS WK
Bengali					1.0				1.0
BrazlPort	0.5								.5
Chinese	4.0	7.0				28	84	84	207.0
EastInd	1.0						56	56	113.0
Farsi					1.0				1.0
Filipino			0.5						.5
Greek	4.0		2.5		1.0		70	70	147.5
HaitCr			2.0						2.0
Hebrew					4.0	3	3	3	13.0
Italian	16.0								16.0
Japans	12.0		3.0						15.0
Korean		5.0	1.5				84	84	174.5
Polish	2.5								2.5
Russn					1.5				1.5
Spansh			89.5	133.5	16.0	2	168	168	577.0
Yugosl			.5						.5

* **Source: Tables 10.4 and 10.6 of Moss and Ludwig, 1991, pp. 259, 264.**
[a] MH = Manhattan Cable.
[b] ACQ = American Cablevision of Queens.
[c] BQ = Brooklyn-Queens Cable.

In November 1989, the revised New York City Charter mandated the creation of the Mayor's Office of Language Services (OLS) (Agencies Face 1992, Campbell 1994) . OLS works with thirty-one city agencies to ensure that services "are provided to all New Yorkers regardless of language barriers" (NYC Language Services Program, June 1992: 1). "Language barriers," OLS says, "cost the City money, interfere with the safety of residents and public employees, and cause misunderstandings, tensions and lost work time" (Language Sensitivity Training 1993: 1). At present OLS has four language professionals who provide interpreting and translation into Spanish, Chinese, Russian and Korean. In addition, the Office publishes a Language Bank Directory of approximately two thousand employees who can interpret in as many as seventy-two languages. OLS has developed Language Identification Cards for use in New York City public agencies in the following 15 languages: Spanish, Chinese, Russian, Korean, Haitian Creole, French, German, Arabic, Vietnamese, Italian, Hindi, Urdu, Hebrew, Yiddish, Polish. Since 1989, publications prepared

Table 10
New York City press in LOTEs*

Language	Name[a]	Year[b]	Frq	Circ	
Arabic	Al-Hoda		m	10,000	
Bengali	Bangali	1991	w	7,000	
	Thikana	1990	w	10,000	
	Shombag	1993	w	3,000	
Chinese	Asian AmericanTimes	1986	w	20,000	
	China Press	1990	d	20,000	
	China Times	1988	w	20,000	
	China Times Weekly News	1980	w	13,000	
	China Tribune		d	10,000	
	International Daily News	1982	d	40,000	
	Neo Asian American Times		d		
	Sing Tao Daily	1966	d	60,000	
	Sing Tao Jih Pao	1966	d	50,000	
	The United Journal	1951	d	30,000	
	World Journal	1967	d	75,000	
Estonian	Vaba Eesti Sona		w	6,000	
French	France Amérique	(1827)	w	30,000	
Finnish	Finnish Newspaper	1954	w	3,000	
	Greenpoint Gasette	1906	w	5,000	Bil
German	Staats-Zeitung und Herold	1834	w	15,000	
	Aufbau (Jewish)	1934	biwk	8,000	
Greek	Campana	1917	2xm	80,000	
	Ellenika Nea		w	5,400	
	Ethnikos Kerix		d	40,000	
	Hellenikos Tachydromos		d	5,000	Bil
	National Herald	1915	d	40,000	
	Orthodox Observer	1971	w	130,000	
	Proini	1977	d	65,000	Bil
	The Reporters	1985	w	10,000	
Gujarati	Naya Padkar	1990	w	8,000	Bil
Haitian Creole	Haiti Observateur	1971	w	32,000	Bil (FrHCrEng)
	Haiti Progrès	1983	w	90,000	Bil (FrHCr)
Hebrew	Hadoar	1921	biwk	4,000	
	Israel Shelanu	1979	w	70,000	
	Maariv Israel Newspaper	1991	w	10,000	
	Yedioth Achronoth	1921	4xwk	25,000	
Hungarian	Hungarian Weekly Nepszava	1896	w	40,000	Bil
	Hungarian World	1902	w	2,000	
Italian	America Oggi	1983	d	70,000	
	Oggi 7	1991	w	20,000	
Jamaican Creole	Jamaican Weekly Gleaner	1954	d	40,000	
Japanese	Asahi Shimbun Intl	1986	d	11,000	
	Nihon Keizai Shimbun	1987	d	15,000	
	OCS News America	1975	biwk	17,000	
	Japan Financial News	1995	w	130	
	New York Nichibei		w	1,500	
	US Japan Business News	1975	w	40,000	

(Continued next page)

Table 10 *(Continued)*
New York City press in LOTEs*

Language	Name[a]	Year[b]	Frq	Circ	
Korean	Chosun Daily News	1986	d	30,000	
	Chosun Iibo	1984	d	5,000	
	Joong-Ang Daily News	1975	d		
	Jung Ang Inc	1969	d	30,000	
	Korea Central Daily	1975	d	27,000	
	Korea Herald	1970	d	60,000	
	Korean Times	1971	d	30,000	
	Saegae Times	1982	w	10,000	
	Sunday Korean Times	1992	w	15,000	
	The News of Korea	1987	w	20,000	
Latvian	Laiks	1946	smw	10,000	
Lithuanian	Darbininkas	1915	w	4,500	
	Laisve		biwk	1,500	
	Tevyne		m	4,500	
Norwegian	Nordisk Tidende	1891	w	6,000	Bil
Polish	Dziennik Nowojorski	1993	d	15,000	
	Polish Daily News	1971	d	30,000	
Russian	Kurier	1992	w	60,000	
	Novorusskoye Slovo	1910	d	65,000	Bil
	Russian Advertising Weekly	1993	w	20,000	
	Russian Weekly	1917	w	1,000	
Spanish	El Diario/La Prensa	1913	d	60,000	
	El Tiempo	1967	w	38,000	
	Impacto	1975	w	57,000	Bil
	La Tribuna Hispana	1988	w	20,000	
	La Voz Hispana	1980	w	68,000	Bil
	Noticias del Mundo	1980	d	28,000	
	Noticiero Colombiano	1983	w	20,000	
	Resumen Newspaper	1971	w	22,000	
Swedish	Norden		w	1,000	Bil
	Nordstjernan-Svea		w	3,500	Bil
Turkish	Hurriyet	1982	d	6,000	
Ukrainian	Robitnik Publishing	1920	bimnth	500	Bil
Urdu	Pakistani Post	1992	w	36,000	
	Urdu Times	1980	w	50,000	
Yiddish	Di yidishe vokh	1954	w	20,000	
	Der Yid		w	7,300	
	Algemeiner zhurnal		w	7,000	
	Yiddish Forward	1897	w	10,000	

* **Source: This table was drawn from data supplied by Ramón Vargas, a graduate student at City College, included in Diloné et al. 1995, and supplemented by Table 17.1 of Bogen 1988.**

[a] The table includes only newspapers published in the New York City metropolitan area in LOTEs. When publication is bilingual it is so indicated.

[b] We have supplied here only information that we have been able to confirm through direct contact with the newspapers.

by the Mayor's Office are translated into Spanish, Chinese, Korean and Haitian Creole, and Russian is being added.

The most progress in providing services in LOTEs in city agencies has been made in the Health Field. In 1986 the New York City Council passed an important local law which states:

> The Board of Health shall require the immediate provision of interpretation services for non-English speaking residents in all hospital emergency rooms located in New York City, when such non-English speaking residents comprise at least ten percent of the patient population of the service area of a particular hospital.

Two years later, New York State's Department of Health passed a similar policy which requires language interpreters for emergency service within ten minutes of a request if the agency has more than 1% LOTE population that does not speak English well (Revised Part 405-Hospital Minimum Standards, 8/22/88 p. 10). Of eighty-three hospitals in New York City, seventy-eight have to provide translation into Spanish according to this policy, fourteen into Italian, five into Chinese, and four into Russian. All the municipal hospitals administered by the Health and Hospital Corporation use the AT&T Language Line Service to supplement translation into Spanish, Italian, Chinese and Russian, and for most other languages.

In 1988 New York City's Local Law 86 required that the Human Resources Administration's (HRA) Income Maintenance Centers provide bilingual staff whenever clients who spoke English poorly were at least ten percent of a Center's caseload. HRA also has a Language Service Coordinator who conducts surveys of bilingual staff and clients and coordinates the publication of a Directory of Community Organizations with staff willing to provide interpretation in forty-three languages. To identify the language of the clients, the Human Resources Administration has also prepared a Language Identification Card in Albanian, Arabic, Chinese, Haitian Creole, Hebrew, Hindi/Urdu, Italian, Russian, Spanish and Vietnamese with the following messages: "Do you speak X? Is someone with you who can interpret for you? Please be seated while I call someone to interpret for you." In 1993 eight percent of the clients of HRA were Spanish speakers who spoke English poorly or not at all, and over eleven percent of the clients of all the programs in HRA in 1993 have limited English speaking ability.

The New York City Police Force started hiring interpreters as receptionists in 1982. In 1992 there were seventy such receptionists in twenty-nine of the seventy-five police precincts. That same year twenty-three percent of the nearly nine million calls to the Emergency Telephone Number, 911, were in Spanish. Three Spanish speaking operators stand by at 911 around the clock (Agencies 1992). New York's 911 also uses the services of the AT&T Language Line. In 1994 the other languages requested by NY 911 from the Language Line were: Akan, Albanian, Amharic, Arabic, Armenian, Bengali, Cantonese, Cambodian, Croatian, Czech, Dutch, Farsi, Finnish, French, Fukienese, German, Haitian Creole, Greek, Hebrew, Hindi, Hungarian, Indonesian, Italian, Japanese, Korean, Latvian, Lithuanian, Malayalam, Mandarin, Norwegian, Polish, Portuguese, Punjabi, Rumanian, Russian, Serbian, Sinhalese, Somali, Spanish, Swahili, Swedish, Tagalog, Taiwanese, Thai, Trigrinya, Toishanese, Toucouleur, Turkish, Urkainian, Urdu, Vietnamese, Yiddish, Yoruba (Cuno, Personal Communication, see note 1).

Bilingual Help Telephone Lines, especially in Spanish and Chinese, are also available at the Department for the Aging, the Bias Hotline of the Human Rights Commission, the Heat and Hot Water Complaint Line of the Department of Housing Preservation and Development, and the Complaint Lines of the Department of Environmental Protection. Both the Help Centers of the Department of Finance which provides tax assistance and the Department of Transportation have Spanish-speaking employees to provide assistance in Spanish (NYC Language Services Program, June 1992: 12).

In April of 1992 the New York City Charter was amended adding a paragraph 18 to Chapter 35, Section 814, which requires appointing interpreters in city agencies where "non-English speaking users comprise at least five percent of the people to be serviced by the agency."

The New York State Courts have ruled that criminal defendants who cannot understand English are entitled to have the proceedings interpreted for them in a language that they understand. Also in Civil trials, the court has authority to appoint an interpreter for any party or witness who does not speak English. Section 387 of the Judiciary Law provides for the temporary appointment of an interpreter when it is necessary. Clearly the number one language in New York City is Spanish, with approximately one hundred and seventy full-time interpreters in the Unified Court System. But again beyond Spanish, per diem interpretation services are provided in forty-nine languages, as Table 11 shows.

LOTEs have also been recently used in a New York State Citizenship Campaign in which the Statue of Liberty says: "Have a voice. Make a difference. Become a U. S. citizen," not only in English, but also in separate brochures written each in Spanish, Haitian Creole, French, Chinese,

Table 11
Rank Order of LOTEs used in New York City's unified court system 1993–1994*

LOTE	Hrs paid per diem interpreters	LOTE	Hrs paid per diem interpreters
Spanish	81,297	Albanian	1,208
Chinese[a]	25,386	Turkish	1,040
Russian[b]	19,770	Japanese	792
Korean	12,242	Portuguese	707
Arabic	11,681	Romanian	509
Polish[c]	9,479	Czech	429
Wolof	7,084	Thai	280
French	5,500	Armenian	236
Creole	4,950	Yiddish	232
Haitian Creole	4,937	Cambodian	230
Greek	4,259	FrenchCreole	217
Urdu[d]	3,880	Sinhala	200
American Sign	3,698	Hungarian	154
Punjabi[e]	3,438	Tagalog	98
Italian	3,132	Macedonian	77
Hindi[f]	2,665	Indonesian	56
Croatian	2,302	Pushtu	56
Vietnamese	2,143	Yoruba	49
Other Indian Langs	1,798	German	21
Bengali[g]	1,709	Malayalam	21
Hebrew	1,509	Bulgarian	14
Farsi	1,444	Hakka	14

* **Source: Unified Court System. Per Diem Interpreter Expenditures. Fiscal Year 1993–94.**

[a] This total was derived from the following figures reported separately: Cantonese-Mandarin 11,716; Cantonese 6,273; Mandarin 4,927; Chinese 2,470.

[b] This total combines 16,902 given for Russian and 2,868 for Russian/Polish combination.

[c] This total combines 6,611 given for Polish and 2,868 for Russian/Polish combination.

[d] This total combines 1,986 given for Urdu and the following combinations: 539 for Bengali–Hindi–Urdu; 898 for Hindi–Punjabi–Urdu; 201 for Hindi–Urdu, 256 for Punjabi–Urdu.

[e] This total combines 2,121 for Punjabi, 161 for Hindi–Punjabi; 898 for Hindi–Punjabi, Urdu; 258 for Punjabi–Urdu.

[f] This figure includes 1,405 reported for Hindi and the following combinations: 161 for Hindi–Punjabi; 898 for Hindi–Punjabi–Urdu; 201 for Hindi–Urdu.

[g] Includes 1,170 for Bengali and 539 for combination Bengali–Hindi–Urdu.

Russian, Korean, Italian, Polish, Arabic and Hindi, and without an English language translation. The use of LOTEs in a citizenship campaign implicitly acknowledges what officially has never been recognized in the United States, that we are a multilingual nation with many LOTE speaking citizens, and that because we're a nation of immigrants, loyalty toward the United States is not the purview of native English speaking monolinguals.

5.3. Language policy in schools

The question of LOTEs in schools is so important and controversial that it is here treated separately; although as we will see, the policy of schools toward LOTEs parallels what we've said before about their promotion in business (private schools) and their temporary tolerance in government agencies (public schools).

Despite the multilingualism of New York City, there are fewer schools that seriously teach a second language in N. Y. than in most cities in Europe, Asia or developing countries. Schools that develop additive bilingualism in New York City are limited to expensive elite schools or private ethnic schools. Among the private bilingual schools in New York City with an additive bilingual goal one finds a Lycée Français similar to that in many other countries. The large business community of the Germans, Japanese and Italians have also spurred the creation of one bilingual school for each of the three groups, with ties to the motherland. And the ethnolinguistic groups with strong religious affiliations all run bilingual schools. Jews have a large system of bilingual day schools, some Hebrew/English, others Yiddish/English, and an even larger system of supplementary schools. Greeks likewise have approximately twenty day schools. Muslims also have a growing number of schools, with Arabic taught only to read the Koran. Armenians have one day school, where Armenian language is taught during one forty-five minute period. In all these schools LOTEs are used as normal expressions of U. S. loyalty. For example, the morning Hebrew prayers in a Hebrew Day primary school are sung to the tune of "Yankee Doodle." During a graduation ceremony in an Armenian school, students say the Pledge of Allegiance to the American flag in traditional Armenian costumes against the background of Mount Ararat, the symbol of Armenian nationhood; and "America the Beautiful" is followed by the *Her Mayr* (García 1988).

Latinos do not have a system of Spanish-English bilingual private schools in New York City, perhaps because of their lower socioeconomic status. Instead, they rely on the public schools to provide whatever Spanish language education exists. Usually Spanish is used only temporarily in transitional bilingual programs, although a very limited number of additive bilingual programs exist. As in the past, the New York City public transitional bilingual programs use LOTEs to teach American History. Recently I witnessed a lesson about the Boston Tea Party taught in Spanish to sixth graders who had recently arrived from the Dominican Republic. The teacher, speaking in Spanish, transformed the phonology of "Boston". The students, speaking little English and not yet familiar with United States geography, didn't recognize Boston as a city. But as avid TV watchers, they knew the meaning of "getting busted". So a student, showing off the little English he knew, remarked in Spanish on how it was good that the Americans had "busted" the British tea, because otherwise the United States wouldn't be independent and free. Even before children become truly bilingual, they express loyalty toward their new country, and LOTEs are successfully used to develop this sense of loyal U. S. citizenship. In fact, the Pledge of Allegiance often serves as the first English repetition drill in the English as a Second Language class.

Students in New York public schools speak one hundred and thirty languages, although ninety-six percent of students who are English language learners speak the sixteen languages that appear in Table 12, with Spanish accounting for two-thirds of the non-English speaking students. There are five hundred and thirty-one New York City public schools with

Table 12
LOTEs for English Language Learners in NYC public schools, 1993–1994*

Language	Number
Spanish	104,654
Chinese	13,652
Russian	7,424
Haitian Creole	7,028
Korean	3.294
Arabic	2,039
Bengali	1,909
Polish	1,637
Urdu	1,600
Vietnamese	1,149
French	935
Albanian	764
Pilipino	711
Hindi	581
Punjabi	537
Italian	519

* **Source: Board of Education of the City of New York, Division of Bilingual Education. Facts and Figures 1993–1994, p. 4**

bilingual programs in the following twelve languages: Spanish, Chinese, Haitian Creole, Russian, Korean, Arabic, Vietnamese, Polish, Bengali, French, Urdu and Albanian. Eighty-five percent of the students are in Spanish-English Bilingual Programs. Educational services in LOTEs for students who are still learning English are provided as part of the Aspira Consent Decree (1974) for Spanish speaking students, and of the Lau Plan (1977) drawn between the New York City Board of Education and the Office of Civil Rights for all others. Furthermore, the Regulations of the New York State Commissioner of Education, Part 154, require that whenever there are twenty English language learners with the same native language in the same grade, educational services in the LOTE or special English as a Second Language programs be provided. LOTEs are widely used in New York City public schools, but only until students learn English.

5.4. New York's language policy. A summary

Two distinct language policies are in place in New York City today. Private businesses have always used LOTEs to sell to the international or ethnic community in New York, and thus a *policy of promotion* continues to be followed. Businesses recognize and promote New Yorkers multilingualism because they know they can sell more in the language of the "heart", even if the customers are bilingual. Government today uses LOTEs only to enable monolingual LOTE speakers to participate in government services, court proceedings or education, and to that end it has adopted a multilingual *policy of tolerance during the transition to English stage*. Government only recognizes New Yorker's multilingualism when their clients are monolingual LOTE speakers, but once they're bilingual, LOTEs have little room in any social public domain in the city. Bilingualism is relegated to the home, and the ethnic community and its institutions.

Glazer and Moynihan (1963: 101) have said that "Spanish ... has a much stronger official position in New York than either Italian or Yiddish ever had." Yet, the difference between the positions of Italian and Yiddish at the end of the century on the one hand, and Spanish today on the other, has a lot to do with the higher level of government involvement today, rather than with the power of the LOTEs themselves. The use of Spanish in public institutions and schools, even with those who do not speak English, continues to enjoy only limited acceptance, despite its mandated existence as a result of judicial decisions and governmental decrees.

6. Conclusion

There has never been official recognition and acceptance of multilingualism in the United States. Yet, this chapter shows that democratic *practices* have historically supported New York's multilingualism. Both the language minority and the language majority have benefited economically, socially and politically from this use of LOTEs in New York. Americans of all kinds, the native born and the foreign born, the wealthy and poor, the cultured and uneducated, have always spoken LOTEs in the city. New York's tolerance toward the use of LOTEs has been a decisive factor in its development, used successfully both to integrate newcomers and to spur economic activity.

As this chapter shows, official institutions in New York use LOTEs when serving the great number of *non-English speakers* in the city. Yet, New York City, like other U. S. contexts, has failed to support the LOTEs of its *English speaking citizens*, relegating them to the home and other private domains. For example, temporary transitional bilingual education programs for English language learners abound in New York City. Yet, developmental bilingual education programs for bilingual ethnolinguistic minorities who speak LOTEs at home or for English monolingual students who would want to become bilingual are almost non-existent in the city. English language monolingualism continues to be the sociolinguistic aim in New York City, as in the rest of U. S. society, and schools carry on this social mandate.

While the United States demands English language monolingualism for true membership in U. S. society, the rest of the world, and most especially the countries of the European Union, have made their citizens' multilingualism a societal priority. To increase the multilingual potential of its citizens, the European Union presently supports bilingual education models, as well as programs such as LINGUA and ERASMUS which send secondary school and university students to study in other countries and in other languages. A multilingual ability is considered a most important economic societal asset in an increasingly interdependent world.

At this historical juncture, it might be appropriate for the U. S. as a nation to reconsider its English monolingualism goal. During the territorial and economic expansion of the United States as a great world power, the imposition of English monolingualism might have served us well socially and politically, regardless of the individual suffering of many. But the period of U. S. expansion without international cooperation is over, and our English monolingualism will not benefit us in a global world. Furthermore, even though English has spread throughout the world, its economic hegemony now competes with that of many other LOTEs, especially, at present, with Japanese. Our English monolingualism no longer holds the key to our economic hegemony.

More than any other nation in the world, the United States has the world and its languages within its territory. The potential for bilingual and multilingual Americans is in our midst. To activate this potential, we would need to understand that English monolingualism can no longer be the sole holder of our economic and social stability. We would need to trust the LOTEs of our bilingual citizens, and to understand that LOTEs can be valuable resources to negotiate our national and international welfare and to protect our interests. In the immediate future, this change in our national linguistic conception seems unlikely. In fact, as the recent trend in English Language legislation suggests, we may be facing a return to more restrictive language policy. New York's City historical use of LOTEs to its advantage may be an important starting point to analyze the benefits that U. S. societal multilingualism might hold.

Notes

1. Many people contributed to the writing of this paper. I would like to thank especially Ricardo Otheguy for his suggestions, comments and critique of an earlier draft of this paper. I am also grateful to Joshua Fishman and to Akie Tomozawa for their careful reading. A presentation of this material was made at the International Linguistics Association, New York, Spring 1996. Much of the contemporary data for this paper was drawn from interviews, telephone conversations and correspondence with many. For his help with the use of the AT&T Language Line in the city, I would like to thank Mike Cuno. For information on Con Edison, the help of Agnes Lugo is gratefully acknowledged. I thank Gladys Romani for giving so freely of her time in the interview she granted me at the Multilingual Center of NYNEX. Joseph Zwilling of the Archdiocese of New York and Frank de Rosa from the Diocese of Brooklyn were most helpful in faxing me information on the use of LOTEs in the Catholic Church. To Michael Miller, I am grateful for having supplied information regarding the Per Diem Court Interpreter program of the New York State Unified Court System. Barry Moreno, Librarian at Ellis Island, was most helpful in making documents available to me. I want to thank Margie McHugh and Victoria Wong from the New York Immigration Coalition for all the information they provided me with, and most especially for a very enjoyable lunch. The help of Chandra Hauptman of the Human Resources Administration is gratefully acknowledged. Valerie Oltarsh, Executive Director of the Office of

Immigrant Affairs, and especially Lillian Li and Carlos Rivera, both from the Office of Language Services, were most generous in meeting with me, answering many questions, and giving me access to many city documents. To Anselma Diloné, William Guerrero, Arcania Jáquez, Reina Salcedo and Ramón Vargas, graduate students in Bilingual Education, I am grateful for an exhaustive survey of ethnolinguistic resources in New York City, submitted as their M. S. Thesis. I am also indebted to Angel Lagomasini, Rosalina Monegro and Sonia Oviedo, also graduate students in bilingual education, for their photographic essay of multilingualism in New York. To all these people and the many other New Yorkers whose names are not mentioned here, I am truly grateful.

2. A recent comprehensive study of New York is offered in Jackson, Kenneth T. (ed.) 1995. *The Encyclopedia of New York City.* New Haven: Yale University Press/The New York Historical Society.
   For an insightful study of today's immigrants in New York City, see especially, Bogen, Elizabeth. 1987. *Immigrants in New York City.* New York: Praeger; see also, Foner, Nancy (ed.) *New Immigrants in New York City.* New York: Columbia University Press. A thorough demographic profile of today's immigration is provided by De Camp, Suzanne. 1991. *The Linguistic minorities of New York City.* New York: Community Service Society, Dept. of Public Policy, Population Studies Unit; and in the 1997 report of The Department of City Planning, *The Newest New Yorkers.* For classic studies of immigrants in New York City, see Glazer, Nathan and Moynihan, Daniel Patrick. 1963 [1970]. *Beyond the melting pot: The Negroes, Puerto Ricans, Jews, Italians, and Irish of New York City.* Cambridge: M. I. T. Press; Bayor, Ronald. 1978. *Neighbors in conflict: The Irish, Germans, Jews, and Italians of New York City, 1929–1941.* Baltimore: John Hopkins University Press. Most insightful for its treatment of immigrant life in the nineteenth century is Ernst, Robert. 1949. *Immigrant life in New York City, 1825–1863.* New York: King's Crown Press.
   For studies of ethnic New York, see Caroline Zachry Institute of Human Development. 1950. *Around the world in New York: A guide to the city's national groups.* New York: Common council for American Unity; see also, Stern, Zelda. 1980. *The Complete guide to ethnic New York.* New York: St. Martin's Press. A recent treatment of the same topic is offered by Leeds, Mark. 1991. *Ethnic New York: A Complete guide to the many faces and cultures of New York.* Lincolnwood, Illinois: NTC Publishing.
   There has been much published about the different ethnolinguistic groups in New York City. For those groups whose languages are treated in this volume, see references at the end of each chapter. Among the groups not included here that have been treated in the sociological literature, see the following: For Koreans, see Kim, Illsoo. 1981. *New urban immigrants: The Korean community in New York.* Princeton: Princeton University Press. For Poles, see Jurewicz, Leslaw (ed.) 1979. *Polish-Americans in the City of New York: An Outline of socioeconomic and cultural needs.* New York: Polish and Slavic Center. For Brazilians, see Margolis, Maxine. 1994. *Little Brazil: An Ethnography of Brazilian immigrants in New York City.* Princeton: Princeton University Press. For Yemenis, see Staub, Shalom. 1989. *Yemenis in New York.* Philadelphia: Balch Institute Cress.
3. See especially, Hoover, Edgar and Raymond Vernon. 1959. *Anatomy of a Metropolis.* Cambridge: Harvard University Press; Hacker, Andrew. 1975. *The New Yorkers: Profile of an American metropolis.* New York: Mason-Charter; Fainstein, Susan S. et. al. (eds.) 1986. *Restructuring the City.* New York: Longman; Noyelle, Thierry. 1989. *New York's Financial Markets.* Boulder: Westview.

4. For studies of New York English, see especially, Babbitt, E. H. 1896. "The English of the Lower Classes in New York City and Vicinity", *Dialect Notes* I, Part IX; Hubbell, Allan Forbes. 1950 [1972]. *The Pronunciation of English in New York City.* New York: Octagon Books; Feinstein, Mark, 1980. "Ethnicity and Topicalization in New York City English", *International Journal of the Sociology of Language* 26: 15–24; Tannen, Deborah. 1990. "Talking New York", *New York 1990* 23, no. 37, Sept. 24: 68–75. The most famous study of English in New York is Labov, William. 1966. *The Social Stratification of English in New York City.* Washington, D. C.:Center for Applied Linguistics. For a study of Puerto Rican English, see Wolfram, Walt. 1974. *Sociolinguistic Aspects of Assimilation; Puerto Rican English in New York City.* Arlington, Va.: Center for Applied Linguistics.
5. Only Spanish in New York City has been studied in the sociolinguistic literature. For Spanish in the Puerto Rican community, see especially, Language Policy Task Force. 1980. *Social dimensions of language use in East Harlem.* New York: Centro de Estudios Puertorriqueños; Language Policy Task Force. 1978. "Language policy and the Puerto Rican community", *Bilingual Review/Revista Bilingüe* 5, 1–2, Jan – August 1–39; Pousada, Alicia and Shana Poplack. 1982. "No case for Convergence: The Puerto Rican Spanish Verb System in a Language Contact Situation", In Fishman, Joshua A. and Gary D. Keller (eds.) *Bilingual education for Hispanic students in the United States.* New York: Teachers College Press, pp. 207–237; Zentella, Ana Celia. 1990. "Returned Migration, Language and Identity: Puerto Rican Bilinguals in Dos Worlds/Two Mundos", *International Journal of the Sociology of Language* 84: 81–100. See also, García, Ofelia et al. 1988. "Spanish language use and attitudes: A study of two New York City communities", *Language in Society* 17: 475–511; Zentella, Ana Celia. 1990. "Lexical leveling in four New York City Spanish dialects: Linguistic and social factors", *Hispania* 73: 1094–1105.
6. The concept of English not being New York's vernacular has been proposed by Ricardo Otheguy. I am grateful to him for sharing this idea with me.
7. Throughout this paper we use the linguistic labels or categories that appear in the census or survey to which reference is made.
8. This volume includes a chapter on Caribbean English Creole and not one on African American English or Ebonics. Although not without controversy (see the discussion by Winer and Jack, this volume, pp. 303–304), Caribbean English Creole falls closer to a LOTE in the continuum of English language varieties than does African American English. Whether African American English can be considered a LOTE has been vehemently argued. There is no question that both African American English and Caribbean English in general contribute to the linguistic heterogeneity of New York City, but the issue of African American English or Ebonics in the city is so important that it deserves a separate study.
9. The U. S. census does not use Haitian Creole as a category. French Creole probably refers mostly to Haitian Creole, but may also include speakers of other French based Creoles.
10. The Johnson Reed Act of 1924 established a quota of 2 percent of the foreign-born of each nationality that had been counted in the 1890 census. In 1927 the quota was based on the proportion of population in the 1920 census.
11. The Immigration Act of 1965 abolished the national origin system. Preference was given to those who had close relatives or occupational skills needed in the United States, as well as refugees. A limit of 170,000 outside the Western hemisphere, 120,000 from the Western Hemisphere, and 20,000 from any country was established.

12. Heinz Kloss (1977) distinguishes between toleration of language rights and promotion of language rights. He also differentiates between the use of LOTEs for the benefit of the ethnolinguistic group, or for the benefit of majority society, calling this last purpose "for expediency."

References

Agencies Face Language Barriers
1992 *New York Times* B, 8: 1, July 14, 1992.

Bogen, Elizabeth
1987 *Immigration in New York*. New York: Praeger.

Botkin, Benjamin Albert (ed.)
1956 *New York City folklore. Legends, tall tales, anecdotes, stories, sagas, heroes and characters, customs, traditions and sayings*. New York: Random House.

Campbell, Gordon J.
1994 "New York City recognising the importance of multilingual communication", *Language International* 6, 1: 36–38.

Clines, Francis X.
1994 "73,000 times in 22 tongues, 1 vow: 'I do.'" *New York Times* 1, 41: 1 (Oct 30, 1994).

Corsi, Edward
1935 *In the shadow of liberty. The chronicle of Ellis Island*. New York: Macmillan Company. In Benjamin Albert, Botkin (ed.), 198–201.

DeCamp, Suzanne
1991 *The linguistic minorities of New York City*. New York: Community Service Society, Dept. of Public Policy, Population Studies Unit.

Department of City Planning
1992a *The Newest New Yorkers: An analysis of immigration into New York City during the 1980s*. June 1992.
1992b *Demographic profiles. A portrait of New York City's Community Districts from the 1980 and 1990 Census of Population and Housing*. August 1992. New York.
1993 *Socioeconomic profiles. A portrait of New York City's community districts from the 1980 and 1990 Censuses of Population and Housing.*, March 1993. New York.
1997 *The Newest New Yorkers*. New York: City of New York.

Diloné, Anselma – William Guerrero – Arcania Jáquez – Reina Salcedo – Ramón Vargas
1995 Ethnolinguistic resources in New York City. [Unpublished M. S. Thesis, City College of New York, School of Education.]

Dinnerstein, Leonard – David M. Reimers
1988 *Ethnic Americans: A history of immigration*. New York: Harper and Row.

Ernst, Robert
1949 *Immigrant life in New York City, 1825–1863*. New York: King's Crown Press.

Fishman, Joshua A.
1966 *Language loyalty in the United States*. The Hague: Mouton.
1972 *Language in sociocultural change*. Stanford: Stanford University Press.
1993 "Yiddish and voting rights in New York, 1915 and 1921", *Language Problems and Language Planning* 18: 1–17.

Federal Writers' Project. New York City
1938a *Italians of New York.* New York: Random House.
1938b *New York Panorama, a comprehensive view of the metropolis.* New York: Random House.
García, Ofelia
1988 "The education of biliterate and bicultural children in ethnic schools in the United States", *Essays by the Spencer Fellows of the National Academy of Education,* Vol. IV, 19–78.
García, Ofelia – Ricardo Otheguy
1994 "The value of speaking a LOTE in U. S. business", *Annals of the American Academy of Political and Social Science* 532: 99–122.
Glazer, Nathan – Daniel Patrick Moynihan
1963 *Beyond the melting pot: The Negroes, Puerto Ricans, Jews, Italians and Irish of New York City.* Cambridge: MIT Press.
[1970] [Reprint edition]
Gross, Alex
1990 "1992 vs Loisaida", *Language International* 2.3: 7–10.
Hansen, Marcus L.
1931 "The minor stock in the American population of 1790", *Annual Report of the American Historical Association for the Year 1931*, Vol. 1.
Howe, Marvine
1992 "Tower of Babel on radio is adding voices", *New York Times* D, 9: 1, September 21, 1992.
Jones, Charisse
1994 "Melting pot still bubbles at I. S. 237", *New York Times* 1, 41: 3 (June 12, 1994).
Kandel, Bethany
1992 "Can you say taxi in Urdu?" *USA Today* A,1: 5 (April 23, 1992).
Kim, Illsoo
1981 *New urban immigrants: The Korean community in New York.* Princeton, New Jersey: Princeton University Press.
Kleiman, Dena
1982 "A surge of immigrants alters New York's face". *New York Times.* September 27, 1982, B: 4.
Klein, Alexander (ed.)
1955 *The Empire City. A treasury of New York.* New York: Rinehart and Company.
Kloss, Heinz
1977 *The American bilingual tradition.* Rowley, Ma.: Newbury House.
La Guardia, Fiorello
1961 *The Making of an insurgent: An autobiography 1882–1919.* New York: Capricorn Book.
Labov, William
1966 *The Social stratification of English in New York City.* Washington, D. C.: Center for Applied Linguistics.
Laguerre, Michel
1984 *American odyssey: Haitians in New York City.* Ithaca, New York: Cornell University Press.

Lait, Jack – Lee Mortimer
1948 *New York: Confidential!* Chicago: Ziff-Davis Publishing Company.

Language Policy Task Force
1978 "Language policy and the Puerto Rican community", *Bilingual Review/Revista Bilingüe* 5, 1–2, Jan-August 1–39.
1980 *Social dimensions of language use in East Harlem.* New York: Centro de Estudios Puertorriqueños.

Language Sensitivity Training Outline and Source Materials
1993 New York: New York City Mayor's Office of Operations, Office of Language Services, November 1, 1993.

Leeds, Mark
1991 *Passport's guide to ethnic New York. A complete guide to the many faces and cultures of New York.* Lincolnwood (Chicago) : NTC Publishing.

Levasseur, A.
1829 *Lafayette in America in 1824 and 1824; Or, journal of a voyage to the United States*, trans. John D. Goodman (Philadelphia: Carey and Lea).

Margolis, Maxine
1994 *Little Brazil: An ethnography of Brazilian immigrants in New York City.* Princeton: Princeton University Press.

Moss, Frank
1897 *The American Metropolis. From Knickerbocker days to the present time. New York City life in all its various phases.* New York: Peter Fenlon Collier, Vol. 1, 2, 3.

Moss, Mitchell – Sarah Ludwig
1991 "The Structure of the media", in: J. H. Mollenkopf – M. Castells (eds.), *Dual city. Restructuring New York.* New York: Russell Sage Foundation.

New York's New World
1990 *New York Newsday,* June 24, 1990.

New York City Language Services Program.
1992 New York: New York City Major's Office of Operations, Office of Language Services, June 1992.

Park, Robert E.
1922 *The Immigrant press and its control.* New York: Harper and Brothers.

Paulston, Christina Bratt
1994 *Linguistic minorities in multilingual settings.* Amsterdam: John Benjamins.

Pedraza, Pedro – John Attinasi – Gerard Hoffman
1980 "Rethinking diglossia" in: Raymond Padilla (ed), *Theory in bilingual education.* Ypsilanti, Michigan: Eastern Michigan University.

Pfanner, Helmut F.
1983 *Exile in New York: German and Austrian writers after 1933.* Detroit: Wayne State University Press.

Pousada, Alicia – Shana Poplack
1982 " No Case for convergence: The Puerto Rican Spanish verb system in a language contact situation", in: Joshua A. Fishman – Gary D. Keller (eds.), *Bilingual education for Hispanic students in the United States.* New York: Teachers College Press, pp. 207–237.

Purdum, Todd S.
1993 "Buttoning every vote". *New York Times* Sec 9:1 (October 3, 1993).

Reimers, David, M.
1985 *Still the golden door. The Third World comes to America.* New York: Columbia University Press.
[1992] [Second edition]
Riis, Jacob A.
1892 *The Children of the poor.* New York: Charles Scribner's Sons.
[1971] [Reprinted New York: Arno Press and The New York Times]
Rosenwaike, Ira
1972 *Population history of New York City.* Syracuse: Syracuse University Press.
Roskolenko, Harry
1971 *1910–1914: The Time that was then. The Lower East Side 1900–1914. An intimate chronicle.* New York: Dial Press.
Salins, Peter. D.
1991 "In living colors: New York's surprising ethnic future", *The New Republic*, January 21, 1991, p. 14 (2).
Sánchez Korrol, Virginia
1983 *From colonia to community: The history of Puerto Ricans in New York City, 1917–1948.* Westport, Conn: Greenwood Press, 1983.
Stern, Zelda
1980 *The Complete guide to ethnic New York.* New York: St. Martin's Press.
Still, Bayrd
1956 *Mirror for Gotham.* New York: New York University Press.
Tannen, Deborah
1981 "New York Jewish conversational style", *International Journal of the Sociology of Language* 30: 133–149.
1990 "Talking New York", *New York 1990.* 23, n. 37, September 24, 1990, pp. 68–75.
Twentieth Century Fund Task Force on the Future of New York City
1980 *New York. World city.* Cambridge, Ma.: Oelgeschlager, Gunn and Hain Publishers.
Williams, William
1912 Ellis Island: Its organization. A Report, December 1912. [Unpublished MS.].
Wolfram, Walt
1974 *Sociolinguistic aspects of assimilation; Puerto Rican English in New York City.* Arlington, Va.: Center for Applied Linguistics.
Youssef, Nadia Haggag
1992 *The Demographics of immigration: A socio-demographic profile of the foreign born population of New York State.* New York: Center for Immigration Studies.
Zentella, Ana Celia
1990a "Lexical leveling in four New York City Spanish dialects: Linguistic and social factors", *Hispania* 73(4): 1094–1105.
1990b "Returned migration, language and identity: Puerto Rican bilinguals in dos worlds/two mundos", *International Journal of the Sociology of Language* 84: 81–100.

II THE LANGUAGE OF EARLY ARRIVALS: STILL ENCOUNTERED

Irish in nineteenth century New York

Kenneth E. Nilsen

"... Brooklyn contains as many persons who speak our vernacular Gaelic as Cork City" (John O'Mahony, editor, *Irish People* (New York), August 24, 1869).

1. The Background

John O'Mahony, the author of the above quotation, was in a good position to know how much Irish was spoken in Brooklyn and the rest of New York in the last century. A native speaker of Gaelic, O'Mahony was forced to flee Ireland after the abortive 1848 rebellion. He arrived in New York from exile in France in 1853, established lodgings in Brooklyn, and, using several Irish language manuscripts which he obtained on loan from fellow Irishmen in New York, he set to work on a translation to English of Geoffrey Keating's seventeenth century history of Ireland which was published in New York in 1857. In following years O'Mahony was to be a main mover in New York's early Irish language movement and also one of the most important figures in the struggle for the independence of Ireland. O'Mahony lived in a New York where one in every four persons had been born in Ireland. Many of these were, in fact, Irish speakers, possibly as many as 100,000. But, although it is generally well known that New York City has been home to many generations of Irish immigrants, it is less well known that many of the Irish who arrived on these shores spoke a language other than English. Indeed many Irish Americans themselves know very little about their ancestral language and until recently Irish American historians have shown little desire or inclination to acknowledge the existence of Irish speakers in this country.

In order to understand the situation of Irish Gaelic in New York in the nineteenth century it would be helpful to have some background about the history of the language. The Irish language, also known as Irish Gaelic, belongs to the Goidelic branch of the Celtic group of Indo-European languages. It is closely related to Scottish Gaelic and Manx Gaelic and more distantly related to Welsh, Cornish and Breton. Irish was once the language of the entire island of Ireland. Literacy developed early in Ireland. Before the introduction of Christianity by St. Patrick in 432 A. D., the Irish had developed their own form of writing called "Ogham" which was used for inscriptions on memorial stones. Approximately 300 of these Ogham stones dating from ca. 400–700 A. D. are known to exist. In the late sixth century, about a century and a half after St. Patrick's mission of bringing the Gospel and Latin learning to Ireland, it is believed the Irish language started to be written in Roman letters. Thus it is generally credited with being the oldest written vernacular of western Europe. Irish learning and literature flourished for centuries and produced a very impressive corpus of early medieval prose, poetry, law tracts and religious and grammatical works.

The Norman Invasion of Ireland in 1169 introduced the English language to parts of the country. The native Gaelic culture proved so strong that the Anglo-Normans instituted the apartheid-like "Statutes of Kilkenny" in 1366 in an attempt to keep themselves segregated from the natives. However, by the fifteenth century the majority of the Anglo-Norman families had been Gaelicized to the point that they were said to be "more Irish than the Irish themselves." During the period 1200–1650 bardic schools supported by the patronage of Gaelic and Norman chieftains alike prospered. However, after the accession of Henry VIII to the throne and his break with the Church of Rome, the Irish, the large majority of whom remained Roman Catholic, and their Gaelic culture were subjected to increased pressure. During the course of the seventeenth century Irish attempts to throw off the English yoke were brutally crushed with the result that the upper echelon of Gaelic society was forced into exile or greatly reduced in status. Without the patronage of a native aristocracy the Gaelic schools of poetry, law and medicine collapsed.

By the end of the seventeenth century only 14% of Ireland was owned by Catholics. By 1778 that figure was reduced to 5%. The Irish had been disenfranchised in their own country. This was accomplished by the notorious Penal Laws which prevented Catholics from holding office, inheriting land, serving in the military or receiving an education. The Irish language had no official recognition and was excluded from all levels of government business. Furthermore, the language was largely denied access to the printing press. Most of the few books printed in Irish in Ireland were Protestant religious works issued in hopes of proselytizing the native Irish. A handful of Catholic devotional works were printed on the Continent in Catholic countries such as France and then smuggled into Ireland. Some Irish did manage to receive an education by means of hedge-schools, poorly constructed hovels built on the side of the road, conducted by itinerant school masters. These school masters were also frequently Irish poets and scholars who kept Irish lore alive by painstakingly copying and circulating manuscripts since there were virtually no printed books in Irish. It may be noted that the traditional script used in most Irish manuscripts was one that dated back to the Middle Ages and is as distinct from "Roman" type as is the German "Fraktur". The question of whether to use the scarce Gaelic type or the usual Roman type when printing Irish books added a further complication to publishing in Irish until recent decades which have seen standard Roman type emerge victorious.

By the third quarter of the eighteenth century as the Penal Laws came to be less rigorously applied, there gradually arose a Catholic middle class who saw clearly that a knowledge of English was essential for economic benefit. By 1800 it is estimated that English was spoken by half of the population of Ireland, mainly in the East (Ó Cuív 1951). Irish was seen more and more as a mark of poverty and backwardness. In the early decades of the nineteenth century the great hero of the Irish people, Daniel O'Connell, known as the Great Emancipator and himself a fluent speaker of Irish, declared that he could witness without shedding a tear the gradual loss of the Irish language. In 1831 the British government established the National School System which gave no recognition to the Irish language, even in areas where Irish was the only language known to the people. The 1841 census listed the population of Ireland at 8,000,000 and it is believed that this figure had risen to 8,500,000 by 1845. Although the percentage of English speakers was rising, as the population of the countryside skyrocketed there may have been more Irish speakers at this time than ever before. The majority of the population depended on one crop for their sustenance: the potato. In 1845, blight struck the potato crop. The most tragic event in Irish history, the Potato Famine, lasted for three years. It is estimated that over one million died of starvation and more than a million emigrated. By the time of the 1851 census the population had fallen to 6.5 million. The tragedy of the Famine is that throughout these years food was being exported to England to pay rents to landlords. The areas hardest hit by this Holocaust were the poorest areas where Irish was the everyday language. The Famine also set the pattern for large-scale emigration from Irish-speaking districts which has continued unabated to the present day. In the 1851 census, the first to include the question of language, only 1.5 million people were returned as Irish speakers.

Throughout the rest of the nineteenth century English replaced Irish as the spoken language in one county after another until only a few scattered Irish-speaking districts remained, mainly in the remote West and representing three different dialects (Ulster, Connacht and Munster). Fortunately, at various times during the century there arose a number of groups which had as their mandate the preservation of the Irish language. The most noteworthy of these was the Gaelic League, founded in Dublin in 1893. This organization sought to stem the loss of Irish as a vernacular language and hoped to reintroduce Irish to areas where it had been lost. The League established branches throughout the country and held night classes and language events. Its campaign was most successful in spreading literacy in the language and within the first ten years of its existence more books were published in Irish than the total of all books published in Irish in the past.

The desire for an Irish Ireland naturally led to a desire to break with English rule. Many of the leaders of the Easter Rebellion of 1916 had studied Irish in Gaelic League classes and some dreamed of establishing an Irish-speaking republic. In 1921 when the Irish Free State was established, it included the revival of Irish as a cornerstone of its existence. Irish was introduced into the school curriculum and was made mandatory for certain positions. The government soon introduced a policy of giving special grants to Irish-speaking districts, which came to be called the Gaeltacht. In spite of this governmental support the Gaeltacht has continued to shrink and it is estimated that today only some 20,000 to 30,000 or 1–2% of the population use Irish as their everyday language. On the other hand, because of the teaching of Irish in the schools, several hundred thousand people have acquired a fair to excellent knowledge of the language. An impressive modern literature has developed in Irish and a significant number of Irish language books are published each year. A Gaeltacht radio service was inaugurated in 1972 and there are plans for an Irish language television service to be started in 1996.

2. *The Irish language in early nineteenth century New York*

From what has been said above about the status of the Irish language in its native land, it should come as no surprise that early references to the language in New York are very limited. Because of the paucity of documentation, historians and linguists in the past have tended to ignore the question and have generally treated the Irish as an English-speaking group. Typical of such works is *A Host of tongues: Language Communities in the United States* by Nancy Faires Conklin and Margaret A. Lourie which frequently refers to Irish immigrants as English speakers and makes no mention of the Irish language. Jay Dolan's study *The Immigrant Church: New York's Irish and German Catholics, 1815–1865* is completely absent of reference to the Irish language although it deals extensively with the question of the German language. Dolan dismisses Gaelic culture by saying that it had passed away "in the late eighteenth century." To find mention of Irish language use in early New York we must search carefully through the available documentation. Early records of the Catholic Church in New York give some evidence of the use of Gaelic. Many of the late eighteenth century and early nineteenth century New York priests were Irish born and we may assume included many who were Irish speakers. The very first New York City Catholic pastor, Father Charles Whelan, who founded St. Peter's Church in 1785, is described as being "more fluent in Gaelic and French than in English" (Cohalan 1983). Father Philip Lariscy who said the first Mass in Brooklyn in 1822 and who labored in Staten Island and several Hudson Valley settlements was well known for his sermons in Irish and "was much in demand because he heard confessions in Irish" (Cohalan 1983). In August, 1824, when an extension was made to the old Saint Patrick's cemetery, "Bishop Connolly, assisted by the Rev. Messrs. O'Gorman and Shanahan, blessed a portion of this cemetery, the Rev. Father O'Gorman preaching in Irish at vespers and making an appeal for funds to pay the cost of the ground" (Corrigan 1900).

Early reports of the celebrations of Saint Patrick's Day by various Irish fraternal organizations occasionally mention that toasts were proffered in Irish and sometimes include the Irish language title of musical pieces that were played. Such manifestations of the language are at best superficial but we know that at least some of the officers of these organizations were Irish speakers. Perhaps the most famous of these was William James MacNeven, an exile from the 1798 Rebellion in Ireland, who came to New York in 1805 and became one of the city's most prominent physicians. Born in Ballynahowna, County Galway in 1764, MacNeven is reputed to have translated Gaelic manuscripts during the period of his captivity in a British prison in 1798. In 1830 MacNeven was one of the initiators of the move to erect a monument in lower Manhattan to his fellow exile Thomas Emmett, brother of the famous Robert Emmett. This monument, which still stands on the south side of historic St. Paul's Church in lower Manhattan at Broadway and Fulton Street, bears an inscription in Irish which John Ridge has identified as the first public appearance of the Irish language in New York. A monument to MacNeven himself, also bearing an Irish language inscription, was later erected on the north side of St. Paul's Church and can still be seen today.

Countless Irish speakers streamed into this country in the first decades of the last century but few left behind any trace of their linguistic orientation for most were illiterate in their own language. One major exception, however, was the monoglot Irish speaker, Patrick Condon, who despite his lack of English was fully literate in his native Irish. With his family he emigrated in 1826 from County Cork to Utica, New York where he wrote letters and poetry in Irish describing life in the New World. After Patrick's death in 1857, his son Pierce moved to Brooklyn and brought with him his late father's manuscript, a photostat of which resides in the New York Public Library.[1] Condon's poems first appeared in print in 1858 in the New York *Irish-American*.

Other pre-Famine Irish speakers in New York include David Reidy who died in the City around 1815 and his distant relation Thomas Crimmins who came to New York in 1836 and, who, many years later recited poetry in Irish to Jeremiah O'Donovan Rossa, the famous New York-based leader of the Irish political group known as the Fenians. Also in New York in pre-Famine days were the Draddy Brothers, who came from a family noted for stone-cutting and Irish manuscripts. As early as 1843 Daniel Draddy, stonecutter, is listed in city directories. It was this family who sculpted the MacNeven monument in 1867.

Many of those arriving in the decades just before the Famine must have been Irish speakers. A search through "Information Wanted" and "Obituaries" of contemporary New York Irish and Catholic newspapers reveals references to a number of individuals from largely Irish-speaking districts. A random sampling of such material from the New York *Freeman's Journal* shows some such individuals who were in New York at the time:

> August 29, 1846 p. 70. Information wanted: John Moriarty, residing in Whitehall, Washington co., New York is very anxious to hear from his brother JAMES MORIARTY a native of the town of Dingle, county Kerry, Ireland, a tailor by trade, and lived, when last heard from, in Cherry St., New York ....
>
> September 19, 1846 p. 93. Died – On Sunday 13th inst. WILLIAM DRADDY, a native of the parish of Ardagh, co. Cork, Ireland, aged 28 years. He emigrated at an early period of his life to this country, and for the last seven years was a resident of the first ward ....

> January 1847. Died – Thomas Mullins, 89, at the residence of his son (Asst. Ald. Mullins of Fourth Ward). A native of Mallow, county Cork, but for the last fourteen years resided in this city ....

Only rarely do we find reference made to the fact that a person spoke Irish, as in Jeremiah O'Donovan's description of a native of County Galway, Michael Burke, who taught in the Brooklyn Orphan Asylum. Of him O'Donovan wrote, "Mr. Burke is both a scholar and poet, and composes admirably in the Irish language" (O'Donovan 1864: 156). More often we are forced to make a guess, based on region of birth and age, whether or not a particular immigrant was an Irish speaker. The case of Patrick Flannery, the piper, may serve as an example. We are told by Francis O'Neill, the historian of Irish American musicians, that Patrick Flannery arrived in New York around 1845 at an advanced age. The blind piper had been born in Ballinasloe, County Galway back in the 1780s at which time 90–100% of that district was Irish-speaking. Thus, we may safely assume that this man who "is entitled to first place among Irish-American pipers" was an Irish speaker. Flannery spent the last ten years of his life in New York playing his pipes and indeed "when the summons to eternity came," as O'Neill tells it, "... he had his pipes buckled on, with the lively strains of 'The Bucks of Oranmore' rolling in rhythmic tones from the chanter, ... as he was entertaining a fascinated audience on the streets of Brooklyn in the year 1855" (O'Neill 1913).

3. The Famine years and after

It was during and immediately after the terrible Potato Famine of 1845–1848 that Irish immigration to New York reached record levels. For the period 1845–1853 over one million Irish entered the United States. In 1848 alone over 150,000 Irish came to the U. S. It is estimated that approximately 28% of the Famine immigrants were Irish speakers. New York was the port of entry for the majority of these. Other nationalities, such as the Germans fleeing revolution at home, also sought refuge in the New World. New York State had such large numbers of immigrants that it was moved in 1848 to pass legislation assuring that newcomers would receive fair treatment upon their arrival. Part of this legislation enjoins boarding houses to have "conspicuously posted ... in the English, German, Dutch, French and Welsh languages a list of the rates of prices." The inclusion of Welsh in this law clearly illustrates the difference between the status of Welsh and Irish. Welsh immigrants amounted at this time to only several thousand, whereas we may assume that approximately 200,000–300,000 Irish speakers arrived here, if we accept that Irish speakers represented only 20–30% of all Irish immigrants. The Welsh, however, were overwhelmingly Welsh-speaking. Probably over 80% of Welsh immigrants at mid-nineteenth century spoke Welsh. Furthermore, the Welsh were far more literate in their own language than the Irish were in theirs. Welsh was widely taught in the schools of Wales. The Welsh clergy were very supportive of their native language. Welsh language chapels had been established in New York as early as the 1830s, and three Welsh language newspapers and a number of books were published in New York City in the 1850s.

As stated above, the overwhelming majority of Irish-speaking immigrants were illiterate in their own language. But some of those arriving, like Patrick Condon, were able to read and write Irish and brought with them any Irish books and manuscripts they had. These literate Irish speakers who came to New York in the Famine years fall generally into two very interesting and separate categories. The first group were political exiles, men who had belonged to the Young Ireland movement and some of whom had taken part in the abortive rebellion in Ireland in 1848. They included men like John O'Mahony, Michael Doheny and Michael Cavanagh. Many of them would continue in America to work for Irish independence, but would also take a lead in the nascent Irish language movement in their new land. The second group of literate Irish-speaking immigrants seem not to have had any interest in Irish freedom. These were Irish-speaking Protestants who had converted from Catholicism and who used the Irish language in New York in their crusade to win the souls of their countrymen over to Protestantism. We will take a closer look at their efforts after investigating the activities of the first group.

Although a number of Irish newspapers existed in America in the first half of the nineteenth century, all of these were totally in English. In June, 1851 there appeared in the New York *Irish-American*, in between two poems in English, a three stanza poem in Irish in praise of a tavern on Duane Street run by James O'Dwyer. It is tempting to speculate that this is the same James O'Dwyer whose widow several years later gave John O'Mahony the loan of an Irish language manuscript of Keating's History of Ireland which O'Mahony, in his Brooklyn lodging, translated to English and published in New York in 1857.

In 1857 the New York *Irish-American* initiated an Irish language column which was to be a regular feature of the paper for much of its fifty-eight year existence. The newspaper had a special Gaelic font made for the column and it would appear that O'Mahony was the editor. The column consisted mainly of traditional poetry and song taken from manuscripts frequently accompanied by English translations made by Michael Doheny. The column occasionally included lessons to learn Irish and from time to time even letters written in Irish. The importance of this weekly article cannot be overstated. At the time no newspaper in Ireland had an Irish language feature, but by 1858, the Dublin *Nation*, following the lead of the *Irish-American*, instituted a Gaelic column. Throughout the rest of the century Irish language initiatives in New York and in Ireland seem to have alternatively spurred each other to further accomplishments.

O'Mahony, Doheny and Cavanagh were instrumental in founding a New York branch of the Ossianic Society which had been formed in Dublin in 1853 with the purpose of publishing works of Irish literature. The New York branch brought shipments of the society's publications to New York and conducted Irish language classes. O'Mahony also started a newspaper in New York in 1859 entitled the *Phoenix*, which expressed strong political opinions in favor of Irish freedom and may be viewed as the early organ of the Fenian movement which would be headed by O'Mahony. The paper, which ran from June, 1859 to approximately 1861, did not have a Gaelic column per se, but it did include some Irish language related articles by contributors like David O'Keeffe, who taught the Irish class for the New York Ossianic Society and who in the 1850s was busy copying Irish manuscripts. O'Keeffe was destined to be an important teacher in the New York Gaelic societies in the late 1870s and throughout the 1880s and came to be known as "the Patriarch."

O'Mahony started another weekly paper *The Irish People* in the mid-1860s. He introduced a "Celtic Department" to this paper which lasted from 1869 to 1871 and consisted mainly of pieces of traditional Irish folk poetry and song, some of which were accompanied by translations into English by M. J. Heffernan of Brooklyn and included the occasional letter written in Irish.

Much of this Irish language literary activity just referred to was conducted largely by individuals who were also involved in the movement for Irish freedom. Indeed, John O'Mahony became the leader of the Fenian movement in the United States.

But, as mentioned above, there was another group of literate Irish speakers who were active in New York in the late 1840s and with increased vigor in the 1850s. These were Irish speakers who had converted to Protestantism in Ireland. After centuries of neglect of the native population, some Protestants in Ireland in the first half of the nineteenth century turned their attention to converting their Catholic neighbors by means of the Irish language. Editions of the Bible and Psalms were circulated in Irish and classes were set up throughout Ireland. This Protestant Crusade met with some minor successes. During the Famine the charge was laid that some Protestant groups offered food and soup to those who would convert. Those who did convert were often ostracized by their community and branded as "soupers", "perverts", and "turncoats." It would appear that many of these converts felt that the best option for them was to emigrate. Some of them ended up in New York where they obtained work in the late 1840s with the American Protestant Society and in the 1850s with its successor, the American and Foreign Christian Union. They worked as *colporteurs*, distributing copies of the Bible and tracts among their fellow Irishmen. The accounts of these *colporteurs* as published in the reports of these societies provide us with the most important evidence to date of the extensive use of the Irish language in New York City and of the presence in New York of substantial numbers of monoglot Irish speakers. They included men like P. J. Leo who lectured *in Irish* in Protestant churches throughout New York and New Jersey to his compatriots; Rev. George MacNamara, a Maynooth-educated ex-priest, who, upon his arrival in New York in 1851, was hired as a *colporteur*; Thomas Jordan and Jeremiah Murray, two converts from Catholicism, who had labored for thirty years in Ireland for the Irish Evangelical Society, and who were immediately hired by the American and Foreign Christian Union upon their arrival in New York, also in 1851. Some of these men attended the Union Theological Seminary and were ordained as ministers. One of these, John Hurley, published in 1855 in New York a paper called the *Irish Evangelist*. Certainly the most interesting find to date has been the twelve handwritten pages of the 1850 journal of Michael McNulty which describes his work in New York as a *colporteur* among his Irish compatriots. McNulty's journal pages contain constant reference to his *teaching* and *reading* of the Bible *in Irish* to his countrymen and conclude with three religious stanzas written in Irish in the Irish script. A few excerpts will suffice to illustrate the general tone of his reports:

> May 10: At the East River where I witnessed the landing of three ships – From there to Water Street where I addressed in the vernacular many countrymen and [distributed] 4 tracts, from there to Rosevelt Street and taught Irish.

> May 11: All the day at the North River where I met the landing of three ships, where I spoke to many and read Irish – from there to Liberty St. and Trinity place No. 10. The latter place the man of the house requested to give him an Irish bible – also in Carlisle Street read Irish to about 65 who gave satisfactory evidence of their attachments.
>
> May 13: In Lawrence Street ... Read more or less in each & taught Irish where no other could be understood.
>
> May 14: At the North River and round at the Battery where I discovered many who wanted Irish testaments ....
>
> May 15: Being a wet day could not travel but read English & Irish in my own house to about 40 from the old country.[2]

McNulty's constant reference to the Irish language is typical of these reports. Many of the *colporteurs* were clearly devotees of their native language but the reports are totally absent of Irish nationalistic goals. It is difficult to gauge how much lasting influence these *colporteurs* had on Irish-speaking Catholics, but what is most striking is the lack of evidence of a Catholic Irish-speaking counteroffensive. One instance of an Irish-speaking priest at this period is Father Joseph P. Burke, the founder of St. Columba's on West 42 Street, who returned to Ireland in June, 1846 due to poor health. But as mentioned earlier, the major study which deals with the Catholic Church in New York City at this time makes no reference to the Irish language although it deals extensively with the question of the German language. The Catholic Church and its stance *vis-à-vis* the Irish language is clearly an area that requires further research.

The evidence of the *colporteurs'* reports bears witness to the fact that the Irish language was indeed widespread in New York City and disputes the image of the nineteenth century Irish immigrant as a monoglot English speaker, an image which was long perpetuated by many historians and linguists. More recent research, however, refers to the "Gaelic-cast" of Irish immigration of this period. In New York City, for many children, Irish was the first language. In a letter to the *Irish World* of March 15, 1873, a native of Brooklyn mentions that he and his siblings were raised speaking Irish. An attempt was even made by one New York ward to have Irish taught in the schools. It has been claimed that the language was used by the Democratic Party to maintain its grip on Irish voters. As late as 1883 there is evidence to show that some politicians may have tried to use some Irish to impress the voters (*Irish-American*, November 10, 1883, p. 5).

In the 1870s readers of the new Irish-American paper the *Irish World* started to exhibit an interest in Irish language affairs. To the forefront of this pursuit was Michael Logan, a native of County Galway and a resident of Brooklyn. Logan established an Irish language class in his local parish hall in Brooklyn in 1873 and founded the Brooklyn Philo-Celtic Society. This society and another founded in Boston in the same year may well have motivated the Irish at home to establish the Society for the Preservation of the Irish Language in Dublin in late 1876. The establishment of this organization in turn prompted the New York Irish to establish Irish classes throughout the New York-New Jersey area and beyond. The rise and progress of these evening classes for the study of Irish are recorded in the pages of the *Irish-American* in the last two decades of the century. The classes had a fine rostrum of teachers including Michael Logan and David O'Keeffe, who as mentioned above, had been active in Irish language affairs in New York as early as the 1850s. Another teacher was the Irish scholar, Daniel Magner, who transcribed numerous extracts from manuscripts for publication in the pages of the *Irish-American.*

Many of the classes were held in church halls often with full participation of the parish priests, some of whom were Irish speakers. Indeed, one of these, Fr. Thomas Fitzgerald of Brooklyn composed a poem of tribute in Irish to his fellow-priest, Fr. Patrick Hennessy of Jersey City, on the latter's silver jubilee.

The classes also produced a fine poet, Patrick ("Padraic") O'Beirne. A native Irish speaker from Donegal, O'Beirne learned to read and write Irish at evening classes in New York. Along with Douglas Hyde, he deserves to be known as one of the originators of a new era of poetry in Irish. His elegy in Irish to Ulysses S. Grant was printed on the first page of the *New York Herald* in 1885. Perhaps his most powerful poem was one written and published in the *Irish-American* in 1887 shortly after the much-beloved priest, Dr. Edward McGlynn was removed from the pastorship of St. Stephen's parish by Archbishop of New York, Michael Corrigan, because of his radical political activities.

One student who attended the early classes with his father was William H. McLees. Born in New York City, McLees lived most of his life in nearby New Jersey and worked for the Sterling Engraving Company, New York. In his spare time, he worked on compiling an English-Irish dictionary which had reached over nine thousand handwritten pages in length by the time of his death in 1953. The manuscript is now in the Archives of the Irish Language Department of University College Dublin (de Bhaldraithe 1979).

In the late 1870s it was estimated that over one thousand people were attending various Irish classes in the New York area. There had been a number of calls for an Irish language periodical. Indeed, in addition to the articles in the *Irish-American*, the paper published in book form reprints of Irish language primers. Irish articles could also be found in the pages of James Haltigan's *Celtic Monthly* and later in his *Celtic Magazine*. In 1881 Jeremiah O'Donovan Rossa, the famous Fenian leader, started his highly political newspaper the *United Irishman* in New York. Rossa was a native Irish speaker from Cork and generally included bits of Irish in his paper. But all of these publications were principally in English with a little bit of Irish relegated to a "Gaelic" or "Celtic" department. Michael Logan decided the time was right to establish a periodical dedicated to the Irish language and in 1881 *An Gaodhal* (The Gael) was born in Brooklyn. The full title of the journal was *An Gaodhal: leabhar-aithris míosamhail tabhartha chum an Teanga Gaedhilge a chosnadh agus a shaorthughadh agus chum féin-riaghla cinidh na hÉireann* which means "The Gael: a monthly publication dedicated to the defense and cultivation of the Irish language and to self-rule for the Irish people." *An Gaodhal* was a bilingual monthly which provided the Irish-reading public in the United States with a fair variety of reading material in Irish, including original poetry and occasional pieces of folklore collected from Irish speakers in this country. When it began, there was no comparable publication in Ireland, but by 1882 the newly-formed Dublin Gaelic Union started to publish its *Gaelic Journal*, almost certainly in emulation of Logan's Brooklyn *Gaodhal*. Logan died in 1899 and *An Gaodhal* continued to be published until 1904.

In June, 1891 Douglas Hyde visited the New York Irish classes and within two years he was among those who founded in Dublin the influential Gaelic League which in many ways emulated the work that was being done in New York.

By the end of the century the *Irish World* finally started an Irish language column and early in this century a new paper called the *Gaelic American* also had a weekly Irish language article. A frequent contributor to the *Gaelic American*'s Irish column and part-time editor of that column was Patrick Ferriter. Ferriter, who was born on the Dingle Peninsula, County Kerry in 1857, was active in Land League agitation in the 1880s and he and his parents were evicted from their holdings. Ferriter was a keen Irish scholar and he greatly impressed the American folklorist Jeremiah Curtin whom he met in Dingle when Curtin was there collecting folktales in 1887. In 1896 Ferriter came to the U. S., living first in Chelsea, Massachusetts. He moved in 1902 to New York City, living at 201 East 42 Street, within a couple of blocks of the site where the New York Public Library was being built. He stayed in New York until 1922 when ill health forced him to move to Chicago where a nephew of his looked after him until he died in 1924. Ferriter's principal employment in this country seems to have been as a night watchman. But it is what he did in his free time that interests us here. Nearly all of that time was devoted to the Irish cause, and primarily the Irish language aspect of it. He had taken down a fair amount of folklore at home in Ireland and he continued this work in the U. S. In fact, by 1924 he had amassed a collection of thirty-eight Irish manuscripts (including one written by David O'Keeffe in New York). Twenty of these Ferriter wrote himself. They include copies of Irish manuscripts that he viewed in various locations such as the Boston Athenaeum. His copy of an Irish manuscript once held by the New York Catholic Club is particularly valuable because the original has since disappeared. Some of the other manuscripts contain a good deal of folklore, songs, poetry, rhymes, and tales which he took down from oral recitation both in Ireland and the U. S. Included also are descriptions of life among Irish speakers, again both in Ireland and the U. S. One such manuscript of over 800 pages was started by Ferriter in 1889 when he was still in Dingle and completed in 1913 when he was in New York. When he died he bequeathed all thirty-eight of his manuscripts to University College, Dublin, as a token of his gratitude that Irish had been made a compulsory subject for matriculation to Irish universities.

4. *The Irish language beyond the 19th century*

By the turn of this century Irish had established a presence in New York, if albeit a marginal one. In this century, although Irish immigration to the city remained high and included many Irish speakers, the percentage of Irish speakers among Irish immigrants was almost certainly not as high as in other cities like Boston and Portland, Maine, which were the preferred destinations for generations of Irish speakers from the Connemara region of County Galway.[3] Indeed, even today the percentage of native Irish speakers among Boston's Irish-born residents may be as high as 10% and in certain sections of that city, such as Dorchester and South Boston, where there are still large concentrations of Irish-speaking Connemara people, one can often hear Irish spoken outside churches after Sunday Mass, on some building sites and in a number of taverns. One can even meet some children there who have some knowledge of Irish.

While the New York area has a fair number of native Irish speakers, they are not now concentrated in any one particular section and they represent probably only 2–3% of Irish-born residents in the region. Most native Irish speakers in the U. S. use the language only with close friends and relatives, and rarely make an effort to pass the language on to their children.

Table 1 presents quantitative data of the number of Irish speakers in New York and the institutional resources available for the Irish language throughout the nineteenth and twentieth century. Even during the two decades in which there were more Irish speakers in New York (1878–1899), the Irish language had little public life in periodicals, radio or classes.

Table 1
Various aspects of Irish language use in New York City and environs, 1800–1995*

Years>	1800–1845	1846–1860	1861–1877	1878–1899	1900–1919	1920–1939	1940–1979	1980–1995
Irish speakers (in thousands)	20	70	75	80	70	40	10	5
Periodicals with Irish content	0	1	3	5	5	5	5	5
Irish classes	0	1	1	20	15	15	15	15
Radio programs with Irish	–	–	–	–	–	0	0	2

*** It should be stressed that the figures given in this table are merely estimates based on the most reliable evidence available.**

The majority of native Irish speakers have traditionally been undemanding and decidedly non-militant with regard to their language. This attitude may derive from a desire to conform not only to American society but also to the standard English-speaking norms of the majority of their fellow Irish countrymen. Only a small percentage of native speakers ever took part in the various organizations devoted to the Irish language, although those native speakers who did participate frequently made significant contributions. Since the 1920s, Irish-born participants in these organizations were far more likely to be native English speakers who had acquired their knowledge of Irish at school in Ireland. However, the Gaelic societies offered Irish-American New Yorkers a valuable service provided by neither the public nor Catholic educational systems: an opportunity to study their ancestral language. Generation after generation of New Yorkers, including the present writer, studied Irish at the New York Gaelic Society which was founded in 1878 and continued offering weekly night Irish classes until the mid-1980s. At various times during this century Irish classes have been offered at institutions of higher learning such as Columbia University in the first half of the century and more recently by New York University and Queens College. An Irish language radio program presented by Dr. Séamas Blake has been on the air for over fifteen years and an excellent selection of Irish language books and tapes is available in Manhattan at the *Irish Book Shop*. A new generation of Irish language organizations has come into being, and since 1993 the *Irish Echo* has published a weekly Irish language column.[4]

The demise of Irish has been predicted often in the past, most recently by an Englishman in a book entitled *The Death of the Irish Language*. But in spite of dire prognostications, the language has survived to the end of the twentieth century; and for the several thousand Irish-speaking New Yorkers, the Irish language continues to live and thrive in New York City to some extent.

Although Irish must have been at least numerically significant at one time in New York, we have seen that it never attained any degree of entitlement. Indeed, as the Irish language was increasingly marginalized in nineteenth-century Ireland, fewer and fewer of those arriving in New York were Irish-speaking and even the Irish speakers themselves saw little point in maintaining a language in a new land that was fast disappearing in its native land.

Notes

1. The photostat copy is bound and on the flyleaf is the following note: "Gift of Miss S. Carty, 211 Berkeley Place, Brooklyn, N. Y. Dec. 1930." Unfortunately the location of the original manuscript is unknown.
2. Journal of Michael McNulty. I am indebted to the Presbyterian Historical Society, Philadelphia, for permission to publish extracts from McNulty's Journal.
3. See K. Nilsen "Thinking of Monday: The Irish Speakers of Portland, Maine," *Eire/Ireland*, 25, 1991, 6–19.
4. In the 1980s, there has been an increase of Irish immigrants to New York City because a special visa lottery has favored the Irish, as well as Poles.

References

Cohalan, Florence D.
1983 *A Popular history of the Archdiocese of New York*. Yonkers, New York: United States Catholic Historical Society.

Conklin, Nancy Faires – Lourie, Margaret A.
1983 *A Host of tongues: Language communities in the United States*. New York: The Free Press.

Corrigan, Michael
1900 "The Catholic cemeteries of New York", *Historical Records and Studies* 1: 372–373.

de Bhaldraithe, Tomás
1979 "Uilliam H. Mac Giolla Íosa – Foclóirí", in: Stiofán Ó hAnnracháin (ed.) *Go Meiriceá Siar*,. [Baile Átha Cliath]: Clóchomhar a d'fhoilsigh do Chumann Merriman.

Dolan, Jay
1975 *The immigrant church: New York's Irish and German Catholics, 1815–1865*. Baltimore: The John Hopkins University Press.

Ó Cuív, Brian
1951 *Irish dialects and Irish-speaking districts*. Dublin: Dublin Institute for Advanced Studies.

O'Donovan, Jeremiah
1864 *A Brief account of the author's interview with his countrymen*. Pittsburgh: by the author.

O'Neill, Francis
1913 *Irish minstrels and musicians*. Chicago: Regan Printing House.

German in New York[1]

John R. Costello

1. Introduction

The majority of the German-speaking population in New York City (NYC) consists of immigrants from Germany.[2] In addition to this group, however, there are three sizable groups of displaced persons which individually differ from the majority to the extent that no description of German in NYC could have a claim to accuracy unless it took them into account. These are the Jews from Germany and Austria, the Danube Swabians, and the Germans from Gottschee, Slovenia. In the following, I shall attempt to describe and contrast these groups, including their attitudes about and their use of German. Unfortunately, because of limitations of space, smaller but equally important groups within New York's German-speaking population, such as immigrants from Switzerland, Austria, and displaced persons from Eastern European countries aside from Rumania and the former Yugoslavia, cannot be dealt with here.

2. Four German-speaking groups in New York City and their European backgrounds

2.1. Immigrants from Germany excluding displaced persons

Over the years, immigrants from Germany have represented all of the sociolinguistic groups of that country. To be sure, attitudes toward the local varieties of speech, and the standard language, have changed at different periods in Germany. Nevertheless, it is in general the case that those living in the north of the country do not hold the local varieties of language (predominantly Low German, so named after the low lands) in high esteem, whereas those living in the south tend to retain their local varieties of speech in many situations in which one might otherwise expect to find the standard language, used in a diglossic[3] role. Put somewhat differently, upward mobility in the north has traditionally been accompanied by disuse of Low German, whereas loss of the use of the local varieties is not as noticeable in the south.

In general, the more education that one receives in Germany, the more likely it is that one has acquired one or more foreign languages there, typically French and/or English, and the more likely it is that competence in foreign languages aside from English will be maintained after immigration to the United States. Since compulsory public education was introduced in Germany in 1872, illiteracy among native Germans is virtually unknown.

2.2. The Jews from Germany and Austria

In most cases, especially in the twentieth century, German-speaking Jews from Germany and Austria have been well educated, having completed the so-called *Gymnasium* (a high school with upper-level courses equivalent to at least the first two years of college in the United States), or several semesters at a university, if not a doctoral or similar program. Most adult Jews leaving Germany between 1933 and 1939 were white collar workers, if not professionals. While a good number of these individuals were able to speak or at least understand the local varieties of speech in the communities where they lived, the standard language was always strongly preferred. Typically, French and/or English had been studied in high school, although proficiency was usually highest in the written forms of these languages, not the spoken. As in the case of the other immigrants from Germany, there was no illiteracy.

2.3. The Danube Swabians

The Danube Swabians are the descendants of persons from the regions of Alsace, Lorraine, the Rhineland-Palatinate, Hessia-Nassau, and Swabia, who in the eighteenth century were resettled in an area known as the Batschka, part of the former Yugoslavian province of Vojvodina, and some adjacent areas. (In much of eastern Europe, the name *Swabian*, which properly refers to the language and the people of the state of Württemberg, is used to refer to all Germans; similarly, Spanish *alemán* and French *allemand* refer to all Germans, although properly, these names refer to the southwestern German-speaking regions, and their local varieties of speech.) Before the outbreak of World War II, there were approximately 250,000 Danube Swabians living in the Batschka, where they represented about 20% of the population. While most of the Danube Swabians were engaged in agriculture, others were active in trade; they controlled about 45% of the region's industry (cf. Nebel 1985: 10). Like the Germans, Austrians, and Swiss, the Danube Swabians are diglossic, speaking local varieties of what is predominantly Palatinate[4] German, as well as Standard German, which most of them mastered well. In addition, depending upon where they lived, many spoke Hungarian and/or Rumanian and/or a Slavic tongue, usually Serbo-Croatian; those who had the opportunity of obtaining a higher education also acquired French and/or English. Of those who later settled in the United States, all are literate.

2.4. The Germans from Gottschee

According to Behaghel (1911: 17), the Germans from the city of Gottschee and the surrounding areas are the descendants of persons who were resettled in Slovenia in the fourteenth century; their place of origin was probably Upper Carinthia or Eastern Tyrol, which today are part of Austria. (The fact that these people consider themselves to be German is almost certainly linked to the designation of the German-speaking territories within the so-called Holy Roman Empire as "The Holy Roman Empire of the German Nation", a term which came into use in the fifteenth century.). The name of the city of Gottschee in Slovenian is Kočevje.

In 1911, the German-speaking population was estimated at approximately 20,000. However, because much of the land was poor from an agricultural point of view, and since there was little opportunity of employment for those who had acquired a higher education, there was significant emigration from the region after World War I, so that at the outbreak of World War II, the German-speaking population had decreased to ca. 11,000. White collar workers and professionals sought to emigrate to Austria and Germany; agricultural families emigrated to the U.S., if they could. As elsewhere in the German-speaking areas, the Gottschee region was diglossic; the local varieties of speech, linguistically of Bavarian stock, co-existed with Standard German. In the early years after World War I, Slovenian and Serbo-Croatian were taught in the public schools, so that those who acquired Standard German did so privately. After some years, Standard German became the language of the local public schools, and as a result, some never acquired Slovenian or Serbo-Croatian. Those who continued their education beyond the minimum number of years acquired French and/or English. Virtually all of the Gottschee Germans are literate.

3. Settlement in the United States

3.1. Immigrants from Germany excluding displaced persons

Sizable groups of immigrants from what is today Germany began to arrive in the English colonies of North America in the late 17th century. It is often said that it took Germany one hundred years to recover from the devastation of the Thirty Years' War (1618–1648); thus it is not surprising that many left the country during that period of recovery. Also, religious persecution did not come to an end once the Thirty Years' War was over. From 1683 until about the time of the Seven Years' War in Europe (1756–1763, or roughly, the end of the French and Indian Wars in North America), the goal of many of the immigrants was the rich farmland of Pennsylvania, particularly those who planned to continue to make their livelihood in agriculture. The extent of this immigration, and the reaction to it on the part of many of the English colonists who had already become established in Pennsylvania, may be seen in the following excerpt from a letter by Benjamin Franklin to Peter Collinson, an English botanist, in 1753:

> ... [t]hey [the Germans] behave however, submissively enough at present to the civil government, which I wish they may continue to do, for I remember when they modestly declined intermeddling with our elections; but now they come in droves and carry all before them, except in one or two counties. Few of their children in the country know English. They import many books from Germany, and, of the six printing houses in the province, two are entirely German, two half German, half English, and but two are entirely English. They have one German newspaper, and one half German. Advertisements intended to be general, are now printed in Dutch [i. e. German] and English. The signs in our streets [i. e. Philadelphia] have inscriptions in both languages, and in some places only in German. They begin of late to make all their bonds and other legal instruments in their own language, (though I think it ought not to be), are allowed good in courts, where the German business so increases that there is continued need of interpreters, and I suppose in a few years, they will also be necessary in the Assembly, to tell one-half of our legislators, what the other half says. In short, unless the stream of importation could be turned from this to other colonies, as you very judiciously propose, they will soon outnumber us, that all the advantages we have, will, in my opinion, not be able to preserve our language, and even our government will be precarious (Beidelman 1898 [1969]: 86).

Of course, this strong influence of German in Philadelphia was not to be permanent. However, something very close to one of Franklin's predictions did occur in the Pennsylvania State Assembly: through the very early years of the nineteenth century, all transactions of that body were translated into German, as we know from resolutions which were passed to cover the expense involved. (Perhaps this is the inspiration behind the erroneous claim that one can hear in Germany to the present day, namely that when the United States Congress took a vote on which language was to be chosen for the newly formed republic, German lost by one vote!) Though attempts were made to induce German immigrants to settle elsewhere, particularly in New York, German immigration to Pennsylvania continued to the extent that in 1873, A. R. Horne, former president of what was then known as Kutztown Normal School (now Kutztown University), stated flatly:

> Pennsylvania is a German State. Fully one half of its inhabitants are of German descent. Possibly 400,000 of its population are not conversant with the English tongue... Half of the aggregate population of [the southeastern] counties and cities, amounting to 2 millions, worship God in the German language, and their children speak German at home (Horne 1873: 79).

Thereafter, sizable numbers of German immigrants settled in areas of Ohio (with concentrations in Cincinnati), Illinois (with concentrations in Chicago), and many areas of Texas (with concentrations around New Braunfels) and New York; smaller numbers settled in all of the English colonies on the eastern seaboard (Learned 1889; Beidelman 1898 [1969]; Robacker 1943; Kloss 1985). The earliest German-speaking immigrants to New York arrived in 1708 or 1709, and settled in Newburgh. Later immigrants settled in Livingston Manor, in the Schoharie and Mohawk Valleys (Learned 1889: 3), and of course, New York City. This immigration peaked at the end of the nineteenth and beginning of the twentieth centuries, although it remained strong during the years between the two world wars, and even after World War II.

In NYC, the preferred neighborhoods for German immigrants who were not displaced persons in the late nineteenth century, and for much of the twentieth century, have been Yorkville in the Borough of Manhattan, and Astoria, Glendale and Ridgewood (which extends into the Borough of Brooklyn) in the Borough of Queens. Over the years, these immigrants have represented all strata of German society, and since Germany is characterized by diglossia, just about every variety of local speech has at one time or another been brought to NYC, in addition to the standard language. Moreover, immigrants who were in fact Germanized Kashubians (a Slavic people distinct from the Poles, living close to the mouth of the Vistula River) brought their "home language" with them, just as the Germanized Wends brought Wendish to the New Braunfels region of

Texas, where it survived for many years. In contrast to areas like Texas, where Low German varieties were predominant, and persisted for many years, and Pennsylvania, where predominantly Palatinate varieties have outlived Standard German (Costello 1986), and persist to the present day, in NYC, no single local variety of German has ever exhibited a disproportionately high number of speakers. Hence in NYC, adherence to local varieties of speech, which are in many cases mutually unintelligible, tends to fade in time, since often, oral communication with other Germans is possible only via the medium of the standard language. On the other hand, in instances where individuals did not acquire a strong mastery of the standard language in Germany, particularly those who had minimal schooling, and who emigrated at an early age, English quickly takes the place of Standard German in communicating with Germans from other dialect areas.

3.2. The Jews from Germany and Austria

Records tell us that there were already Jews in NYC, then still New Amsterdam, when in 1654, twenty-three Jews arrived there after their plans to return to Amsterdam from Brazil had been thwarted (Burke 1979: 6). These individuals, however, were not German-speaking Jews, but rather Portuguese-speaking Sephardic Jews. German-speaking (and other Ashkenazic) Jews[5] began to arrive in New York soon after the British gained control of the city in 1664, but large numbers of these immigrants started to appear only after 1860. Between that year and 1880, 50,000 German-speaking Jews emigrated to the United States; thereafter, the main source of Jewish immigration was from Russia. Comparatively little information is readily available concerning the immigration of German-speaking Jews in other areas of colonial America; however, Learned (1889: 10) mentions the settlement of “a company of German Jews” near Schaefferstown, Pennsylvania, in 1729. It was known that they had a synagogue, and by 1732, a cemetery. This Jewish community is no longer in existence, except in the memory of some of today’s inhabitants of Schaefferstown. In the twentieth century, the immigration of German-speaking Jews peaked between the years 1933 and 1945, clearly as a result of the persecution and atrocities inflicted upon the Jewish population by the National Socialist regime in Germany, and in other areas under the control or influence of that government, during those years.

Although the Jewish immigrants from Germany settled in all areas of the United States, as well as in and around NYC in the 1930's and 1940's, sizable numbers congregated in Washington Heights in Manhattan, and Jackson Heights in the Borough of Queens. The number of German-speaking Jews in these communities, however, has declined considerably over the years, and for a variety of reasons. For one thing, as these individuals improved their command of English, and assimilated to the ways of their adopted country, they became less dependent on the support which they had derived from their first associations. Also, a good number of them married spouses from other language backgrounds. In the late 1940's and early 1950's, many of them joined the other urban dwellers who were moving to the suburbs. A further factor is that in recent years, many who had remained in the city throughout their careers, decided to leave it upon retirement.

3.3. The Danube Swabians

Events in 1944 and 1945 in Europe in general, and in the Batschka and adjacent areas in particular, led to the relocation of the Danube Swabians to parts of Austria and Germany (Nebel 1985: 12, and the references cited there, for details). Because of the Displaced Persons Act of 1948,[6] many of these individuals were able to emigrate to the United States. Today, about 1,000 live in the NYC area, mostly in Ridgewood and Glendale. As Nebel (1985: 9) indicates, other areas of the United States where Danube Swabians have settled include Akron, Chicago, Cincinnati, Cleveland, Detroit, Los Angeles, Milwaukee, Philadelphia, Rochester, St. Louis, and Trenton; outside the United States, Danube Swabians have settled in Canada, Brazil, and Argentina.

3.4. The Germans from Gottschee

Almost the entire German-speaking population of Gottschee and the surrounding areas was expelled at the start of the Italian occupation in 1941. The immediate site of their relocation was Austria, but many subsequently went on to Germany. Like the Danube Swabians, many of them emigrated to the United States in 1953 and thereafter, with the passing of the Displaced Persons Act and the Refugee Relief Act. Today, some 3,000 live in the NYC area, particularly in the communities of Ridgewood, Glendale, Maspeth, and Middle Village. Sizable numbers of them have also settled in Canada, and in the midwest of the United States.

4. Language use

For well over one hundred years, almost all German-speaking immigrants in the United States have eventually learned English, if for no other reason than out of practical necessity. In the early years of migration, most of them arrived in the United States knowing no English at all; in the twentieth century, however, many of the better educated immigrants have arrived with at least a "classroom" knowledge of the language, and since World War II, younger immigrants often have a very good command of English from the start. Nevertheless, German continues to be used in a variety of ways by the majority of the immigrants, although with very definite limitations.

The publication of German language books and newspapers has had a very long history in America; in fact, it dates back to the colonial period. According to Robacker (1943: 28), a thirty-four page pamphlet entitled *Der in der Amerikanischen Waldnusz Prediger* 'The Preacher in the American Wilderness' by Georg Weiss was published in 1729 by Andrew Bradford in Philadelphia; and in the following year, a book entitled *Mystische Sprüche* 'Mystical Proverbs', by Konrad Beissel, was published by Benjamin Franklin, also in Philadelphia. According to Robacker (1943: 31) and Beidelman (1969 [1898]: 79), Christopher Sauer's newspaper, the Germantown *Zeitung* 'Newspaper' began to appear in 1739. For a very fine account of the voluminous German-language publications in America, including books, newspapers, and periodicals, that appeared from these beginnings until well into the nineteenth century, the reader is referred to Robacker 1943.

Although Philadelphia has the distinction of being the home of the first German-language newspaper in America, New York's record is also impressive: the newspaper which is today commonly called the *New Yorker Staats-Zeitung* 'The New York State Newspaper' has been published since 1834. Decades ago, the newspaper merged with the *New Jersey Herald*; it now serves the New York and New Jersey German-speaking communities under both titles. In addition to this, several pages devoted to events in the Philadelphia area appear under the rubric *Philadelphia Gazette Democrat*, and likewise, pages devoted to events in Florida appear under the rubric *Florida Express*. Thus, the paper serves far more than the immediate NYC area. To be sure, the readership has declined steadily over the years; formerly a daily, then a semiweekly, the paper now appears only once a week. Nevertheless, it is run by a young, energetic staff, and its future looks bright.

A younger German language newspaper published in NYC is the *Aufbau* [Construction], which describes itself as "America's only German-Jewish Publication". Founded in 1934, it is now 60 years old. Originally it appeared biweekly, but from 1939 to 1985 it appeared weekly. Since that time, it has again been appearing biweekly. At its peak, in the early 1950's, the paper had a circulation of 45,000. Today its circulation is 8,000, but of course, the number of readers is higher than that. The readership of the paper goes far beyond the German-Jewish population of the NYC area; in fact, the paper has readers all over the United States, and as far away as Zimbabwe and South Korea.

American radio broadcasts in German have been aired on Sunday afternoons for decades. Currently a program entitled Grüsse aus der Heimat 'Greetings from Home' may be heard on Sunday afternoons on Station WFUV-FM Public Radio from Fordham University, in the Borough of the Bronx, in NYC; its listening range includes all of NYC, and extends into New Jersey and Connecticut. This program, which is listener-supported, offers music from operas, operettas, musicals, and other films, folk-songs, popular songs, etc. It also airs news from Germany and Austria, special reports, commentaries, interviews, and live narrated sketches from Germany. In addition, it announces local cultural events, and events sponsored by local German-American clubs. By way of contrast, not Standard German, but rather radio broadcasts in the Pennsylvania German dialect[7] may be heard on Thursday evenings on radio station WBYO-FM in Boyertown and surrounding areas in Pennsylvania. The themes of this program, humorously called *Die Wunnerfitz Schtunn* 'The Nosy-body Hour', which has been aired for over twenty years, center around things Pennsylvania German; the format is basically one in which a topic is introduced by the program host, after which listeners call in to the station, and discuss the topic with the host over the air.

Although there are no regular television broadcasts in Standard German which originate in the United States, German-language programs originating in Germany, namely *Deutsches Fernsehen in Amerika* 'German Television in America' may now be received via satellite-cable on over 160 systems in most major cities in the United States.

In the NYC area, religious services are conducted weekly in German, in three Lutheran churches, one in Brooklyn, and two in Manhattan. In addition, one Manhattan Roman Catholic church offers Mass in German on the first Sunday of each month. In the much older German communities of Pennsylvania, some churches conduct an annual service in Standard German. What is more common, however, is the so-called Dutch

Sunday School (or Dialect Service), which is a service conducted in the Pennsylvania German dialect. These services have gained in popularity over the years, so that they occur more frequently today than they did decades ago. Typically, they are held on a Sunday afternoon. Regular church services held in Standard German were phased out in Pennsylvania during World War I.

One of the main German-language cultural organizations in NYC is the *Literarischer Verein* 'Literary Society', founded in 1905, which states as its *raison d'être* the *Pflege der deutschen Sprache*, 'Cultivation of the German Language'. Since 1940 this organization and its activities have been sponsored by the endowment of the Literary Society Foundation, Inc. Except during the summer months and some holidays, the *Literarischer Verein* offers German-language lectures or films every Friday evening. The lectures are usually about German literature, past or present, or about other areas of world culture, politics, the sciences, and so on. Films are of the highest caliber. Also at the forefront of German-language cultural activities in NYC is the *Deutsches Haus* 'German House' at New York University, which offers German-language lectures and films, and sponsors concerts, conferences, exhibits on German art and culture, and so on. The Consulate General of the Federal Republic of Germany, and the Goethe House (funded by the German government), support German language and culture in the New York area as well. Also, German films are shown at the German Film Club, hosted by a Lutheran church in Yorkville. The two German-language movie theaters that once existed in NYC, the Wagner Theater in Queens, and the Casino Theater in Manhattan, have been closed for decades.

5. *Language maintenance*

5.1. *Immigrants from Germany exclusive of displaced persons*

Time has brought about numerous changes in the use of German in the neighborhoods of NYC which have, or had, large German-speaking populations. Yorkville, where through the 1960's one heard much German in the streets and business establishments, is today no longer a German-speaking neighborhood. Most of the German restaurants and stores were not able to meet the drastic rent increases that have become typical for Manhattan in recent decades. To be sure, Yorkville's German-speaking churches, and the *Liederkranz Club*, the site of many German-American cultural and social events, remain, but many of the persons who attend functions at these institutions are no longer from the immediate neighborhood.

Astoria, which generations ago had a sizable German-speaking population – one heard the language of the neighborhood referred to as "Steinway Street German" – is also no longer a German-speaking community. Today Astoria is known as a Greek-speaking neighborhood.

By comparison with Yorkville and Astoria, the Ridgewood-Glendale area has retained much of its German-speaking population; losses here may be attributed mainly to deaths, a desire to move to the suburbs, or a desire to relocate – usually to a warmer climate – upon retirement. Among the immigrants themselves, German is retained in informal daily life if one's spouse is also German-speaking. This includes shopping, and many other business transactions. Also, German is used in the numerous social clubs to which many of the immigrants belong; these may be clubs whose members originated in a certain locality in Germany, or whose members enjoy a particular activity, such as singing. As a rule, these individuals favor the retention of German by themselves and their children, although they recognize that a knowledge of English is a necessity in order to survive and prosper in the United States. Their command of their local variety of speech is retained if their spouse speaks the same variety of German, and if they have the opportunity to speak that variety with friends and relatives. Also, if both parents speak a local variety of German, they tend to speak this variety to their children. On the other hand, if one's spouse is German-speaking, but does not speak one's local variety of German, the standard language – or something approximating it – is spoken at home, and to one's children.

The degree to which the children of German-speaking immigrants master and use German is extremely variable. As a rule, unless both parents are German-speaking, the children will not acquire the language. Nevertheless, even in such cases, there may be a caretaker, often a grandparent, who will teach the children German, and especially in cases where that person's English is poor, the children will master German quite well. However, once the children are no longer in daily contact with that caretaker, language proficiency begins to deteriorate. Children whose parents bring them up to speak German frequently begin to speak English to their parents once they begin to have contact with English-speaking children, or once they attend school. If parents do not insist that the children speak German to them, the children's spoken proficiency quickly declines, and may become nonexistent. Nevertheless, if the parents continue to speak German to the children under these circumstances, the children's ability to understand German remains intact.

In many cases where active spoken proficiency is retained by the children of German-speaking immigrants, the parents want their children also to be able to read and write German. Unfortunately, in such cases, whether the parents are the sole teachers or whether the children are taught German in a private German-language school, or even in a public school where instruction in German is offered, the results are usually disappointing. Such children may learn to read German tolerably well, but as a rule, their written German is noticeably deficient, even in cases where the student is exposed to Standard German at home. As a general rule, these children will rarely read something in German as a matter of personal choice, part of the reason being that very little of what is published in German, including German-language newspapers published in the U. S., has anything to do with life in New York, or the United States.

Children of immigrants who are brought up to speak German, and who continue to speak it to their parents, nevertheless tend not to use the language with anyone else, unless they have to. Most importantly, they will not use it with persons their own age who speak German, unless these people cannot speak English. Even in cases where such children have a German-speaking spouse who is either an immigrant or the child of an immigrant, English will be the preferred language.

In cases where immigrants marry spouses who are not German-speaking, it is a rare occurrence that this spouse acquires German, that German is used in informal daily life, and that their children acquire German. More commonly, the German-speaking individual speaks only English to the spouse and children. While this individual's attitude toward German often remains positive, the use and mastery of the language often decline. (In some instances, the immigrant's attitude toward German becomes neutral; not surprisingly, in these cases, the language often falls into disuse, and mastery deteriorates very rapidly.) If this individual has the opportunity to use both the local variety of German and the standard language to friends and relatives, language skills may be maintained fairly well. Even in such cases, however, active ability, i. e. speaking, and especially writing the standard language, are more difficult to maintain than understanding and reading.

5.2. The Jews from Germany and Austria

In most cases, assimilation to the American way of life has proceeded rapidly among the Jewish immigrants from Germany and Austria. Perhaps some aspects of the assimilation process were initially slower for those who lived in the communities of Washington Heights and Jackson Heights, but as was mentioned in Section 3.2, many of the Jewish immigrants have gradually left these communities and settled elsewhere, and thus have become as Americanized as the rest of the members of their group.

During the early years in America, immigrants were much assisted by Jewish immigrants from Germany and Austria who had come to America earlier, and who had already established themselves. Also, they derived a great deal of assistance from the newspaper *Aufbau*, which gave them much practical information about their adopted country, and often, about opportunities for employment. Moreover, the newspaper functioned, and still functions, as a medium for persons wishing to establish contact with family and friends going back to their years in Europe.

The attitude of the Jewish immigrants toward German, and their use and maintenance of the language, is characterized by great variation. On one end of the scale, an individual will continue to look at German as her or his native language, as the language in which they received their education, and as the language of a rich culture in which they grew up: *die Sprache der Dichter und Denker* 'the language of poets and thinkers'. These individuals cleave to authors like Goethe, Schiller, Lessing, Heine, and Kant, who have produced some of the most lyrical, liberal, and enlightened writings that the world has ever known. Also, many of these individuals feel that the more languages one knows, the better. Frequently these are the views of individuals who had already entered one of the professions before 1933, or whose studies at a university were interrupted after Hitler came to power. When the spouses of these individuals are also German-speaking, the language tends to be maintained in informal daily life, and their children are fluent in spoken and written German. In many such cases, the children read and write German to the extent that they have been able to study at German universities.

On the other end of the spectrum are those individuals who essentially wanted to forget everything about Germany or Austria, including the language. If such individuals married spouses who were not German-speaking, the mastery of German deteriorated rapidly, especially among those who had not finished the *Gymnasium* in Europe. Such persons made every effort to speak only English, and certainly did not encourage their children to learn German. However, when such individuals married German-speaking spouses, they often maintained an excellent command of spoken German, since it was easier for them to converse with their spouses in their native language. In many such cases, the children are able to understand a great deal of German, though their parents did nothing to encourage this.

Yet other immigrants, while always mindful of what caused them to leave Germany or Austria, felt that although they were now Americans, they were also "German-Jewish", and thus have maintained their bilingualism and biculturalism to varying degrees.

In the early years after emigration, there were social clubs, cultural clubs, and athletic clubs to which many younger German-speaking Jews belonged. German was spoken in these organizations. However, as the members married and started families, and as assimilation progressed, these activities played less and less of a role in their lives, so that today, only a few of these clubs are still in existence, e. g. the New World Club, Club of the Habonim [Sons], and the Jewish Unity Club of New Jersey. Lectures or other events may now be in German or English.

5.3. The Danube Swabians and the Germans from Gottschee

The maintenance of German among the Danube Swabians and the Germans from Gottschee is relatively high among the immigrants, especially among the immigrants who were married to members of their respective groups when they arrived in the U. S., or who married members of their respective groups once they settled here. Another factor which contributes to their maintenance of German is residence in the Ridgewood-Glendale area, thus being in close proximity to the friends and relatives of one's respective group. Furthermore, many members of these groups work in establishments with other individuals of their respective groups. Here, attitudes toward the maintenance of German are positive, and degree of proficiency remains high, although the importance of acquiring English is also recognized. While the children of the immigrants are brought up to speak German, and many of them retain an active knowledge of the language into adulthood, they tend to use it interchangeably with English, and they tend not to teach German to their children. In the social clubs, the immigrants themselves speak German, whereas their children use English. In the athletic clubs (e. g. *Blau-Weiss Gottschee*, a large soccer club named after the colors of Gottschee, blue and white), where the players are all American born, English has been the language of its members for decades.

5.4. Language maintenance among the four groups

One may conclude from the above that the shift from German to English by many German-speaking immigrants in New York City, and their offsprings, may be attributed to existent conditions as well as non-existent ones, i. e. to developments that have taken place in their communities, as well as to conditions conducive to language maintenance that were never present in their communities. Of the former, we recognize what might be called "dilution", the relocation of individuals out of former German-speaking neighborhoods, attrition due to deaths, the (involuntary) relocation of German-speaking commercial establishments, and the arrival of other ethnic groups and commercial establishments.

Among the non-existent conditions for language maintenance, we may mention specifically the absence of private – with the exception of the *Deutsche Schule*, discussed in section 6 – or public German-speaking schools (or even schools with a predominance of German-speakers), the paucity of religious establishments in which German is the dominant language, and the absence of readily-available German-language media and popular entertainment which relate to life in the United States.

It must also be born in mind that the large waves of immigration of German-speaking individuals took place in the 1930s, 1940s and 1950s. Had such immigration continued through the 1990s, the presence of these immigrants would have provided a significant linguistic reinforcement of what had begun decades earlier. Clearly the absence of this reinforcement, and the other missing factors mentioned above, have contributed in no small measure to the gradual but relentless shift away from German and toward English.

6. *Excursus: Swiss, Austrian, and German nationals working in New York City, and the Deutsche Schule New York 'German School of New York'*

By way of contrast with the German-speaking groups in New York City discussed above, there is a comparatively small group of German-speaking individuals living in and around New York City who are not immigrants; rather they have been assigned to work in the New York City area for a specific period of time, after which they will return to Switzerland, Austria, or Germany. These individuals are employed by their national governments, or large firms from their native countries that are heavily engaged in international trade. As a group, they are well educated, and have strong ties to their native countries. However, because their assignments are usually of several years' duration, they live in the Greater New York area with their spouses and children.

In many cases, these individuals choose not to send their children to American schools; rather, they send their children to the *Deutsche Schule New York*, a private school located just north of New York City, in White Plains. The original school building itself, and the property, were purchased by the *Deutsche Schule Corporation* from the City of White Plains in 1980. The main purpose of the *Deutsche Schule* is to provide a school in the New York City area which completely adheres to the curriculum of schools in the Federal Republic of Germany, and which offers the *Abitur* [an examination, the passing of which enables one to enter German universities] after completion of the "thirteenth grade". All instruction is in German; French and English are studied as foreign languages, even though students who have lived in the United States for several years often known English quite well. Thus, no matter when a child should leave a school in Germany and enter the *Deutsche Schule*, or leave the *Deutsche Schule* to return to school in Germany, the difference would be no greater than changing schools within Germany.

The school has grown considerably since 1980, when it offered instruction only through the end of the *Grundschule* (roughly through pre-high school). Since that time, it has added two large wings, and, as mentioned above, goes as far as the thirteenth grade. Currently there are approximately 360 pupils in attendance; about 65% of the pupils are German, about 9% Swiss, 7% Austrians, 7% Americans, and 12% represent numerous other nationalities.

One might well wonder to what extent the foreign nationals from Switzerland, Austria, and Germany, and the *Deutsche Schule*, have interacted with the German immigrants described in the sections above. Perhaps not too surprisingly, the interaction has been practically non-existent. For the most part, the backgrounds of the immigrants are vastly different from those of the foreign nationals: the immigrants arrived in the United States earlier, left Europe when it was economically, politically, and socially quite different from what it is today, came, for the most part, from very different educational and occupational backgrounds, retained little if any concrete ties to Europe, and were resolved to settle permanently in the United States. In some ways, the Europe of today, and its inhabitants, would be as strange to the immigrants as was the United States and its inhabitants upon their arrival; certainly this would be the case for their children.

Interestingly, most of the foreign nationals from Switzerland, Austria, and Germany temporarily assigned to the Greater New York area wish to experience as much of the cultural life of New York as possible while they are here, and many of them are eager to meet and mix with Americans, as well. However, because most of these individuals live in parts of Manhattan and the suburbs where rents and real estate are rather expensive, they are simply unaware of the existence of German-speaking groups described in the sections above, and even if they were aware of them, they would find that they had little in common with them.

The situation is similar with respect to the *Deutsche Schule*, and its pupils. The school is acutely aware of the fact that it is all but unknown except to the foreign nationals who send their children there, and as part of its recent efforts, still in its beginning stages, to provide its students with more opportunities to experience American life, it has sought to reach out to the Westchester County community in general, and to the American schools of the area. Thus most of the faculty and students connected with the school are either unaware, or only remotely aware, of the German-speaking groups described in the sections above, and there has been no interaction at all.

One might speculate as to whether the *Deutsche Schule* could have had an impact on the German-speaking immigrant groups, particularly with respect to language maintenance, had it been founded earlier, perhaps in the 1950's. In all likelihood, however, the effect would have been negligible. For one thing, the commute from Manhattan, Brooklyn, or Queens to White Plains and back, each day, would have been a strong deterrent, with respect to the time and expense involved. The tuition would have been an additional deterrent, especially for immigrants who arrived in the United States with no resources, and who were in most cases struggling to establish themselves; in the 1994–1995 school year, the tuition ranged from \$6,300 for grades 1–4, to \$7,950 for grades 11–13. Finally, although it is possible to earn a New York State Regents Diploma at the school, the *Deutsche Schule* is essentially a German institution on American soil; it does not seek to prepare its pupils for a future in the United States, but rather for a future in Germany.

7. Conclusion

If one compares the vitality of Pennsylvania German (particularly among the Mennonites and Amish), whose first speakers came to America over 310 years ago, and which still has many thousands of native speakers (including infants who are just now learning to speak), with each of the four German-speaking communities in the NYC area, one cannot escape the conclusion that environment is a major factor affecting language use, proficiency, and maintenance. That a European language competing with English could be maintained in North American communities for over three centuries, is nothing short of amazing, considering the size of the Mennonite and Amish groups. Clearly the rural-agricultural environment, offering speakers of a minority language ample opportunity to retreat to their native language daily, is greatly conducive to language maintenance, even under conditions where outside support for their efforts has been nonexistent, and in fact, discouragement, and often outright hostility, have been the order of the day almost from the time that the first speakers arrived. By comparison, one might think that the support and tolerance offered in an urban area like NYC might ensure the maintenance of a minority language like German for many generations; yet, unless current immigration patterns change, German may well be a dead language in NYC before Pennsylvania German passes out of existence among the Plain groups in Pennsylvania.

Nevertheless, the matter of language maintenance is too complex to be explained on the basis of only one factor, environment. Speakers' views on assimilation to the dominant culture must also be taken into consideration. Also crucial to an understanding of language maintenance are the views which speakers have about adaptation in their native language and culture, a factor which is similar, but not identical to assimilation (Kraybill 1989). The study of German in the urban environment, today still in its infancy, will without doubt elucidate additional factors and their interrelationships in questions of language maintenance, and will thereby contribute in no small degree to our overall understanding of the phenomenon that we call language.

Notes

1. I would like to thank Mr. Henry Marx of *Aufbau* and Mr. Egon Stadelmann of the *New Yorker Staats-Zeitung* who provided invaluable perspective by sharing with me insights gained over decades of service to the German-speaking communities of New York. I am also very much obliged to Mr. Wolfgang Dipscheid, Principal of the Deutsche Schule New York, who graciously took time from his very busy schedule to explain the functioning of his school, and kindly provided me with fascinating material concerning its origin and development. In addition, I would also like to express my appreciation to the many other people without whose help this paper could not have been written; unfortunately, it is not possible to mention all of them by name.
2. According to statistics of the 1990 census, there were 395,230 persons who reported German ancestry in New York City; this represents approximately 14% of the 2,900,879 persons who reported German ancestry in New York State, and not quite 1% of the 45,583,932 persons who reported German ancestry in the United States.

3. The term *diglossic* refers to *diglossia*, a linguistic situation in which typically, two varieties of a language are used for different purposes. Many linguists refer to these as informal and formal. The informal variety is usually used for ordinary, everyday spoken communication. The formal variety is often grammatically more complicated than the informal one, and is usually used for written communication, and on occasions when formal speech is required. The formal variety, which may represent the language of an earlier period, or the language of another speech community, is often acquired as part of the formal education process (Ferguson 1959: 336 and Costello 1986). In some publications, the term *diglossia* may also be used to represent linguistic conditions which in some ways differ considerably from those described above.
4. The *Palatinate* is that area of western Germany bordered by the Saarland and France to the west and south, the Rhine River, Baden, and Hessia to the east, and the Rhineland to the north.
5. We may assume that many of these individuals spoke Yiddish as well as German. In his book *Geshikhte fun der yidisher shprakh* [*History of the Yiddish Languagage]*, first published in 1973, but quoted here from the 1980 English translation, Max Weinreich wrote, "Although western Yiddish began to wither toward the end of the eighteenth century, it can still be partly studied from living informants. . ." (p. 241, see also, Weinreich 1980: 444, 724–725).
6. The history of legislation limiting immigration to the United States is extensive. With respect to the immigration of persons displaced because of World War II, the events leading to it, and its consequences, the following legislation is particularly relevant. The National Origins Act of 1924, which became effective in 1929, allowed the immigration of only approximately 154,000 individuals a year from countries beyond the Western Hemisphere. In addition, immigration was intentionally limited according to nationality, so that approximately 127,000 persons per year could immigrate from western and northern European countries. However, because of the large numbers of persons displaced after World War II, the United States Congress passed the Displaced Persons Act of 1948, and the Refugee Relief Act of 1953, which enabled approximately 600,000 Europeans to immigrate.
7. Although 17th and 18th century German immigrants to Pennsylvania, already referred to in section 3.1 above, originated in many regions of that country, the majority of the immigrants were from the Palatinate area (cf. note 4 above). The varieties of German which the immigrants and their descendants spoke gradually blended into one fairly homogeneous variety of speech which is today known as Pennsylvania German (or colloquially, Pennsylvania Dutch); however, the dominant element in this variety is that of the Palatinate. This variety of German very much resembles that of the Danube Swabians, since they both reflect the Palatinate element. On the other hand, Pennsylvania German is in many ways quite distinct from Standard German, (which has most of its roots in dialects of Central German) and other regional varieties of German which have been transplanted to New York City. The individuals using Pennsylvania German may be divided into two groups, which are known colloquially as the Plain Dutch and the Fancy Dutch. The Plain Dutch are largely the descendants of Mennonite and Amish settlers who continue to speak Pennsylvania German as part of their efforts, inspired by religious beliefs, to remain apart, as much as possible, from the society around them. The Fancy Dutch are the descendants of settlers who belonged to the Lutheran and Reformed churches; as a rule, they find it necessary and desirable to integrate themselves into American society, and one of the results of this integration is the steadily decreasing use of Pennsylvania German among them (Costello 1978, 1985, and 1989).

References

Behaghel, Otto
1911 *Geschichte der deutschen Sprache.* (3rd edition.) Strassburg: Karl J. Trübner.
Beidelman, William
1898 *The Story of the Pennsylvania Germans.*
[1969] [Reprint edition. Detroit: Gale Research Company].
Burke, Ellin M.
1979 "New York 1654–1800" in: Ellin M. Burke – Ann G. Perry (eds.), *The Jewish community in early New York 1654–1800.* New York: Fraunces Tavern Museum, 6–8.
Census of Population
1990 *Ancestry of the population in the United States.* Washington DC: U. S. Government Printing Office. (Issued August 1993).
1990 *Social and economic characteristics.* New York. Washington DC: U. S. Government Printing Office. (Issued September 1993).
1990 *The foreign born population in the United States.* Washington DC: U. S. Government Printing Office. (Issued July 1993).
Costello, John R.
1978 "Syntactic change and second language acquisition: the case for Pennsylvania German", *Linguistics* 213: 29–50.
1985 "Pennnsylvania German: social and linguistic aspects", in: Heinz Kloss (ed.) *Deutsch als Muttersprache in den Vereinigten Staaten.* Stuttgart: Franz Steiner Verlag Wiesbaden, 66–76.
1986 "Diglossia at twilight; German and Pennsylvania 'Dutch' in the mid-nineteenth century", in: Werner Enninger (ed.) *Studies on the languages and the verbal behavior of the Pennsylvania Germans I.* Stuttgart: Franz Steiner Verlag Wiesbaden, 1–24.
1989 "Innovations increasing syntactic complexity in the native language of bilingual children from 5 to 10: the case for Pennsylvania German", in: Werner Enninger – Joachim Raith – Karl-Heinz Wandt (eds.) *Studies on the languages and the verbal behavior of the Pennsylvania Germans II.* Stuttgart: Franz Steiner Verlag Wiesbaden, 3–16.
Ferguson, Charles
1959 "Diglossia", *WORD* 15: 325–340.
Horne, A. R.
1873 "Pennsylvania German", *Pennsylvania Dutchman* l: 79–83.
Kloss, Heinz (ed.)
1985 *Deutsch als Muttersprache in den Vereinigten Staaten.* Stuttgart: Franz Steiner Verlag Wiesbaden.
Kraybill, Donald B.
1989 *The Riddle of Amish culture.* Baltimore: The Johns Hopkins University Press.
Learned, Marion Dexter
1889 *The Pennsylvania German dialect.* Baltimore: Isaac Friedenwald.
Nebel, Jeanne J.
1985 *The Danube Swabians.* Sersheim: Verein zur Pflege donauschwäbischer Heimatkunde e. V.

Robacker, Earl F.
1943 *Pennsylvania German literature.* Philadelphia: University of Pennsylvania Press.

Weinreich, Max
1973 *History of the Yiddish language.*
[1980] [Translated by Shlomo Noble, with the assistance of Joshua A. Fishman. Chicago: The University of Chicago Press].

Yiddish in New York: Communicating a culture of place[1]

Hannah Kliger and Rakhmiel Peltz

1. Language: a lens on the landscape

Yiddish writers, readers and speakers have long exhibited a special relationship with New York, the city that was home to so many East European Jewish immigrants and their descendants. Especially for those who reached New York and never left it, the nature of the language and culture of their ethnolinguistic community was inextricably tied to an evolving sense of place, that place being the city streets where Yiddish was heard. We have decided to explore that unique connection between citizens and their city, communicators of Yiddish and their community. For it is true, New York is unlike any other place in America in its centrality for Yiddish-language users. We set out to find out what we know about life in New York City as experienced by those who live it, in Yiddish.

The somewhat unconventional perspective we have adopted for this essay on Yiddish language and Yiddish life in New York City assumes a stance that we share with Schieffelin, that language can be a lens through which to search for clues about "the nature of culture and how cultural knowledge and beliefs are transmitted..." (1986: 183). In that vein, we have focused on the demonstration of conceptualizations about the conditions of their New York environs by those who express themselves in Yiddish. In other words, collecting what Hummon has called "commonplaces about communities" (1990: xiv) seems an important, if as yet uncharted, approach to understanding how language and place intersect. Analyzing language about a place and in a place, both, can help reveal the panoramas that people are prone to incorporate into their sense of self and their sense of community. Hummon summarizes this viewpoint aptly when he states that "community identity answers the question, 'Who am I?' but does so by countering, 'Where am I?' or, more fundamentally, 'where in the landscape of community forms do I belong?' It identifies the individual with place..." (1990: 142). We intend to survey, in a necessarily exploratory way, the articulation of allegiance on a grass-roots level, rather than offer the standard overview of the formal agencies representing Yiddish language in the city of New York.

The topic of Yiddish in New York has been treated to date mainly in terms of the contributions of the immigrants to Yiddish culture in the field of literary creativity (Harshav 1986; Wisse 1988; Howe 1976; Sanders 1969; Teller 1968) and in such institutions as the Yiddish press (Soltes 1925; Doroshkin 1969; Howe 1976) and the Yiddish theater (Cypkin 1986; Sandrow 1977). Lifson (1965: 502) recounts how in 1925–1926, thirteen Yiddish theaters, including three in Brooklyn, competed for popularity among New York theater audiences. In the 1990s, these New York-based cultural institutions in Yiddish survive, although drastically diminished. The Folksbiene Theater presents one production each season and performances by other groups can occasionally be viewed. Two weekly newspapers are published, *Der algemeyner zhurnal*, and the once vibrant immigrant daily, *Der forverts*. The former was founded in the 1970s and currently attracts a larger circulation than its competitor, appealing to Orthodox and especially Hasidic Jews. A variety of literary and political journals still circulate (Fishman 1985: 335), including the *Tsukunft*, the longest running periodical in Yiddish literary history, having celebrated its one hundredth anniversary in 1992.

We have chosen to turn our attention to "local knowledge" (Sanders 1993: 114) that Yiddish speakers in New York City exhibit, in their vernacular, about the intimate attachment that exists between their venue and themselves. From our own previous research on culture and communication in communities of immigrants and their children (Kliger 1990; Peltz 1989), feelings of rootedness and emotional attachment to place loom high in explaining identity changes. We agree with Davis (1991: 6) that:

> people who share a common relation to the place of residence – a place where they have their homes, raise their children, and relate to each other more as neighbors than as coworkers – can and do forge solidarities on the basis of interests that are inherent in that relation to that place.

If the relation to New York City streets, neighborhoods, physical and human markers is central for the personal and group identities of Jewish residents, we are interested in how that connection is expressed in the ethnic mother tongue and how it is observed in the ways that communication is organized. Residence in New York creates a uniquely shared identity for the city's Yiddish speakers, and that community also exists as a collectivity of shared hopes and emotional bonds (Suttles 1972: 265; Bender 1978: 7; Varenne 1986).

Yiddish has been associated with Ashkenazic Jewry for most of its history, both arising with beginnings in the Germanic lands of the ninth century. Eventually these Jews moved eastward from Western and Central Europe, being centered in Poland, Ukraine, Belorussia, the Baltic states, Hungary and Rumania by the eighteenth century. Further emigration brought Yiddish from Eastern Europe to the Western Hemisphere, Palestine (later the state of Israel), South Africa and Australia.

Although the first immigrants to arrive in New York City in the seventeenth century were Sephardic Jews, deriving from Spain and Portugal, by the middle of the eighteenth century Yiddish-speaking Jews were the majority (Doroshkin 1969: 49). The mass immigration of East European Jews to the United States took place between 1881 and 1924, mostly from the Russian and Austro-Hungarian empires. These Yiddish-speaking Jews were concentrated in the large urban centers, with two-thirds of the Jews in the ten largest cities, 1.6 million in 1927–1928, living in New York (Doroshkin 1969: 68). Smaller waves of Yiddish-speaking immigrants arrived after World War II and again starting in the 1970s, when the Soviet Union eased its emigration policy.

Yiddish language evolved over the centuries as a fusion of elements modified from several stock languages. The main components of Yiddish are Germanic, Semitic (derived from Hebrew and Aramaic), and Slavic (derived from Czech, Polish, Ukrainian and Belorussian). Within European society, the Yiddish vernacular coexisted in a diglossic relationship with Hebrew, which was generally limited to sacred functions and religious texts. Although the Germanic component is predominant in spoken and written Yiddish, the Slavic component is integrated in the language, including in constructions that are Germanic in form but modeled after Slavic usage. As is the condition of language in general, Yiddish is differentiated geographically and exhibits a variety of societal registers. Yet, despite differences, a speaker in its Northwestern extreme in Amsterdam could be understood by a speaker in Odessa in Southeastern Europe. The Yiddish heartland of Eastern Europe that thrived for hundreds of years was decimated by Nazi Germany during World War II.

Few immigrants who arrived during the period of mass immigration are alive today. The waves of subsequent immigration were markedly smaller. Therefore, the American Jewish population today consists of an aged population of children of immigrants, the second generation, and larger numbers of third, fourth and subsequent generations. Qualitative studies show an intense exposure to Yiddish during the first years of life for the children of immigrants, but this is not followed later on with active Yiddish speaking (Peltz 1991). The following figures for individuals claiming Yiddish as mother tongue demonstrate fluctuations: 1.8 million in 1940, an estimated 1.0 million in 1960, 1.6 million in 1970, an estimated 1.2 million in 1979 (Fishman et al. 1985: 130, 147). The authors (Fishman et al: 1985: 146) who compiled these statistics explain that for Yiddish, as for other major languages, the second and third generation increased their claims of mother tongue usage from 1960 to 1970. However, "Yiddish, which in 1970 had pulled out of its steep 1940 to 1960 decline, registered a 24% drop in 1979, thereby once again achieving the rare distinction of being the most rapidly declining non-English mother-tongue among 'the big six' (indeed, among non-English mother tongues in the USA as a whole)".

Of the 1.6 million Yiddish mother-tongue claimants in 1970, 0.7 million were from the state of New York, reflecting the geographic concentration of the original immigrants (Fishman et al. 1985: 183). In 1982, 1,168 local religious units reported Yiddish usage, as did 422 schools (Fishman et al. 1985: 200). These institutions are found largely in the more religiously observant Orthodox sphere of Jewish life. In general, the demands of Jewish religious observance are associated with concentrated residence, commercial establishments that provide food that complies with religious dietary requirements, and nearby institutions for prayer and study. In the early part of the century, Boro Park in Brooklyn became a residential area for observant Jews (Moore 1992: 259). After World War II, other areas in Brooklyn, such as Williamsburg and Crown Heights, became centers for Hasidic Jewish life.

Hasidism, a form of fervent religious devotion characterized by intense emotional prayer and spiritual transcendence, arose in eighteenth century Eastern Europe largely in opposition to the strict text-based study methods of rabbinic Judaism. It became the dominant form of Jewish Orthodoxy in large parts of Eastern Europe. After World War II, New York City, and especially the borough of Brooklyn, became a world center for Hasidic communal life. Living in tight-knit insular subgroups, Hasidim had many children and built neighborhood institutions where Yiddish was most often the language of discourse. Different Hasidic adherents produced their own weeklies and monthlies, and published primers for teaching their children.

Fishman (1982, 1983), in his essays devoted to the more recent demographic data regarding Yiddish, has underscored that it is in the ultra-Orthodox Hasidic sector that Yiddish is the first language of family life, of the neighborhood synagogue and of the school. In contrast to these daily language-based activities transmitted from generation to generation in the primary institutions of the community, secular Jewish circles sponsor the more intermittent Yiddish-language activities of secondary institutions. The occasional theatrical performance or the publication of printed periodicals do not preserve the intergenerational bond in the same enduring way. Thus, the oscillations in the census data showing an increase in Yiddish mother-tongue declarations in 1970 and a decrease in 1979 can be accounted for by the articulation by secular younger people, first, of their dissatisfaction with American society through an expressed interest in ethnicity and, subsequently, a relative lack of ethnic identification. In the year 2000, it is predicted that one million individuals in the United States will report Yiddish as their mother tongue. However, in terms of sustained language maintenance and use, Fishman (1983: 3–4) highlights the 26,000 youngsters in Hasidic circles, mostly in Brooklyn. In the year 2000, they will have increased their numbers by 20% since 1985, and it is for them that Yiddish will be the first and likely only language. The larger proportion of non-Hasidic Jews in the city, as they become distanced from the immigrant generation, turn less to Yiddish for their linguistic and communal needs.

The question of how members construct the dimensions of their community and, then, communicate those parameters to themselves and to others is a process worthy of investigation. What matters in these conversations is the meaning of such discourse, the topic to which we now turn. This was underscored in a study of contemporary Jewish clubs in New York City formed by immigrants with a common link to a European hometown (Kliger 1992: 119–136). It was revealing, for example, to monitor members' assessments of their communities of origin. Post-World War II refugees who settled in New York in the 1940s and early 1950s spoke of their Polish hometown cities of Lodz or Warsaw in terms and tones quite distinct from their compatriots who had settled in the U.S. earlier. Their children and grandchildren cannot necessarily accurately depict the geographical borders or historical legacy of the Old World communities to which they are tied by virtue of their cultural and linguistic ancestry. To understand these developments, it is important to note the context that gives contour to the continual discussions about identity. For each cohort, their Lodz is a different place. But, then, so is the New York City they each live in. As one urban historian of New York has concluded: "To move to a new neighborhood – to change the view from the kitchen window – meant to exchange an old ethnic identity for a new one, to abandon tradition, for modernity" (Moore 1992: 253). And it is, after all, within the boundary of New York, the new world community Jews joined and helped build, that the struggle to give voice to multiple visions of self occurs. This compelling challenge is faced by many ethnic enclaves, generation after generation, as they try to make sense of reality.

2. *At home in New York: language as the link*

In trying to find the language(s) to represent their loyalties as Jewish New Yorkers rooted in the Yiddish-centered milieu of the Ashkenazic Jewish tradition, immigrants were quite innovative. In many areas of the city that they populated, "the Yiddish language of the street, home, and business, allowed Jews to develop a sense of Jewish identity..." (Sorin 1990: 16). The dominance of Yiddish conferred a cohesive sense of neighborhood. Although, as Moore (1992: 255) cites, "Jewish neighborhoods on the fringes of the city shared a common ethnic 'language' of cultural pluralism", Yiddish language and culture ensured the unique Jewish flavor of the surroundings that the Jewish residents themselves constructed, in the traditions of all "imagined communities" (Anderson 1991). Some sections in New York's boroughs even became associated with Yiddish names. Manhattan's Riverside Drive, for example, was known as "Allrightniks Row" when East European Jews came to the area. The slang term resulted from the back and forth interpolation between the English word "allright" and the American Yiddish phrase "olraytnik" that evolved to indicate a person who had succeeded financially and was now comfortably set up. When the place name "Allrightniks Row" was utilized, it was meant to reflect the arrival and all-encompassing presence of upwardly mobile Yiddish speakers on Manhattan's upper west side (Allen 1993: 238). While Riverside Drive was transformed into Allrightniks Row, Second Avenue in lower Manhattan was distinguished as the Yiddish Broadway, since many Yiddish theaters flourished there in the early part of the twentieth century. This similitude between New York landmarks and the signposts of Jewish New York was extended by tagging the Cafe Royal, the social hub of Second Avenue's theater crowd, the Yiddish Sardi's (Allen 1993: 61).

The practice of assigning Yiddish alternatives to official place names was in fact quite common in Europe. Although the propensity to generate Yiddish-language versions of neighborhoods or streets in America is less apparent, unauthoritative names were designated by Yiddish speakers for some of the regions where they resided. Particularly among the immigrant generation, a folk toponymy emerged that is notable for the ways in which it reveals attitudes and attachments of a people in social and linguistic transition. A listing of such appellations published in 1973 includes the following: *levone* [Yiddish word for moon] instead of Livonia Avenue in Brooklyn, Essex Street in Manhattan becomes *esikstrit*, borrowing the Yiddish word for vinegar. In another example, the inhabitants of Mosholu Parkway in the Bronx spoke of the "*parkvey* that was Moyshele's" [Yiddish name] (Shekhter 1973: 56–57). These adjustments should not be seen as mere mispronunciations, but rather as cleverly (if not always consciously) construed strategies whereby immigrants could bring their worldview to bear on their accommodation to New York. Irving Howe has said that some of "the difficulties experienced in learning English were not merely technical, like mastering the "th" and "w" sounds or coping with the chaos of English spelling; they were basically cultural" (Howe 1976: 227). We tend to agree. Indeed, it seems that adjustment to New York culture is more readily facilitated when newcomers can wander through the city streets, including figuratively and linguistically, without suddenly being forced to abandon the intimacy and security of familiar Yiddish speech.

The immigrant language can serve as the cultural anchor for a world in transition, both for the immigrant and for the children. Yiddish is the signal of the intimacy of home, of endearment, of the parents who take care of you. This nurturance extends into the larger circle of family, friends, fellow immigrants from the same hometown and neighbors, all the way onto the streets of the neighborhood. Moving beyond the "nurturing neighborhood" (Sorin 1990) can be a frightening experience, even for those children who are born in New York City.

Henry Roth's classic novel of immigrant life in New York, *Call It Sleep* (1991 [1934]), is a saga of an immigrant child, David, from the time he arrives in the United States at age two until age eight. The work is a linguistic marvel because Roth builds a complex but consistent code whereby the major language of the immigrant home, first in Brooklyn's Brownsville and then on the Lower East Side, is Yiddish, portrayed by Roth as standard English (Kleederman 1974). The children on the street and among themselves speak in a New York dialect of English, sometimes with a few borrowed Yiddish words, transcribed in the text to reflect pronunciation. Adult immigrants, Jews and non-Jews, speak to people outside their group in an accented English that is influenced by their mother tongue. Added to these are Hebrew and Aramaic of the religious school, and Polish that David's mother uses to keep secrets from him.

At no point does this well tailored language system break down in David's mind; he controls all parts and knows their place. Language is present in the foreground as intense, mind-boggling events and emotions confuse and overwhelm David, as we follow his education in matters of sex, love, family relations, physical abuse and violence. Yet in this passionately psychological novel, language does not appear as a threat or puzzle for David, even though the different components seem to collide against each other. As the process of becoming American ensues, language represents hearth and home for the immigrant child.

This does not mean that the rest of the world adjusts to David's delicately balanced language system. Right off, we see that the young adult immigrants, David's parents, do not fare as well. When the immigrant couple is reunited upon the wife and child's arrival at Ellis Island, marital conflict and cultural disintegration are clearly presaged in the symbol of broken Yiddish, one of the few times that standard English is not used by Roth (1991: 16).

Not only is there disorder in David's family system, but the outside non-Jewish world does not accept his language strategies. In a frightening scene in which David gets lost on the city streets, this English-Yiddish bilingual cannot make the name of his street understood (Roth 1991: 97–100). The phonology followed by Jewish residents may be part of the system of appropriating the streets of New York as part of their Jewish world, but it is not always conducive for communicating with non-Jews. David seems destined to be a prisoner of the Jewish street, able to communicate only with those who speak Yiddish and Jewish English. The ambivalence toward Yiddish starts early. The children are enclosed by a protective web that shields them in their first years from the public language that is their key to mobility. As we see, in the case of little David on the streets of Brooklyn, it is terrifying to be fettered by the language of your youth.

Echoing the fiction of Roth, himself an immigrant child who came to the United States at age two and grew up on New York's Lower East Side, is the autobiographical essay by the literary critic Irving Howe (1946: 364), a child of immigrants who was raised in the East Bronx. On his first day in kindergarten, he identified the fork that the teacher held up by the Yiddish word *gupl*. Shamed by the laughter of the whole class, five-year old Irving informed his parents that afternoon that he would never again speak Yiddish to them. This silence of the second generation belies a knowledge of the language and culture, at the same time that it halts transmission to the next generation.

The children of immigrants, growing up in the neighborhoods of secondary settlement were not deprived of a Yiddish cultural milieu, as Howe attests (1982: 2–3), but they were often unaware of its dimensions. Although a far cry from the vibrancy of the Lower East Side, Howe's East Bronx of the 1920s and 1930s was dominated by spoken Yiddish. The English of the young, in addition, had a unique intonation, analogous to that described by Roth. Crotona Park, where Howe played ball, was a meeting place for Yiddish literati. Yiddish theater was performed at the McKinley Square Theater, a few blocks from his apartment, and a secular Yiddish school stood on another street. Yiddish did indeed spread throughout the New York neighborhoods, but the degree of involvement of descendants of the immigrants was far less than that of parents and grandparents.

The interplay of languages on city streets, as well as in public and private forums, is a telling indicator of continuity and discontinuity in communicative competencies among community members who speak Yiddish. The character of Yiddish language behavior in the city needs also to be scrutinized in those arenas where being a Yiddish reader, and not only a Yiddish speaker, figures prominently. A 1965 study of the Yiddish readership frequenting New York public libraries was imaginative, if somewhat unsystematic, in that ethnographic observations at a selected subsample of these sites complemented the author's audit of circulation figures for Yiddish books (Faust 1973: 283–285). Thus, a visit to Hamilton Fish Park Library on Manhattan's Lower East Side confirmed that those who enter the building to read Yiddish books or to choose from the available variety of Yiddish periodicals were mostly elderly individuals; librarians estimated that a total of 150 Yiddish volumes were checked out per month. Seward Park Library circulation statistics showed that in 1959, 1,769 books were circulated, and 1,906 books went out in 1962, but borrowers are known to come from other districts to examine some of the special and rare editions housed at that branch. Specific figures were compiled from libraries throughout neighborhoods in the Bronx and Brooklyn, while more extended fieldwork documented how the latter borough's Williamsburg branch serviced its residents.

Data on the distribution of Yiddish newspapers and Yiddish and Hebrew books throughout the United States in a nationwide study by N. Goldberg (1948) uncovered a drop overall in the figures for Yiddish dailies in the time period between 1918 and 1947, but the decline is sharper in the cities outside of New York. The comparative tabulations disclose that New York City furnished approximately 70 per cent of the total number of newspaper subscribers, in some years as much as 84 per cent (Goldberg 1948: 42–56).

3. *The language of poetry, the poetry of place*

Not only speakers and readers, but also Yiddish writers developed a constant, continuing association with New York. American Yiddish poetry is an important locus for discovering how a sense of belonging is forged through the community's language practices. American Yiddish poets sing of their connection to the city of New York in a variety of voices, from the writings of the Introspectivists, a school of modernist Yiddish poets who emphasized experimentation in poetic form and language, largely inaccessible to the masses, to the unpretentious verses that were pronounced at political rallies or widely performed at social gatherings.[2]

The panorama of poetic creativity in Yiddish in New York includes the words of Mina Bordo-Rivkin, who in 1954 wrote in Far Rockaway, Queens of the budding romances that flowered during the pilgrimages of the young to the Atlantic Ocean (Mayzl 1955: 709–710). H. Royzenblat, too, was enchanted by the love between a young couple visiting the oceanside amusement park in Coney Island (Mayzl 1955: 238–240). Y. Slonim, who came to the United States at age two in 1885, wrote "On Vandover Avenue" in 1942 about his return to the Bronx of his youth, a journey that evoked special memories of the literary, socialist, and Zionist clubs that assembled in Crotona Park and Claremont Park (Mayzl 1955: 308–310). He was himself affiliated with the literary group, *Di yunge*, and remembers how he would play in the park as a boy with the writers-to-be, Dilon and Ignatov. It was later, in the park, that his own poetry would mature and he would fall in love with his future wife. The poem in which he describes these sentiments is laden with ambivalence, for he misses the optimistic excitement of unknown prospects and fails to convey this feeling to his sons, who accompany him on his nostalgic visit. The symbolism of the absence of intergenerational continuity is clear, as the sons look on with love, sensing their father's joy and sorrow, yet they remain closed off from the historic cultural experience of his younger years.

Several poets, especially among the Introspectivists, were taken with the image of the city and used the New York cityscape as an abstraction of the American metropolis (Harshav 1986: 43). The city is seen, symbolically, as a hub where dreams are built, more than as a locale for developing one's identity. In his book *In New York*, for example, M. L. Halpern uses the city image to express feelings of homelessness (Hellerstein 1982: xiv, xix). Leyeles, the Introspectivist who is best known for introducing into Yiddish poetry the highly structured forms of European poetry, uses "Wall Street" as a symbol of the uncaring gods of contemporary capitalist society (Leyeles 1926: 37; Cooperman – Cooperman 1967: 153–155). In other poems, he proclaims his love for places, streets, and edifices, such as the Manhattan Bridge, Madison Square Garden and Broadway, but he is unconvincing about his affinity for these urban sites and structures (Leyeles 1926: 38–39, 47–48, 54). More often, we find the city as the backdrop for a polemic on social inequity, such as in Ester Shumyatsher's "My New York Street Sings". The song that cries out from the joyous, noisy Manhattan streets is the wail of poverty, inciting the poet to declare that Manhattan will have to pay for this (Mayzl 1955: 777–778).

When the Yiddish immigrant poet feels at home in New York, it is largely because the city embraces an entire universe of languages and cultures:

It's a city of merriment,
A city of many nations,
All tongues are here evident
In noise or adoration...

You're never astray,
You're always at home...
Nowhere here a stranger –
Everywhere, free, free...

(Lyesin, in Cooperman – Cooperman 1967: 37–38)

New York also represents freedom from anti-Semitism and its dangers:

My home is now New York, the free city of nations,
The city where church bells ring away unheard.
And where no blood flows in the name of a god.

(Halpern 1919 [1982]: 51)

Not only is the strong international, tolerant ambiance of the city attractive, but the Jewish presence is undeniably reassuring. To Hirshbeyn, the Hudson is more appealing than other rivers because of the million and a half Jews living in the city (Mayzl 1955: 265–266). Chatham Square in Lower Manhattan is the subject of several poems because Jews are buried there, refugees from Portugal in the seventeenth century who were provided with a haven (Gross, in Cooperman – Cooperman 1967: 344; Shvarts, in Rozhanski 1977: 71–74). The Lower East Side is home to piety, tradition, and continuity, i. e. *vu yidish nusekh yoyvlt* 'where Yiddish is celebrated', according to Opalov (Mayzl 1955: 622–623). As for the language, the essay "On East Broadway" states that Yiddish is stylish, no longer a mere "jargon" (Shapiro, in Mayzl 1955: 244–246).

One Yiddish poet, Leyvik, writes of sitting in Hester Park on the Lower East Side, yet envisioning his parents' graves in Russia (Harshav 1986: 730–731). The pull of his birthplace at that moment is stronger than "the towering city", yet he feels virtually enveloped by the compact and circumscribed Jewish tract that has been recreated on the Lower East Side (Harshav 1986: 695). Another writer, Vaynshteyn, poignantly laments the last lingering sounds of the Old World on this new territory:

Tsu hern zey redn vert dir epes troyerik-bang,
Vos fun shtetldikn yid geblibn iz bloyz a klang.
[To hear them speak makes you sad and forlorn,
That only a sound remains of the shtetl Jew.]
(Mayzl 1955: 832–833, authors' translation)

Years later, the poet Arn Tseytlin will write his "New York Elegy", testifying that he himself and "the dying language of my verse...have been put out on the street like an old piece of furniture, a lost remnant of a world" (Mayzl 1955: 731–732, authors' translation). Tsetylin managed to reach the shores of New York at the beginning of World War II, yet lost his family in the Nazi onslaught. When Tseytlin stands by the Hudson, he thinks of the Jordan and the Vistula, of Jewish life in the land of Israel and in Poland (Cooperman – Cooperman 1967: 159). The literary critic Sh. Niger (1941: 24), who spent most of his career in New York, reflected that the immigrants looked for all developments of Yiddish culture to emanate from Eastern Europe. When that source was obliterated, the Yiddish poets of New York mourned their fate and became the guardians of Yiddish language and culture.

4. *Becoming American: language in transition*

The relationship of New York Jews to Jewish New York was also characterized by a collaborative team of Yiddish poets and writers who worked under the auspices of the New York City Unit of the Federal Writers' Project of the Works Progress Administration. This Yiddish Writers' Group, in two Yiddish-language volumes describing Jewish hometown associations and Jewish family clubs in New York City during the early years of this century, published results from a survey of approximately 2000 organizations, including findings on Yiddish-related language use, educational achievements, media habits, and leisure time preferences (Federal Writers' Project, 1938; 1939; Kliger 1992). In addition, the writers contributed flavorful chapters reporting on exchanges taking place in restaurants, meeting halls, and immigrant institutions in New York City. Against the backdrop of these urban settings, the Yiddish-language deliberations invariably center on the quest for community.

Yiddish-speaking Jews established their presence in New York and confirmed, to themselves and to other city dwellers, their intention to remain a vital component of the metropolis. In the internal communal networks they created by themselves and for themselves, their attempts to perpetuate language, culture, and identity were shaped by the encroachment of English-language influences. Indeed, in the very same immigrant clubs described in the WPA study, one author found signs of the infiltration of English at the gatherings he attended, where Yiddish was ostensibly the language of choice. As a result, he prepared a guide to conducting a meeting in correct Yiddish, offering proper Yiddish speech constructions for uniformly discussing the affairs of the organization at its assemblies (Itskovits 1944: 114–120).

Similar counsel was forthcoming from another observer, actually a listener, who classified Yiddish broadcasts on New York's radio station WEVD according to patterns of pronunciation and unsuitable borrowings from English or German. These inconsistencies and other "contaminations" (Gutmans 1958) were deemed inappropriate for a language heard on the airwaves by an estimated 175,000 listeners in the New York area, in other words, a public language.

Outside of the community's own organizations, Yiddish was evidently also ranked an official language by municipal authorities. Press releases with information deemed newsworthy for the general public were disseminated from offices in City Hall in numerous languages, including Yiddish. Appraising one such document, a mimeographed sheet from the Office of Civil Defense, M. Mark laments the multitude of errors, "at least one mistake on each of forty lines", and ponders whether other foreign languages are similarly mishandled and mixed with English (Mark 1952: 89–91).

Where questions arise about language maintenance and language shift, be it in the inner realm of family and communal life or in the domain of civic governance, the politics of identity can never be far behind. This theme of the interrelation of language and ideology surfaced in a maneuver by Republicans in New York who, during the World War I years, suggested an amendment to the New York State constitution that would mandate literacy in English for all potential voters in New York elections. In his absorbing analysis of this campaign, Fishman (1993a) relates that the initial proposal was put forth at a time when the prerequisite for U. S. citizenship was knowing how to read *any* language, with Yiddish most definitely regarded as an admissible option. Clearly, a change in policy such as was submitted in 1915 would weaken the power at the polls of New York's Jews. Present in this constituency were the Yiddish-literate voters whose participation in elections could be counted on in greater proportions than other groups, and whose ticket tended to be Democratic and socialist-leaning.

Some New Yorkers responded to this contest, when it first arose, as if it were a conflict about the Jewish vote; the vitality of the Yiddish voice was defended by others, notably the renowned attorney and leader of the American Jewish Committee, Louis Marshall. The only Yiddish newspaper that supported the proposed change framed the issue not as a Jewish one, but as an immigration matter. The other dailies were vehemently opposed, and eventually the legislature canceled the motion. However, when the same amendment was recommended in 1921, voice and vote were entwined in a different kind of configuration. By this time, according to Fishman (1993b), bilingualism was more prevalent in the New York Jewish community. And, the rhetoric in the Yiddish press and on the streets was circumscribed to arguments about American ideals and principles of American democracy. This time the amendment was accepted, a portent of things to come in 1924 when the mass immigration from Southern and Eastern Europe that had brought hundreds of thousands of Yiddish speakers to New York City was halted. These dwindling numbers, together with the inevitable acclimatization of first- and second-generation Jews to American society, inextricably altered the commitment to Yiddish language and culture. Communication in Yiddish and about the continuity of Yiddish would carry on, but in ways that would reflect the new circumstances of its champions.

Succeeding generations in the Jewish community in New York were involved with the ethnic language, Yiddish, differentially. As with other immigrant-based communities, the changes in language behavior cannot be separated from changes in group identification (Nahirny and Fishman 1965). One place to scrutinize these dynamics is in the particular case of the New York secular Jewish afternoon schools, where the vicissitudes of

Yiddish language instruction verify a shifting balance between bilingualism and biculturalism not only in the classroom, but in the ethnic community at large (Kliger – Peltz 1990). These schools were sponsored by several organizations of differing political and cultural complexion. Jewish children, in the afternoon hours after attending public schools, studied such non-religious subjects as history, literature and Jewish folkways with Yiddish as the language of instruction.

The first wave to enter the Yiddish schools were immigrant children and children of immigrants who knew Yiddish from home. With the cessation of immigration, the schools soon served pupils who heard little or no Yiddish from their parents. In 1935, in New York City, there were 6,800 school children in attendance in the secular Jewish schools, representing 9.3% of all students in Jewish schools (Mark 1948). In 1951, enrollment in these schools constituted only 4% of the Jewish student population in New York City (Ruffman 1957). Nationwide studies in 1959 (Dushkin – Engelman) and in 1968 (Institute of Jewish Affairs 1971) substantiate this downward trend in enrollment and in the number of schools. Still, the efficacy of the program offered by the network of Yiddish schools was validated by the Greater New York study for 1951 (Ruffman 1957), certifying that students from Yiddish afternoon schools scored higher in examinations on Jewish history, Jewish holidays, and Hebrew than did students from synagogue-affiliated Hebrew afternoon schools. Interestingly, graduates of the Yiddish schools in New York City displayed the most positive opinions of all students about their Jewish education. At this time in history, most Jewish children receiving a Jewish education in New York City were attending supplementary schools after public school in the neighborhood Orthodox synagogues. The curriculum consisted largely of the liturgy of the prayer book and Bible stories. Only students from the Orthodox yeshiva day schools performed better than those from the Yiddish schools. The yeshivas were full day schools for pupils who did not attend public school. They were usually under the auspices of more strictly observant Orthodox authorities than the neighborhood synagogues. In 1960, 47 of these 87 religious day schools in New York City taught Yiddish (Poll 1981: 214–216).

Throughout their history, the Yiddish secular schools in New York were grappling with a fate they shared with all proponents of the Yiddish language. This destiny was irrevocably recast by American realities and events in Europe, starting with suspended immigration from Eastern Europe in 1924, the rise of Nazism in the 1930s, the annihilation of the Yiddish heartland and the majority of its speakers during World II, and the establishment of the state of Israel. The schools also felt deeply the repercussions of economic, residential and social changes within the American Jewish community. The human, linguistic, and cultural resources required to bolster the cause of Yiddish language instruction had become greatly diminished.

Unfortunately, appropriate teaching materials for the new era in the development of the secular schools were not produced (Parker 1981). The Jewish Teachers' Seminary and Peoples' University in New York City prepared several generations of Yiddish educators (Shteynboym 1978–1979), but this training institute closed in 1977. Residential patterns shifted drastically in the neighborhoods that sustained these schools. By the last quarter of the twentieth century, it became obvious to its patrons that the secular Yiddish school system was unable to supplement and authenticate its language maintenance efforts with viable forms of support rooted in the immediate environment of the children and their families, the neighborhoods of the city.

5. *Daily lives, daily languages: Yiddish on the streets of New York*

To probe further the relationship between the course of Yiddish linguistic and cultural continuity and the connectedness of community members to their urban surroundings, it is useful to review features of language that have been inspected in situ, as it were, on the sidewalks of New York. The sparseness of the data deserves an explanation. How is it that such a large urban Jewish population has not been examined to gain insight into face-to-face communication patterns in its ethnic mother tongue? The politics of scholarship on spoken Yiddish reflects a strong bent towards normativism and the absence of ethnographic observation of actual language behavior in Yiddish (Peltz 1990). Moreover, linguistic analysis of Yiddish in its East European setting has been favored because the spoken language in its new American environment was viewed to be in a state of disintegration (Weinreich 1941: 34).

This does not mean that New York City Yiddish speakers have not been the subject of investigation. In a study that attempted to evaluate the complex dialectical situation in New York City, Disenhouse (1974) chose informants from four major religious subgroups – Reform, Conservative, Orthodox, and Hasidic Jews – to determine whether the manner of pronouncing certain phonological variables in English, including in loan words from Yiddish, signifies beliefs about ethnic identification. Jofen (1964) and the *Language and Culture Atlas of Ashkenazic Jewry* (Herzog et al. 1969; Herzog 1992) examined the speech of city residents, but the research design was limited to dialectological aspects of their language, with Eastern Europe as the basis. Yiddish cultural activists, when tested for word naming and usage and compared with Puerto Rican Spanish speakers, were shown to be stronger in Yiddish in cultural and ethnic behavior domains, whereas English was more prevalent in home and work domains (Ronch et al. 1969). Labov (1966 [1982]: 121, 132) in his well-known study of English speech on the Lower East Side had to qualify the inclusion into the category of native English speakers two women who immigrated at age five, supposedly because of the Yiddish influence in their speech. The characterization of the special linguistic qualities of Jewish speakers of English has described the influence of Yiddish on such English speech (Gold 1985).

When we survey Yiddish language behavior observed in the city's neighborhoods, we come across Weinreich's (1941: 34) observation of remarks overheard in a Lower East Side shop: the word for word loan translation *mit a shlos un mit on a shlos* 'with a lock and without a lock' (Yiddish "without" is simply "*on*"). In Brooklyn's Brownsville neighborhood, a largely working class enclave of secondary settlement that was 80% Jewish in the first decades of the twentieth century, a young Italian friend of the American-born Jewish boys could speak Yiddish and was called by the Yiddish name "*Shimmele*" instead of Jimmy (Sorin 1990: 16).

It is among the Hasidim of New York that researchers have most fruitfully been able to study the predicament of English and Yiddish bilingualism. In the only study to concentrate on children born in America, Jochnowitz (1968) found that children of the Lubavitch Hasidim, a large sect centered in Crown Heights that actively seeks proselytes among secular Jews, retained much of the dialectal features of their parents and were not influenced greatly by the standard Yiddish of the radio or other dialects present in Crown Heights, nor did he find a strong influence of Yiddish on the observed phonology of English. Girls spoke English more readily because in the primary grades they have secular instruction in English in the afternoon, whereas the boys' entire school-day is in Yiddish.

Most of the findings relate to Hasidic residents of Brooklyn neighborhoods that maintain Yiddish. The growth of these ultra-Orthodox communities reverses the older trend in a neighborhood like Boro Park, where by 1918 English had replaced Yiddish in most synagogues as the language of sermons and announcements (Mayer 1979: 27). As late as 1973, a local Hasidic rabbi with poor command of English was forced to turn to the language nonetheless, in order to satisfy his second and third generation modern Orthodox congregation who had meager knowledge of Yiddish (Mayer 1979: 110). Although Boro Park had become a major Hasidic neighborhood by the 1960s, its diverse Jewish complexion included non-observant residents. Today, some Hasidim are attracted to the more traditional and insular atmosphere of Williamburg:

> Over here the kids would speak mainly Yiddish – not mainly but *only* Yiddish; over there you hear kids speaking English. In other words the barriers between Jews and secular people are much greater over here than over there ... I want to raise my kids in the values here in Williamsburg rather than those in Borough Park (Mintz 1992: 111)

Yiddish figures prominently in the cultural agenda of the Brooklyn Hasidic neighborhoods. In 1960–1961, Brooklyn contained more than half of the Jewish day schools in the United States that taught in Yiddish. Of the 47 day schools teaching Yiddish then in the city, 35 were in Brooklyn (Poll 1981: 214–216). One mother in Boro Park was reportedly concerned about her children's knowledge of English, feeling that the educational program of total immersion in Yiddish and Hebrew in the early school years was too drastic (Mintz 1992: 178).

In the 1970s, the same Brooklyn neighborhoods also witnessed conflicts that involved the very Yiddish cultural institutions that served them. Satmar Hasidim, a sect deriving from Hungary who maintain strict separation from the secular world and oppose the official state and government of Israel, were accused of ransacking and burning to the ground the offices of *Der algemeyner zhurnal* in Boro Park, a Yiddish weekly that supports Lubavitch. Harassing phone calls were made to subscribers, distributors and advertisers in Williamsburg and a local candy store that carried the paper was destroyed by fire (Mintz 1992: 57). In 1989, Yiddish made news again. A coalition of Puerto Rican, other Latino, and Black residents in Brooklyn filed complaints against the developer of the new Brooklyn Villas condominium apartments for failing to dispense information outside the Hasidic community. The only major advertising had been in the Yiddish weekly *Di tsaytung* and information packets were printed only in Yiddish (Mintz 1992: 262–264).

The most recently arrived cohort of Yiddish speakers to have populated Brooklyn, mainly, and other neighborhoods are the Soviet Jewish immigrants who, according to Markowitz (1993: 155), "seek work and residential situations where they can use Yiddish in everyday life. Many ...boast that their fluency in Yiddish enabled them to... find apartments and first jobs in New York." She cites a study by the Federation of Jewish Philanthropies of New York (1985: 11) that concluded that 68 percent of the Soviet Jewish immigrant interviewees understand Yiddish, and 43 percent speak the language. In New York, continues Markowitz, this Jewish language becomes the *lingua franca* of many Soviet immigrants, allowing them to communicate in public arenas with Americans. This dramatic transition in the status of Yiddish for this group, from a secret Jewish code to a public language with its own press and radio stations, attests to and verifies the change that the immigrants' Jewish identity undergoes as a result of migration. Elevation of Yiddish to one of the several languages used in public by New York's varied ethnic and immigrant groups legitimizes its speakers as well.

6. *Language and the culture of community: communication in context*

In this essay, we have viewed the acquisition of certain Yiddish linguistic practices as a dynamic ongoing process. And, we have found it rewarding to consider the connections between language and locality. "Speakers develop linguistic patterns as they act in their various communities," according to Eckert – McConnell-Ginet, such that "in practice, social meaning, social identity, community membership, and the symbolic value of linguistic form are constantly and mutually constructed" (Eckert – McConnell-Ginet 1992: 473). In our pursuit of what these authors call "living social practices in local communities," (Eckert – McConnell-Ginet 1992: 462) in this study of Yiddish in New York City, we have undoubtedly posed new dilemmas. We point to complexities that still need to be unraveled: the similarities and disparities in ethnocultural behavior of the first and second generations, the contrasts in the cultural landscape of neighborhoods of primary, secondary and subsequent settlement, the effects of short-lived residence in an area on personal and group identification with a neighborhood or with the city as a whole. Hopefully, the less traditional route we have taken has offered some discoveries, too, and new pathways for examining the embeddedness of Yiddish language and culture in the lives of Jews in New York City.

There are, it should be clear by now, many ways to learn about the linguistic differences that exist among New York's Yiddish speakers and readers. The rich texture of city life, as experienced and expressed by members of the ethnolinguistic minority, can be captured via a variety of methodologies. We have tried to bring forward an assortment of data as evidence for how the key to community is in the patterns of communication that the ethnic group develops. For the immigrants in New York City, and for their children, the ties were strengthened by Yiddish.

Notes

1. Both authors contributed equally to the research and writing of this article; their names appear in alphabetical order.
2. All poetry quoted in this section was written and published in Yiddish. We present English translations of these texts.

References

Allen, Irving Lewis
1993 *The City in slang: New York life and popular speech.* New York and Oxford: Oxford University Press.

Anderson, Benedict
1991 *Imagined communities.* rev. ed. London and New York: Verso.

Bender, Thomas
1978 *Community and social change in America.* Baltimore: The Johns Hopkins University Press.

Cooperman, Jechiel B. – Sarah H. Cooperman
1967 *America in Yiddish poetry.* New York: Exposition Press.

Cypkin, Diane
1986 Second Avenue: The Yiddish Broadway. [Unpublished Ph.D. dissertation, New York University, New York.]

Davis, John Emmeus
1991 *Contested ground: Collective action and the urban neighborhood.* Ithaca: Cornell University Press.

Disenhouse, David. S.
1974 Phonological manifestations of ethnic identification: The Jewish community of New York City. [Unpublished Ph.D. dissertation, New York University, New York.]

Doroshkin, Milton
1969 *Yiddish in America: Social and cultural foundations.* Cranbury, New Jersey: Associated University Presses.

Dushkin, A. M. – U. A. Engelman
1959 *Jewish education in the United States.* New York: American Association for Jewish Education.

Eckert, Penelope – Sally McConnell-Ginet
1992 "Think practically and look locally: Language and gender as community-based practice", *Annual Review of Anthropology* 21: 461–490.

Faust, Ray
1973 "Di tsirkulatsye fun yidishe bikher in di nyu-yorker shtotishe bibliotekn un di leyenershaft" [The Circulation of Yiddish books in the New York Public libraries and the readership]. *Yivo bleter* 44: 283–285

Federal Writers' Project
1938 *Di yidishe landsmanshaftn fun nyu york* [The Jewish Landsmanshaftn of New York]. New York: Yiddish Writers' Union.

Federal Writers' Project
1939 *Yidishe familyes un familye krayzn fun nyu york* [Jewish families and family circles of New York]. New York: Yiddish Writers' Union.

Federation of Jewish Philanthropies
1985 Jewish identification and affiliation among Soviet Jewish immigrants in New York – A needs assessment and planning study. New York: Federation of Jewish Philanthropies. [Unpublished MS.]

Fishman, Joshua A. [Shikl]
1982 "Yidish, modernizatsye un reetnifikatsye: an ernster un faktndiker tsugang tsu der itstiker problematik." [Yiddish, modernization and reethnification: a serious and factual approach to the present problem]. *Afn shvel* 248: 1–7.
1983 "Vos vet vayter zayn? Vos vet undz nokh blaybn?" [What will the future look like? What will remain for us?]. *Afn shvel* 251: 2–4.
1993a "Yidish un shtimrekht in nyu-york, 1915 un 1921" [Yiddish and voting rights in New York, 1915 and 1921]. *Afn shvel* 291, Part I: 11–14.
1993b "Yidish un shtimrekht in nyu-york, 1915 un 1921" [Yiddish and voting rights in New York, 1915 and 1921]. *Afn shvel* 292, Part II: 11–14.

Fishman, Joshua A. (ed.)
1981 *Never say die!: A Thousand years of Yiddish in Jewish life and letters.* The Hague: Mouton.

Fishman, Joshua A., et al.
1985 *The Rise and fall of the ethnic revival.* Berlin, New York, Amsterdam: Mouton Publishers.

Gold, David
1985 "Jewish English", in: Joshua A. Fishman (ed.) *Readings in the sociology of Jewish languages.* Leiden: E. J. Brill, 280–298.

Goldberg, N.
1948 "Di tsirkulatsye fun yidishe tsaytungen un yidishe un hebreyishe bikher in di fareynikte shtatn, 1918–1947" [The circulation of Yiddish newspapers and Yiddish and Hebrew books in the United States, 1918–1947]. *Gedank un lebn* 5: 42–56.

Gutmans, T.
1958 "Di shprakh fun a yidisher radyo-stantsye in nyu-york" [Usage of Yiddish on the Radio Station WEVD]. *Yidishe shprakh* 18, 3: 65–72.

Halpern, Moyshe-Leyb
1982 [1919, 1927, 1954] *In nyu york* [In New York] in: Kathryn Hellerstein (ed., transl.). Philadelphia: The Jewish Publication Society of America.

Harshav, Benjamin – Barbara Harshav
1986 *American Yiddish poetry: A bilingual anthology.* Berkeley: University of California Press.

Hellerstein, Kathryn
1982 "Introduction" in Halpern, xi – xxv.
Herzog, Marvin I. (ed.)
1992 *The Language and culture atlas of Ashkenazic Jewry.* Vol. 1, Tubingen: Niemeyer Verlag.
Herzog, Marvin I. – Wita Ravid – Uriel Weinreich (eds.)
1969 *The Field of Yiddish* Vol. 3, The Hague: Mouton.
Howe, Irving
1946 "The Lost young intellectual: A Marginal man, twice alienated." *Commentary* 2, 361–367.
1976 *World of our fathers.* New York: Harcourt Brace Jovanovich.
1982 *A Margin of hope: An intellectual autobiography.* New York: Harcourt Brace Jovanovich.
Hummon, David M.
1990 *Commonplaces: community ideology and identity in American culture.* Albany: State University of New York Press.
Institute of Jewish Affairs and the World Jewish Congress.
1971 The Jewish Communities of the World. London: Andre Deutsch.
Itskovits, H.
1944 "A zitsung oyf a reynem yidish" [How to conduct a meeting in correct Yiddish] *Yidishe shprakh* 4, 3–6: 114–120.
Jochnowitz, George
1968 "Bilingualism and dialect mixture among Lubavitcher Hasidic children", *American Speech* 43: 182–200.
Jofen, Jean
1964 *A Linguistic atlas of Eastern European Yiddish.* New York, privately published.
Kleederman, Frances Farber
1974 A Study of Language in Henry Roth's *Call it sleep*: Bilingual markers of a culture in transition. [Unpublished Ph.D. dissertation, New York University, New York.
Kliger, Hannah
1990 "In Support of their society: The organizational dynamics of immigrant life in the United States and Israel," in: K. Olitzky (ed.), *We are leaving Mother Russia: Chapters in the Russian-Jewish Experience.* Cincinnati: American Jewish Archives Press, 33–53.
1992 *Jewish hometown associations and family circles in New York: The WPA Yiddish writers' group study.* Bloomington: Indiana University Press.
Kliger, Hannah and Rakhmiel Peltz
1990 "The Secular Yiddish School in the United States in Sociohistorical Perspective: Language School or Culture School?:" *Linguistics and Education* 2: 1–19.
Labov, William
1966 *The Social stratification of English in New York City.* Washington, D. C.: Center for Applied Linguistics.
[1982] [Reprint edition].
Leyeles, A.
1926 *Rondos un andere lider [Rondos and other poems].* New York: Farlag "In-zikh".

Lifson, David S.
1965 *The Yiddish theater in America.* New York: Thomas Yoseloff.

Mark, Mendl
1952 "Dos ofitsyele yidish fun der shtot nyu-york" [Yiddish in the Releases of the City of New York]. *Yidishe shprakh* 12, 3: 91.

Mark, Yudl
1948 "Draysik yor yidishe shuln in amerike 1918–1948" [Thirty Years of Yiddish Schools in America 1918–48]. *Gedank un lebn* 5: 1–41.

Markowitz, Fran
1993 *A Community in spite of itself: Soviet Jewish emigres in New York.* Washington and London: Smithsonian Institute Press.

Mayer, Egon
1979 *From Suburb to Shtetl: The Jews of Boro Park.* Philadelphia: Temple University Press.

Mayzl, Nakhmen, ed.
1955 *Amerike in yidishn vort [America in Yiddish literature].* New York: Yiddisher kultur farband.

Mintz, Jerome R.
1992 *Hasidic people: A Place in the New World.* Cambridge, Massachusetts: Harvard University Press.

Moore, Deborah Dash
1992 "On the fringes of the city: Jewish neighborhoods in three boroughs," in: D. Ward – O. Zunz (ed.), *The Landscape of modernity: Essays on New York City 1900–1940.* New York: Russell Sage Foundation, 252–272.

Nahirny, V. C. and J. A. Fishman
1965 "American immigrant groups: Ethnic identification and the problem of generations", *The Sociological Review* 13: 311–326.

Niger, Shmuel
1941 "Lomir zey kashern (a briv in redaktsye)" [Let's Make Them Kosher (A letter to the editor)]. *Yidishe shprakh* 1: 21–24.

Parker, Sandra
1981 "An Educational assessment of the Yiddish secular school movements in the United States", in: J. A. Fishman (ed.), 495–511.

Peltz, Rakhmiel
1989 "'It Used to be like Jerusalem': South Philadelphia, portal to the city and enduring Jewish community," in: G. Stern (ed.) *Traditions in transition: Jewish culture in Philadelphia 1840–1940.* Philadelphia: Balch Institute for Ethnic Studies, 43–63.
1990 "Di politik fun forshn di geredte shprakh in di fareynikte shtatn un in sovetnfarband" [The Politics of researching spoken Yiddish in the USA and the USSR]. *Oksforder yidish* 1: 141 – 158.
1991 "Ethnic identity and aging: Children of Jewish immigrants return to their first language," in: J. R. Dow (ed.), *Language and ethnicity:Focusschrift in honor of Joshua A. Fishman.* Amsterdam and Philadelphia: John Benjamins, 183–205.

Poll, Solomon
1981 "The Role of Yiddish in American Ultra-Orthodox and Hassidic communities", in: J. Fishman (ed.), 197 – 218.

Ronch, Judah – Robert Cooper – Joshua Fishman
1969 "Word naming and usage scores for a sample of Yiddish-English bilinguals", *Modern Language Journal* 53: 232–235.

Roth, Henry
1934 *Call It Sleep*. New York: The Noonday Press.
[1991] [Reprint edition].

Rozhanski, Shmuel, ed.
1977 *Nord-amerikanish [The Yiddish literature of North America]*. Buenos Aires: Ateneo Literario en el Iwo.

Ruffman, L. L. (ed.)
1957 *Survey of Jewish education in Greater New York 1951–1952: Findings and recommendations*. New York: Jewish Education Committee.

Sanders, Ronald
1969 *The Downtown Jews*. New York: Harper and Row.

Sanders, Scott Russell
1993 *Staying put: Making a home in a restless world*. Boston: Beacon Press.

Sandrow, Nahma
1977 *Vagabond stars: A World history of Yiddish theater*. New York: Harper and Row.

Schieffelin, Bambi
1986 "Language Socialization", *Annual Review of Anthropology* 15: 163–191.

Shekhter, Mordkhe
1973 "Folkishe Toponimik" ['Folk Toponymy']. *Yidishe shprakh* 32: 1–3, 6 – 7.

Shteynboym, Y.
1978–1979 *Di geshikhte fun yidishn lerer-seminar un folks-universitet in nyu-york 1918 – 1968* [The history of the Jewish Teachers' Seminary and Peoples' University in New York 1918–1968]. Jerusalem.

Soltes, Mordecai
1925 *The Yiddish press: An Americanizing agency*. New York: Teachers College, Columbia University.

Sorin, Gerald
1990 *The Nurturing neighborhood: The Brownsville Boys Club and Jewish community in urban America, 1940–1990*. New York and London: New York University Press.

Suttles, Gerald D.
1972 *The Social construction of communities*. Chicago: The University of Chicago Press.

Teller, Judd L.
1968 *Strangers and natives: The Evolution of the American Jew from 1921 to the present*. New York: The Delacorte Press.

Varenne, Herve
1986 " 'Drop in anytime': Community and authenticity in American everyday life", in: Herve Varene (ed.), *Symbolizing America*. Lincoln: University of Nebraska Press, 209–228.

Weinreich, Max
1941 "Vegn englishe elementn in undzer kultursprakh" [On English elements in our language of high culture). *Yidishe shprakh* 1: 33–44.

Wisse, Ruth
1988 *A Little love in big Manhattan: Two Yiddish poets*. Cambridge: Harvard University Press.

III THE LANGUAGES WITH VITALITY IN THE PAST AND THE PRESENT

Italian in New York*

Hermann W. Haller

1. Introduction

The story of the Italian language in the United States is intimately tied to the history of Italian immigration. It is a story as diverse as the people who came for a peaceful and laborious colonization of new lands with hopes for better lives. First, there were adventurers who dared to cross the Atlantic ocean, followed by Jesuit missionaries from the seventeenth century on. Then there were political thinkers such as Filippo Mazzei, a Tuscan physician and agronomist whose name is closely associated with the American Revolution. Among the few thousands of mostly Northern Italians who came during the first century of the American Republic there were the laborers, but also entrepreneurs and refugees, charismatic figures like Garibaldi who would be instrumental in shaping Italy's political unification, participants in the American Civil War, and professors such as Lorenzo Da Ponte, the librettist of Mozart and first professor of Italian at Columbia University. There were also sculptors, painters, architects, and the musicians who brought Italian opera to America in the early nineteenth century.

2. Patterns of Italian migration to the United States

The Italian migrations took off in the 1860s, coinciding with Italy's political unification. Beginning with 1880, the number of immigrants rose to 10,000 annually, above 50,000 in 1890, and to more than 100,000 in 1900. The migration between 1900 and 1914 can be likened to an exodus; in the year 1913 alone 376,776 Italians arrived, making up half of all immigrants to the United States (Gastaldo 1987: 152). Between 1880 and 1927 more than five million Italians left their country. While the first immigrants came from Northern regions such as Liguria, Lombardy, Veneto and Friuli, the vast majority during this period – over 80% – were Southern Italians,[1] originating from the regions of Campania and Sicily,

Lazio and Calabria, Abruzzo, Apulia and Basilicata. Most had been induced to leave by poverty, the result of age-old oppressions exerted on the region by foreign colonialists, and of a feudal hierarchical structure that inhibited social mobility. For many Southerners the new Italian unification proved to be disappointing economically, and natural disasters only furthered the emigration fever (Mangione – Morreale 1993: 31–108). The emigrants fled oppression and depravation, driven by their dreams of becoming prosperous and returning soon to the home and families they had left behind.

A vast majority of the immigrants – but by no means all, as Tuttle (1990: 97) showed in his study of Venetians in California – were illiterate or had only little formal education. Most came from rural areas and had some farming and fishing experience, others were artisans, few professionals. New York became the door to the United States, and most emigrés settled in the Northeast. Eventually however, more restrictive policies – e. g. the Literacy Test Act of 1917 – slowed the pace of immigration, particularly in the decade preceding World War II.

After a spectacular decline following the 1920s, immigration resumed again in the 1960s and 1970s. While compounding the characteristics of earlier times – arrivals were predominantly family members who had come from Southern, economically depressed areas –, the more recent emigration tended to be better educated, and frequently also more Italianized. According to statistics, after 1979 only some 5,000 people arrived annually.[2] In recent years, Italy has become a country of immigration, due to changing social and economic conditions, ranking it fifth among the top industrialized nations.

A brief account of the history of the Italian language and of the sociolinguistic panorama of modern Italy explains why spoken dialects were the dominant varieties brought to American shores. Standard Italian is based on fourteenth-century literary Tuscan, the language written by Boccaccio and Petrarch, and codified by Cardinal Pietro Bembo in his *Prose della volgar lingua*, published in 1525. His proposal of a highly cultivated literary model produced an idiom that for many centuries lived predominantly in books. The perennial deep political and social fragmentation of the peninsula prevented this variety from spreading among a population that spoke a myriad of dialects, many of which were mutually unintelligible. A glimpse at the maps of Jaberg and Jud's *Sprach- und Sachatlas Italiens und der Südschweiz* (1928–1940) make the dialectal fragmentation abundantly evident: it did not only involve strong variation in phonemes – such as, e. g., the presence of umlaut North of the

Table 1
Immigrants from Italy according to decades compared with total immigration to the U. S., 1821–1990*

	Immigration from Italy	Total Immigration to U. S.
1821–1830	409	143,439
1831–1840	2,253	599,125
1841–1850	1,870	1,713,251
1851–1860	9,231	2,598,214
1861–1870	11,725	2,314,824
1871–1880	55,759	2,812,191
1881–1890	307,309	5,246,613
1891–1900	651,893	3,687,564
1901–1910	2,045,877	8,795,386
1911–1920	1,109,524	5,735,811
1921–1930	455,315	4,107,209
1931–1940	68,028	528,431
1941–1950	57,661	1,035,039
1951–1960	185,491	2,515,479
1961–1970	204,111	3,321,677
1971–1980	129,368	4,493,314
1981–1990	32,900	7,338,000

* **Source: G. Battistella 1989: 102; for the most recent decade *Statistical Abstract of the U. S. 1993*, U. S. Department of Commerce 1993.**

linguistic border between La Spezia and Rimini (Milanese *lüna* vs. Tuscan *luna*) –, but also in morpho-syntax and in the lexicon. The word for "boy", e. g., is *caruso* / *piccireddu* in Sicilian, *quatraru* in Calabrese, *guaglione* in Neapolitan, *ragazzo* in Tuscan, *fiöl* in Milanese, *masnà* in Piedmontese, *frut* in Friulan, and *toso* in Venetian, to cite but one example for a number of dialects.

This situation explains why in 1861, at the time of Italy's unification, only some 2.5% of the population were able to speak the Tuscan-based Standard (De Mauro 1972: 43), a group that was made up of the educated elite minority, of Tuscans, and also of Romans, due to early Italianization of their dialect (Vignuzzi 1988a: 610–613). Even though this figure has been disputed and enlarged by some linguists (Castellani 1982: 3–26 proposes 9.52%; see also the discussion in Bruni 1992: xix – xxxiii), it gives evidence of how there was no popular base to the Standard language, as there was in other nations, such as France or Germany. In fact, writers such as Leopardi were keenly aware of how the Italian literary language was perceived as a dead language, "una lingua morta". A revival occurred partly with the work of Carlo Manzoni, whose historical novel *I Promessi Sposi* [The Betrothed] (1827), though still based on cultivated Florentine, rejuvenated Italian, bringing it closer to the spoken reality. The novel was considered a sort of gospel for the future Standard language, read by generations of Italian students. However, several decades would be needed to eradicate illiteracy and to educate dialect speakers in the Standard. De Mauro (1972) shows how in the early years of unification students were frequently exposed to semi-literate or even illiterate teachers.

Table 2
Illiteracy (in %) in selected Italian regions, 1861–1951*

	1861	1911	1951
Italy	75	40	14
Sicily	89	58	25
Calabria	86	70	32
Apulia	86	60	24
Basilicata	86	65	29
Campania	86	54	23
Abruzzi	86	58	19
Lazio	68	33	10
Toscana	74	37	11
Veneto	65	25	7
Liguria	54	17	4
Piedmont	54	11	3

*** Source: T. De Mauro 1972: 95.**

The diffusion of the Standard was facilitated and accelerated by the industrial age, mandatory instruction which became law in 1859, the migrations from rural to urban areas – particularly to large cities like Rome and Milan –, and the mass media.

It was ironically in the trenches of the first World War that Italians from different regions, speaking different dialects, shook hands for the first time. With the new contacts and migrations of vast segments of the population, Italians became increasingly bilingual, speaking both standard and dialect. Yet at the same time, the form of the dialects began to change also, through the increasing exposure to Italian. *Regiolects*, i. e. forms of regional Italian, at the crossroad between Italian and dialect, began to be used widely. Popular Italian, a simplified interlanguage acquired by exclusive dialect speakers, became equally part of the sociolinguistic continuum of varieties (Berruto 1987: 13–15, 105–138).[3] And the Standard, used for the first time by millions of dialect speakers, underwent changes, not only in adopting regionalisms (such as, e. g., Lombard *bevuto* [St.It. *ubriaco*] 'drunk', Roman *fasullo* 'not authentic', Sicilian *intrallazzo* 'manoeuvre'), but also in simplifying syntactic structure. Ever since the 1950s, television exerted one of the strongest influences on the diffusion of the Standard among the population at large.

As we approach the next millennium, more than half of the Italian population uses Standard Italian exclusively. The language surveys carried out by DOXA and ISTAT illustrate how Standard Italian is the language used generally by 42% of the population in the family, by 45% if the interlocutors are friends, and by 65%, if they are strangers. The respective figures for the dialect are 32%, 26% and 14% (Russo 1991: 37). While these proportions vary with age, social stratum, level of formal instruction, and region – the Northeast and the South being notorious dialect strongholds –, dialect attrition is occurring today particularly in small towns (pop. less than 100.000) (Vignuzzi 1988b: 243).

The Italian language brought to North America was consequently of diverse form, according to time, region, and social characteristics of immigrants. While privileged emigrés were conversant in the Standard and the dialect, it is reasonable to assume that during the peak years, and even later, the majority of immigrants spoke dialect as their predominant variety, with varying degrees of passive competence in the Italian learned at school. After crossing the ocean for thousands of miles, they arrived in a foreign land, without a consciousness of being "Italians", deprived of a Standard, and without the knowledge of English, the language of the new land. The hardships faced by these immigrants, who were lured to America by stories and promises from family members already in America, or by greedy agents and *padroni* eager to exploit their plight, and their various destinies in the new land have been described in a rich documentary and scholarly literature written by Jerre Mangione (1943), Richard Gambino (1975), Richard Alba (1985), Rudolph Vecoli (1987), Salvatore LaGumina (1988), and Anthony LaRuffa (1988), to name but a few. Many migrants returned after few years of hard work; in fact, it is estimated that about half of those who had come to the U. S. between 1880 and 1924 went back to Italy (Mangione – Morreale 1992: 89).[4]

New York City was the point of entry for Italian immigrants, with famed Ellis Island as the obligatory gate to the New World. Those admitted settled mostly in urban America, establishing "Little Italies". However, there were also successful farming settlements, as Margaret Meade's mother, the social science pioneer Emily Fogg Meade painstakingly documented in her study *The Italian on the Land* (1907). The cities of New York, Buffalo, Boston, Philadelphia, Baltimore, and Chicago became major centers of attraction. Earlier mostly Northern Italian immigrants had ventured to the West, settling in the San Francisco area. Greater New York became in time the most important haven for Italian immigrants, and a strong Italian presence is felt to this day.

Table 3
Regional distribution (in %) of Italian Americans, 1960 and 1980*

	Northeast	NorthCentral	South	West
First Gen 1960	70.3	15.2	4.6	9.9
Second Gen 1960	69.2	14.8	6.3	9.7
First Gen 1980[a]	68.2	14.4	7.2	10.0
MultipleAnc 1980	48.2	19.8	15.0	16.8

* **Source: P. Gastaldo 1987: 154.**

[a] No comparative data are available for the second generation from 1980 census reports (Gastaldo 1987: 155).

The first New York settlements took hold of the Mulberry Street district. As in other cities, groups from the same city speaking the same dialect lived in tenement buildings along the same street, forming enclaves which copied village and regional boundaries of the country left behind. The settlers later moved to Greenwich Village,[5] East Harlem, the Bronx, Queens, and Staten Island. The immigrants were employed as day laborers in various industries, from textiles to cigar manufacturing and railroad construction. They frequently worked in squalid conditions and for minimal wages. Many would eventually participate actively in the early labor movements. From a social and linguistic point of view, despite the lack of a strong documentation, it seems obvious that the language factor constituted a prime obstacle for the majority of immigrants. While well educated Italians mastered a form of the standard language – some of these would earn their money as scribes, writing letters to their illiterate clients' families in Italy[6] –, the majority of immigrants moved between their dialect, the language of their home town, and English, the language which was expected of them, especially in the climate of the melting pot ideology prevalent in the early twentieth century. At the same time, immigrants became increasingly aware of the importance of education.

As De Mauro (1972: 54–57) notes, the migration overseas acted as a "school of italianization" on two counts. Dialect speakers had abandoned Italy in large numbers, with the subsequent loss of the dialect presence in society at large; at the same time they grew aware for the first time of the importance of literacy and of the Standard language as the only means of written communication, and as the only instrument to move up socially. Thus emigrés encouraged their families' education (and Italianization) in a way not seen before.

3. *Italian as an immigrant language*

It is interesting to note the absence of references to language in much of the literature on Italian Americans and their history, except for anecdotes. One of the most recent accounts of Italian American history by Jerre Mangione and Ben Morreale, *La storia*, has, except for its title and a few transcriptions of Sicilian songs or proverbs, only one or two notes concerning language use. This is even more surprising, if considering that the richly documented book also discusses literary texts. Yet it is by no means an exception, and the silence may be an expression of linguistic uneasiness.[7] Especially among second or third generation Italian Americans, one comes frequently across negative attitudes towards the language varieties used in their communities. Others regret instead the loss of their linguistic heritage. Still others are in the process of recuperating Italian as a language of culture.[8] If language is a primary marker of ethnic identity, what Italian languages were and are used in the United States, in what forms, and in what contexts?

Among the 12,183,692 Italian Americans counted in the 1980 U. S. census (including multiple ancestry), 930,201 (7.6%) claimed to be born abroad (Battistella 1989: 144), while close to 1.5 million individuals age 5 and above claimed to speak Italian[9] at home. Of the total population, 2,811,811 Italian Americans lived in New York State. Among these, some 458,887 persons claimed to use Italian at home, with more than 286,515 or 60% living in the five boroughs of New York City.

For 1990, of the 14,664,550 Italian Americans reported by the U. S. Census Ancestry List, 1,308,648 persons five years of age and above reported the use of Italian at home. For New York State, with its Italian American population of 2,837,904, the figure was 400,218; in New York City 203,935 of the 838,780 Italian Americans counted in the census claimed to use Italian. Brooklyn and Queens with their dense ethnic populations particularly of Bensonhurst, Ridgewood, Ozone Park, had most Italian American residents and speakers of Italian (Brooklyn pop. 263,800 vs. 78,000 speakers; Queens pop. 252,690 vs. 65,781 speakers), followed by Staten Island (pop. 150,321 vs. 18,191 speakers), the Bronx (pop. 92,584 vs. 28,371 speakers), and Manhattan (pop. 79,385 vs. 13,592 speakers).[10] If adding to these figures the large numbers of Italian Americans residing in the immediately surrounding areas (Westchester and Nassau counties, New Jersey), it becomes clearly evident that the greater New York metropolitan area constitutes the largest "Italian" city abroad.[11]

Table 4
Italian American population vs. language use, 1980 and 1990. U. S. and New York State*

	1990	1980
Italian American population, USA	14,664,550	12,183,692
Italian used at home by people above age 5	1,308,648	1,499,146
Italian American population, New York State	2,837,904	2,822,911
Italian used at home by people above age 5	400,218	499,951

* **Source: U. S. Census.**

Other states with a large Italian American population reported in the 1990 census include New Jersey (1,459 million), California (1,448 million), Pennsylvania (1,375 million), followed by the states of Massachusetts, Florida, Illinois, Ohio, Connecticut, and Rhode Island. While the Northeast made up more than 55% of all Italian Americans for that period, the midwestern states accounted for over 14%, California for over 10%. If we compare these census figures with those for earlier decades, the similar distributions point to the relative stability of the Italian American population throughout the twentieth century.

As can be seen, the largest concentration of Italian speakers is found in the New York region.[12] Elsewhere, the numbers of those who claim to speak Italian at home is far from being proportional to the Italian American population in these states. For 1990, the U. S. average of 8.9% – a decrease from 12.3% since 1980 – rises to 14% in New York State, and to 24% in New York City. In New Jersey, 154,160 Italian Americans claimed to use Italian at home (10.5%), in Pennsylvania that figure was 103,844 (7.5%); and in California it was 111,133 (7.6%). These figures illustrate a gradual decline of Italian in the immigrant communities since the years of the exodus.

3.1. Language varieties

"Italian", as it is spoken in the Italian American communities today, and as it is reported in the census figures, consists of a continuum of varieties, ranging from a dialectal Italian H(igh) variety to the L(ow) dialect and hybrid varieties, the latter including admixture from English. Rather than the standard H variety used in contemporary Italy, one finds a H variety with dialectal features, an Italian that shares many elements of the popular Italian mentioned above.

Dialectal elements in this H variety appear in the pronunciation, e. g., in the voicing of consonants between vowels (*allargade*=allargate 'enlarged'), assimilation of *-rl-* (*parrano* = parlano 'they speak'), occasional aspiration of initial *p-* by some Calabrese speakers (*phiù* = più 'more'). Predominant features of popular Italian include a reduced pronominal system (*ci* danno soldi = gli danno soldi 'they give them money'), *che* with a variety of functions, e. g. to express time (ho lasciato l'Italia *che* avevo diciannove anni = *quando* … 'I left Italy *when* I was eighteen years old'), or relation (la temperatura *che* non mi sono potuto adattare = alla quale… 'the temperature I couldn't get used to'). Other elements that are due to contact with Southern dialects are found in the use of auxiliaries (si *hanno* sviluppate [St.It. si *sono* sviluppate] 'they have developed'; *ho* venuto [St.It. *sono* venuto 'I came'], in analogical plural formation (*strade grande* [St.It. *strade grandi*] 'large streets'), and in double comparative (*più meglio* for St.It. *meglio* 'better'). Dialect contact is also found in the vocabulary. Expressions such as *teneva la febbre* [St.It. *aveva la febbre]* 'he/she had a fever' are indicative of a Neapolitan speaker, *cuatrarella* [St.It. *bambina*] 'child' points to Calabrese origin.

Language contact with English in this variety is relatively rare, and usually limited to concepts for which one doesn't readily find an equivalent in Italian (lavorare in *accounting* = ragioneria, lavori di *filing* = schedatura, *jobless* =disoccupato, etc.).

The following is a sample oral text of this H variety. The speaker is a woman who at the time of the interview had lived in the U. S. for 17 years, after emigrating from Calabria at age 11:

> [Question: *Ricorda la Sua emigrazione in America?*] Mi ricordo tutto. (…) Per primo è statu 'n po' negativo, perché non parlavo l'inglese maa andando a scola…ho praticato di più e…pharlo a lingua americana. [Q: *Che lingue parli a casa?*] Well, con la mia famiglia parliamo menzo calabrese menzo americano – mezza. Per prim'anno è sta' un po' difficile però continuando è stato più miglior perché ho mparato a lingua inglese. (…) … Quelli che erano più piccoli si sono imparato la lingua più presto di me

> perché quelli che erano piccoli sono andato dal kindergarten on,però per me è stato un po' difficile perché sono venuta aca quando ero nella quinta media, nella quinta elementhare, ed è stu' un po' difficile... [Q: *Sei mai tornata in Italia per una visita?*] sí certamente...Ci sono stata un po' di anni faaa ed è stu un'esperienza molto difficile perché non sapevo tante parole che non... sapevo prima, perché parlando calabrese è di... è molto più facile del parlare nella lingua italiana (...) [Q:*Hai trovato cambiamenti nei dialetti?*] Sí ho trovato un po' molto perché ho 'vuto visite dei cugini che abitavano in Torino... loro parlavano la vera lingua italiana invece io sapevo most – oh boy! – capivo solamente capivo tutto però non potevo esprimermi (Haller 1993: 157–158).

This non-Standard H variety differs from speaker to speaker, and also between groups of different regional origin. However, unlike in past decades, when dialect groups tended to be segregated or isolated, the H variety seems to share many elements among speakers from different dialect backgrounds, moving in the direction of an informal popular Italian speech variety.

Other L speech varieties present in the language continuum of the communities include the dialect and the hybrid "Italian American" speech form with its borrowings from English. However, these varieties tend to be used less today, and they may gradually disappear in speakers belonging to the third and fourth generations. It is a well known but little researched fact, that among older first generation immigrants one finds archaic elements in their dialect speech which by now have disappeared in Italy due to their contact with Italian, which is instead absent in the U. S. linguistic enclaves. The mixed or hybrid variety has been much exploited for the purpose of anecdotes. Menarini (1947), a pioneer in the study of Italian among immigrants in the U. S., includes many such words in his description, and many are still in use today. They are English loans which were Italianized by the immigrants, such as *carro* 'car' (St.It. macchina/automobile), *marchetta* 'market' (St.It. *mercato*), *grosseria* 'grocery' (St.It. *generi alimentari*), *farma* 'farm' (St.It. *fattoria*), *giobba* 'job' (St.It. *lavoro*, but semantically not equivalent), *bisinisse* 'business' (St.It. *affari*); *storo* 'store' (St.It. *negozio*). In some cases, the expressions are calques, i. e. loan translations from English, such as *guarda bene* 'he/she looks good' (St.It. *è bello,–a*), *pizzapaia* 'pizza pie' (St.It. *pizza*).

The hybrid variety was also exploited for popular sketches performed in New York cabarets frequented by Italian immigrants during the early decades of the century. Edoardo Migliaccio, nicknamed Farfariello, and Carlo Ferrazzano wrote and performed the so-called *macchiette coloniali*, which were very popular (Mangione – Morreale 1993: 311–314). The following scene by Ferrazzano is from *Orré for Italy: scuperchiatevi li cape!* [Hurrah for Italy: take your hats off!]:

> Na sera dentro na barra (*bar*)[13] americana, dove il patrone era americano, lo visco (*whisky*) era americano, la birra era americana, ce stava na ghenga de loffari (*a gang of loafers*) tutti americani: solo io non ero americano; quanno a tutto nu mumento me metteno mmezzo e me dicettono: "Alò spaghetti! (disparaging for "Italian") Iu (*You*) mericano men (*American man*)?" "No! no! mi Italy men!" "Iu blacco enze (*black hand*, i. e. criminal)? "No, no!" "Iu laico (*like*) chistu contri?" "No, no! Mi laico mio contri! Mi laico Italy!" A questo punto mi chiavaieno lo primo fait (*they began to fight, gave me the first punch*). Dice: "Orré for America!" Io tuosto: "Orré for Italy!" Nato fait. [...] N'ato fait e n'ato fait, fino a che me facettono addurmentare, ma però, orré for America nun o dicette! [...] (Haller 1993: 30 n.3).[14]

3.2. Language use

The continuum of language varieties in the sociolinguistic spectrum of the Italian American community shows a definitive departure from that of Italy. As Saltarelli (1986: 110–112) showed in his proposal for a typology of immigrant languages, most Italians historically spoke non-Standard varieties in unstable contexts, without being functionally bilingual. A dialectal or popular form of Italian on the one hand and English on the other are found in lieu of Standard Italian as the H varieties; a hybrid form of speech is the result of the immigrants' language contact with American English. The latter is a transient speech register whose vocabulary testifies to the social and economic hardship and drama of immigration.

Language use varies with age and gender, generation, the amount of formal instruction, and social contexts. Older and first generation persons with only little formal education tend to use dialect and dialectal Italian more exclusively; some know little English after many years of residence. Better educated first generation individuals are frequently bilingual, sometimes trilingual, using dialectal forms at home, the H variety with Italians from different regions, and English in all other contexts. For the second generation, diglossia tends to be the norm, with English as the dominant variety, and dialectal Italian as the language of the home. My own field studies of the 1980s, based on interviews with representative groups of New York Italian Americans of different generations point to significant language shift already in the second generation. This group grew up typically with the dialectal or hybrid variety of their parents, and then underwent the trauma of switching to English at school and with peers, where their non-Standard L1 variety was rejected or treated disparagingly. Many individuals thus decided not to cultivate Italian, except in its "domestic" variety. For third generation Italian Americans, Italian was often only a dim memory, made up of some words heard from grandparents. Mixed ancestry and upward social mobility contributed further to language shift among Italian Americans.

Especially in the speech of second and third generation individuals, language attrition in "troubled contexts" is evidenced by redundancies, lacunae, long pauses.

3.3. The Italian language in the mass media

Italian language mass media have long played an important role for immigrant communities. The newspaper *Eco d'Italia* began to appear as early as 1859, a few decades prior to the mass migrations from Italy. Among the daily papers written in Italian, *Il Progresso Italo-Americano* became the most important, published for more than a century until 1983, when it was substituted by *America Oggi*.

In 1920, there were no fewer than 11 daily, 66 weekly, and two monthly papers printed in Italian. The daily papers alone accounted for a circulation of 330,000. The decline of immigration was accompanied also by the decline of the foreign-language ethnic press. In 1960, the considerable number of 18 papers (5 dailies, 12 weeklies, and one monthly) showed a huge decline in circulation. Still, Italian is today the only major European immigrant language to continue a daily newspaper in the United States (Haller 1988). A definitive increase, both in the number of publications and in circulation, is seen conversely, at least until the 1940s, in the bilingual and English-language press directed at Italian Americans. This trend mirrors language shift in the Italian American community quite clearly.

Table 5
Italian-, bilingual and English-language newspapers and periodicals, 1920–1980*

	1920	1940	1960	1980
Italian	79–584,000	42–369,000	21–270,000	10–122,500
Bilingual	18– 59,000	39–174,000	20–164,000	4– 31,000
English	–	5– 27,000	5– 47,000	1– 1,800

*** Sources from Fishman (1966) and *Ayer's Directory*. The figures indicate the number of papers and the circulation.**

A study of the language of *Il Progresso* (Haller 1993: 89–99) analyzed for the period of the late Seventies shows, in addition to some archaic features, a very limited use of anglicisms, in contrast with the high numbers found in Italian newspapers in Italy for the same period. This would be indicative of a stronger conservatism or purist effort on the part of journalists operating in a linguistic enclave surrounded by the hegemony of English.

Since the 1930s, Standard Italian appeared also in radio transmissions directed at immigrant communities. Here again, there has been a steady decline from the 229 stations across the country in 1960 airing 609 hours weekly in Italian to the 135 stations transmitting 412 weekly hours in 1983. In that year, New York State had still the largest number of stations, a total of 39 transmitting 94 weekly hours or close to 20% of all Italian-language radio transmissions in the U. S., with five stations in the metropolitan area. Transmissions in the Northeast made up more than 50% of the total, reflecting the demographic distribution of Italian Americans. California, on the other hand, with its large ethnic population, presents an exception, with some six stations transmitting 10 hours weekly (Haller 1993: 84–88). During the past ten years, Italian-language radio programs have further declined. For 1993 we find 86 stations nationwide broadcasting some 232 weekly hours; New York State is leading with 20 stations and 48 hours; New York has two stations and four hours. However, if one adds two Italian radio stations broadcasting round the clock, though accessible by subscription only (ICN in Queens), the New York area appears to have the largest number of programs and weekly hours.[15] The data again reflect the strong language shift and loss that took place in Italian American communities, particularly on the West Coast – California today has only three stations and seven hours weekly. In general, for the most recent years, one observes a shift from Italian to English, and from speech to music.

Italian-language television programs on the other hand seem to flourish, again mostly in New York. The 17 weekly hours of Standard Italian-

Table 6
Italian-language radio transmissions in the U. S., 1960–1993*

	1960	1980	1993
Number of stations	229	135	86
Number of weekly hours	609	412	232 (resp. 400)

* **Source: Fishman 1966, Haller 1993).**

language television (6 hrs on Sunday, 2 hrs Monday through Friday, 1 hr on Saturday), produced and broadcast in New York by RAI, the Italian Radio and TV corporation, includes only a dim fifteen minutes of locally produced community-related news (interviews). Although it is difficult to know or estimate the effect of these programs on language loyalty, it is estimated that between 600,000 and 1 million viewers tune in at least once a week. Italian television could thus serve as one of the potentially strongest means of diffusion of contemporary Italian among Italian Americans and Italophiles.[16]

4. *Italian as a language of culture today*

The gradual decline of Italian as a community language[17] is accompanied by a simultaneous increase during the past decade of interest in contemporary Italian civilization in general, and also in the Italian language. This is occurring at a particularly felicitous moment in time, since by now Italian is no longer an exclusive literary idiom, but has instead a broad social base. A recent study by Tullio De Mauro et al. (1993) demonstrates how there has been steady progress toward unification of spoken Italian across large Italian urban areas. At the same time, the dialects in Italy have gradually lost ground to the Standard and are becoming more and more "domestic" languages.

4.1. Language attitudes

A study on language attitude among Italian Americans in New York carried out in the late 1980s confirms some of the developments described above. Without any intent of being statistically representative, the study was based both on a direct questionnaire survey and on the indirect matched-guise technique (Haller 1993: 37–58). The latter method directed a specific group of selected "judges" from the community to evaluate the speakers of a prepared tape according to an adjective scale with positive/negative attributes concerning affect, status, and ethnicity. The tape included several brief conversations in the following varieties: English with an Italian accent; (Sicilian/Neapolitan) Regional Italian; Sicilian/Neapolitan Dialect; Hybrid Variety.

Both methodologies yielded similar results. English is clearly considered the language with the highest status by all judges. All Italian varieties are seen as the language of the roots, of ethnic identity, of the family, varieties with important affective functions. However, there seems to be some difference in attitude between first and second generation judges. The former are more purist oriented, favoring Standard languages, while the latter tend to be more tolerant toward non-Standard varieties. Many of those born in Italy – mostly with a dialect heritage – experienced the social stigmas of being deprived of a functional standard, and they are more willing to deemphasize the need for dialect. Those born in America, by now fully fluent in English, feel no more the potential limitations of dialects, and in fact view dialectal speech and the hybrid variety as positive symbols of ethnicity, varieties which allow bonding between family members of different generations.

Some answers to direct survey questions are particularly noteworthy. A majority is in favor of trilingualism among Italian Americans (English/Italian/Dialect); they all favor acquisition of Italian as L2 for their offsprings and also support bilingual education. Standard Italian is seen as a poetic, musical, colorful, and romantic language; dialect as comical, honest, dramatic, the language of roots, family, and home (Haller 1993: 49). While these results may of course be linked to judges with a strong orientation toward preserving the cultural and linguistic heritage, it is nonetheless dramatically obvious that they are a reflection of ideal objectives rather than of any linguistic reality.

To some extent, language behaviour and language attitudes appear to be consistent with the "three types of Italian Americans" described by Tomasi (1980). The author defines as "Italian Residents in the U. S." first generation individuals who grew up in Italy and arrived as adults, maintaining their ties with Italy, without any particular identity conflict. The second group constitutes the Italian Americans belonging predominantly to the second generation, and whose socialization was divided between the "Italian home" and the American contexts. Its divided loyalty led either to the acceptance of the mainstream and loss of the heritage or to a return to the ethnic roots. The third group, "Americans of Italian origin" of third and fourth generation individuals, lacking any particular cultural disorientation, can opt to freely explore its ethnic roots.[18]

4.2. The teaching of Italian

Italian has been taught in the United States since the colonial period. Between 1775 and 1861 foreign languages could be studied in the major cities of the Atlantic coast, frequently by way of private lessons. According to a study by J. Fucilla (1967), in the period between 1820 and 1861

Italian was taught in 714 private schools across 28 states and the District of Columbia, including 116 Virginia and 115 New York State schools (Lèbano 1992: 217). After a slow start,[19] the popularity of Italian took off in the 1920s. According to Fucilla, 898 students took courses in Italian in seven New York City schools in 1921–1922, and that number rose to 16,000 students in fifty-five schools in 1937–1938 (a total of 75,000 students studied Italian in 257 public and private schools in seventeen states in 1936–1937). However, during the two World Wars, the teaching of Italian declined dramatically. In 1962–1963 there were only 25,777 students enrolled in Italian in fifteen states. Italian was in competition with French and Spanish, the two foreign languages most traditionally taught in the United States.

At the college and university level, foreign languages were first taught at the College of William and Mary, followed by others. In New York it was Lorenzo Da Ponte who in 1825 began the teaching of Italian language and literature at Columbia. However, German and French were still the two most popular languages until the late nineteenth century, when Italian studies began to flourish in institutions of higher learning up to the beginning of WWII. The numbers began to rise again vigorously during the fifties and sixties; in 1965 close to 20,000 college and university students were registered in Italian courses.

During the 1980s and early 1990s, the teaching of Italian grew steadily both at the secondary school and at the college and university levels. According to a 1987 survey (Lèbano 1992), there were 62,430 students taking courses of Italian in 458 public and 79 private primary and secondary schools throughout the nation. New York State, where Italian is offered already in kindergarten, had the largest numbers, a total of 244 among the 855 schools surveyed, offering Italian to 40,981 students.[20] Among these, some 15,500 students alone (38%) were concentrated in the five boroughs of New York. Massachusetts (5,028), New Jersey (4,100), Connecticut (2,771), Rhode Island (2,177) were states with enrollments higher than 2,000. At the college and university level, Italian was offered in some 400 schools nationwide, with 39,029 students enrolled in courses. A more recent comparative chart (Lèbano 1993) illustrates the growth of Italian in higher education from 34,367 students in 1983 to 44,102 in 1990 (the larger number of 49,726 students of Italian was produced by an independent survey prepared by the Modern Language Association for 1990–1991). Throughout the decade, New York State was leading with 7,103 students in 1983 and 8,210 in 1990; in New York City alone there were 3,602 college students of Italian in 1983 and 3,390 in 1990 (Lèbano 1993: 546–560).[21]

Table 7
Number of students and colleges/universities offering Italian in the U. S. and in New York State, 1983–1990*

	1983	1985	1987	1990
Enrollments				
U. S.	34,367	40,014	39,118	44,102
N. Y. State	7,103 (=20.6%)	8,633 (=21.5%)	7,734 (=19.7%)	8,210 (=18.6%)
Institutions				
U. S.	375	399	353	370
N. Y. State	64 (=17%)	71 (=17.8%)	57 (=16.1%)	60 (=16.2%)

* **Source: E. Lèbano 1993: 493.**

In addition to public and private schools and to several after-school programs, the study of Italian language and culture has also been and continues to be promoted by such institutions as the *Italian Cultural Institute* (presently engaged in a large-scale inititative, coordinated with the support of the Italian government through the two *università per stranieri*, Siena and Perugia, and aimed at improving teacher preparation and at increasing course offerings); the *Scuola di New York Guglielmo Marconi* with its officially approved experimental bilingual/bicultural curriculum available to Italian, Italian American and American students; the *Casa Italiana* at Columbia University and at New York University; organizations such as the *American Association of Teachers of Italian*, the *American Association of Italian Studies*; and a variety of cultural circles.

The above figures illustrate that the teaching of Italian is healthy and more or less stationary. The largest concentrations are found in the state of New York, particularly in New York City, where much of the interest is owed to the large Italian American community. However, there are areas in the United States, where Italian is popular despite a very low number of students of Italian heritage (Cravens 1986: 121).

As the statistics suggest, the history of the teaching of Italian is not always related directly to the demography of the Italian American population. Even today, the approximate number of 110,000 students pursuing Italian nationwide, or the considerable number of 19,000 students of Italian for New York City are but a small group, if contrasting it to the Italian American population earlier described. In fact, the teaching of

Italian – and the lack of Italian bilingual programs[22] – indirectly reflect the language shift and loss that has taken place in the community. It is also related to ambiguous general policies in regard to foreign language acquisition in the United States. Italian was long considered an "ethnic" language, the language of immigrants, and as such not particularly encouraged by school authorities. Of course there was the language of Dante, the language of music and high culture, pursued by the elite. For many college bound Italian Americans, Italian was conceivably not especially appealing either, since it was perceived as the hybrid variety used at home, or the language of a group that had exploited and indeed exiled them, an alien language, typified as "Harvard Italian" by a character of A. Innaurato's Broadway play *Gemini* that ran in New York for over a decade. For most Italian Americans, Italy was identified with a home town or a region.

Contemporary students of Italian find themselves in a more refreshing environment. Particularly third and fourth generation Italian Americans study the language in search of their roots. The changing image of Italy, the desire to visit the country of their ancestors, the awareness of Italy as a country with a great culture are all motivations, valid for many English-speaking countries where Italian is studied (Baldelli 1987, Vignuzzi 1986).

5. *Conclusion and outlook*

The Italian language varieties present in New York must be viewed against the backdrop of the linguistic history of Italy and within the framework of the history of Italian immigration to the U. S. Through time, the linguistic background of migrants shifted from dominant dialectophony to dialect/Standard bilingualism of various degrees, depending on social characteristics. The Italians who came during the peak years of 1880–1924 – some 5 million – spoke dialects that were not only different from the literary Standard, but diverged widely among each other. While different dialect groups first tended to move to different areas in the United States, and to form enclaves within their communities, with the gradual decline of immigration these communities became more mixed, and some dialect leveling took place. Traditionally, the city of New York – and the Northeast – was the privileged place of settlement, particularly among Southern Italian immigrants. Side by side with its early cultivation as a literary language mostly in private schools, Italian lived in the United States predominantly as a *spoken* community language. Due to assimilation pressures and economic conditioning, emigrés generally tended not to cultivate their rich linguistic heritage beyond the varieties used within the boundaries of home and ethnic community. Cross-generational language shift was furthered by the low prestige of the dialect and the hybrid variety. The endemic division in the old country between the language of a small elite and that of the masses was brought also to the new land, and it is documented today by the relatively small segment of a very large Italian American population that claims to speak any Italian at home. In fact, it is probably fair to state that cultural interest is not reflected by a strong loyalty towards the language heritage.

The presence of the Italian language in what was once a large ethnic press served as a link between the home land and the Italian American community, and provided instructions for living in America. While later supplemented by Italian-language radio and TV, the decline of the ethnic-language mass media accompanied that of immigration, even if at a somewhat slower pace. As a school subject, Italian grew more popular after the period of mass migration, with a huge decline setting in with the advent of the second World War.

Today, as we approach a new millennium, Italian finds itself at an important crossroad. It is a language that is very much alive in New York, in fact, New York City is still the most important "Italian city" in the U. S. As a community language, its varieties are used widely, continuing to guarantee affective bonds between different generations of speakers. Yet, Italian is also more available as the language of a great culture, both in the written media and on television. Despite – and maybe because of – the strong cross-generational language attrition of Italian as a community language, the gap between "high" and "low" Italian has also been narrowing. On the one hand, with the decline of a strong new immigration during recent years, Italian as a community language tends to grow thinner. On the other hand, the strong attachment to the values of Italian civilization, the new debates on ethnicity and diversity, and also the reevaluation of dialects as social and historical varieties, are strong motives for a return to the Italian language – the dominant Standard language of contemporary Italy. The new popularity of Italian in the schools seems to confirm this new direction. Lastly, the vibrant economic ties, communications, and cultural interactions between Italy and the United States will further contribute to shaping the future of the Italian language abroad.

Notes

* I wish to acknowledge the assistance in my research by Ms. Eda Henao, Ph.D candidate in comparative literature, Graduate School, City University of New York, as well by the Calandra Institute of the City University of New York. I also wish to thank the following individuals for information provided concerning institutions promoting Italian language and culture in New York: Ms. Dolores N. Mita (State Education Department), Prof. Gianclaudio Macchiarella (Italian Cultural Institute), Dr. Gabriele Del Re (Scuola di New York), Dr. John Acampore (Bilingual Programs / N. Y. Board of Education).

1. According to Gastaldo (1987), the U. S. became the preferred destination for Southern Italians; Northern and Central Italians generally preferred other destinations, such as Argentina and later Australia.
2. These figures are likely to be higher, if one considers recent findings concerning undocumented immigration, estimated at 67,000 for the U. S., and at 26,800 for New York State. (*Immigration and Naturalization Service*. Compiled by Population Division, New York City Department of City Planning, 1993).
3. The concept of *popular Italian* has been much debated, beginning with Manlio Cortelazzo, *Lineamenti di italiano popolare*. Pisa: Pacini, 1972.
4. For a discussion of the linguistic problems related to return migration see Immacolata Tempesta. *Lingua ed emigrazione*. Lecce: Milella, 1978; and Alberto Sobrero, "Indagine sugli emigrati di ritorno: lo specifico linguistico delle donne", *Studi Emigrazione* 22, 1985: 399–410.
5. See e. g. Donald Tricarico, *The Italians of Greenwich Village: The Social Structure and Transformation of an Ethnic Community*. Staten Island, N. Y.: Center for Migration Studies, 1984.
6. For a linguistic analysis of letters written by immigrants see Celestina Milani, "Osservazioni sulla lingua di emigrati italiani in USA: un carteggio inedito", *Saggi di linguistica e letteratura in memoria di Paolo Zolli*. Padua: Antenore, 1991, 279–288.
7. A certain lack of linguistic integrity is noted not infrequently in misspellings of Italian words; see on this point Luisa Del Giudice's review of *Italian-American Folklore* by Frances M. Malpezzi and William M. Clements. *Italian Americana* 12, 1993: 105–107.
8. The linguistic literature is also somewhat scarce and frequently sketchy, if not outright anecdotal in character. There are many exceptions, of course. Robert J. Di Pietro and Yole Correa-Zoli have done important work. Somewhat more attention has been paid to the Italian language in Canada, with work by Gianrenzo Clivio, Marcel Danesi, Jana Vizmuller-Zocco, and others. My essay is based largely on linguistic data gathered during the 1980's in the New York metropolitan area and presented in my book *Una lingua perduta e ritrovata* (1993). The focus is here on language use in the Italian American communities.
9. These numbers were self-reported and must therefore be read with caution. They do not yield specific information concerning language variety, context and frequency of use.
10. For New York City census data see *City of New York, Department of City Planning. Population Division, June 1992*. For census data on New York State and other states see *1990 Census of Population. Social and Economic Characteristics*. Washington, D. C., Department of Commerce, Bureau of the Census 1993. For the U. S. census summary cfr. *CD Rom Census of Population and Housing Summary*. Tape File 3C, U. S. Department of Commerce, Bureau of Census 1994.

11. For Nassau County 41,496 people claim to speak Italian at home, in Westchester the 1993 census yields 36,861 speakers. It is difficult to give an accurate account of the number of Italian Americans living in the U. S., due mostly to the fluctuations in the declarations of ancestry. The same inconsistencies must be kept in mind for the number of speakers. The question on the foreign language use formulated by the U. S. census bureau only yields very general data on Italian language use in the U. S.
12. This is probably also the case for the Standard speaking elite, considering the large number of international businesses operating in the New York area. No specific figures were available for this group.
13. The corresponding American terms are given in parenthesis.
14. "One evening in an American bar where the owner was American, the whisky was American, the beer was American, there was a gang of loafers, all American, only I was not American, when suddenly they were in front of me shouting: "Hello spaghetti! Are you American?" "No, no! I am Italian!" "Are you a black hand?" "No, no!" "Do you like this country?" "No, no! I like Italy!" At that point they punched me. They said: "Hurrah for America!" And me right away: "Hurrah for Italy!" Another punch...Another punch, and another punch, but I never said "Hurrah for Italy!" – The text is filled with dialect and hybrid vocabulary.
15. Other states broadcasting Italian radio include Massachusetts (8 stations – 29 weekly hours), Florida (6 sts – 24 hrs), Connecticut (8 sts – 23 hrs), Pennsylvania (8 sts – 23 hrs), Ohio (8 sts – 18 hrs), Illinois (2 sts – 11 hrs), Rhode Island (3 sts –10 hrs), New Jersey (4 sts – 5 hrs; resp. 5 sts – 173 hrs). Eight other states broadcast 5 hours and less weekly. Source: *Broadcast and Cable Yearbook 1993*.Vol. 1, New Providence, N. J.: Bowker 1993, p.B566.
16. Segments of the same RAI program are broadcast in San Francisco (½ hr a week), in Philadelphia, and in a few other cities.
17. Strong language shift and attrition have been reported also for Australia, a country with a more recent large Italian immigration (see Camilla Bettoni, "Language variety among Italians: anglicisation, attrition and attitudes", in Suzanne Romaine (ed.),*Language in Australia*. Cambridge: Cambridge University Press, 1991, 263–269); in Latin America it appears to have proceeded at a slower pace (see, e. g., Loredana Corrà and Flavia Ursini, "Dialetti italiani all'estero", in Günter Holtus, Michael Metzeltin, and Max Pfister (eds.), *La dialettologia oggi. Studi offerti a Manlio Cortelazzo*. Tübingen: Narr, 1988, 373–393).
18. The ethnic interest is reflected in a myriad of organizations (for a list see Ezio Marchetto, *A Directory of Italian American Associations in the Tri-State Area*. New York: Center for Migration Studies, 1989), some of which have specific regional focus, such as, e. g., the *Famija Piemontèisa*, a group that has its own *Notissiari* and meets in New York, cultivating the Piedmontese dialect. There are also poets writing in the dialect, and there is a journal, *Arba Sicula*, which cultivates the Sicilian dialect.
19. See e. g. the statement from the memoirs of L. Covello, printed in 1958: "During this period (the 1900's), the Italian language was completely ignored. In fact, throughout my whole elementary school career, I do not recall one mention of Italy or the Italian language or what famous Italians had done in the world with the possible exception of Columbus, who was pretty popular in America. We soon got the idea that Italian meant something inferior, and a barrier was erected between children of Italian origin and their parents. This was the accepted process of Americanization. We were becoming

Americans by learning how to be ashamed of our parents" (*From the Margins. Writings in Italian Americana*. Eds. Anthony Julian Tamburri, Paolo A. Giordano, Fred L. Gardaphé. West Lafayette, IN: Purdue University Press, 1991, 7).

20. For 1993, the New York State Education Department reports instead 35,187 students of Italian.
21. In evaluating these figures, it must be kept in mind that several schools with programs failed to answer the questionnaire on which Lèbano's survey is based. The figures do not take into account the number of students acquiring the language through private tutoring.
22. Italian bilingual programs were flourishing in the 1970s.
    The New York Board of Education now offers bilingual education predominantly to speakers of Spanish, Chinese, Russian, and other languages, a reflection of the change in demography and immigration patterns.

References

Alba, Richard D.
1985 *Italian Americans. Into the twilight of ethnicity*. Englewood Cliffs, N. J.: Prentice Hall.

Baldelli, Ignazio (ed.)
1987 *La lingua italiana nel mondo.Indagine sulle motivazioni allo studio dell'italiano.* Rome: Istituto della Enciclopedia Italiana.

Battistella, Graziano (ed.)
1989 *Italian Americans in the 80's.A Sociodemographic profile*. New York: Center for Migration Studies.

Berruto, Gaetano
1987 *La sociolinguistica dell'italiano contemporaneo*. Rome: La Nuova Italia Scientifica.

Bettoni, Camilla, ed.
1986 *Italian abroad. Studies on language contact in English-speaking countries. Altro Polo*. Sydney: Frederick May Foundation.

Bruni, Francesco
1992 *L'italiano nelle regioni. Lingua nazionale e identità regionali*. Turin: UTET.

Castellani, Arrigo
1982 "Quanti erano gl'italofoni nel 1861?", *Studi linguistici italiani* 8: 3–26.

Correa-Zoli, Yole
1981 "The Language of Italian Americans", in: Ferguson, Charles – Shirley B. Heath (eds.) *Language in the USA*. Cambridge: Cambridge University Press, 239–256.

Cravens, Thomas D.
1986 "Sistemi a contrasto: l'italiano come lingua straniera negli Stati Uniti", in: AA. VV. *L'italiano negli Stati Uniti. Il Veltro* 30 (1–2): 121–129.

De Mauro, Tullio
1972 *Storia linguistica dell'Italia unita*. Bari: Laterza.

De Mauro, Tullio – Mancini Federico – Vedovelli Massimo –Miriam Voghera
1993 *Lessico di frequenza dell'italiano parlato*. Milan: ETAS.

Fishman, Joshua A.
1966 Language loyalty in the United States. The Hague: Mouton

Fogg Meade, Emily
1907 "Italians on the land. A Study in immigration", *Bulletin of the Bureau of Labor* 70 (Washington, D. C.): 1–87.

Fucilla, Joseph G.
1967 *The Teaching of Italian in the United States. A documentary survey.* New Brunswick, N. J.: American Association of Teachers of Italian.

Gambino, Richard
1975 *Blood of my Blood.* New York: Anchor Books.

Gastaldo, Piero
1987 "Gli americani di origine italiana: chi sono, dove sono, quanti sono", in *Euroamericani. La popolazione di origine italiana negli Stati Uniti*, vol.1, Turin: Fondazione Agnelli, 149–199.

Haller, Hermann W.
1988 "Ethnic-Language mass media and language loyalty in the United States today: The Case of French, German and Italian", *Word* 39: 187–200.
1993 *Una lingua peruta e ritrovata. L'italiano degli italo-americani.* Florence: La Nuova Italia.

Jaberg, Karl, – Jakob Jud
1928–1940 *Sprach- und Sachatlas Italiens und der Südschweiz.* Zofingen: Ringier.

La Gumina, Salvatore J.
1988 *From Steerage to suburb: Long Island Italians.* New York: Center for Migration Studies.

La Ruffa, Anthony L.
1988 *Monte Carmelo. An Italian-American community in the Bronx.* New York-London: Gordon & Breach.

Lèbano, Edoardo A.
1992 "L'insegnamento dell'italiano negli Stati Uniti", in: AA. VV. *L'insegnamento della lingua italiano all'estero.* Turin: Fondazione Giovanni Agnelli, 195–221.
1993 "Report on the teaching of Italian in American institutions of higher learning (1981–1990)", *Italica* 70: 489–587.

Mangione, Jerre
1943 *Mount Allegro.* Boston: Houghton Mifflin.

Mangione, Jerre – Ben Morreale
1993 *La Storia. Five centuries of the Italian American experience.* New York: Harper Collins.

Menarini, Alberto
1947 *Ai margini della lingua.*Florence:Sansoni.

Russo, Domenico
1991 "Un aggiornamento sulle cifre dell'italofonia", *Italiano e oltre* 1: 36–38.

Saltarelli, Mario
1986 "Aspetti descrittivi dell'italiano negli Stati Uniti", in: Bettoni, Camilla (ed.), 105–112.

Tomasi, Silvano
1980 *Italian culture in the United States.* Turin: Fondazione Giovanni Agnelli.

Tuttle, Edward F.
1990 "Veneti in California. Premesse di un'indagine", in: Padoan, Giorgio (ed.) *Presenza, cultura, lingua e tradizioni dei veneti nel mondo.* Parte II. Venice: Regione Veneto, 97–117.

Vecoli, Rudolph J., ed.
1987 *Italian immigrants in rural and small town America.* New York: American Italian Historical Association.

Vignuzzi, Ugo
1986 "Why study Italian? A survey of the English-speaking world", in: Bettoni, Camilla (ed.), 171–204.
1988a "Areallinguistik VII. Marche, Umbrien,Lazio", in: Holtus, Günter – Michael Metzeltin – Christian Schmitt (eds.), *Lexikon der romanistischen Linguistik.* Vol. 4. Tübingen: Niemeyer, 606–642.
1988b "Chi parla ancora in dialetto?" *Italiano e oltre* 3: 241–245.

Greek in New York

Chrysie M. Costantakos and John N. Spiridakis

1. Ethnicity and linguistic survival

Although the United States is a multilingual society, there has been in this country a long tradition of abandonment of the mother tongue among linguistic minorities, a situation which has led to the basic attitude that language shift is a natural step expected from a psychologically mature minority population. "There is some *prima facie* evidence that, while large scale language shift is usually considered indicative of a progressive attitude in the Americas and in Africa, in both Europe and Asia language loyalty is considered to be natural as well as wholesome" (Kloss 1966: 145).

Nathan Glazer (1966 [1978]: 359) described the phenomenon of ethnic language non-maintenance in the United States as follows:

> This country, which can find within its borders native speakers of the most outlandish and exotic languages – and very often sizable numbers of them – seems to be one of the most linguistically limited of the great nations in its international contacts. Tens of millions of people in this country were raised speaking languages other than English, yet these Americans are, it seems, tongue-tied abroad and unable to make use of the huge literature published in other languages – including, commonly, the ones they or their parents used in their childhood.

In such a milieu, as a result, the question of ethnic language continuity takes on a distinct significance. To those who find linguistic survival indispensable to ethnic continuity, disappearance of language may be tantamount to ethnic extinction. Ethnicity itself has had widely varying definitions, many of which assume linguistic distinctiveness as an essential component.

National characteristics, traits, manners of thought, action, and speech are transmitted from generation to generation through the medium of language. Stephan George Chaconas (1942) reviews the work of Korais, the outstanding Greek philologist of the eighteenth century, and his concept that language makes and preserves nationality. To Korais, nationality was only circumscribed by language, and therefore, all persons who spoke Greek were Greek nationals and purveyors of the Greek spirit.

Greeks have always considered their Greek language to be a binding force to their ethnic identity. They struggled for its survival during many periods of foreign domination, evidenced by the endurance and maintenance of the Greek language during four hundred years of occupation by the Ottoman Empire at which time the learning of the Greek language was forbidden. *Krifa-Skolia* 'Hidden Schools', operated clandestinely under the cover of darkness to maintain the language during this period (Spiridakis 1994).

In the United States Greeks continued their devotion to their native tongue and made efforts for its maintenance and continuity. Despite the efforts, however, the Greek language has suffered losses because of the migratory and adjustment history of Greek Americans. This paper will examine some of these trends in the Greek American community of New York City.

2. Greek migration and settlement in the United States and New York City

Greeks as a group were among the last of the groups of Europeans to emigrate to the United States. Immigration from Greece continued to be in limited numbers until the last decade of the nineteenth century (Costantakos 1980; Kourvetaris 1990; Moskos 1989; Saloutos 1964; Scourby 1984). Of the 19,000 Greeks who immigrated to North America in the latter part of the nineteenth century according to official census data (INS 1976), fully 16,000 arrived during the 1890's. The figure grew tenfold to 167,500 during the first decade of the twentieth century, and by 1940 no fewer than a half million Greek immigrants had come to the United States. The peak early years of Greek immigration were 1907, 1914 after the Balkan Wars, and 1922 following the Asia Minor Catastrophe, the War of Greece and the Ottoman Empire (1919–1923).

One important consideration with regard to Greek immigration is the basic distinction between "immigration from Greece" and "Greek immigration" which by extension has a bearing on the basic question of the definition of a "Greek". "Immigration from Greece" refers to immigration from Greece proper while "Greek immigration" encompasses those of Greek descent, irrespective of their country of origin. This is a major source of difficulty concerning numbers applicable to Greek immigration since those persons of Greek descent, such as Greeks from Turkey, Egypt, Asia Minor, Cyprus and formerly the Dodecanese Islands who were not or are not Greek subjects would not be included in the official list of immigrants from Greece, but would be included in the list of the country they happened to be subjects of at the time of their arrival to the United States (Costantakos 1980).

Greek immigration, as defined, falls into four general periods: 1890–1922, 1923–1939, 1940–1959, and 1960 to the present. The first of these periods was, by far, the most trying. At that juncture the majority of those who migrated were young males, many of them teenagers, without families and without the support of an ethnic community organizational structure. They had neither English language nor work skills, and they were often the victims of unscrupulous labor agents. Greek men came to the new world for economic reasons, to improve their lot, help their families and most often to provide for their sisters' dowry, *prika*, an obligation traditionally born by fathers and brothers. Brothers were also expected to postpone their marriages until their sisters were married and placed in the protection of their husbands. Marriages in Greece were arranged through a match-making procedure, *proxenio*, and the intervention of a matchmaker, *proxeniti* or *proxenitra*, the female counterpart. It was an arrangement between families and included financial considerations such as the provision of a dowry, *prika*, as the financial contribution of the bride who traditionally was not expected to work outside the home. Marriages based on love, the American ideal, was a concept alien to the Greek culture. Coming to the new world was considered a temporary interlude for the early Greek immigrants who dreamed of their return to Greece and whose concern remained the struggles of the "mother country", most especially the liberation of Greek-speaking areas of the Mediterranean: Thrace, Epirus, Macedonia, and Asia Minor, areas still dominated by the Ottoman Empire.

The majority of Greeks during this period came from the Peloponnese, the Greek islands, the Greek mainland, and the Ottoman Empire. Those from the Peloponnese were among the first to immigrate and continued coming in greater numbers. They came for economic reasons with the intention to return to Greece. The primary reason for their departure was the drop in the price of currants, the main money crop, repeated crop failures, poor soil conditions, floods, earthquakes, oppressive taxation, government instability, and difficulty in making a living. Most were unskilled laborers, had little education, and came from agricultural areas (Saloutos 1964). Scourby (1984) cites sources indicating an illiteracy rate among Greek immigrants of approximately 27 percent between 1900–1908. In 1910, 24 percent were unable to read or write, but by 1920, due to compulsory education in Greece, the rate dropped to 22 percent.

The substantial wave of Greeks who arrived in the United States before 1920 settled in three different areas. First, some went to the Western states to work in railroads and mines; second, others went to the New England mill towns to work in the shoe and textile factories; and third, yet others went to Northeastern cities, especially New York and Chicago, to work in factories and work as peddlers in the service trades.

Greeks were often targets of hostility, as witnessed by violent encounters in Utah, Idaho, and Nebraska. By the 1920's, many Greeks began to leave the mines and railroads to establish restaurants or confectioneries, hotels, and other businesses. Some Greeks prospered by investing in real estate. It can be said that by the early 1920's and following the war between Greece and the Ottoman Empire which fixed the boundaries of Greece, the Greek community in the United States was looked upon in more permanent terms. The impact of the Asia Minor defeat (1922), migration from Greece which progressively included females and resulted in the family orientation of the Greek community, and the emergence of Greek American formal organizations and ethnic institutions contributed to this stabilization. Speaking of marriage and family life for Greek men, it should be noted that a number of them chose not to marry, the decision at times based on the realization that they could not financially support a wife and raise a family. Employment of the wife for the most part was unthinkable as it would reflect negatively on the ability of the husband to provide for his family. A number of the early Greek migrants intermarried for reasons which included the lack of Greek women in America. Yet there were those who made the financial sacrifice to travel to Greece to procure a bride, usually through family arrangements, and those who made a marital choice through a mail-order arrangement, settling for a "picture bride" who came to America either accompanied by a member of her family or alone. Such marriages were a means of finding a husband for women whose families could not provide a "dowry". Many of those brides were much younger in age and came from the agricultural parts of the country. Both the intermarriages and the across-the-ocean marital arrangements had understandably a significant influence on Greek language maintenance and rate of acculturation albeit in opposing ways. At the same time, a number of Greeks who could not adjust and make it in the New World repatriated (Saloutos 1956). Although many Greeks lost their holdings during the depression, Greek communities began to witness movement to middle-class status.

The Johnson-Reed Act of 1924 restricted immigration and set the Greek quota at one hundred immigrants per year. This contrasted with 28,000 Greeks who came to the United States in 1921, the last year of relatively open immigration. In 1929, the annual Greek quota was raised to three hundred and seven, where it remained for most of the next three decades. Non-quota entrants were allowed principally through the mechanism of wives joining husbands. The Greek entry into the United States averaged about two thousand per year between 1925 to 1930 (Costantakos 1980; Moskos 1989; Scourby 1984).

The halt in mass immigration had two profound consequences, one immediate and the other long term. First, there was a frantic scramble to acquire American citizenship on the part of those already in the United States. In 1920, only one in six Greek male immigrants had acquired American citizenship, but by 1930 half of these immigrants had become naturalized Americans. Second, without the transfusion of new arrivals from Greece, American born Greeks eventually replaced foreign born Greeks as the core Greek American population, except for cities like New York where the foreign born outnumbered the native born. In 1920, only one in four Greek Americans was born in this country, but by 1940 American born Greeks were the majority. Makeshift Greek Orthodox Churches and Greek schools began to be systematically replaced by structures which indicated permanency and rootedness. The Greek advance into the middle class was profoundly set back by the depression, and the thirties were grim years for most Greek Americans. Many marginal Greek-owned businesses collapsed and working class Greeks witnessed a tremendous drop in earning power and availability of jobs. The outflow of Greeks back to the old country exceeded the number coming to the United States during this troubled economic time (Moskos 1989).

The period of 1940–1965, referred to as the period of respectability, brought Greece into World War II (Saloutos 1964). The successes of the Greek army in fighting the forces of Mussolini had an exhilarating effect on the Greek American community, and pride in Greek ethnicity soared. This was followed by a long and brutal civil Greek war between government supporters and communists, which lasted until 1949. One of the historic consequences of the civil war was the 1947 Truman Doctrine which initiated a military alliance between Athens and Washington, an alliance which over the next generation led to an increasing U. S. influence in Greek political and economic life.

The fifties were a time of general serenity in the Greek American community. Many Greeks had prospered during the war and post war years.

Under special refugee legislation in 1948, it was possible to borrow from future annual quota numbers. By 1952, the Greek quota, set to three hundred and seven annually, had been mortgaged to the year two thousand fourteen. Hope for less restrictive immigration policies did not materialize and the new McCarran-Walter Act of 1952 only raised the Greek quota to three hundred and eight. Legislation passed in 1953 and 1954, however, permitted non-quota Greeks to enter either as displaced persons or through preferences given to close relatives. A number of Greeks came under student visas and eventually managed to become permanent residents and later citizens. About seventy thousand Greeks came under those provisions between the end of World War II and 1965 (Moskos 1989). The fresh wave of immigrants replenished Hellenism in America. Many of the entrants concentrated in the big cities, especially New York City.

The Immigration Act of 1965 abolished the country of origin basis for selecting immigrants. From 1965 to 1971 about 15,000 Greeks came to the U. S. annually, a number in decline since the mid-seventies, when the figure stabilized at approximately 8,000 annually. New York City attracted by far the largest number of recent arrivals. These late Greek immigrants were better educated than the earlier generations; they did not come exclusively from small agricultural communities, and there were as many women as men. In contrast to the early immigrants, these new immigrants came to stay, and found an established organizational structure to facilitate their adjustment.

To attempt to describe the present size of Greek America nationwide is extremely difficult. Estimates vary from a high of 3,000,000 according to the Greek Orthodox Archdiocese, to the Greek Embassy estimate of 2,000,000, to a low of 1,250,000 extrapolated from available census, immigration data, and ratios of births to deaths. On the basis of the latter estimate, the generational distribution of Greek-Americans in the late 1980's is calculated to be approximately 250,000 first generation, 400,000 second generation, 250,000 third generation, and 100,000 fourth generation (Moskos 1989).

New York State has the largest number of Greek Americans, almost one-sixth of the total country, followed by California, Illinois, Massachusetts, New Jersey, Pennsylvania, Ohio, Florida, Michigan, and Maryland. Greek America continues to remain an overwhelmingly urban phenomenon, concentrated in New York, Chicago, Boston, Los Angeles, Northern New Jersey, Detroit, San Francisco Bay area, and Philadelphia in descending order (Moskos 1989). New York City alone is home to the largest Greek American community in North America (approximately 200,000 population). This number has been challenged by the Hellenic American Neighborhood Action Committee (H.A.N.A.C.), a publicly supported New York City social agency which estimates that the city is home to at least 439,000 Greek Americans. In fact, a recent estimate puts the Greek American population of the Astoria section of Queens in New York City at between 60,000–70,000, which makes New York City the largest home of Greeks outside of mainland Greece and Cyprus (Hatzidimitriou 1995). Other sizable New York City concentrations of Greeks are to be found in Bay Ridge, Brooklyn, and Washington Heights in Manhattan, the numbers of the latter having declined in recent years.

The earliest New York City Greek neighborhood (Moskos 1989) was centered around Madison Street between Catherine and Pearl Streets in Manhattan's Lower East Side, but this area never developed into a definitive ethnic enclave. Other smaller Greek neighborhoods were scattered throughout Manhattan and in the other boroughs. After World War I, a substantial number of Greek immigrants settled along Eighth Avenue between 14th and 45th Streets (Hatzidimitriou 1995).

The Greeks in New York City, like other immigrant groups, pursued their economic goals along two routes: they cultivated the commercial needs of their own ethnic group while at the same time vying for control over the city's larger commercial and manufacturing interests. The fur industry was an important source of employment for Greeks in New York City from early on. They also operated florist shops, bootblack parlors, coffee shops, confectioneries, and wholesale businesses. Very few Greeks worked in factories. Those who did not have their own business and did not work in other Greek enterprises went through the push-cart peddler route (Moskos 1989).

At the present time, three types of Greek American communities can be discerned in New York City and elsewhere in the country: A predominantly post World War II Greek American community made up of the more recent immigrants, a mixed Greek American community of early and late Greek immigrants and their families, and a Greek American community comprised of the native born second and third generations and beyond.

The first two are for the most part ethnic urban communities of hard working entrepreneurs, and white and blue collar workers of lower middle class life styles. Most Greek Americans of the first two groups reside close to their parishes, the organizational structure whose center is the Greek Orthodox Church (Kourvetaris 1988). Exempted from the first two groups is a group of upper middle class and upper class Greek Americans, highly successful in both business and professions who reside in the most desirable areas of urban centers, such as areas of Manhattan in New York City.

The third group, is an increasingly suburban community of professionals and business owners of middle and upper-middle class lifestyles (Kourvetaris 1988). Progressively, the pervasive trend toward suburbanization of middle class America is also followed by Greek Americans, such movement attributed to the rising affluence of the group, reputed to be second or equal to the Jewish group.

3. The language of the Greeks

The official language of Greece is Greek. Other languages, Albanian, Armenian, Bulgarian, Macedonian, Rumanian, Romany, and Turkish are also spoken in Greece, although not officially. English in Greece is increasingly used for international trade and tourism. German is gaining ground because of tourism. French was always a second language of the elite and educated.

The language of the Greeks is an Indo-European language in its origin. The language is attested to from around the Fourteenth Century B. C., the earliest evidence coming from inscriptions discovered on the island of Crete, and Mycenae, known as Linear B, and named by Evans a half century before, written in an Archaic Greek syllabary (composed of syllables). This is known as *Mycenaean Greek*, which needs to be distinguished from the later *Classical or Ancient Greek*, dating from the Eighth Century B. C., when texts such as the epic poems of *The Iliad* and *The Odyssey* were written in the Greek alphabet. Several major dialect groups are in evidence at that time such as Doric, Ionic and Aeolic. The great period of classical drama, history, philosophy and poetry lasted until the Fourth Century B. C. In the succeeding decades of the post-classical era, the vocabulary became more simplified, as Alexander the Great spread out in the conquest of the then known civilized world. Hebrew, Aramaic and Latin were influential molders. From the Fourth Century B. C. and for about 800 years, a variety known as *Koine 'Common' or Hellenistic Greek* was spoken throughout the Eastern Mediterranean. In its written form, this was the language of the New Testament. A period of *Byzantine Greek* followed, beginning with the creation of the Byzantine Empire in 330 A. D. It lasted until the Fifteenth Century, the end of the Byzantine

Empire. The four hundred year occupation of Greece by the Ottoman Empire brought about the contributions from the language of the Turks to medieval Greek vocabulary.

In the third decade of the nineteenth century, Greece fought and won independence, ushering in the foundation of the varieties of *Modern Greek* in use today. *Modern Greek* has two main varieties, *Demotike* 'Popular Language' which is based on the spoken language and is widely used in everyday communication, and, *Katharevousa* 'Pure Language' which reflects the classical language more closely, and was found in official documents, newspapers and other formal contexts.[1]

It was only in 1976 that the Greek government recognized the *Demotike* "Demotic" as the official language of the nation. This was followed by a renewed effort toward the simplification of the language introducing the simplified *Monotoniko* orthography.[2] The change to Demotic has become fully implemented and is used by virtually all writers and the media today (Demakopoulos 1989).

In the United States with the passing of time, and the succession of the native born generations, Greeks have developed a pattern of speech which they call "Gringlish" replete with words and phrases from English (Bardis 1976). "Gringlish" thrives either because there is no exact equivalent in the standard Greek vocabulary, or the counterpart is too difficult for the Greek American to remember or too cumbersome to reproduce (Demakopoulos 1989).

4. *Institutional support of the Greek language: The Church*

Central to the life of the Greek American community has been the church. Whenever a group of Greeks settled together in any large numbers, especially in bigger cities like New York, they would most likely form an association, name it after some historic classic Greek person or place, and have it serve as the governing body of the community. From its beginning, such a body concentrated on the founding of a church to be followed by a school, and the arrangement for the arrival of a priest provided by the official church of Greece, and who more often than not served in the dual capacity of clergyman and Greek school teacher.

The first Greek Orthodox Church was founded in 1864 in New Orleans, Louisiana by a small colony of Greek merchants. The establishment of Greek Orthodoxy in America began towards the end of the last century with the founding of churches in bigger centers such as New York City (Costantakos 1980).

The first Greek Orthodox Church of New York City was established in 1892. Approximately 500 Greeks met in a small hotel on Roosevelt Street where they organized the Society of "Athena" and determined to secure a priest and found a church. The Holy Synod of Greece responded to the request and sent a priest to serve the newly established Parish of Holy Trinity.

While a number of Greek communities and churches were established early in the present century, the year 1922 marked the beginning of organized ecclesiastical life of Greek America, through the incorporation of the Greek Orthodox Archdiocese of North and South America under the statutes of the State of New York, with New York City as the headquarters. There are approximately 550 churches in the United States today and another 70 in Canada and Latin America. Metropolitan New York claims twenty-three Greek Orthodox parishes with additional churches on Long Island. There are also a number of other Greek Orthodox Churches not under the jurisdiction of the Archdiocese which follow the old Gregorian calendar. In the five boroughs of New York, the distribution of parishes is: Manhattan 11, Queens 6, Brooklyn 4, Bronx 1 and Richmond 1. Also, a dozen more parishes are distributed throughout Westchester and Long Island (Greek Orthodox Archdiocese of North and South America Yearbook 1994).

A panoply of Archdiocesan institutions such as an orphanage, homes for the aged, a summer camp in Greece for Greek American youths, a national shrine in Florida, programs for religious instruction, and sponsored cultural events add to the portrait of Greek America. The keystone of the Archdiocesan institutional structure is Holy Cross Seminary, a Graduate School of Theology, located in Brookline, Massachusetts. An undergraduate liberal arts college, the Hellenic College, the Hellenic College Press, a teachers' academy, an Archdiocesan newspaper, *The Orthodox Observer*, currently bilingual and by far the most widely distributed publication, support the perpetuation of religion, culture and ethnic language. Tied to the church structure is the *Philoptochos Society* (Friends of the Poor) formally organized as such from women's groups which tends to the needs of disadvantaged individuals and families, preserves the Orthodox faith and educates the young.

Vaporis (1984) eloquently traces the influence of the church structure in the maintenance of the Greek language in the United States. From the beginnings of the formal establishment of the Archdiocesan structure, the church never stopped supporting the teaching of Greek to young Greek American children. To this end the church administration established afternoon Greek schools in every locality where more than ten Greek American children older than six years of age resided. The church also established Orthodox Sunday Schools for the teaching of the faith, the instruction to be given in the Greek language. Sunday Schools did not exist in Greece where such instruction was part of the regular school curriculum.

Vaporis (1984) also notes the active contribution of the church to Greek press in the United States, and its support for the publication of books and journals in Greek of historical, philosophical, theological and philological content. The church has also established scholarships for study in Greece and has founded and supports the Ionian Village in Greece, to which 400–500 Greek American youths are sent annually. Assistance for the development of Greek theater, music, dance, and cultural activities has also been provided by the church. In Astoria, a special Greek Cultural Center was established in 1986.

In addition, in cooperation with the educational authorities of the State and the City of New York, the church has secured recognition of the Greek language as being on an equal status with other foreign languages for academic credit (Hatziemmanuel 1982: 186).

The language question has found its battleground in church usage. As early as 1927, a Boston Bishop stated that the Greek Orthodox could be considered faithful even if they did not know the Greek language (Papaioannou 1976). The Greek Church hierarchy, however, has kept a conservative stance with regard to this issue. Proposals to consider English were seriously introduced in the 1950's, but the Archdiocese authorized English only in sermons. In addition, the youth organization GOYA (Greek Orthodox Youth of America) was permitted to use English as its official language. It was in 1964 that the Clergy-Laity Congress, under pressure from the old migrants, fearful of losing the youth and the native born generations, allowed certain readings and prayers in the Liturgy to be repeated in English.

The year 1970 marked an important development, as the Archbishop of North and South America, in a personal appeal, asked for the introduction of an English liturgy to accommodate communities of native born congregations.

The language traditionalists joined forces with the recent migrant constituency to oppose changes. As a result, Greek language use in church today varies widely. In urban areas such as New York with its replenished immigrant neighborhoods, the services are offered almost entirely in Greek. In mixed foreign/native born parishes, certain parts of the liturgy are conducted in English, with the service in English or in both languages in suburban areas of mostly native-born Greek Americans. Wedding ceremonies, especially those involving mixed marriages, draw from both languages. In effect, a "local option" system is operative today as regards use of the Greek language.

With regard to Sunday School religious instruction, the de-ethnization is striking. Whereas the teaching of the religious dogma was done originally in Greek, it is currently conducted in English. The change represents a gradual development. At first, instruction was conducted orally and from books obtained from Greece. Later, the Archdiocese in the United States printed books in Greek with inclusion of translations of difficult words or terms. Following this change, bilingual materials appeared only to move eventually to completely English texts (Costantakos 1980).

Closely associated with the development of the Greek church was the development of Greek schools which culminated in a parochial school system under the auspices of the Greek Archdiocese.

5. *Greek language education*

The first school for Greek language studies still stands in St. Augustine, Florida. It was established in 1777 after the first group of Greek immigrants to the U. S. settled in New Smyrna, Florida. Two forms of organized Greek education developed. One was the full time day (parochial) school and the other the afternoon (parochial) school where young children received Greek language instruction after attending public school. The duration of instruction and the number of days varied from parish to parish depending on the organizational structure and resource availability. The handful of day schools established before World War I replicated primary schools in Greece. The teachers were the priests in their dual capacity or teachers from Greece. The books were published in Greece using rather puristic language. Learning was by rote in a highly disciplinary environment. Such schools conformed with the immigrant's dream of returning to the motherland.

At the beginning, the language of instruction in day schools was Greek, with English taught as a foreign language. In time, as the need for accreditation arose, English became the main language for instruction, but the Greek language, religion, history and culture continued to be heavily stressed.

In another organizational movement, the schools came under Archdiocesan governance and became part of the Parochial School System of the Greek Orthodox Church of North and South America. Though the system has not developed extensively, it presently includes 24 day schools in the United States, Canada and South America, with a total enrollment of 6,386 students for the 1993–1994 school year, and 400 afternoon schools which provide instruction in the Greek language, culture, history and religion to 40,000 students, ages 6–15 (Greek Orthodox Archdiocese of North and South America Yearbook 1994).

There are twelve day schools in the New York metropolitan area, three in Chicago with the rest scattered in Florida, California, Massachusetts, Texas, Canada and South America. The directory of Greek American schools includes 2 schools in Manhattan, 1 in the Bronx, 4 in Brooklyn, 4 in Queens and 1 in Garrison, New York (Greek Orthodox Archdiocese of North and South America Yearbook 1994). There are also some independent Greek schools which cooperate and receive support from the Archdiocese.

As the numbers indicate, the Greek day schools reach only a small segment of Greek American youth. The afternoon schools have had a much greater impact. Held for the most part on the church premises, but also at public schools in New York City, it is the school that Greek Americans usually mean when they refer to "Greek School".

The Greek Orthodox Archdiocese continues to stress Greek language literacy through its Department of Education and its implementation of programs in the community schools. The teacher-training department of St. Basil's Academy prepares teachers for the various schools, in addition to teachers who have received pedagogical training in Greece. With the cooperation of Greece's Ministry of Education, an annual seminar of three weeks is conducted yearly. Greece's interest in the problem of de-Hellenization of the U. S. native born generations is also reflected in measures taken since 1976 when the Greek Parliament debated the issue of language preservation and decided on measures to assist in the literacy effort. To this end, a Counselor of Education was appointed at the Greek Consulate General in New York City with the purpose of providing assistance to Greek education programs in New York City and of advising the Minister of Education in Greece as to the language education progress of the Greek American community (Hatziemmanuel 1982: 181–191).

Up until the 1960's, the methods and reading materials of Greek parochial school classrooms were oriented toward children who had been raised in Greece or who spoke Greek at home. The books and curricula were imported from Greece, and teaching methods were not relevant to the needs and interests of children learning Greek as a second language in New York City (Spiridakis 1987).

Attempts to include Greek language in public schools in the United States date back to the 1930's, when the community of Chicago put pressure on the Board of Education to include Greek in the public school curriculum. By 1935, through the efforts of the Hellenic Education League, Greek was introduced in Chicago's public schools where it remained until 1961.

The Bilingual Education Act of 1968 provided for bilingual programs in Greek where a sufficient number of non-English speaking children warranted the special curricula. Greek bilingual education programs were established in cities such as New York, Chicago, Lowell, Massachusetts, and Tarpon Springs, Florida.

In the 1970's, the NYC public school district which included Astoria, Queens, had identified over 2,500 Greek immigrant children whose proficiency in English was quite limited. Bilingual classes, taught in Greek and English, were structured and implemented in several schools in the district. Bilingual teachers were recruited for these classes. Many of the teachers migrated from the parochial schools responding to the lure of higher pay and enhanced benefits.

The public school Greek bilingual programs were initially tailored to meet the dual language and cultural needs of Greek immigrant children. Greek parochial school advocates expressed consternation that these new immigrants were not enrolling in the parochial schools. However, the public schools were free, offered Greek language instruction, and taught English as a second language. Greek parochial schools were not specifically geared to meet the needs of recent arrivals, who needed English as a second language classes and responded well to the use of Greek for subject matter instruction throughout the school day which the public bilingual class offered (Spiridakis 1987).

The teaching of Greek is essential for Greek language maintenance. Konstantellou (1990) notes that,

> ... at the present moment in its history with immigration from Greece decreasing to a near halt and with new generations of Greek Americans increasingly losing touch with their Greek heritage there is an acute awareness that community survival depends on education (p. 125).

Certain elementary schools in the Astoria public school district today offer Greek as a second language for enrichment. The two public high schools in the district also offer modern Greek classes. Programs of Modern Greek studies have been established through the efforts of Greek immigrant intellectuals who have held university positions. They have disseminated translations of Greek literary works into English and have initiated publications and journals often with the support of Greek benefactors (Moskos 1989: 85). Today there are approximately thirty programs of Greek studies at various U. S. universities (Kourvetaris 1990: 62).

6. *Organizational and community influences*

From the beginning, Greek immigrants have had a predilection for forming topical (home-town) or regional societies. As early as 1900, in New York alone, there were thirty such societies in existence. They included business associations, a ladies charitable group, a volunteer military company, and an athletic association (Burgess 1913: 76).

The first organization in New York, Athena, was established in 1891. "Athena", as well as some other of the earliest organizations, were Pan-Hellenic in nature, having as members Greeks from all parts of Greece. Group and language identification was more important at the time than local, topical loyalties.

As more immigrants arrived from the same villages and localities, and settled in the same cities in the United States, organizations started to reflect allegiances based on local Greek geographical roots. Funds were raised to build schools, bridges, churches, and roads in their own Greek villages.

After World War I, and the disaster in Asia Minor in 1922, most Greeks who had held to the idea of repatriation, chose to remain in the United States. New types of organizations emerged which were oriented to helping immigrants become citizens and make the U. S. their home.

Numerous professional and community groups, Greek-American Veteran Associations, a Greek-American Athletes Association, charitable organizations, and topical, cultural, and recreational groups tied to Greek tenets, make up the organizational structure of the Greek-American community. There are presently 446 such Greek American organizations reported nationwide. The most numerous (107) and perhaps the most characteristically Greek are in metropolitan New York (Greek Orthodox Archdiocese of North and South America Yearbook 1994).

The two most influential Hellenic associations have been AHEPA (American Hellenic Educational Progressive Association) and GAPA (Greek American Progressive Association). The basic philosophy of the two organizations is to be found in the first word of their name, American and Greek.

AHEPA was first organized in 1922, and came into being as a reaction to the anti-foreign attitudes which were sweeping the country during the post World War I years. From its inception, AHEPA was denounced as pseudo-patriotic, disloyal to the Greek Orthodox Church, to Greek schools and Hellenism. The attacks on AHEPA for its use of the English language instead of Greek at meetings (justified by AHEPA on the grounds that Greeks were living in the United States and this necessitated improvement of their facility in the English language) mirrored the turmoil precipitated by the 1970's church decision to allow the use of English in church.

Those who believed that AHEPA was repudiating Hellenism founded GAPA in 1933 to preserve the Greek tradition in the U. S., most especially the Greek language. GAPA thrived on the assumption that Americanization meant the abandonment of Greek traditions and Greek. GAPA supported expansion of Greek schools, organizational activities of Greek mothers, and Greek musical and athletic events. GAPA waged relentless efforts to retain the Greek language and culture. While GAPA membership has declined, AHEPA has remained the largest, most active group in New York City and in the United States.

Even as the sidewalks of Astoria, Queens, have become populated with other than Greek immigrants in the 1990's, the Greek ethnic presence remains dominant in ways other than organizational activity. Astoria, with its numerous Greek restaurants, recently celebrated the dedication of "Athens Square Park" which boasts a sculpture of Socrates. Greek-American banks, medical offices, law offices, real estate offices, and shops are still found throughout this "Greek-town". The only hospital in Astoria offers patients' rights fliers in Greek. The Greek language can be heard throughout this community where the environment and economy continue to support it.

The Annual Greek Independence Day Parade committee is centered in Astoria. The parade up New York City's Fifth Avenue each year is attended by thousands of Greek-Americans. The city acknowledges an official Greek Heritage Week with an annual celebration including Greek poems, songs, and dances performed by Greek children from public and parochial schools.

7. Greek media and ethnic language

The Greek press along with the church and school has played a prominent role in preserving the Greek language and culture. It has kept the immigrants in touch with events in their country of origin and more importantly,

> it became an educational vehicle for learning the Greek language, particularly among the women whose literacy rate was lower than that of the males. Women have reported in interviews their frustration and then, at last their success in merging letter with letter, word with word, phrase with phrase to complete a sentence that would yield some news of their homeland as well as their adopted country (Scourby 1984: 97).

The first Greek newspaper in this country *New World* was published in Boston in 1892. Since that time well over a hundred different Greek newspapers have appeared at one time or another. The peak period of Greek journalism in America was the time between World War I and the depression.

Two dailies published in New York City dominated the scene. The first was the *Atlantis*, a conservative daily of royalist leanings in terms of the politics of the motherland. It was founded in New York in 1894 and in 1972 it succumbed to financial and labor pressures and ceased publication. The second daily, *The National Herald*, was founded in New York in 1915. It rivaled the *Atlantis* as an advocate of liberalism and anti-royalist positions. Several socialist papers emerged between the two world wars, but those and other Greek publications never surpassed the influence of these two New York dailies. Over the years while other papers had a short lived existence, those two New York dailies enjoyed a loyal following and a nationwide circulation. *The National Herald* remains the flagship Greek language paper in New York City and elsewhere (Spiridakis 1979).

The language of the Greek press in Greece and in the U. S. in the early 1900's was *Katharevousa* – the language associated with educated Greeks and the elite class. For the Greek immigrant, *Katharevousa* was a difficult language to understand, especially since the early newcomers had little, if any education. These early immigrants in effect were forced to learn two languages: English, the language of the new world, instrumental for survival; *Katharevousa*, in order to stay in touch with news from the country left behind and in the midst of continuing political turmoil.

While the early Greek immigrants grappled with understanding *Katharevousa*, the language of the Church, schools and government, scholars in Greece and in the USA debated the efficacy of its use in the United States, as well as in Greece. As the Athenian correspondent to the United Nations observed,

> ... supporting *Katharevousa* a language never spoken by the people, helped to alienate the often illiterate Greek immigrant [who] learned a bit of *Katherevousanica* (high class Greek words) but also forgot his own Demotiki language ... and for that the leaders of the Greek-American community, the Greek government, and the Greek press are to blame (Granitsas 1959).

Although the Greek Orthodox Church was committed to *Katharevousa*, the "Demotic" is now used almost exclusively in the United States. *Katharevousa* remains the language of ecclesiastical writings and in use in elitist literary circles.

Since 1977, the Greek American community in New York was introduced to another daily, the *Proini* [the Morning Daily]. The *Proini* reflects a rather socialist viewpoint often in contradiction to U. S. foreign policy. *Proini* is sold mainly in New York City while the *National Herald* continues to have a nationwide subscription base. Both dailies are published in the "Demotic" language and now have two new publications in English, setting new standards for Greek American periodicals. *Greek Accent*, a bimonthly publication of the *National Herald*, appeared in 1980 presenting both Greek and Greek American topics. *The Greek American*, a weekly newspaper founded in 1986, and produced by the *Proini* is of more serious and thought provoking content. An earlier newspaper in English, *The Hellenic Times*, also published in New York City, gives candid opinions on cultural events in New York. There are also several other weeklies, biweeklies, and monthlies found in a few of the larger cities with Greek American populations in both the Greek and the English language. It should also be noted that today eight different Athens and Salonika newspapers are flown to New York and Chicago daily (Moskos 1989).

While the Greek press played a constructive role in meeting the nostalgic yearnings of the Greek immigrant, and contributed in the perpetuation of the ethnic language, it was also quick to respond to the erosion of Greek language proficiency, as early as 1923, with the publication of *The Democrat*, the first Greek-American newspaper published in English. Especially since the 1940's, several newspapers, periodicals and journals have sought a wider audience among American born Greeks. Greek language newspapers have been progressively replaced by either bilingual or solely English language papers.

The prediction regarding future Greek reading generations is grim, though this perhaps unfortunate picture is counterbalanced by a growing number of Greek radio programs in America. Today, there are in the United States and Canada 81 radio programs (10 of them in New York) and 38 television programs, (9 in New York) the electronic media drawing both readers and advertisers away from the Greek press. Their programs are offered in both Greek and English and their content relates to events in Greece, the Greek American subcommunity, and the larger American community (Moskos 1989). In New York City, there is a 24 hour Greek cable television channel. One of the Greek radio programs, "The Sounds of Greece", has been aired for over 25 years.

It should be noted that some of the first language films and recordings of Greek music were produced in New York City. Local Greek language broadcasts that are syndicated elsewhere have also been produced in New York City as far back as the thirties. Up until the 1960's, an Astoria movie theater showed Greek films on Sundays, usually without subtitles. There exists also video distribution and cable networks of Greek programming in New York City. Greek records, tapes and videotapes are sold at numerous stores in New York City. In addition, present transportation and instant communication electronic networks allow for daily publications to be made available to the Greek American readership (Hatzidimitriou 1995). Travel to Greece has been another avenue that has enhanced the use of Greek in the city.

8. Greek language and cultural continuity in New York City

Several Greek scholars have pointed to diminishing or non-existent ethnic language proficiency among native-born Greek Americans (Kourvetaris 1988, 1990; Moskos 1989; Scourby 1984). Studies of Greek communities reflect a decline in the link made between Greek ethnicity and Greek language, but not a diminishing Greek identification. The Greek Orthodox Church and the family emerge as the significant sources of subcultural continuity, with the Greek language losing ground as one moves along the generational continuum.

A study (Costantakos 1982) of two hundred eleven Greek American respondents, representing three generations of Greek Americans in the metropolitan New York City area probed attitudes toward the Greek language as well as the relation of language proficiency to ethnic identification. The study found that attitudes toward the Greek language remain positive despite considerable language shift, and that ethnic identification is strongest among those whose language proficiency is greatest.

A sample of statements by the respondents reflects the positive attitudes toward the Greek language:

> I have positive feelings about the Greek language … It is that sense of belonging, peoplehood, the little things that no one else understands.

> It would be nice if one could travel to Greece to revitalize the culture and also improve the language.

> I do not know what realistic goals are. I think preservation of language is important. I cannot see the Greek Orthodox Church disassociated from Greek language. If you take cultural aspects away, which to me means language to a great extent, there is nothing left. Even I, who feel inadequate in language, do not like church and aspects of the structure, enjoy the ritual in the Greek language.

> I'd rather see that services are not conducted in English. Service and liturgy will lose something. It would be nice to understand what is going on, though. A sermon could be given in English. Pretty much like what is going on right now. Of course, people can get instruction in Sunday school. I do not see merging of churches desirable. I'd rather see them as they are.

> Use of English? At the beginning, I was totally against it. Now, I think it may not be a bad idea to use some English for the youth, and the ones who do not understand. Of course, we should not go to the extreme of changing everything. Our trouble today is that we cater to the young. Maybe the priest can say the Creed in English after he says it in Greek. Use English in sermon, not all in English … Never … .

The shift from Greek to English in church, as the sample statements indicate, is not overwhelmingly favored by Greek-Americans in New York City, whether in terms of liturgy or sermons. A number of the respondents who did not speak Greek or comprehend the language of the liturgy, still expressed enjoyment in the mysticism of the ritual and did not wish it to be changed. Some drew a parallel to the uplifting experience of listening to an operatic score in languages other than English. There was, however, greater agreement for the change to English sermons. This change is a significant indicator of language shift since as Hofman (1966: 133) indicates,

> use of the mother tongue in church sermons seems to be the most meaningful index of language maintenance because the sermon is probably most sensitive to the linguistic needs and preference of the congregations as a whole.

As Greek Americans become progressively heterogeneous in composition generationally, ethnically, and in terms of social class membership, the Greek language becomes progressively weakened as a process of subcultural continuity. Yet, as reflected in the study, there is great desire for maintenance and continuity of the Greek language, and ethnic identity remains considerably stronger among those whose Greek language proficiency is greatest.

9. Conclusions

Preoccupation with the maintenance of the Greek language and legacy became a prime concern of the early Greeks. Since most intended to return to the homeland, they insisted that their children learn the language of their ancestors. Greek was spoken at home, for the most part limited to the exigencies of daily living. The intensity of the desire for Greek language maintenance is exemplified by the fact that every time a new community was organized, the establishment of the church was followed by a Greek language school or class. Religion, language, and tradition were inseparably linked; there was no dichotomy between religion and nationality. The family, every organization, community resources of the church, the school, the Greek press, and the voluntary organizations, promoted formal and informal schooling for the purpose of language use and preservation.

In the United States despite rather extensive efforts by the Greek American community, in New York City and elsewhere, Greek language use has been eroded and gradual language shift has taken place. Among second generation Greek Americans there has been a progressive reluctance to adhere to all cultural components of Greek ethnicity. Although ethnicity for this generation was still identified with religion, tradition and language, the Greek language was giving way to English, and Greek nationality to a Greek Orthodox religious affiliation, a shift assuming greater strength with the third and subsequent generations.

The younger generations favor preservation of religion and aspects of culture without necessarily using the Greek language to achieve it. The native born generations still express positive attitudes toward the ethnic language, while in reality fewer of the third generation speak Greek. There is also diminished study of the Greek language and Greek school attendance with the native born generations. This is true, even in New York City, with its large concentration of Greek Americans and dynamic ethnic activity in many aspects of Greek community life.

The weakening of this ethnic identification process is reflected in several studies and writings related to Greek language preservation (Bardis 1976; Costantakos 1982; Konstantellou 1990; Kourvetaris 1990; Moskos 1989; Orfanos – Tsemberis 1987; Psomiades 1987; Sarantopoulos 1990;

Scourby 1984; Spiridakis 1994). Bardis (1976: 31–35) gives a thoughtful analysis of the reasons for the Greek language erosion. He speaks of the limited education of the Greek immigrants and its weakening effect on Hellenism in the United States, the restrictive immigration laws which prevented replenishment of the Greek communities for prolonged periods of time, and the decline in nationalistic sentiment following the Asia Minor defeat of 1922. He adds as reasons the American depression of the 1930's which led to a weakening of Hellenism, the complexity of the Greek language, the limited impact of Greek schools which proved to be inadequate in terms of teacher qualifications and resources, the general outlook of some influential organizations like AHEPA (American Hellenic Educational Progressive Association) which espoused the use of the English language, the U. S. policy of Americanization and assimilation, the U. S. public schools, the social upward mobility characteristic of Greeks, intermarriage, and the politics of the Greek American communities.

Scholars of Greek ethnicity assume different positions with regard to predicting Greek language maintenance in the United States. Positions range from the inevitability of language loss and the shift of Greek Orthodoxy in the American context, to a more optimistic position which calls for reassessment of the language maintenance potential through educational changes in approaches to language learning. The approaches include the use of electronic media, support for programs of Greek Studies with emphasis on Modern Greek Literature and History and Culture, and exchange programs with Greece. Language efforts in New York City reflect this most positive outlook toward Greek language preservation. Can the future be predicted within such opposing positions? Can the clock be turned back? Only time can give us the answer.

Notes

1. The *diglossia* in Greece, the struggle between *Katharevousa* and *Demotike*, has been a thorny one as it became a social, political, religious, even an ideological issue, rather than just a linguistic one. *Katharevousa* (puristic, primarily written) was the official language of the past while the *Demotike* ("Demotic") was the spoken language, resulting in two different linguistic systems of words, grammatical and syntactical rules. For example the word "fruit" in *Katharevousa* is *oporika* while it is *frouta* in the *Demotike*. One goes to the *oinopoleion* [liquor store] to buy *oinos* [wine] (the word used by Homer) and not *krasi*, the word in the Demotic. The *Katharevousa* speaking person would say, "*Ta thakria kateklisan ek neou tous ophthalmous mou*" [Tears filled again my eyes] instead of "*Ta thakria yemisan pali ta matia mou*" in the "Demotic". Educated men and women often prefer to address the language as it has evolved as *Kathomiloumeni* or "Common

Spoken" a simplified approach to the two linguistic systems, as the term *Demotike* represents various Demotic forms and a somewhat arbitrary choice of what is the correct Demotic.

2. The *Monotoniko* ["Monotonic"] system was proclaimed by Presidential Decree in Greece on April 22, 1982 and is now taught in all schools, employed by all governmental agencies and the media in Greece and in the diaspora. It replaced the "Polytonic" system which was introduced in Hellenistic times. (There were no accents in *Ancient Greek*.) As the name indicates, the "monotonic" system employs one accent, the acute (′).

References

Bardis, Panos D.
1976 *The future of the Greek language in the United States*. San Francisco, CA: R. and E. Research Associates.

Burgess, Thomas
1913 *Greeks in America*. Boston, MA: Sherman, French and Co.

Chaconas, Stephen George
1942 *Adamantios Korais: A study in Greek nationalism*. New York, NY: Columbia University Press.

Costantakos, Chrysie M.
1980 *The American Greek subculture: Processes of continuity*. New York, NY: Arno Press.
1982 "Ethnic language as a variable in subcultural continuity", in: Harry J. Psomiades – Alice Scourby (ed.), 137–170.

Demakopoulos, Steve A.
1989 *Do you speak Greek*? New York: Private Publication.

Glazer, Nathan
1966 "The process and problems of language maintenance: An integrative review", in: Fishman, Joshua A. *Language loyalty in the United States*. The Hague: Mouton.
[1978] [Reprinted New York: Arno Press, 358–368]

Granitsas, Spyros
1959 "The Greek language in America", *Argonautes:* 267–270. (Translation from Greek to English by Alexander Spiridakis).

Greek Orthodox Archdiocese of North and South America
1994 *1994 Yearbook*. New York, NY.

Hatzidimitriou, Constantine G.
1995 "The Greek American community in New York", in: Kenneth T. Jackson (ed.), *The Encyclopedia of New York City*. New Haven: Yale University Press, 503–504.

Hatziemmanuel, Emmanuel
1982 "Hellenic Orthodox education in America", in: Harry J. Psomiades – Alice Scourby (eds.), 181–189.

Hofman, John E.
1966 "Mother tongue retentiveness in ethnic parishes", in: Joshua A. Fishman, *Language loyalty in the United States*. The Hague: Mouton, 127–155.

Immigration and Naturalization Service
1976 *1976 Annual Report*, U. S. Government Printing Office.

Kloss, Heinz
1966 "Types of multilingual communities: A discussion of ten variables", *Sociological Inquiry* 36 (2): 135–145.
Konstantellou, Eva
1990 "Education as a means of empowerment for minority cultures: Strategies for the Greek American community", *Journal of Modern Hellenism* 7: 125–139.
Kourvetaris, George A.
1988 "The Greek American family", in: C. H. Mindel and R. W. Habenstein (eds.), *Ethnic families in America.* New York: Elsevier, 76–108.
1990 "The futuristics of Greek America", *Journal of Modern Hellenism* 7: 45–66.
Moskos, Charles C.
1989 *Greek Americans: Struggle and success.* 2nd. ed. New Brunswick, NJ: Transaction Publishers.
Orfanos, Spyros D. – Harry J. Psomiades – John Spiridakis, eds.
1987 *Education and Greek Americans: Process and Prospects.* New York: Pella Press.
Orfanos, Spyros D. – Tsemberis, Sam J.
1987 "A needs assessment of Greek American schools in New York City", in Spyros D. Orphanos –Harry J. Psomiades – John Spiridakis (eds.).
Papaioannou, George
1976 *From Mars Hill to Manhattan: The Greek Orthodox in America under Athenagoras I.* Minneapolis, MN: Light and Life Publishing Co.
Psomiades, Harry J.
1987 "Greece and Greek America: The future of the Greek American community in Education and Greek Americans: Process and prospects", in Spyros D. Orfanos – Harry J. Psomiades – John Spiridakis (eds), 91–102.
Psomiades, Harry J. – Alice Scourby (ed.)
1982 *The Greek American community in transition.* New York, NY: Pella Press.
Saloutos, Theodore
1956 *They remember America.* Berkeley and Los Angeles, CA: University of California Press.
1964 *The Greeks in the United States.* Cambridge, MA: Harvard University Press.
Sarantopoulos, S.
1990 "Modern Greek education: A new audience", *Journal of Modern Hellenism* 7: 117–124.
Scourby, Alice
1984 *The Greek Americans.* Boston, MA: Twayne Publishers.
Spiridakis, Alexander
1979 "The Historic beginning of the *National Herald*" *Special anniversary issue: 65 years of service to Greek Americans. The National Herald.*
Spiridakis, John
1987 "Greek bilingual education: Policies and possibilities", Spyros D. Orfanos – Harry J. Psomiades – John Spiridakis (eds.), 73–90.
1994 "The pursuit of Greek bilingual education", *Journal of Modern Hellenism* 9: 19–33.
Vaporis, N. M.
1984 "The Church and the preservation of the Greek language in America", in Anne Pharmakides – Kostas Kazazis – Nomikos M. Vaporis – Athan Anagnostopoulos – Harry J. Psomiades (eds.), *The teaching of modern Greek in the English speaking world.* Brookline, MA.: Hellenic College Press, 71 – 75.

Spanish in New York[1]

Ana Celia Zentella

1. Introduction

I remember the signs in shop windows when I was growing up in the South Bronx in the 1950s: *Aquí se habla español* 'Spanish spoken here'. My mother and father made their purchases in English because they had been in New York City (NYC) for decades and spoke it with ease, but increasing numbers of Puerto Rican immigrants were aided by Spanish-speaking merchants, often Sephardic Jews. Their centuries-old Spanish, maintained in the diaspora since the expulsion of the Jews and Moors from Spain in 1492, was rekindled to serve the burgeoning Puerto Rican community. Puerto Ricans formed the earliest Spanish-speaking settlements in New York at the end of the 19th century, and they have constituted the majority of the city's Spanish speakers during the 20th century, but as we approach the 21st century the varieties of Spanish heard in New York's stores and subways include those of all Latin America and Spain. Most of the signs that announced *Aquí se habla español* are gone because it is assumed that at least one clerk will be able to attend to customers' needs in Latino neighborhoods, although it is impossible to predict which variety of Spanish s/he will speak.

The official Hispanic population of NYC grew from 16% in 1970 to 20% in 1980, and in 1990 the 1,783,511 Latinos in NYC comprised a quarter of the city's total population. It is projected that Latinos will outnumber African Americans by the year 2000 and outpace Anglos and African Americans by 2010, when they are expected to make up 35% of the city's population (Bouvier – Briggs 1988). References to "Latinos" or "Hispanics" – the Spanish term is preferred by most activists but the English term is favored by government officials – obscure significant differences in the historical, political, economic, and linguistic histories of nearly two dozen groups. Because of those differences, and because their identification with the homeland remains strong, groups prefer to be identified by their national origin, e. g., Puerto Rican, Mexican, Cuban, instead of by a pan-ethnic label like *Latino* or *Hispano*, or as a hyphenated American. Significantly, a national survey conducted among Mexicans, Puerto Ricans and Cubans found that 80% or more "do not see themselves as very similar culturally or politically" (de la Garza et al 1992: 8). The variety of Spanish that each group speaks is the most distinctive marker of its individuality, but the Spanish language also is their most powerful unifier, thanks to more than 300 years of Spanish colonization. Because the dialects of Latin American Spanish are more mutually intelligible than some dialects in Spain (Zamora Vicente 1979), speakers resent being asked "Do you speak Puerto Rican, Dominican etc?" The unity of the Spanish language is due to the proximity of the nations, the normalizing efforts of the Royal Academy of the Spanish Language, and the fact that some countries in Latin America were still part of the Spanish empire less than 100 years ago. Still, there are notable distinctions in some of the words and sounds favored by each group, and in the attitudes and customs surrounding the use of language. Because some dialects of Spanish are considered more prestigious than others, certain groups of speakers suffer from linguistic insecurity which may affect their maintenance of Spanish negatively. This chapter provides a brief overview of the dialects of Spanish spoken by the major Spanish-speaking communities in NYC, and discusses the historical, socio-economic and political forces which shape their linguistic diversity and which will determine whether or not a pan-Latino NYC Spanish lies in NYC's future.

2. Puerto Ricans and the increasing diversity

A pioneering Puerto Rican community existed in the Brooklyn Navy Yard area even before Puerto Rico became a United States colony in 1898, and migrants who came after the U.S. granted island residents citizenship in 1917 moved into other areas. When my mother and father arrived in NYC in the 1920s – Mami from Puerto Rico and Papi from Mexico – they met and married in the small community of Spanish-speakers from Spain and Latin America who had settled in Central and East Harlem in Manhattan. Mami knew more English than her fellow Spanish-speakers because the U.S. had imposed English-only in the schools and courts of Puerto Rico soon after the 1898 invasion and she was fortunate enough to have graduated from eighth grade, but the 50-year-long English-only policy resulted in more dropouts than English speakers. The arrival of approximately 50,000 Puerto Ricans a year during the post World War II decade (1945–1955) prompted the *Aquí se habla español* signs. Washington's "escape valve" policies – designed to defuse the nationalist powder keg that the widespread poverty and unemployment of Puerto Rico represented – included mass emigration as their centerpiece. The establishment of direct San Juan-New York airline service provided the garment industry with skilled machine operators and made NYC the center of Puerto Rican migration. By 1950, there were 245,880 Puerto Ricans in NYC, and so many were concentrated in Manhattan's East Harlem that it was known as *El Barrio* 'the neighborhood'. In the decades after Puerto Rico was declared a Commonwealth of the United States in 1952, city urban relocation policies helped make the South Bronx (Mott Haven, Hunts Point) the NYC area with the highest Puerto Rican concentration. Other significant *barrios* were created in Manhattan and Brooklyn, some of which were re-labeled with Spanish names, e. g., *Loisaida* (recalling both 'Lower East Side' and *Loíza Aldea,* a town in Puerto Rico) and *Los Sures* ('the Southside'). Towards the end of the 20th century, Puerto Ricans made up 20% or more of eleven areas in NYC.

Table 1
Puerto Rican neighborhoods[a] in NYC, 1987*

Bronx neighborhoods	% Puerto Rican
Mott Haven/Hunts Point	53.2%
University Heights/Fordham	41.5
Soundview/Parkchester	39.1
Highbridge/Grand Concourse	33.1
Kingsbridge Heights/Moshulu	28.2
Manhattan neighborhoods	
East Harlem (*El Barrio*)	36.3
Lower East Side (*Loisaida*)/Chinatown	21.8
Brooklyn neighborhoods	
Bushwick	49.6
Sunset Park	32.1
Williamsburg (*Los Sures*)/Greenpoint	27.7
East New York/Starrett City	21.0

*** Source: Falcón et al 1989: 6.**

[a] Neighborhoods with Puerto Rican concentrations of 20% or more.

Puerto Ricans were the first group to make the presence of Spanish felt in NYC and they still account for the majority of the city's Spanish speakers, but at a decreasing rate. In 1980 Puerto Ricans constituted 61% of New York's Latinos but by 1990 that figure had dropped to 50%. The mix of Spanish-speakers intensifed as immigration from several Latin American countries began to out-pace the rate of Puerto Rican arrivals in the 1980's. The Dominican community grew by 165%, and so many settled in the upper west side of Manhattan (11,392 Dominicans are registered in one Washington Heights zip code) that the area is referred to as *Quisqueya* (the Taíno name for the island of Hispaniola that the Dominican Republic shares with Haiti) *plátano* 'plantain land', or *el platanal* 'plantain grove'. In other sections of the city, e. g., Manhattan's Lower East Side, Brooklyn's Sunset Park, and Tremont in the Bronx, Dominicans live in close contact with Puerto Ricans. More educated and prosperous Dominicans are concentrated in the Elmhurst-Corona section of Queens, an area which they share with newcomers from various Central and South American countries. In the 1990's, The Dominican Republic alone accounted for one out of five immigrants to the city (Dept. of City Planning, 1997).

The only other Latino group besides Puerto Ricans and Dominicans that has at least one identifiable ethnic neighborhood in NYC is the Colombian community. "Little Colombia" or "*Chapinero*" (a middle class suburb in Bogotá) in Queens traces its beginnings to the few hundred educated Colombians who emigrated to Jackson Heights at the end of World War I. It grew after WWII when the political unrest at home caused many to flee *la violencia* 'the violence', and in the 1970s high rates of unemployment in Colombia contributed to its further expansion (Orlov – Ueda 1980). In 1990 Jackson Heights was home to almost half of all Colombians in NYC, and the area has attracted increasing numbers of newer arrivals, e. g., Ecuadorians, Argentineans (Hays 1993). The extent of Jackson Heights' Latino diversity is obvious in the proliferation of restaurants and groceries in close proximity, e. g., La Colombianita, Fiesta México, La Uruguaya, La Bonaerense, and Inti Raymi: Peruvian Cuisine/*Cocina Peruana*. War in Central America was responsible for making the number of Salvadorans in NYC grow the most dramatically – 280% between 1980–1990 – 50% of whom live in Queens. Perhaps a "Little El Salvador" will be established in the future, as well as "Little Ecuadors" etc., and even a "Little Mexico" is possible.

The largest concentrations of Mexicans in the U. S. traditionally have been in the Southwest and California. When my father and his friends founded the *Centro Mexicano de Nueva York* circa 1930, its membership included many non-Mexicans because few immigrants left Mexico for NYC. As late as 1980, there were less than 13,000 Mexicans in NYC, but just before my father died in 1987, he welcomed many newcomers to the *Centro*. The amnesty provided by the 1986 Immigration Reform and Control Act contributed to a 173% increase in the number of Mexicans in NYC, and put New York State in tenth place in terms of the number of Mexican residents in the country (Valdés de Montano – Smith 1994). No definable Mexican neighborhood exists yet, but *taquerías* 'taco stands' have replaced several of the *cuchifrito* restaurants that sold typical Puerto Rican food in El Barrio and parts of the Bronx.

The only Latino group to decline in NYC in the 1980s was the Cuban population, despite the arrival of 125,000 Mariel boatlift "entrants" in 1980. They formed the Third Wave of Cubans to arrive, after the First Wave that fled the Cuban Revolution (1959–1965), and the Second Wave

Table 2
Percent distribution of Hispanics by descent, NYC 1990*
(Department of City Planning, 1993: Table A)

Hispanics	Total	% of all
Total Hispanics	1,783,511	100.0%
Puerto Rican	896,763	50.3
Dominican	332,713	18.7
Colombian	84,454	4.7
Ecuadorian	78,444	4.4
Mexican	61,722	3.5
Cuban	56,041	3.1
Salvadoran	23,926	1.3
Peruvian	23,257	1.3
Panamanian	22,707	1.3
Honduran	22,167	1.2
Spaniard	20,148	1.1
Guatemalan	15,765	0.9
Argentinean	13,934	0.8
Nicaraguan	9,660	0.5
CostaRican	6,920	0.4
Chilean	6,721	0.4
Venezuelan	4,172	0.2
Bolivian	3,465	0.2
Uruguayan	3,233	0.2

* **Sources: 1990 Census Summary Tape File I and Summary Tape File 3. For populations under 20,000 the source is: 1990 Census Public Use Microdata Sample A.**

(1965–1973) that was characterized by family reunification (García – Otheguy 1988). The Cuban community in NYC, which had preceeded Dominicans on the upper west side and in Elmhust-Corona, grew smaller while Cuban communities in Dade County and West New York-Union City grew larger: more than 70% of the Cubans in the U. S. are concentrated in Florida and New Jersey. Nevertheless, Cubans were among the six groups that contributed more than 50,000 to NYC's total Latino population in 1990 (see table 2).

The reliability of the figures in Table 2 has been questioned. Census Bureau officials admit that the Latino community was undercounted, e. g., the undercount for Mexicans alone was estimated at 6,000 in New York State (Valdés de Montano – Smith 1994). Leaders of the Dominican community believe that including undocumented immigrants more than doubles their numbers in NYC. Notwithstanding these limitations, Table 2 establishes some important contrasts. The great majority of Spanish dialects have at least 3,000 speakers in NYC: the only Spanish-speaking country in the western hemisphere that is not represented is Paraguay. All groups trail far behind Puerto Ricans, who along with the second and sixth place Dominicans and Cubans, respectively, make Caribbean Spanish the dialect that is spoken by 72% of NYC's Latinos.

3. *Latin American Spanish*

3.1. *History and Lexicon*

The Caribbean is one of the five geographic zones of Latin American Spanish first proposed by the Dominican linguist Pedro Henríquez Ureña in 1921 (Henríquez Ureña 1940). In it, he included much of Venezuela and the Atlantic coast of Colombia as well as Puerto Rico, Cuba, and the Dominican Republic. The other four regions are: Chile, the Andes (Peru, Ecuador, Bolivia, northwest Argentina, most of Colombia and part of Venezuela), the Río Plata (Argentina, Uruguay, Paraguay), and Mexico (Mexico, Central America, Southwest U. S.). The linguistic features of these dialect areas and their major subdivisions are summarized in various overviews of Latin American Spanish, including Lope Blanch 1968, Rosario 1970, Canfield 1981, Cotton and Sharp 1988, and Moreno de Alba 1988. Henríquez Ureña based his divisions on the common geography, history, and substratum of indigenous languages that united each zone, and although scholars have questioned the validity and usefulness of such broad dialect areas and proposed other formulations (cf. Moreno de Alba 1988 for a review), his classification remains useful. This is particularly true for the Spanish Antilles: all three islands were explored during Columbus' first and second trips, and had established cities before Cortés arrived in Mexico. Columbus's landing on the northcoast of the Dominican Republic in 1492 and the settlement of Santo Domingo in 1496 made Quisqueya the cradle of Spanish in the "New World".

San Juan in Puerto Rico (established by Ponce de León in 1508) and Havana in Cuba (1514) also provided important ports of entry and resupply for the Spanish galleons that dropped off new settlers and slaves on their way to the South American mainland. The early extermination of the Taínos makes it difficult to determine the extent of their linguistic influence beyond the lexicon. Nevertheless, most studies maintain that the Taíno contribution was greater than the African (Alvarez Nazario 1961, López Morales 1971, Megenney 1982, 1990), due to "*la rápida acomodación del negro a los patrones culturales del europeo dominador*" [the rapid accomodation of the black man to the cultural patterns of the European ruler] (Rosario 1969: 13). The extent of African influence on the Spanish of the area, particularly in the Dominican Republic, is being re-investigated (Green 1993). As for the regional origin of the peninsular Spanish brought to the Caribbean, immigration figures from southern Spain and characteristics of Andalusian Spanish favor Andalusia over Castile (Cotton – Sharp 1988). The Spanish that is spoken in NYC by the descendants of the Taíno-African-Spanish mix that took place five hundred years ago in the Caribbean reflects its original multicultural heritage, as it continues to integrate new linguistic contributions and to influence features of other dialects of Spanish.

Elsewhere I have described the lexical levelling that is occuring in NYC among Puerto Ricans, Dominicans, Cubans, and Colombians (Zentella 1990a). Each group maintains its ways of speaking, especially for in-group conversations, but almost everyone picks up features of another dialect, primarily the lexicon. I have talked with Mexican newcomers who abandoned their traditional *chile* in favor of the Caribbean word for hot sauce (*pique*), Ecuadorian taxi-drivers who referred to *chavos* 'money' like Puerto Ricans, and speakers from many countries who have adopted *guagua*, the Caribbean term for 'bus'. Close contact in neighborhoods, schools, and the work place, and especially intermarriage, makes some dialect levelling inevitable. The prevalence of speakers of Caribbean Spanish suggests that the levelling should take on an overwhelmingly Caribbean flavor, but social and linguistic factors that stigmatize Caribbean Spanish militate against that tendency.

3.2. Linguistic security and insecurity

Negative attitudes towards Caribbean Spanish frequently are expressed by all Spanish speakers, including Dominicans, Cubans, and Puerto Ricans. Their linguistic security, expressed as evaluations of their dialect as positive or negative and as superior or inferior to others (Labov 1966), is in stark contrast to that of other Spanish speakers, especially Colombians. In response to the question, "Should the Spanish of your group be the one taught in NYC schools?", only Colombians (n=51) responded "yes" in the majority (64%). Most of the Puerto Rican (n=73), Cuban (n=20), and Dominican (n=50) subjects answered in the negative: 60%, 61%, and 80% respectively. The majority stressed the importance of teaching a general standard Spanish in their response, but the extent of linguistic insecurity among Dominicans was further underscored by the percent who believed their Spanish should not be the dialect of choice for classrooms because it was *incorrecto* 'incorrect' or *malo* 'bad'. In stating their reasons, only 2% of the Colombians, 13% of the Puerto Ricans, and 19% of the Cubans expressed negative opinions of their dialect, but 35% of the Dominicans expressed negative opinions about Dominican Spanish (Zentella 1990a).

Latino linguistic security/insecurity can be traced to social and linguistic factors that are interrelated. In the first place, the educational level of the subjects – which has important implications for their socio-economic status – is mirrored in the pattern. Fewer Colombians (16%) and Puerto Ricans (19%) had ended their education at the elementary level, and Cubans had the highest percent with some graduate schooling (25%). Dominicans had the largest percent who did not go on to secondary school (34%) and the smallest percent who went on to graduate school (8%). The fact that those who had completed fewer years of formal education expressed more condemnation of their Spanish is not surprising. Since Puerto Ricans and Dominicans in NYC have a much lower rate of college graduates (6% each) compared to Colombians (11%) and Cubans (18%) (Department of City Planning 1993), it seems logical that the latter groups would feel more linguistically secure than the former. But the correlation between education and linguistic security in my NYC study was not a stable one. Some Colombians who had studied only a few years were prouder of their groups' Spanish than some Dominicans who had studied many more years. Dominican linguistic insecurity reflected a more widespread rejection of Dominican Spanish by the other groups, explicity verbalized in the high level of dismay they said they would express if someone were to tell them that they sounded like a Dominican. Puerto Rican Spanish was rejected to a slightly lesser degree, and Colombian Spanish was praised the most.

The political, socio-economic, and racial factors that are at work in establishing the hierarchy of prestige among these dialects cannot be ignored. The negative impact of U. S. language policies in Puerto Rico (Zentella 1981) and of decades of dictatorial repression in the Dominican Republic, as well as the lower incomes and darker skins of Dominicans and Puerto Ricans in NYC, place them at the bottom of the language status ladder. In 1989, 39% of Dominican families and 36% of Puerto Rican families lived below poverty level, compared with 15% of the city's Colombian families (Department of City Planning 1993). The percent of Cuban families in poverty rose to 14% in 1992 (IPRP 1993) because of the immigrants from Mariel and the more recent *balseros* 'raft people', but it remains significantly lower than that of most other Latino groups. The influx of black and unskilled Cubans since 1980 and the arrival of an increasing number of Puerto Rican professionals over the last decade have diversified the variety of class dialects from the Caribbean that are heard in New York, but unequal comparisons between working class Puerto Rican and Dominican speech on the one hand and middle class Cuban, Central and South American speech on the other continue to abound. Usually, negative attitudes are not expressed in racial or class terms. They are couched in criticisms of Caribbean Spanish, particularly how it is pronounced, while the dialectal differences of all other regions and classes are conveniently down-played or ignored.

3.3. Pronunciation

3.3.1. Caribbean Spanish pronunciation

The phonology of the Caribbean was inherited from Andalusian Spanish, and some of its features may have been influenced by the African language mixtures during the extensive slave trade in the Caribbean. Most noteworthy is the instability of word/syllable final -s, particularly in informal speech. As in *Andalucía* to this day, it can be rendered as an aspirated /h/, as in 'he', or be dropped altogether. In Puerto Rican, Dominican, and Cuban Spanish, e. g., *Nosotros gastamos* 'We spend' can sound like *Nosotroh gahtamoh* or *Nosotro gatamo.* Deletion is more prominent among the less educated in every group, but quantitative research by Terrell (1982a,b) proved that Dominicans deleted more than Puerto Ricans and Cubans – in ascending order – no matter what the educational level. Dominicans who had attended university omitted syllable/word final -s 76% of the time, and deletion was almost categorical (94%) among those who had not gone beyond elementary school.

Cultural attitudes toward the retention of -s in the Caribbean explain the high deletion rates. Among Dominicans, those who stress -s are accused of *hablando fisno* 'talking fine/high class', (with an intrusive -s in *fino*) or *comiendo espagueti* 'eating spaghetti', and there is the added connotation of effeminacy when men do it. In NYC, therefore, social pressures on Caribbean speakers to aspirate or delete -s conflict with the insistence on its enunciation by higher status speakers from other regions. This conflict contributes to feelings of linguistic insecurity, particularly for those groups with the highest deletion rates. It is as if U. S. Americans were made to feel ashamed of their English because they pronounce words like "water" and "butter" with a flap sound that is like a Spanish r in the middle of the word instead of the British t, when adoption of the British pronunciations would earn them ridicule. My solution, and that of many others who are aware of the negative attitudes and are bidialectal, is to reserve my informal Caribbean Spanish for in-group members, and switch to a more conservative variety for formal communication with outsiders.

In addition to the features that distinguish Caribbean Spanish speakers as a group, each country is known for its intonation, i.e, the particular rise and fall voice pattern that identifies each group, and at least one distinctive phonological feature:

a. Puerto Rican Spanish
The trilled r, written as single r at the beginning of words and as double rr in the middle of words, may be pronounced as a velar R which can be raspy like the German ch in *Achtung* or *Bach*. It is similar to the Spaniards' pronunciation of j or g before i/e, all of which are transcribed as /x/.

b. Dominican Spanish
The most salient aspect of Dominican Spanish is the substitution of /i/ for -r in syllable final position, e. g., *doctor>doctoi* 'doctor', *cuarto>cuaito* 'room' or 'money', characteristic of the northern Cibao region, the original home of many NYC Dominicans. Speakers from the south are distinguished by the -r that replaces syllable final l in their speech (*tal vez>tar ve* 'perhaps'), and those from the capital are known for replacing syllable final r with l (*carne>calne* 'meat').

c. Cuban Spanish
Traditionally, Cubans have been distinguished by the absence of syllable final -l and -r and the doubling of the following consonant, e. g., *Alberto> Abbetto.*

3.3.2. Central and South American Spanish pronunciation
The varieties of Spanish that are spoken in the Caribbean are considered more "radical" (Guitart 1982) than Central and South American dialects because they drop or change several consonants, particularly syllable/word-final -s, even though some inland/highland varieties of Spanish delete vowels. Rosenblat (1970: 136) described the contrasting pattern of "*las tierras altas y las tierras bajas"* [highlands and lowlands] with a humorous analogy based on "dietary" habits:

> *Yo las distingo, de manera caricaturesca, por el régimen alimenticio: las tierras altas se comen las vocales, las tierras bajas se comen las consonantes.*
>
> [I distinguish them, in caricature form, by their diet: the highlands eat their vowels and the lowlands eat their consonants.]

Inland Mexican, Central, and South American dialects were less exposed to Andalusian Spanish than the Caribbean ports, and some inland areas were off limits to Blacks, so inland dialects tend to conserve syllable final -s like the Castilian dialect of north central Spain. Speakers of conservative dialects tend to be highly critical of radical speakers from the coasts, and Guitart (1982) claims that radical speakers are more likely to imitate conservative pronunciation than vice versa. But illegal immigrants who try to "pass" as Puerto Rican citizens, and South/Central American activists who identify with the plight of Puerto Ricans and Dominicans have found it useful to blend in linguistically by adopting -s deletion. Additionally, contraction and deletion are normal processes present in every dialect, e. g., the replacement of syllable/word initial /s-/ by /h/ is not unknown in some varieties of Central and South American Spanish, so that *si pasamos* 'if we pass by' can become */hi pahamos/.*

3.4. Variations in Grammar: Pronoun placement, frequency, and forms

I have concentrated on pronunciation because it is the focal point of most criticisms, and because Spanish dialects vary less in grammar. Of the nine supposedly widespread differences in Caribbean Spanish listed by Rosario (1970), most are frequent in all Spanish, e. g., preference for the periphrastic future (*ir a* 'to go to' + infinitive) instead of the future verb form. Only the placement of personal pronouns before the verb in questions clearly separates Caribbean Spanish from other varieties, e. g., *¿Cómo tú te llamas?* instead of *¿Cómo te llamas tú?* 'What's your name'? One feature that Rosario does not mention is the redundant use of pronouns which Spanish does not require. The deletion of syllable final -s on second person verbs in Caribbean Spanish makes many first, second and third person verbs undistinguishable, e. g., *yo, tú, Ud., él, ella: hablaba)*, and may trigger the expression of more personal pronouns to aid in subject identification. Furthermore, pronouns may be employed more frequently by English dominant bilinguals because English requires them, e. g., redundant first person pronouns were employed by a young *cubana*: "*... son los puertorriqueños que* **yo** he conocido aquí porque cuando **yo** fui a Puerto Rico ..." 'those are the Puerto Ricans that **I** have met here because when **I** went to Puerto Rico ...'.

The most distinctive use of pronouns in the Spanish-speaking world occurs in some parts of Central and South America. The second person singular pronoun for familiarity or informality is usually *tú*, but the archaic *vos* and its accompanying verb forms are preserved in a few regions, e. g., *vos sos* vs. *tú eres* for 'you (familiar) are'. Central American and Argentinean friends in NYC speak with *vos* among themselves, but like the Salvadorans and Hondurans surrounded by Mexicans in Houston (Lipski 1979), many are adopting *tú*, particularly when speaking with other Latinos informally. In general, the traditional distinction between the polite and familiar forms (*Usted [Ud.]* and *tú/vos*) is less pervasive in the Caribbean than in Central and South America, where formal *Ud.* sometimes is extended to parent-child communication.

Different and changing social norms are involved: what seems an appropriately respectful form of address to some groups is interpreted as cold and distancing by others, particularly when used within the family. A study of pronoun usage by Dominican and Puerto Rican immigrants in NYC in the early 1970s found an age-related pattern: speakers reported that they maintained the Caribbean habit of addressing others as *tú* and being addressed as *tú* (=reciprocal *tú*)) in early childhood, moved to non-reciprocal *Ud.* at the onset of adolescence as a sign of growing maturity (adolescents addressed elders as *Ud.* but were addressed with *tú*), and increased reciprocal *tú* for solidarity in adulthood (Keller 1975). More recently, I have heard it argued that the use of *tú* (*tuteo)* has increased at the expense of *Ud.* because of a loss of crucial cultural values such as *respeto* 'respect'. A more positive interpretation is that the preference for *tú* is due to greater feelings of equality and comradeship among

Latinos in the U. S. Additionally, there is the possibility that the omnibus "you" English pronoun, which makes no polite vs. familiar distinction, is contributing to the change.

3.5. The influence of English

The tendency to blame English for every difference in U. S. Spanish has been criticized because it ignores similar changes that are occurring in Latin America among speakers who do not know English, and universal processes affecting language change (Silva-Corvalán 1986). But the influence of English is inevitable given the close but unequal contact – in power and status – between NY's English and Spanish speakers. Even purist Hispanists who chide the members of the second and third generations for speaking an English-influenced Spanish or "Spanglish" are not immune. After a few years in NYC, the impact of English is visible in almost everyone's Spanish (see below). As is traditionally the case in language contact situations all over the world (Weinreich 1968), the lexicon is most affected, as follows:

1. English words, often representing new or different cultural realities encountered in NYC, are borrowed and frequently transformed by Spanish pronunciation and grammar in the process, e. g., *biles* 'bills', *la boila* 'the boiler', *un jolope* 'a hold-up'. These words are known as "loans", or specifically "anglicisms" when they are borrowed from English.

2. Spanish words that are phonologically similar to English words but differ in meaning may take on the English meaning, e. g., *librería* ('bookstore' replaces *biblioteca* for 'library', *papel* ('paper', i.e, stationery) replaces *periódico* for 'newspaper'. García – Otheguy (1988) label these "merged word calques" because of the overlap in form and semantic field.

3. English words or phrases may be translated literally into Spanish, e. g., "to lose weight" = *perder peso* instead of *rebajar.* The lack of phonological resemblance, e. g., between English "lose" and Spanish *perder,* distinguishes "independent word calques" from the merged word calques (see 2 above) in García – Otheguy's framework (1988). Finally, "phrasal calques" are composed of "a series of elements that belong to the Spanish language but are being used as they would be if they were English elements" (García – Otheguy 1988: 182), e. g., "Prescriptions filled here" = *Recetas* (or *prescripciones) llenadas aquí* instead of *Aquí se despachan recetas* (Varela 1992).

Loans and calques usually are part of what is included when people criticize "Spanglish", but the term also refers to speech that contains Spanish and English segments, as in the following:

> I remember when he was born *que nació bien prietito, que* he was real black and my father said *que no era hijo de'l* because *era tan negro.*
>
> [I remember when he was born 'that he was born real dark, that' he was real black and my father said 'that it wasn't his son' because 'he was so black'.]

This recollection by a seven year old boy of his baby brother's birth reveals crucial cultural knowledge about racial diversity in Puerto Rican families and excellent bilingual skills. His switching without hesitation at appropriate points before/after conjunctions, dependent and independent clauses —all of which he knew how to say in both languages —is characteristic of fluent adult bilinguals for whom code-switching is a significant discourse strategy.

Contrary to the belief that "Spanglish" is a chaotic hodge-podge used by people who are deficient in one or both languages – signaling the deterioration of both Spanish and English – the rule governed nature and important functions of Spanish-English alternation beyond that of filling in for vocabulary gaps have been proven conclusively (see collections by Durán 1981; Amastae – Elías-Olivares 1982). Most of the research has been conducted among U. S. Mexicans and Puerto Ricans, but other bilingual Latinos report code-switching in the same way and for the same reasons, including – but not limited to – quotation, emphasis, translation, aggravation and mitigation of requests, and bonding with fellow bilinguals. Language alternation has passionate detractors and supporters: some view it with alarm as evidence of cultural confusion and others embrace it as evidence of adaptability and creativity. Those Latinos – often well educated members of the first generations – who insist that Spanish and English should never be mixed, repudiate the bilingual speech and poetry of their younger and/or less educated compatriots. Purists repudiate "Spanglish" as an epithet, along with identity labels like "Nuyorican" and "Dominican York" or "Chicano", because of their insistence on a idealized language and identity that is static and unrealistic. Instead of promoting Spanish maintenance, the net effect of Spanglish bashing is the promotion of language shift, with negative repercussions for the communities' academic and bilingual excellence. Latinos who end up convinced that their Spanish is bad or *mata'o* 'killed', rush to adopt English and eventually do kill off their Spanish. After all, when they speak a Hispanized English most Latinos sound alike so it is easier to avoid being singled out for criticism. Some speakers of Caribbean Spanish, who report higher levels of language alternation than Central or South Americans, adopt code-switching as a step toward greater English proficiency in an attempt to escape being discriminated against because of their stigmatized Spanish, color, and socio-economic condition (García et al. 1988, Zentella 1990a).[2] In the end, the effort backfires because their code-switching becomes the symbol of their stigmatized racial, class, and linguistic status.

Other bilinguals, however, like the writers of *Nuyorican Poetry* (Algarín – Piñero 1975), are generating a process of semantic inversion of the sort experienced by African Americans with "black" and "African". From their perspective, the terms "Nuyorican", "Dominican York", "Chicano" and "Spanglish" do not constitute a repudiation or degeneration of the homeland's culture and language, but a graphic way of displaying membership in two worlds – a proud straddling of cultural borders. The linguistic cross-over that it encourages is reflected in the appearance of English lyrics in *salsa* dance music and the creation of Spanish "raps" by English dominant bilinguals who identify with both languages proudly, e. g., Latin Empire, Latin Alliance.

4. *The Spanish media*

New Yorkers who are used to hearing Spanish all around them remain incredulous when told that the language is being lost at a rapid rate, as Veltman (1988) has documented nationwide, and as I corroborate below. In addition to the many Latino faces they see, the proliferation of newspapers, signs, and advertisements in Spanish and the availability of all-day radio and television programming contribute to the impression that Spanish will never die out, and even that English is in danger of being displaced. While it is true that "the Hispanic media has rocketed to unprecented heights", there is some debate as to whether the Spanish media contribute "to preserve the traditions and values of the Hispanic immigrants and to facilitate their integration to the North American culture" (Paladin 1994: 3) or whether it is a big business that sells self-hate. The type of Spanish that is used in different formats varies in ways that shed light on the issue.

As Paladin 1994: 3 indicates the expansion of the Spanish media has been formidable:

> In 1991 there were 32 television stations with dozens of affiliates, 11 newspapers, 160 weekly magazines and 54 scientific and literary magazines in the United States .... *Univisión* is the fifth largest network in the U. S.

> reaching 92% of the Hispanic households via 37 broadcast affiliates and more than 600 cable affiliates .... On the other hand, the number of Hispanic radio stations has grown from 322 to 390 since 1990.

In New York City, the print media is clearly divided along regional, national, and local lines. At least 23 dailies in Spanish can be bought at newstands in Latino neighborhoods throughout the city, although some of them can be found only in certain areas.[3] Two of the dailies are produced locally, and they have the largest circulation: *El Diario/La Prensa*, New York's oldest Spanish daily (81 years old), sells 60,000 copies a day, with the greatest number of readers in the Bronx. *Noticias del Mundo*, 14 years old, has 28,000 readers. The next most widely read daily is *El Nacional,* a leading paper in the Dominican Republic which circulates 25,000 copies of a special New York edition every day. The remainder come from the countries and cities of Latin America which contribute the largest number of immigrants in New York City:

– In addition to *El Nacional,* five more dailies come from the Dominican Republic : *El Listín Diario, Hoy, El Siglo, Ultima Hora, El Jaya* (*El Jaya* is published in el Cibao and the rest are published in the capital). Most are available in Washington Heights and the Lower East Side (Manhattan), Jackson Heights/Corona (Queens), Bushwick (Brooklyn) and the South Bronx.

– 4 from Colombia, in the Jackson Heights area of Queens:
  2 from Bogotá, the capital: *El Espectador*, *El Tiempo*
  1 from Medellín: *El Colombiano*
  1 from Cali: *El País*

– 3 from Ecuador:
  1 from Guayaquil, *El Universo,* in Washington Heights
  1 from Quito, *El Comercio,* in Washington Heights
  1 from Cuenca, *El Mercurio*, in Jackson Heights/Corona

– 2 from Honduras, both in the South Bronx:
  1 from Tegucigalpa, the capital, *La Tribuna*
  1 from San Pedro Sula, *Tiempo*

– 2 from Guatemala City, both available in Jackson Hts/Corona: *Gráfico* and *Prensa Libre*

– 1 each from the following cities:
  San Juan, Puerto Rico's *El Vocero*, widely available
  Miami, Florida's *Diario Las Américas*, in Washington Heights
  San Salvador, El Salvador's *El Universo,* in Washington Heights
  San José, Costa Rica's *La Nación,* in Jackson Hts/Corona

Several important facts are gleaned from this summary of dailies: many first generation immigrants are literate in Spanish and they make an economic sacrifice to keep up with events in their homelands via the national newspapers, for which they pay an average of $1.25 per day.[4] Most surprising is the presence of newspapers from El Salvador and Ecuador in Washington Heights, communities that are not highly visible among the Dominican majority in that area. Following a time honored practice in New York, newer immigrants enter the poorest neighborhoods, contributing to the dialectal levelling discussed above.

At the local level, more than nine weeklies, several of them free, are designed to meet the needs of specific communities. *El Especial* and *Impacto* are sold most widely and address a broader range of Latinos than others which print more items of interest to the Cuban (*El Tiempo, El Continental)*, Dominican (*Visión Hispana, Eco Latino)*, Colombian (*Noticiero Colombiano e Hispano)*, Mexican (*El Sol de México y Latinoamérica)*, and South American (*Resumen*) communities. As neighborhoods become home to a greater diversity of Latinos, the newspapers adapt their contents to appeal to the newer residents. For example, *El Sol*, a free weekly published in Queens, was originally *El Sol de Colombia*. As its readership changed, the reference to Colombia was dropped, although the editor continues to favor a Colombian Spanish style.

Whereas the dailies from Latin America are written in the national variety of standard Spanish and are likely to include local words and expressions, the two that are published in New York try to reach out to a variety of nationalities and limit their regionalisms accordingly. As one editor explained it, the general practice is to write a Spanish that is "*accesible a todo el mundo*" [accesible to everybody], but when various lexical alternatives conflict, it is likely that the form most commonly heard in New York will be chosen, namely the Caribbean or specifically Puerto Rican term.

In a revealing comparison of the ethnic press in the U. S., García et al. (1985) found that the Spanish press expresses more negativity toward its ethnic mother tongue and its ethnicity than the French, German, or Yiddish presses. The NY Spanish press has expanded but it has not changed significantly in this regard. Each paper criticizes the others' Spanish in private, e. g., one *Noticias del Mundo* staffer said that subscribers often characterized their Spanish as more refined – "*con más cordura*" [with greater restraint] – than that of *El Diario/La Prensa*, which was "*muy común*" [very common], while the editor of another paper described the Spanish of *Noticias del Mundo* as "*un desastre*" [a disaster]. Spurred on by a regular "watch your p's and q's" column in the Cuban oriented *Diario Las Américas* from Miami, a columnist for *El Diario-La Prensa* recently announced the formation of *Proyecto MADE* (Por un Manejo Adecuado del Español) 'Project MADE, For an Adequate Command of Spanish' (Chávez-Vásquez 1994a). Its avowed purpose is to combat the "*violentos cambios lingüísticos*" [violent linguistic changes] that are "*injustificables*" [unjustifiable] and "*ofensivos*" [offensive] (Chávez-Vásquez 1994b). Apparently, violation of the adjective-noun placement rule is not targetted because the article included three such violations, e. g., *graciosas anécdotas* 'funny anecdotes' follows the English pattern (noun-adjective) instead of the Spanish norm, *anécdotas graciosas*. The organizers of many well intentioned prescriptivist efforts often get caught in the inevitable web of the linguistic changes they censure.[5]

In regard to anglicisms, a favorite pet peeve of the Spanish press, NY editors with extensive experience adopt a policy that nods to the purists but achieves their principal objective – communicating with the largest possible readership. They go to great lengths to avoid anglicisms, but recognize that some English words are so widespread that the Spanish version might prove incomprehensible. In those cases, they use the anglicism and sometimes follow it with a translation in parentheses, e. g., "welfare (*bienestar público*)".

In recognition of the importance of English to their readership, *El Diario/La Prensa* translates its editorial and *Noticias del Mundo* publishes a bilingual page for children. These efforts also serve those in the majority community who are trying to learn Spanish, the foreign language most studied in New York's high schools and universities. The Spanish press has long made overtures to English speakers, and the mainstream English press is beginning to pursue Spanish readership. None of the English dailies has a section in Spanish, but in November of 1994 the *Daily News* began to circulate 250,000 free copies of *Noticias de los Pueblos Latinoamericanos*. It had approximately twelve pages of text devoted to the most important events in Latin America and New York's Latino communities, and was supported completely by advertisers. *Noticias de los Pueblos Latinoamericanos* was discontinued in 1995.

Even when newspapers are free, their success is limited by the number of people literate in Spanish and the extent of their distribution network. Radio and TV transcend these limitations and are part of every Latino's daily life. Two of the four Spanish radio stations are at the top of the charts in NYC: La Mega (97.9FM) and Radio WADO (1280AM). The former plays the rhythms popular with youths and includes at least one bilingual program, while the latter has a long history of offering music and programs that appeal to a broader range of Latin American immigrants. Both stations provide news from many homelands. The news reporters and talk show hosts usually speak a more standard Caribbean Spanish than the disc jockeys, and the most informal and regionally linked Spanish is heard on the programs that are directed at specific nationalities. The music programs attract a multi-generational audience because the lyrics and patter are within everyone's reach. Overall, Spanish radio is much more reflective of life in New York than Spanish television in programming, advertisements, and in the type of Spanish that is spoken, because most radio programs are produced locally and many people call in.

Since "research shows that TV watching is the major form of entertainment for U. S. Latinos" (Fernández 1994: 14), it is important to take a close look at television programming. Two Spanish-language broadcast networks, *Univisión* and *Telemundo*, and one cable network, *Galavisión*, compete for markets all across the United States and in Latin America. In New York, *Univisión* (channel 41) is available approximately 19 hours a day for a total of 130 hours a week, *Telemundo* (channel 47) has 84 hours of programming, and *Galavisión* provides 192 hours to those who subscribe.[6] The great bulk of the shows come from Latin America, primarily Mexico, and except for daily newscasts and a few hours devoted to educational and religious programs and talk shows, most offer entertainment. Soap operas and movies made in Mexico and Venezuela are the most popular programs, although they often are criticized for their racist, sexist, and classist themes. Whatever the ideological effects, the lexical impact is clear. My students know how to say 'male friend/buddy' in Mexican Spanish (*cuate*) and 'maid' in Venezuelan Spanish (*cachifa*), as well as other regional vocabulary, although their pronunciation and grammar do not change. The only time they hear the variety of Spanish that is spoken in their homes is when reporters take to the streets in Latin America or during shows transmitted from their homeland. For example, five cable channels transmit about five erratic hours per week each from the Dominican Republic, and much of their comedy depends on knowing regional dialectal differences.

The supra-standard spoken by newscasters and by the spokespersons for the blue-chip advertisers, which is always difficult to locate nationally, is consonant with their looks, which also are bleached of Latino diversity – most are very light skinned and often blonde because "white sells":

> There are proportionately less black faces on Spanish-language TV than on its Anglo counterpart, and the more important the show or the ad the fewer Indian features that will appear. Try to sell black faces, try to sell Indian faces, and you will no longer be in the TV business. Spanish language TV reflects the racism endemic in the community. Except that it does more than reflect it: it streamlines it and makes a business of it (Fernández 1994: 81).

And big business it is, with the Latino market's current purchasing power at $ 206 billion. When some Latinos organized a protest against the lack of diverse racial/ethnic types on *Univisión*, the management candidly admitted that it was a business decision meant to achieve the highest ratings. The protesters did not target the Spanish of the anchors, probably because a Spanish expunged of local idiosyncracies is easier for a wider audience to understand. But those who subscribe to the translations available for English premium cable TV (192 hours weekly each on Disney, HBO, and Showtime) hear the Spanish of Spain. Thus it turns out that the electronic media is stratified linguistically and economically, i. e., the cheapest and most easily available format, radio, is the one that incorporates the most local Spanish. As the medium gets more expensive – Spanish broadcast television, Spanish cable and English cable – the variety of Spanish that is preferred is more and more distant. The net effect is that the young shy away from Spanish TV and even their elders prefer English TV as soon as they can understand it, because they get more choices and higher quality programming. Thus, Spanish TV offers little in the way of Spanish maintenance for the second generation while English TV helps pave the way for the first generation's shift to English.

5. *Language shift*

5.1. Generational Language Shift among Puerto Ricans

The great majority of Latinos in NYC speak English, making recent immigrants most responsible for keeping Spanish alive. Those who arrive at a young age make the transition from Spanish monolinguals to English dominant bilinguals within a few years, precipitated by schooling and aided by their devotion to English TV, movies, radio. Birthplace is the most significant determinant of language loss or maintenance. Children born in the U. S. are more likely to become English monolinguals than those born in the homeland, especially those of the third generation. Beginning with the 1980 census and escalating in the 1990 census, less than half of all Puerto Ricans in NYC were born in Puerto Rico. This augurs greater language loss for Puerto Ricans than for all other Latinos, most of whom were born in their homeland.

I observed language shift in one lower working class East Harlem *bloque* 'block' where, in 1979, 20 Puerto Rican families lived with 26 children between 3 and 20 years old – four of whom had been born in Puerto Rico but had come to NYC before they were eight years old – and eleven infants (Zentella 1997). Most of the children (61%) were more proficent in English than Spanish, but only one was an English monolingual. By 1993, the original 37 children and 25 more – including siblings and children of the first group – had moved conclusively toward the English end of the language proficiency spectrum (see Table 3).

Table 3
Language proficiency spectrum of *El Bloque*'s children: 1980–1993

	SM	SD	SB	BB	EB	ED	EM	Eng?
1980 (n=26)	0%	8%	8%	23%	38%	19%	4%	0%
1993 (n=62)	0%	0%	0%	7%	22%	37%	17%	17%

SM = Monolingual in Spanish, limited English comprehension
SD = Spanish dominant, weak English [limited vocab, tenses]
SB = Spanish dominant bilingual, fluent English
BB = Balanced bilingual, near equal fluency in both languages
EB = English dominant bilingual, fluent Spanish
ED = English dominant, weak Spanish [limited vocab, tenses]
EM = English dominant, limited Spanish comprehension
Eng ? = either English dominant or English monolingual (based on the evaluation of others)

Citywide figures for Puerto Ricans corroborate *el bloque's* trend: "sixty-three percent of all Puerto Ricans aged five and over reported a "strong" command of English in 1990, up from 53 percent in 1980" (Department of City Planning 1993: 4). The increase in English proficiency extended to the island-born, whose strong English speakers went from 37% to 46% over the decade. Improved English proficiency need not be at the expense of Spanish, but that was the unfortunate outcome for almost all former members of *el bloque*. In 13 years, English monolinguals (EM) had risen 13% among those I interviewed, and those who had moved away were evaluated by their relatives as either English dominant

(ED) or monolingual in English. At the other end of the scale, there was no longer anyone more proficient in Spanish than English, and the percent of bilinguals who were equally at ease in both languages (BB) had decreased three-fold. Four generational groups were identified, each one of which manifested a higher degree of language shift:

I = born in PR, immigrated before 8 years of age
50% = Balanced Bilinguals, 50% = English dominant Bilinguals

II = born in US, has/had at least one caregiver born in PR who immigrated in post-teens
44% = BB & EB, 56% = ED,EM,E?

III = born in US, has/had Group I caregiver(s)
6% = BB & EB, 94% = ED, EM, E?

IV = born in US, has/had Group II caregiver(s)
100% = ED, EM, E?

The three groups of speakers who were born in the U. S. (NYC) exhibited distinct levels of Spanish proficiency that were related to the birthplace of their parents and the age at which immigrant parents came to NYC. Parents who arrived after they had established a strong base in Spanish and had completed most or all of their schooling in Puerto Rico were most likely to speak Spanish to each other and to raise their children in Spanish. Those who came as young children or who were born in NYC became English dominant and usually spoke more English than Spanish to their partners and children. On Fishman's (1991) eight level measure of community language shift – at level eight only a few old speakers are left – the former members of *el bloque* were between stages five and six.

After studying language maintenance efforts all over the world, Fishman (1991: 91) concludes that nothing "can substitute for the re-establishment of young families of child-bearing age in which Xish is the normal medium or co-medium of communication and/or of other culturally appropriate home, family, neighborhood and community intergenerational activity." The young parents I observed were raising their children primarily in English, and their Spanish was limited to several tenses. Spanish was part of their children's lives because poverty kept them living with or near Spanish dominant grandparents in Spanish-speaking neighborhoods. Visits to Puerto Rico were rare, but visitors from the island brought the children in contact with relatives who were monolingual in Spanish, and local schools had increasing numbers of Mexican and Dominican children whose parents spoke to them in Spanish. Most of the third generation offspring of *el bloque* understood a little basic Spanish, but they would not be able to raise a fourth generation of bilinguals unless they went to school in Puerto Rico and/or married a newcomer.

Language shift in the NYPR community must be interpreted in the light of community-specific definitions of bilingualism and identity. The parents of *el bloque* considered children bilingual if they understood and obeyed Spanish requests; most did not insist that children respond in Spanish since almost all elders understood English. It was possible for children with only passive or receptive skills in Spanish to follow the community's frequent switching between Spanish and English, but a small and growing number had to rely on English translations. As a result, the relationship between Puerto Rican identity and Spanish has been transformed: the majority of the second generation and even some members of the first generation believe that it is possible to be a Puerto Rican without speaking Spanish (Attinasi 1979, Zentella 1990b). The idea of a non-Spanish speaking Puerto Rican, anathema to island residents, takes root in NYC to accommodate the growing number of young Puerto Ricans who identify with the culture but cannot speak the language. In order to include everyone in the larger pan-Puerto Rican family, Puerto Ricanness is re-defined in NYC without pre-requisites of birthplace and/or language: you are a Puerto Rican "if you have Puerto Rican blood in you."

5.2. Language shift and English language proficiency

Immigrants from other Latin American countries have not been subjected to the imposition of English on their native land the way Puerto Ricans have, and most still belong to the first generation, unlike Puerto Ricans, but there are many indications that their working classes are undergoing a similar process of generational language shift. As the ranking in Table 4 indicates, communities that reported the smallest percent of people who spoke only English at home also had the smallest percent of members who spoke English very well of those who spoke only Spanish or both Spanish and English at home.

Table 4 refutes the common belief that Spanish speakers do not know or want to speak English. Not surprisingly, the newest immigrant groups have the lowest figures in both columns. We can assume that with time more Guatemalans, Salvadorans, Dominicans, Ecuadorians, Colombians, Peruvians, and Nicaraguans will speak English "very well", significantly beyond the 31–37% that already do. As that percent increases, so will the percent of those who speak only English at home, presently 7%

Table 4
Percent that speaks only English at home, compared with percent of others who speak English very well*

Hispanic Origin	Speak only English at home	Don't speak only Eng at home, but speak it *Very Well*[a]
1. Guatemala	3%	34%
2. El Salvador	4%	31%
3. Dominican Republic	4%	34%
4. Ecuador	4%	37%
5. Colombia	5%	35%
6. Peru	5%	37%
7. Nicaragua	7%	37%
8. Argentina	9%	52%
9. Honduras	10%	39%
10. Chile	11%	45%
11. Puerto Rico	13%	58%
12. Cuba	13%	47%
13. Costa Rica	14%	62%
14. Mexico	15%	31%
15. Venezuela	19%	55%
16. Panama	22%	69%

* **Source: Percentages, based on persons 5 years and older, were calculated from numbers provided for New York City in the US Census, Table 192, Social Characteristics for Selected Hispanic Groups: 1990, CP-2-34.**

[a] The Census asks if each person *who speaks a language other than English at home* (which may be interpreted as including those who speak only Spanish and those who speak Spanish in addition to English) speaks English "very well", "well", "not well", or "not at all". The last three proficiency levels are not broken down in this table, and the proficiency of those who speak only English at home is not included in the second column.

or less. Since it is likely that most of those who speak only English at home would evaluate themselves as speaking it "very well" if asked, adding the two columns in Table 4 provides a better idea of the extent of advanced English proficiency in each community. That rate exceeds one third in the first seven groups, which range from 35%–44%, and rises dramatically in the groups with a longer immigration history.

The relationship between newness of immigration and place in the scale holds for many groups, but not all. Puerto Ricans are not in last place, as might be expected given the length and strength of their immigration stream. Although 58% of those Puerto Ricans who spoke a language other than English at home reported they spoke English "very well", only 13% of all Puerto Ricans 5 years and older never spoke Spanish at home, a rate lower than that of three other groups with fewer highly proficient English speakers. Greater access to their island homeland via plane and telephone may account for this difference. The majority (69%) of the Mexicans who speak Spanish at home, in contrast, reported they did not speak English very well, yet another 15% reported speaking only English at home. The implications for communication in households where members do not speak the same language are unclear without ethnographic data to supplement census figures. Children who are monolingual in English may become estranged from Spanish monolingual elders, as Wong-Fillmore's research (1991) with early childhood programs maintains. Or, non-reciprocal bilingual conversations in which children speak in English and adults answer in Spanish may be the norm, as was the case in the families of *el bloque* whose parents were members of the first generation.

The self reports of some groups may have been influenced by different perceptions of what constitutes speaking English "very well". Perhaps some groups base their evaluation on their ability to get along in English and others base it on their literacy skills in the language. Still others may be attempting to provide evidence of assimilation by reporting that family members, especially young children, speak no Spanish. Notwithstanding these possibilities, the overall pattern in Table 4 is consistent: the more English Latinos know, the more English is the only language they speak at home. Panamanians exemplify this pattern the best. They occupy the last place in both columns, which puts them in first place in terms of English ability. More than one fifth (22%) of the city's Panamanians speak only English at home, and in addition, 69% of those who speak Spanish or Spanish and English at home speak English "very well". In total then, 91% of NY's Panamanians reported high levels of English ability. These figures can be explained as a result of anglophone West Indian immigration to Panama, the U. S. presence in the Panama Canal, and residential patterns in NYC. Many Panamanian immigrants come knowing English, and in NYC they live near English speaking Caribbeans and African Americans, predominantly in Brooklyn. The percent of Panamanian families living in poverty in NYC (13%), however, is higher than that of groups with less English ability, e. g., Chilean (8%), Argentinean (10%), Peruvian (12%), and Venezuelan (12%). The idea that the more a group speaks English, the better off it will be economically, does not always hold true.

The Argentinean community represents an interesting exception in that 91% of Argentineans in NYC speak some Spanish at home, but the majority of that group (52%) reports speaking English very well. Argentinean bilingualism is no doubt related to their education (43% had "some college or higher") and occupations (28% were in "managerial and professional specialty occupations"), as well as their racial and class congruence with the dominant society. Advantages for the Latino elite in NYC include professional jobs, elevated incomes, and bilingualism. For too many others, high levels of English proficiency do not necessarily result in higher incomes or education, and progress in English is achieved at the expense of Spanish. Without the experience and the resources to counteract negative attitudes towards Spanish and the power of the English media, and without widespread availability of bilingual programs which maintain and develop Spanish and English skills, language shift by the third generation is inevitable. Children who are now speaking English at home will raise their children in English, barring marriage with a recent immigrant or an extraordinary committment to do otherwise.

6. *Latino unity re: bilingualism*

It is important to underscore the fact that despite major contrasts in education, occupations, and years in the U. S. that separate Latinos on the one hand, and the inexorable shift to English that all are experiencing on the other hand, all Latino groups shared high levels of Spanish use at home in 1990. Latino unity concerning loyalty to the home language and a desire to improve in English was a significant finding in a study that included Dominicans, Cubans, Puerto Ricans, and Central and South Americans in NYC (n = 294) (García et al. 1988: 508):

> Communities with differences in social class and ethnic composition, as well as different Hispanic national origin groups, have great interest in speaking English well, great loyalty toward Spanish as the means of communication with others in the country of origin and the family in the United States and as a resource for the ethnic community, and great desire to have the schools teach Spanish to their children.

Similarly, the four groups reported on in Zentella 1990a overwhelmingly wanted bilingualism for their children:

Colombians	Puerto Ricans	Cubans	Dominicans
100%	97%	95%	94%

The few Puerto Ricans, Cubans, and Dominicans who did not want their children to be bilingual believed that their children would be more successful in this country if they became English monolinguals; no one favored raising Spanish monolinguals. The differences were not statistically significant, but the unanimity of the Colombians in favor of bilingualism and the last place of the Dominicans mirrored each group's level of linguistic security/insecurity, discussed above. It is doubtful that any Latino group will achieve the level of bilingualism that it desires for its future generations, but that desire *is* achieving high levels of Latino unity – among groups that are otherwise divided – on language policy issues of local and national importance, e. g., against English-only laws and in favor of bilingual ballots and bilingual education (Rosario 1994).

7. Governmental and educational services in Spanish

Insecurity about spiraling budgets and intractable social problems have led to a rise in anti-Latino violence in NYC over the last decade.[7] Hispanophobia also is at the root of a national movement to make English the official language of the United States, couched in terms of fear of losing English as the *lingua franca* despite evidence to the contrary (Crawford 1992; Zentella 1994b). During the 1980's fifteen states passed constitutional amendments making English their official language. In New York State, Senator Marchi proposed such an amendment (#2514) in 1989, but the opposition has kept the legislation in committee up to now. Many people on both sides of the issue are confused about the scope of the amendment. If it were to become law, most Spanish advertisements would not disappear because they are produced by private companies, e. g., the telephone company's Spanish Yellow Pages, and the government-funded public service announcements that qualify as "directions or other informational devices" (#2514, line 11) would remain also. Targeted for elimination, however, are bilingual ballots and education that goes beyond providing "supplemental instructional programs for pupils of limited English proficiency" (NY State Amendment Proposal #2514, line 10). At least one NYC candidate for the State Assembly in 1994 campaigned on an English-only platform.[8]

At present, government funds provide for bilingual 911 operators. There are 150 full time interpreters in the city's courts – all Spanish speaking. Districts where at least 10% of the population is limited to a language other than English must provide a ballot in that language: they are available in predominantly Spanish- and Chinese-speaking areas. In the interests of health, efficiency, and public safety, hospitals try to provide Spanish-speaking personnel and help in other languages.[9] Puerto Ricans and other Latinos in NYC are overwhelmingly in support of bilingual services and against English-only laws that would eliminate bilingual ballots and bilingual education (Zentella 1990c, Rosario 1994).[10]

In the wider community, bilingual education is hotly debated. The program was established in 1974 as a result of a consent decree between the Board of Education and Aspira, a Puerto Rican educational agency, "for students whose Engish language deficiency prevents them from effectively participating in the learning process and who can more effectively participate in Spanish" (Consent Decree cited in Facts and Figures 1993–94, Board of Education/ Division of Bilingual Education). In 1993–1994, 15% of the 1,015,756 students enrolled in NYC public schools were identified as Limited English Proficient (LEP), and 57% of them were enrolled in bilingual education (84,517).[11] Spanish-speakers made up 68% of the LEP students and 84% of the students in bilingual education, but children from eleven other language backgrounds were also served by bilingual programs.[12] Well-grounded national research found that NYC has some outstanding bilingual programs in which there is "a direct and consistent correlation between Spanish-language development and student gains" in English language, reading, and math (Crawford 1992: 230), but no newspaper mentioned this. In contrast, a report based on unsound methodology that compared the city's bilingual education to English as a Second Language unfavorably enjoyed extensive coverage (Dillon 1994; *Daily News* 1994; Leo 1994). One encouraging sign is that, despite unfair press, there is increasing interest in two-way bilingual programs, in which children from language minorities and English monolinguals learn each other's language as well as their own.

8. *Conclusions*

References to Latinos, Hispanics, Spanish, and Spanish speakers in NYC obscure many important differences in language form, use, and attitudes. These differences follow regional and national boundary lines above all, and each Latino group prefers to be recognized individually because it sees itself as distinct from the others. The specific history of each Spanish-speaking group, including the origin and dialects of its first settlers and subsequent invaders in the homeland, and the regional, racial and class origin of different waves of immigrants to the new land – as well as their reasons for emigrating and the welcome they receive – shape the present and future of Spanish in NYC as well as their educational and socio-economic progress. The most complete understanding of this complex language picture requires an anthro*political* linguistics (Zentella 1994a).

Latino unity is being simultaneously strengthened by support for the Spanish language in general and weakened by attacks on specific dialects in particular. Puerto Ricans, who constitute half of the Latinos in NYC, leave their homeland because of conditions created by direct U. S. economic and political control of the island; they arrive as U. S. citizens from a Caribbean island that is an unincorporated territory of the United States with an official bilingual policy for the government, after being subjected to a half century of English imposition in the schools and courts. For linguistic, racial, and socio-economic reasons, Caribbean Spanish – the variety spoken by the majority of Spanish speakers in NYC – does not enjoy the prestige of other dialects, and negative attitudes, coupled with the shift from more island-born to more US-born Puerto Ricans in NYC, create a degree of linguistic insecurity that promotes language shift and a re-definition of Puerto Rican identity. Other groups with similar backgrounds, e. g., Dominicans, can be expected to follow suit while whiter, wealthier, better educated, and more linguistically secure Latinos may be more successful at achieving advanced levels of bilingualism in speaking and writing. All groups, however, are unlikely to pass Spanish on to the next generations, despite their fervent desire to do so, if they do not make special efforts to raise their children bilingually. These include insisting on Spanish at home and demanding developmental – not transitional – bilingual education in the public schools, and Spanish for Native Speakers courses at the university level.

The replacement of Spanish by English may be encouraging news for advocates of English-only, but the loss of native ability in any language should be lamented for individual, group, and national reasons. NYC is home to one of the largest and most diverse concentrations of Spanish speakers, at a time in the history of this nation when multilingual and multicultural skills are necessary for the resolution of educational, economic, and political problems. Lack of concrete support for the bilingualism of its Latinos – and speakers of other languages – is tantamount to discarding a national treasure. Only a nation-wide committment to making multiculturalism less of a slogan and more of a reality will avert language loss among Spanish speakers and others, and enable us to extend the benefits of bilingualism to all. More than 500 years of Caribbean experiences at integrating different races, cultures, and languages continue in *La Gran Manzana* 'The Big Apple', as multiple dialects of Spanish come into contact with many varieties of English and other languages. Spanish speaking communities that recognize and respect the differences among themselves but are united in their defense of bilingualism should be in the forefront of the opening of New York's linguistic and cultural frontiers.

Notes

1. Thanks to the editors, Ofelia García and Joshua Fishman, and to my colleagues John Holm and José Manuel Torres Santiago, for their comments and suggestions.
2. The notion that darker skinned Latinos are more likely to maintain their Spanish in an effort to distinguish themselves from African Americans deserves to be investigated.
3. I am grateful to Juan Lulio Blanchard, a student of Ofelia García, for collecting newspapers from throughout the city for me, and for gathering data about their publication. Given the vast number of newstands in New York, the list provided here does not pretend to be exhaustive.
4. The more than two dozen magazines in Spanish, almost all of which are imported and some of which are translations of U. S. magazines, e. g., *Mecánica Popular [Popular Mechanics]* and *Selecciones de Reader's Digest*, are much more expensive. Although not mentioned in my analysis, the magazines seem similar in linguistic policy and objectives to the national TV networks.
5. In a personal response to my letter of inquiry about MADE, in which I pointed out the noun-adjective violations, Ms. Chávez-Vásquez correctly noted that adjective-noun placement in Spanish can serve to mark emphasis. She also acknowledged the inevitable influence of English on Spanish and adopted a realistic attitude toward cultural and linguistic change: "*Soy realista en que (sic) el sentido de que acepto las consecuencias del choque cultural y por ende idiomático.*" [I am a realist in that I accept the consequences of cultural and consequently linguistic clash.] (Chávez-Vásquez, personal communication).
6. I am indebted to Celeste Fondeur, Ofelia García's student, for the information presented on the number of TV stations and programs.
7. The Latino Coalition for Racial Justice keeps track of bias incidents like the Sept. 1994 murder of Manuel Aucaquizhpi, an Ecuadorian immigrant who was beaten to death by a gang of Italian American youths who were "yelling obscene epithets about Mexicans" (Steinhauer 1994:39).
8. Frank Borzellieri, the Republican challenger in the 38th district, Queens, where "Hispanics are the largest minority with 26% of the population", campaigned for "eliminating foreign languages from government-issued documents and banning from public schools books he considered anti-American, like biographies of Martin Luther King, Jr." (Onishi 1994).
9. Clinic and hospital needs for Spanish, Chinese, Russian, and Haitian Creole speakers are partially met by programs like Hunter College's Community Interpreter course. An English-only law that was voted down in Suffolk county in 1989 was so repressive that it would have forbidden county health workers from communicating with patients in any language except English (Schmitt 1989).

10. The majority of all other ethnic groups also supported bilingual services, but many also were in favor of making English the official language, presumably because they did not understand the law's repercussions.
11. The LEP label has been critized because it conjures up leprous images. Casanova (1991) offers SOL, Speakers of Other Languages, as a substitute.
12. Bilingual education includes English as a Second (ESL) instruction, native language arts instruction, and social studies, science, and math using the native language and English as media of instruction. Programs are available in Spanish, Chinese, Haitian Creole, Russian, Korean, Arabic, Vietnamese, Polish, Bengali, French, Urdu, and Albanian. In 1993–1994 another 63,014 LEPs received ESL only, and 5%, or nearly 7,000 students, received neither bilingual education nor ESL.

References

Algarín, Miguel – Miguel Piñero (eds.)
1975 *Nuyorican Poetry.* New York: William Morrow and Co.

Alvarez Nazario, Manuel
1961 *El elemento afro-negroide en el español de Puerto Rico.* Río Piedras, Puerto Rico: Editorial de la Universidad de Puerto Rico.
1977 *El influjo indígena en el español de Puerto Rico.* Río Piedras, Puerto Rico: Editorial de la Universidad de Puerto Rico.
1982 *Orígenes y desarrollo del español en Puerto Rico.* Río Piedras, Puerto Rico: Editorial de la Universidad de Puerto Rico.

Amastae, Jon – Lucía Elías Olivares (eds.)
1982 *Spanish in the United States: Sociolinguistic aspects.* Cambridge: Cambridge University Press.

Attinasi, John
1979 "Language attitudes in a New York Puerto Rican community", in: Raymond Padilla (ed.), *Bilingual education and public policy in the United States.* Ypsilanti, MI: Eastern Michigan University, 408–461.

Bean, Frank D. – Marta Tienda
1987 *The Hispanic population of the United States.* New York: Russell Sage.

Bouvier, Leon and Vernon Briggs
1988 The *Population and labor force of New York: 1990–2050.* Washington, D.C.: Population Reference Bureau.

Canfield, Lincoln
1981 *Spanish Pronunciation in the Americas.* Chicago: University of Chicago Press.

Casanova, Ursula
1991 "Bilingual education: Politics or pedagogy?", in: Ofelia García (ed.), *Bilingual Education: Focusschrift in honor of Joshua A. Fishman on the occasion of his 65th birthday.* Amsterdam/Philadelphia: John Benjamins, 167–180.

Chávez-Vásquez, Gloria
1994a "La fuerza del idioma", *El Diario/LaPrensa,* domingo, 11 septiembre, 21.
1994b Estimado(a) amigo(a) ,PROYECTO MADE subscription', letter, October 15.

Cotton, Eleanor Greet – John Sharp
1988 *Spanish in the Americas.* Washington, D.C.: Georgetown University Press.

Crawford, James
1992 *Hold your tongue: Bilingualism and the politics of "English Only".* Reading, Mass.: Addison Wesley.
Daily News
1994 "Talking turkey about English", Editorial, Oct 21, 1994: 24.
de la Garza, Rodolfo – Angelo Falcón – Chris García – John García
1992 *Latino national political survey: Summary of findings.* New York: Institute for Puerto Rican Policy.
Department of City Planning
1993 Demographic and socioeconomic profiles, selected tabulations, selected Hispanic origin groups, NYC and Boroughs [Unpublished MS.]
1997 *The Newest New Yorkers.* New York: City of New York.
Dillon, Sam
1994 "Report faults bilingual education in New York", *New York Times*, Oct. 20: A1.
Durán, Richard (ed.)
1981 *Latino language and communicative behavior.* Norwood, N. J.: Ablex Press.
Falcón, Angelo – Minerva Delgado – Gerson Borrero (eds.)
1989 *Towards a Puerto Rican-Latino agenda for New York City.* New York: Institute for Puerto Rican Policy.
Fernández, Enrique
1994 "Our mirror, ourselves: Latino-made Latino images in the media", *Culturefront* 3, no 2.
Fishman, Joshua
1991 *Reversing language shift.* Clevedon, England: Multilingual Matters.
García, Ofelia – Ricardo Otheguy
1988 "The Language situation of Cuban Americans", in: Sandra McKay and Sau-ling Cynthia Wong, (eds.), 166–192.
García, Ofelia – Joshua Fishman – Silvia Burunat – Michael Gertner
1985 "The Hispanic press in the United States: contents and prospects", in: Joshua Fishman, *The Rise and fall of the ethnic revival.* Berlin: Mouton, 343 – 362.
García, Ofelia – Isabel Evangelista – Mabel Martínez – Carmen Disla – Bonifacio Paulino
1988 "Spanish language use and attitudes: A study of two New York city communities", *Language in Society* 17: 475 – 512.
Green, Kate
1993 The genesis and development of Dominican vernacular Spanish: Evidence of creolization? [Unpublished Dissertation proposal, CUNY Graduate Center.]
Guitart, Jorge
1982 "Conservative vs. radical dialects in Spanish: Implications for language instruction", in: Joshua Fishman – Gary Keller (eds.), *Bilingual education for Hispanic students in the U. S.* New York: Teachers College Press, 167–190.
Hays, Constance
1993 "To Markets! To Markets!" *New York Times*, section 13, November 28, 14–16.
Henríquez Ureña, Pedro
1940 *El español en Santo Domingo.* Buenos Aires: La Universidad de Buenos Aires.

Institute for Puerto Rican Policy (IPRP)
1993 "Puerto Ricans and other Latinos in the United States: March 1992", *Datanote on the Puerto Rican Community* #14.

Keller, Gary
1975 "Spanish *tú* and *Ud*: Patterns of interchange", in: William Milán, John Staczek and Juan Zamora (eds.), *1974 Colloquium on Spanish and Portuguese Linguistics*. Washington, D. C.: Georgetown University Press, 84–96.

Labov, William
1966 *The social stratification of English in New York City*. Washington, D. C.: Center for Applied Linguistics.

Leo, John
1994 "Some straight talk on a bad bilingual plan", *Daily News*, Nov. 2 [Reprinted from *US NEWS and World Report*].

Lipski, John
1979 Pronominal hybridization of Central American Spanish in the United States. [Unpublished MS.]

Lope Blanch, Juan
1968 *El español de América*. Madrid: Ediciones Alcalá.

López Morales, Humberto
1971 *Estudios sobre el español de Cuba*. Long Island City, N. Y.: Las Américas Publishing Co.

Mann, Evelyn – Salvo, Joseph
1984 *Characteristics of New Hispanic immigrants to New York City: A comparison of Puerto Rican and non-Puerto Rican Hispanics*. New York: Department of City Planning.

McKay, Sandra and Sau-ling Cynthia Wong (eds.)
1988 *Language Diversity: Problem or resource*. New York: Newbury House.

Megenney, William
1982 "Elementos subsaháricos en el español dominicano", in: Orlando Alba (ed.), *El español del Caribe*. Santiago, R. D.: Universidad Católica Madre y Maestra.
1990 *Africa en Santo Domingo: Su herencia lingüística*. Santo Domingo: Editorial Tiempo.

Moreno de Alba, José
1988 *El español en América*. México, D. F.: Fondo De Cultura Económica.

Navarro Tomás, Tomás
1948 *El español de Puerto Rico*. Río Piedras, Puerto Rico: Editorial de la Universidad de Puerto Rico.

Onishi, Norimitsu
1994 "An 'America-first' challenger is resonating in English Only", *NY Times*, Nov. 6, 1994.

Orlov, Ann – Ueda, Reed
1980 "Central and South Americans", in: Stephen Thernstrom (ed.), *Harvard encyclopedia of American ethnic groups*. Cambridge, Mass.: Harvard University Press.

Paladin, Karina
1994 "The Hispanic media in the United States", *Mexican Notebook*, Vol 3, No. 9, December, 3–5.

Rosario, Rubén del
1970 *El español de América.* Sharon, Conn.: Troutman Press.
Rosario, Sandra
1994 American identity and the language question: Should English be the official language of the United States? Paper presented at Hunter College Mellon Fellows annual luncheon, April 21. [Unpublished MS.]
Rosenblat, Angel
1962 "La diversidad lingüística americana", in: Rosario, 1970: 132–140.
Schmitt, E.
1989 "English-only bill ignited debate and fear on L. I.", *New York Times*, February 14, B3.
Silva-Corvalán, Carmen
1986 "Bilingualism and language change: The extension of *estar* in Los Angeles Spanish", *Language* 62: 587–608.
Steinhauer, Jennifer
1994 "Killing of immigrant stuns a Brooklyn area", *NY Times,* Oct. 1994.
Terrell, Tracy
1982a "Current trends in the investigation of Cuban and Puerto Rican phonology", in: John Amastae – Lucía Elías- Olivares (eds.), 47–70.
1982b "Relexificación en el español dominicano: Implicaciones para la educación", in: Orlando Alba (ed.), *El español del Caribe: Ponencias del VI simposio de dialectología.* Santiago, R. D.: Universidad Católica Madre y Maestra.
Valdés de Montano, Luz María – Smith, Robert
1994 *Mexican migration to the New York City metropolitan area: An Analysis of selected socio-demographic traits and the links being formed between a Mexican sending region and New York.* New York: Tinker Foundation.
Varela, Beatriz
1992 *El español cubano-americano.* New York: Senda Nueva de Ediciones.
Veltman, Carl
1988 *The future of the Spanish language in the United States.* New York/Washington, DC: Hispanic Policy Development Project.
Weinrich, Uriel
1968 *Languages in Contact.* The Hague: Mouton.
Wong Fillmore, Lily
1991 "When learning a second language means losing the first", *Early Childhood Research Quarterly* 6(3): 323–46.
Zamora Munné, Juan
1976 *Indigenismos en la lengua de los conquistadores.* Río Piedras, P. R.: Editorial Universitaria.
Zamora Vicente, Alonso
1979 *Dialectología española.* 2ed. Madrid: Gredos.
Zentella, Ana Celia
1981 "Language variety among Puerto Ricans", in: Charles A. Ferguson – Shirley Brice Heath (eds.), *Language in the U. S. A.* Cambridge; Cambridge University Press, 218–238.
1990a "Lexical leveling in four New York City Spanish dialects: Linguistic and social factors", *Hispania* 73 (4): 1094–1105.

1990b "Returned migration, language, and identity: Puerto Rican bilinguals in dos worlds/two mundos", in: Florian Coulmas (ed.), *Spanish in the U. S. A.: New quandries and prospects* [Special issue]. *International Journal of the Sociology of Language* 84: 81–100.

1990c "Who supports English-Only and why?: The Influence of social variables and questionnaire methodology", in: Karen Adams – David Brink (eds.), *Perspectives on Official English: The campaign for English as the official language of the USA*. Berlin/New York: Mouton de Gruyter, 160–177.

1994a Towards an anthropolitical linguistic perspective on the Spanish competence of U. S. Latinos. Paper delivered at NWAV, New Ways of Analyzing Variation. Stanford University, Oct. 21. [Unpublished MS.]

1994b The Anti-Spanish thrust of the English-Only movement. Paper delivered at American Anthropological Association, Atlanta, Ga., Nov. 30. [Unpublished MS.]

1997 *Growing up bilingual: Puerto Rican children in New York City.* Oxford: Basil Blackwell.

Hebrew in New York

Alvin I. Schiff

1. Origins and development

Hebrew is an ancient language well over three thousand years old. While there are Canaanite, Akkadian, Amorite and Egyptian linguistic antecedents which are considered by some as pre-biblical forms of the language we now know as Hebrew, the Bible is the first corpus of texts written in Hebrew. In its biblical form it was a fully fashioned literary vehicle.

There has been a special relationship between the Jewish people and their ancestral language from the time the first Jew, Abraham, according to Jewish rabbinic tradition, spoke in the language of the Bible. A citation in a *Midrash* (a collection of commentaries and interpretations on the Bible) notes that the word *ha-ivri* [the Hebrew] in describing Abraham, suggests that the language and the person of the first Jew are essentially the same.

Hebrew continued to be the language of Abraham's descendants, the Israelites, when they were enslaved in Egypt for two hundred and ten years. The *Midrash* observes that the Israelites survived their exile experience in Egypt and were redeemed because, among other things, "they did not change their language" (*Midrash Rabbah Leviticus*: 32, 5).

Hebrew was the *vernacular* of the Israelite masses from the time they conquered the Land of Canaan, after their Exodus from Egypt, through the periods of the Judges, Prophets and Kings until the end of the First Commonwealth with the destruction of the First Temple in Jerusalem in 586 B. C. E. Thereafter, it was the vernacular only of some of the Babylonian exiles who resettled in Judea a half-century later. For the rest of the Jewish population of Palestine, Aramaic replaced Hebrew as the spoken language.

Thereafter, in each succeeding era – the Second Commonwealth (500 B. C. E. – 70 C. E.), the Persian Empire exile (300 B. C. E. – 900 C. E.), the Spanish period (1000–1492), the Ashkenazic periods in Germany and Poland (1200–1939) – Hebrew underwent changes in vocabulary, grammar, phonetics and syntax. In essence, these changes reflected the various ways Hebrew was used as a system of representation of ideas and communication (Bickerton 1990: 47–70). As Jews resided in countries all over the globe, their ancestral language was influenced in different times and places by Aramaic, Greek, Latin, Arabic, Spanish, French, German, Polish and Yiddish (Horowitz 1960: 256–289). This led to regional differences in Hebrew language usage. Nevertheless, Hebrew maintained a uniformity throughout.

The use of Hebrew as the language of prayer and study during the last two millennia, since the destruction of the Second Temple in Jerusalem in 70 C. E. and the subsequent scattering of Jews all over the globe, is one of the ingredients contributing to the survival of the Jewish people. Their singular use of Hebraic prayers strengthened their attachment to the land of their forefathers as they faced Jerusalem in their daily prayers – morning, afternoon and evening – and as it reinforced their sense of belonging to the Jewish people. In his wanderings in the Diaspora, "the less recourse the Jew had to his ancient tongue in his daily speech, the more he clung to it as a symbol. Hebrew became a sacred language, an indispensable element of the Jewish religion"(Halkin 1942: 122).

"And you shall teach them diligently to your children," (Deuteronomy 6: 7) the Bible instructs. A cardinal principle of the Jewish faith, Jewish learning occupies a central position in Judaism. Study of the Bible, its Hebraic commentaries, and related post-biblical sources was ingrained into the fabric of Jewish culture.

2. *Modern Hebrew*

The development of Hebrew as a modern vernacular corresponds, in a practical way, to the development of the modern Jewish State. Although Hebrew was spoken in Palestine by small groups of Jews for centuries prior to the late 19th century efforts to establish a modern Jewish State in the region, the actual revival of Hebrew as a modern language began in Palestine in the latter decades of the nineteenth century with the arrival from Eastern Europe of Zionist pioneers, among them Eliezer Ben-Yehuda (1857–1922). Along with other pioneers of modern Hebrew language and literature in Europe, chiefly Mendle Mokher Sefarim (1836–1917), a founding father of the Hebrew realist novel, and Ahad Ha'am (1856–1927), Hebraist thinker and Zionist leader who authoritatively made the case for the centrality of the Hebrew language in modern Jewish culture, Ben-Yehuda was determined to revive ancient Hebrew and make it the common language of a new State. These Zionist pioneers believed fervently that Jewish rebirth in Palestine was not possible without the revival of the Hebrew language. Without a language capable of expressing all the nuances of life, both ancient and modern, the national rebirth of the Jewish people in its land was a meaningless anachronism.

Ben-Yehuda and his associates and followers engaged in *milhemet ha-safah*, a language war, fighting for a place in Palestine with other languages. They propagated Hebrew in everyday life by teaching adults and by establishing cultural institutions and an educational system in which Hebrew, with almost no exceptions, became the only language used (Glinert 1991).

The revival of Hebrew as a modern language required overcoming a variety of linguistic problems concerning pronunciation, spelling, vocabulary and grammar. The Sephardic (oriental) variant was established as the standard pronunciation (as opposed to Ashkenazic Hebrew deriving from Western and Eastern Europe).

The most outstanding achievement of the modern revival period is the transformation of a "dead" language to a language of everyday use. In truth, the Hebrew language never "died", as it remained an active medium of religious expression wherever Jews wandered and settled. Its revival utilized words from the vast liturgical, rabbinical and literary works in mishnaic, medieval and contemporary times, many of which dealt with matters of science, medicine and even mathematics and astronomy. The four thousand words invented by Ben Yehuda and the thousands of new words introduced into modern Hebrew during the last century were derived largely from these sources.

Hebrew, then, is both classical and modern at once, not to be compared to the difference between classical and modern Greek. Unlike Sanskrit, Hebrew did not give way to a modern counterpart (in the case of Sanskrit – Hindustani), hardly similar to its progenitor. Unlike Latin, Hebrew was not confined at any time to church ritual, but was considered an appropriate language of communion between the Jew and his Maker (Schiff 1981: 2).

Hebrew in modern times has emerged as an *altneuschprache* (an old-new language) which is the vernacular of some five million Jews and non-Jews in Israel. It is this *altneuschprache* as used in the United States, particularly in New York City, that is the focus of this essay.

3. New World historical perspective

3.1. The early period 1654–1880

The Jewish immigrants who came to the United States in the seventeenth and eighteenth centuries were largely of Sephardic origin (descendants of Jews who lived in Spain or Portugal before their expulsion in 1492). Their essential relationship with the Hebrew language was their reading knowledge of prayers. While there were in each generation several Jews who were known to be Hebraists (Marcus 1953: 426), Jewish scholarship and Hebrew speaking Jews were virtually unknown (Grinstein 1945: 24).

In his address at the consecration of the Mill Street synagogue in 1818, Major Mordecai Manuel Noah, the preeminent Jewish communal leader of his time, spoke of the necessity of teaching Hebrew "for with the loss of Hebrew language may be added the downfall of the House of Israel" (Grinstein 1945: 255). By and large, his plea fell on deaf ears. The use of Hebrew continued to be limited to rote prayer recitation, writing inscriptions on tombstones, recording birth dates, marriages and deaths, liturgical readings at wedding and circumcision ceremonies, memorial prayers and the "sale" of *aliyot* (the custom of auctioning the honors of reciting a blessing over the Torah) during synagogue services.

There are indications that some people had more than passing familiarity with the Hebrew language. Occasionally, Hebrew advertisements appeared in the Jewish press. In 1826, a Hebrew circular appealing for funds for which to purchase a synagogue building was sent by Congregation Bnai Jeshurun in New York to various synagogues in the United States. Hebrew was the language used for Kashrut seals ascertaining that foods were kosher. In 1835, a Hebrew grammar and the first volume of a Hebrew concordance were published by a printer who established a Hebrew printing shop in 1820 (Grinstein 1945: 350).

From 1840 until 1880, when masses of Jews began coming from Eastern Europe, the Jewish immigrants were mostly from Germany and Western Europe. They established liberal Reform synagogues and used German as well as Hebrew in their prayer services. Over time, English became the main medium of worship in the Reform congregations.[1]

Hebrew pronunciation varied with the immigrant's origin. By and large, the early settlers in the seventeenth and eighteenth centuries used the Sephardic pronunciation while the immigrants from Western and Eastern Europe employed the Ashkenazic pronunciation.

Whatever the level and extent of Hebrew language usage in America prior to 1880, the number of Jews in the United States, as a whole, and in each of the cities where Jews resided was "too small to provide the atmosphere for Hebraic cultural activity" (Halkin 1942: 125).

3.2. The East European period 1880–1960

With the great East European migrations from 1880 to 1920, new influences were introduced in the use of Hebrew as the Jewish population in the United States soared. In 1880, there were approximately 100,000 Jews in New York City. By 1960, there were well over 500,000. Twenty years later, this number had tripled.

The main influence on the use of Hebrew as a modern language was the development of *Zionism* (the worldwide Jewish movement begun at the end of the nineteenth century for the establishment in Palestine of a national homeland for the Jews in response to growing anti-Semitism and continued oppression of Jews) and *Haskalah* (the eighteenth and nineteenth century enlightenment movement of German, Central and East European Jews to modernize Judaism and make it cosmopolitan by promoting secular knowledge and culture and encouraging the adoption of the dress, customs and language of the general population). Proponents of Haskalah and Zionism wanted to modernize the Hebrew language and make it a common everyday medium of expression.

Among the masses that came to America during this period were dedicated Zionists and followers of Ahad Ha'am, Hebraist thinker and Zionist leader who pioneered the use of Hebrew for Jewish cultural and national communication, and Ben Yehuda who helped develop Hebrew into a spoken language (Mintz 1993: 42). They brought with them the zeal,[2] knowledge and ability to energize small pockets of Hebrew devotees at the turn of the century. In 1882, a *Hovevi Zion* 'Lovers of Zion' society was founded in New York (Urofsky 1975: 82). Its members, along with other Zionists, devoted themselves zealously to Palestinian colonization and to the rebirth of Hebrew. Also, in New York, the first Hebrew speaking society *Mephitze Sephat Ever Vesiphrutah* 'The Promoters of The Language of *Ever* and Its Literature' was founded in 1902:

> Each of its weekly meetings on Sunday evenings offered a well prepared lecture which was followed by discussion from the floor, all in Hebrew. It became a lasting sensation. Its sessions drew 150–300 participants through the season. Out-of-town visitors came to see the miracle of spoken Hebrew, and upon returning home, spread the news that Hebrew was becoming again a living tongue (*The Jewish Communal Register 1918: 567*).

In 1909, *Achieber*, another Hebrew language society, was organized to promote Hebrew aggressively. It arranged Hebrew lectures throughout the city and encouraged Hebrew writers to ply their trade. In 1913, it founded *Hatoren*, first a monthly and then a weekly Hebrew journal. By 1918, there were ten Hebrew speaking organizations with a total membership of 500 in New York City (*The Jewish Communal Register* 1918: 568). One of the groups, *Agudah Ivrith* of the College of the City of New York, made its goal the creation of a Hebrew stage which lasted several years.

Outside of New York there were twenty Hebrew speaking clubs. One of their most prominent activities was sponsoring evening courses in Hebrew for adults. In addition, there were Hebrew speaking clubs in many Hebrew schools. In 1917, there were "several thousand whose language of conversation is Hebrew either steadily or intermittently". At least ten public lectures were given in Hebrew each week during the World War I period (*The Jewish Communal Register* 1918: 569).

In 1914, Henrietta Szold, as president of *Hadassah* (the Women's Zionist organization in the United States), organized adult Hebrew study groups and youth camps to spread the use of Hebrew (Urofsky 1975: 143). In 1918, the Zionist Congress in Pittsburgh issued six guiding principles, the sixth of which was "Hebrew, the national language of the Jewish people shall be the medium of public instruction" (Urofsky 1975: 256).

Zionist pronouncements and efforts had effect only on small groups of committed followers. Among these was a select group of outstanding Hebrew scholars, writers, poets and teachers in the 1920's, 30's and 40's who, as a direct expression of Ahad Ha'am's ideology, set a high standard for American Hebraism. Their influence on the general Jewish population was hardly noticeable as they spawned a short-lived Hebraic movement for the elite. Yet, almost all Jews during those years, even non-Zionists, with the exception of the ultra-Orthodox and most of the secular Yiddishists, recognized the promotion of Hebrew as a positive Jewish value (Patai 1971: 132). And, although only a limited number of Jews were Hebrew scholars and/or Hebrew speakers, most Jewish males had a basic familiarity with the language (Mintz 1993: 44). A significant aspect of Hebrew language usage was the introduction of Hebrew Zionist songs into the Jewish community in the 1920's. Thousands of Jewish youth in schools, camps and Zionist youth groups would sing these songs in the 1930's, 1940's and 1950's. Hundreds of Hebrew songsters were published during this time.

One of the moderately successful results of Hebraic Zionist influence was the founding of Hebrew camps. The first camp, *Achvah* (1926–1940), for Hebrew speaking teenagers in New York City was followed by the establishment of *Massad* in 1943. At its peak in 1968, there were three Massad camps with over 1200 campers and counselors all speaking Hebrew for eight weeks during the summer months. *Massad* closed in 1982.

Other Hebrew camps include *Camp Yavneh* (founded in 1944 by the Hebrew College of Brookline, Massachusetts) and the *Ramah* camps (established in 1946 by the Conservative movement). During the 1950's some 3,000 campers were immersed during the summer months in Hebrew speaking programs. Currently, their stress is on Judaica rather than Hebrew.

4. *Hebrew language usage in educational settings*

4.1. The early period 1654–1880

From the time Jews set foot on the soil of America in 1654, the immigrants provided their children with a Jewish education according to the traditions of the country from which they originated. In most instances, this included some form of Hebrew language instruction, generally limited to "mechanical reading, liturgy, a smattering of the *Pentateuch* in the original, elementary Hebrew grammar, preparation of boys for *Bar Mitzvah* (special synagogue service at age thirteen) and laws and ceremonies of the Jewish religion" (Fromer 1969: 16).

Where Bible was studied in the original in the traditional synagogue day schools and in private classes, it was taught by the translation method into the vernacular since Hebrew was considered to be a "dead" language on a par with Latin or Greek. As such, Hebrew was variously translated into German by the German immigrants, into Yiddish by the East European Jews and into English by the American born (Grinstein 1969: 29). Some teachers introduced Hebrew grammar as they translated the Bible from the Hebrew, explaining the root of each verb, its tense and gender.

The traditional program of Hebrew studies in the day school began with the Hebrew alphabet, then moved on to syllables and words in the *Siddur* (the daily and Sabbath prayer book), and then to *Pentateuch* translation. Occasionally, Hebrew writing was added. One or two hours each day were usually devoted to Hebrew.

In the one day Sunday or Sabbath schools, first organized in 1838 in Philadelphia, little or no attention was paid to Hebrew language. However, in the traditional synagogue afternoon schools, Hebrew language – reading, *Siddur*, grammar and Bible translation – was incorporated into the program much the same way it was studied in the day schools.

Several efforts to establish Hebrew high schools met with little success, as did attempts to establish schools of higher Jewish learning.

4.2. From 1880 until the present time

With the arrival of East European immigrants, the tenor of Jewish education changed. The immigrant *Zionists* and *Maskilim* (enlightened, liberal Jews who advocated and supported *Haskalah*) brought with them the desire and oftentimes the know-how to infuse Hebrew language instruction into the Jewish education programs. They even developed the beginnings of *ivrit b' ivrit*, the method of using Hebrew as a medium of instruction for all Judaic subjects. However, the attempts to teach Hebrew as a spoken language was limited to a few afternoon schools where knowledgeable and enthusiastic secular and religious Zionist educators were able to influence the direction of Jewish schooling (Wolowelsky 1990, 1991).

Ivrit b'ivrit schools opened in New York as well as in Boston, Philadelphia, Chicago, Detroit, Indianapolis, Pittsburgh and San Francisco. These schools, enrolling, in total, during the peak 1930's and 1940's, some 15,000 students each year, were the exception and not the rule. The vast majority of schools established by East European immigrants were patterned after the *hadarim* in Europe where Bible and Talmud were taught via translation into Yiddish. In the United States the Bible and Talmud were translated into English. The translation method involved the recitation by the teacher of the Hebraic text followed by line-by-line or phrase-by-phrase translation. The students were then required to repeat the text and translation, first in unison and then individually.

A more pervasive influence of *Haskalah* on Hebrew language in the United States was the founding of eleven Hebrew Teachers Colleges between 1987 and 1929 – in New York (five colleges) and in Philadelphia, Boston, Chicago, Cleveland, Baltimore and Pittsburgh. All instruction in these institutions was in Hebrew. Hebrew language, grammar and literature represented the major area of concentration of most of the colleges (Dushkin 1970: 65,73). Students were trained to teach Jewish subjects and Hebrew language using Hebrew as a medium of instruction.

The enrollment in the Hebrew Teachers Colleges peaked in the 1950's at about 3,000 students. By 1966, it declined to 1,800 students, as secular colleges introduced Judaic studies and Hebrew language programs, and as Jewish youths lost interest in these types of programs (Schiff 1967: 83). Over time, it became more difficult for the Hebrew Teachers Colleges (which all became Colleges of Jewish Studies by 1975) to conduct class work entirely in Hebrew, since the Jewish feeder schools were no longer Hebraic (Schiff 1988). In 1994, about one thousand students attended these schools where the language of instruction is largely English.

The influence of *Zionism* and *Haskalah* on Hebrew language usage in Jewish schools was short lived as *synagogue afternoon schools* began in the 1930's to replace the *communal Hebraic Talmud Torah schools*, known generally as "Hebrew Schools", which provided supplemental Jewish religious education to Jewish students after public school hours. *Congregational Jewish education* emphasized the study of prayer, Jewish laws and customs, Jewish holidays, Jewish history and preparation for *Bar/Bat Mitzvah*. This was accompanied by a reduction of the number of weekly hours of instruction from 10–12 hours for 48 weeks to 4–5 hours for 36 weeks. Together, these developments reduced the role of Hebrew language in the schools (Schiff 1988) in which 270,000 pupils (60% of the total 1993 American Jewish school population of 450,000) are enrolled.

The growth of the *modern Jewish day school* (the all-day educational institution in which students study both general and Jewish subjects) since 1940 has added a major dimension to the use of Hebrew language in the United States, especially in New York City. The Judaic studies programs in these schools are intensive, averaging about 20 hours per week. There is much variation among the day schools regarding emphasis on Hebrew language, ranging from minimal attention in the Reform day schools (comprising about 2% of the pupil population), to intensive study of biblical and post-biblical texts, Talmud, and commentaries, mostly translating them into Yiddish in the *Hasidic* and ultra-Orthodox *yeshivot* (comprising about 40% of the enrollment), and to a balanced curriculum of Hebraic studies with a variety of emphases on Hebrew language in modern Orthodox schools (44%), in community day schools (5%), and in Conservative Solomon Schechter schools (9%). About 25% of all day school students are exposed to *ivrit b'ivrit* instruction.

Hebrew language was introduced into the New York public school system in 1929. By 1942 there were three thousand students in sixteen junior, senior and evening high schools in the city. With the elimination of language requirements in the high schools and the movement of Jews to the suburbs, Hebrew language instruction in New York City public schools all but disappeared by 1970, after it peaked to over 7,000 students in twenty-four public junior and senior high schools in the 1950's.

Hebrew language and Hebrew text study was basic to many early American colleges. Ten universities established before the American Revolution included Hebrew among the "learned languages" of the curriculum. Among these schools were Harvard, Yale, and Dartmouth, which made the study of Hebrew obligatory. In Harvard, whose first two presidents were Hebrew scholars, all freshmen were required to study Hebrew for one full year (Goldman 1993).

The study of Hebrew in colleges declined during the eighteenth century and all but disappeared by the nineteenth century. However, the custom of giving valedictory addressees in Hebrew, as well as in Greek and in Latin, continued in several universities until the onset of the twentieth century.

During contemporary times, the growth in Hebrew language and Jewish studies programs in U. S. universities began in the 1930's. By 1966, there were sixty-four institutions offering Hebrew courses of which twenty-five had an undergraduate Hebrew major (Band 1967: 258). By 1989, the National Association of Professors of Hebrew identified ninety-three Modern Hebrew programs in U. S. colleges and universities with an enrollment of 5,115 students. Only about half of the modern Hebrew programs extended beyond the second level. The dropout rate after the first year course was due to the fact that "most of the students have no real interest in Hebrew" (Morahg 1993: 22).

There is a strong relationship between Israel and enrollment in Hebrew language courses, particularly for those who continued on to second, third or fourth levels of Hebrew language. A 1993 University of Wisconsin survey of 322 undergraduates enrolled in Modern Hebrew programs demonstrated that the most powerful factors motivating the study of Hebrew were "travel to Israel" (88%), "interest in Israel" (85%), and "ability to talk to Israelis" (82%).

The establishment of the State of Israel in 1948 motivated the organization of *Ulpanim* (study institutes in modern Hebrew language according to new Israeli methods of language teaching which stress oral comprehension, conversation and daily terminology) for adults throughout the United States and particularly in New York. However, only a minuscule segment of the adult Jewish population has availed itself of this Hebraic study opportunity. During the peak years of Ulpan programming in the 1950's and 1960's, some ten thousand Jewish adults throughout the Unites States would study Hebrew annually for periods of three months to several years.

Currently, the major effort in Ulpan teaching takes place at the Ulpan Center in New York and several other cities with large Jewish populations sponsored by the World Zionist Organization. Four hundred and fifty adults were enrolled in the New York Ulpan Center in 1993 in the various program levels which range from beginner Hebrew to advanced level where students learn to read Israeli newspapers and speak Hebrew fluently. Classes meet for two to six hours per week for nine to fourteen weeks. Students can progress from one level to another over a period of one or two years (Pinchuk 1994). According to a survey of adult programs in Hebrew language, one of the major problems regarding adult study of Hebrew in American *Ulpanim* is the use of Israeli texts and materials prepared for immigrants in Israel:

> In Israel, Hebrew is taught (to newcomers) as a second language in an Ulpan with the entire society reinforcing the lessons of the Ulpan, but in the United States, Hebrew is a foreign language and receives no societal reinforcement (Wassertzug 1993).

5. *Current Hebrew usage in the United States*

5.1. The variety of Hebrew language users

Jews came to the shores of America in several waves. Each group of immigrants brought with them linguistic baggage that included, among others, the language of the country from which they migrated (Spanish, Portuguese, German, Dutch, Russian, Polish, Hungarian, etc.), Hebrew (their ancestral language of prayer and Judaic study), and often a Jewish language peculiar to their residential setting – essentially *Ladino* by Sephardim immigrants from Spanish speaking lands, and *Yiddish* by those coming from Eastern European countries.

As a result of the acculturation-deculturation syndrome that has affected American Jewry and the accompanying transposition of intellectual and cultural interest away from Judaism by a majority of Jews once they arrived in the United States from European lands, the active users of Hebrew, even if mostly only in prayer and Judaic study, are relatively few, probably not more than twenty percent of the *five million core* Jews in the United States and not more than forty percent of the Jewish population of *one million* in New York City.

According to the 1991 New York Jewish Population Study, of the one million Jews residing in New York City (over two-thirds of them in Brooklyn and Manhattan) and 400,000 in the suburban counties (Nassau, Suffolk and Westchester), slightly more than one quarter claim to speak Hebrew and 16% claim they can read a Hebrew newspaper (Horowitz 1993: 51).

More males (30%) than females (23%) speak Hebrew. More young adults speak Hebrew than older adults. Generational differences are also apparent. Forty-one percent of first generation Jews (this figure includes many Israeli immigrants) claim to speak Hebrew, compared to 24% and 21% of second and third/fourth generation adults. There is obviously a relationship between those who have Israeli ties and use of Hebrew language. Seventy-seven percent of first generation American Jews, 47% second generation and 33% third/fourth generation Jews have close friends or family in Israel. Sixty-six percent of first generation, 48% and 31%

respectively of second and third/fourth generation adults have visited Israel (Horowitz 1993: 52).

There are other generational differences regarding the use of Hebrew. Thirty percent of first generation Jews attend synagogue weekly, compared to 17% of second generation and 10% of third/fourth generation Jews. Seventy-three percent of first generation Jews, compared to 65% of second generation and 54% of third/fourth generation adults, attend synagogue on High Holidays where they are exposed to Hebrew in the prayer service. In other activities where Hebrew terms and or Hebrew blessings are used – Israeli Independence Day celebration, Holocaust commemoration, Purim celebration and lighting Sabbath and Hanukkah candles – first generation Jews are much more involved than second, third and fourth generation adults (Horowitz 1993: 63).

The variety of contemporary Hebrew language users in New York City may be divided into several categories: the *daveners* 'daily worshippers', occasional worshippers, lifetime "learners", occasional learners, students, speakers and readers. Moreover, there is an ideological base to the use of Hebrew. Hasidic and Ultra-Orthodox, centrist or modern Orthodox, Conservative, Reconstructionist and Reform, and secular Jews all relate to Hebrew language usage in distinct ways.

The Hasidic and Ultra-Orthodox (about 110,000 or 11% of the City's Jewish population) use Hebrew essentially in the same manner as did their predecessors in Eastern Europe. The Jewish culture of their communities in New York is not much different from the *shtetl* way of life of their ancestors in Eastern Europe in the 18th and 19th centuries. For the Hasidic and Ultra-Orthodox Jews, Hebrew is *leshon hakodesh*, a Holy Tongue, referred to as *loshn koydesh* in their Yiddish usage, employed solely for prayer and Torah study. It is not to be used for any other purpose. Even in Israel, they prefer to use Yiddish as their daily vernacular rather than the language of the country.

The Ultra-Orthodox and Hasidic Jews, largely concentrated in Brooklyn and Rockland County, about 30 miles north of New York City, are the daily *daveners* and daily learners. Adult males spend as much as two hours a day in Hebrew prayers. Many young males, up to the age of thirty and more, spend most of their waking hours studying Judaic texts. Many working males devote as much time as possible to learning Torah – Pentateuch, Talmud and Commentaries, and Hasidic lore. But these are orally translated and discussed in Yiddish. Most Hasidic and Ultra-Orthodox Jews are trilingual: Yiddish is their Jewish language, the vernacular of their home; English is the language of their business activity and association with non-Jews and Jews who do not speak Yiddish; and Hebrew is their internal language, their sacred language of study and prayer. Their communities in Borough Park and Williamsburg, Brooklyn, and in Monsey, New York are essentially Yiddish speaking islands. Their daily Yiddish conversation with family and friends is punctuated with Hebraic religious terminology. Since Hasidim are forbidden, by and large, to watch TV, listen to secular radio programs and read English newspapers in their homes, contact with English is limited to external associations.

This trilingual attribute is two millennia old. As Spolsky and Cooper (1991: 33) have said, "multilingualism clearly predates the destruction of the Second Temple in 70 C. E. By the first century, a pattern had developed whereby Jews knew and used Hebrew for religious and literary purposes, spoke a Jewish vernacular (Aramaic) and also, as members of a minority group, knew and used non-Jewish language".

Like the Ultra-Orthodox and Hasidic Jews, *Centrist or Modern Orthodox Jews*, (population about 120,000 or 12% of the city's Jewish residents) pray solely in Hebrew and study biblical, post-biblical and rabbinical literature in the original Hebrew. As they differ in their relationship to Western society, modern Orthodox differ also in their relationship to modern Hebrew. While giving the Hebrew language the respect it deserves as a Holy Tongue, modern Orthodox Jews believe in its use as a living form of expression – as a vernacular, although Hebrew rarely reaches that level without extensive Israeli exposure.

Conservative, Reconstructionist and Reform Jews live largely in the suburban counties of Greater New York – Nassau, Suffolk and Westchester – and in the suburbs of all the cities where Jews reside. *Conservative Jews* (population 290,000 or 29% of Jews in New York City) pray in Hebrew. While the Hebraic content of their prayer books is similar to the modern Orthodox, their Hebrew prayer service is interspersed with English prayers.

While the *Reconstructionist* prayer book is essentially in Hebrew, the Hebraic liturgy of Reconstructionist Jews (15,000 or 1.5% of Jews in New York City) is generously interspersed with English prayers. The prayer book used by *Reform Jews* (300,000 or 30% of the Jewish population in New York City) is basically a Hebrew-English liturgical text. Whereas prayer books used by Reform synagogues in the mid-nineteenth century with the introduction of Reform in the United States were entirely in Hebrew (Grinstein 1945: 356,362), Hebrew as a language of worship and study was eliminated essentially within the Reform wing of Judaism as it developed in the United States in the nineteenth century. Currently, there appears to be a revival of interest by Reform Jewish leaders in increasing the use of Hebrew in worship (*Union Prayer Book 1922*; *Gates of Prayer, The New Union Prayer Book* 1975).

One of the ways in which the ideological groups differ in the extent of the use of Hebrew prayers is in the amount of time worshippers spend in prayer. The active Reform worshippers (about twenty percent of the total Reform population) attend one service a week – usually on a Friday evening for one-and-a-half to two-and-a-half hours including the sermon. The active Reconstructionist worshippers (about twenty percent of the total Reconstructionist population) attend Friday evening and Saturday morning services for one-and-a-half to two-and-a-half hours including a sermon and/or discussion period. The active Conservative worshippers (about 20 percent of the total Conservative population in New York City) attend synagogue on Friday evening for one-and-a-half to two-and-a-half hours and on Saturday morning for two to two-and-a-half hours. Some Conservative Jews worship daily. The active Orthodox worshippers (about 80 percent of the total Orthodox population) attend morning, afternoon and evening services in synagogue during the weekdays or pray at home twenty-five minutes to one-and-a-half hours each day, on Friday evening for one hour, and Saturday morning for three hours.

The use of Hebrew liturgy is not limited to the synagogue. The devout Jew – particularly the male – recites Hebrew blessings upon rising, after taking care of his personal needs, before partaking of food, after eating (a lengthy grace after each meal), before retiring at night, upon hearing thunder, seeing lightning, seeing a rainbow in the sky or an ocean, upon smelling fragrances, upon seeing an outstanding Torah or secular scholar or head of state, upon baking *hallah* (Sabbath or festival bread) and upon hearing good or bad tidings.

At the Sabbath and Festival table, *zemirot* 'Hebrew liturgical poems' are sung. At life cycle events – *brit milah* 'circumcision ceremonies naming the baby boys and girls', *pidyon haben* 'redemption of the first born male child at 30 days', *Bar/Bat Mitzvah* and weddings – special ceremonies are conducted in Hebrew. When he travels, the devout Jew recites *tefillat haderech* 'the wayfarers' prayer'. At every religious occasion he hears a *d'rashah* 'a homily' in Yiddish or English containing numerous Hebraic religious terms and biblical quotations.

While the vast majority of American Jews are of Ashkenazic origin, a small yet significant part of the American Jewish population has Sephardic roots, estimated at 200,000 to 250,000 (Alcosser 1994; Lieberman

1994; Levy 1994). The most identifiable segment of this population are the Syrian Jews – thirty-five thousand in New York and fifteen thousand elsewhere in the United States. They usually congregate in their own communities and, as a group, have a special relationship to Hebrew. According to Dr. Zevulun Lieberman, Mayhem professor of Sephardic Studies at Yeshiva University and Syrian Jewish Community *Hakham* 'rabbinical scholar', eighty to ninety percent of Syrian Jews in New York spend about thirty minutes each day in Hebrew prayer; sixty percent can speak Hebrew although they do not engage regularly in Hebrew conversation; twenty to thirty percent of the adults participate in Judaic-Hebraic classes weekly. Almost all Syrian Jewish children attend Hebraic, *ivrit b'ivrit* day schools patterned after the Syrian Jewish custom in Alepo, Syria, whereby all instruction in Jewish Studies beginning with the third grade takes place in Hebrew (Lieberman 1994). In the New York day schools, they are exposed to three to four hours of Hebraic learning daily.

The rest of the Sephardic Jewish population in the United States is not as conversant in Hebrew as the Syrian Jews, but uses Hebrew more regularly than other non-Orthodox American Jews. According to Edward Alcosser, the executive vice president of *American Sephardi Federation*, more than one third of Sephardim (excluding the Israelis) pray daily in Hebrew, fifteen to twenty minutes each day; about one-half attend Sabbath and Holiday services fairly regularly and recite and listen to Hebrew prayers and readings from the Bible for about two hours at each service. Almost all can read Hebrew phonetically. About forty percent understand written and spoken Hebrew. Moreover, Hebrew is interlaced in the everyday vernacular of first generation Sephardim who speak Ladino, Farsi, or Arabic. Ninety percent of Sephardic children receive some kind of Jewish education in which they learn to read Hebrew prayers as well as other Judaic subjects.

About forty thousand Sephardim in the United States are recent immigrants from Iran. Most of them reside in New York. They speak Farsi at home and have a good reading knowledge of Hebrew (Alcosser 1994).

In order to promote the use of Hebrew as a modern vehicle of communication, particularly as a medium of Hebraic cultural expression, the *Histadruth Ivrith* 'the Hebrew Language and Culture Association' of America was founded in 1920. In 1930, it organized the *Hanoar Haivri*, the Hebrew Youth Organization, which existed for some twenty years and, at its zenith, had several thousand Hebrew speaking members.

The major activity of *Histadruth Ivrith* has been the sponsorship of Hebrew language periodicals – the *Hadoar*, a weekly for adults with advanced Hebrew knowledge, and *Lamishpahah* for those with intermediate understanding of Hebrew. In the 1940's the *Hadoar Lanoar*, a simplified juvenile Hebrew monthly, and *Musaf Lakorai Hatzair*, an intermediate monthly youth magazine, were carried as supplements to the *Hadoar*.

5.2. The Hebrew Readers

During medieval and contemporary times, the publishing of religious Hebraic literature was second nature to the Jew. In Europe, during the late nineteenth century, the *Haskalah* and Hebrew language revival movements saw the publication of a variety of journals, dailies, weeklies and occasional books in modern Hebrew on secular, cultural, non-rabbinic topics, especially on contemporary Judaism and Palestine. In Eastern Europe, writers and poets like Chaim Nachman Bialik, Shaul Tchernichowsky and Ahad Ha'am created a modern genre of Hebrew literature read by a core of Hebraic devotees schooled in Jewish religious tradition who opted for a secular-cultural-national approach to Jewish life. This literature influenced significantly the development of modern Hebrew, particularly the style of written communication.

In early America, until the end of the nineteenth century, there was little publishing of any sort.[3] The Hebrew texts – essentially Bibles, prayer books and related Hebraic materials – used by Jewish immigrants in the U. S. were bought with them from their countries of origin or sent to them once they arrived.

From the time of the arrival of East European Jews, prodigious efforts were made to publish in Hebrew.[4] Since 1881, when *haM'assef ba-Arez heHadashah* [The Journal in the New Land] appeared only once as the literary organ of the New York based *Society of Lovers of Hebrew in The United States*, at least seventy different Hebrew periodicals were published. With the exception of two pedagogic magazines issued in Chicago, all the periodicals were published in New York City.

The bulk of the publications were cultural, literary efforts –mostly monthly magazines and annuals – appearing during the last decade of the nineteenth century and the first three decades of the twentieth century. Readership of these periodicals varied from a handful – twenty subscribers in the case of the *Hashiloah* (1900–1902) to several hundred (*The Jewish Communal Register* 1918: 568).

One modern Hebrew periodical currently being published had its beginnings in the early part of the twentieth century. *Hadoar* first appeared as a daily in 1921 and became a weekly in 1923. Its peak readership was about 15,000 in the early 1940's (Halkin 1942). As of 1993, it became a bi-weekly with a circulation of 4,000 and estimated readership of 10,000 (Galanter 1994). Most of the subscribers and readers of modern Hebrew periodicals during the first half of the twentieth century were Jewish educators (Learsi 1954: 97).

From 1903 to 1972, a dozen periodicals were published on rabbinical issues and Judaica. These were relatively long-lived. Four of the journals – *haPardes (1913*), *Bitzaron* (1939), *Or Hamizrach* (1954) and *Hadarom* (1957) – are still being issued. Since 1972, many additional occasional periodicals and books on rabbinical issues, Jewish studies, *halakhah* 'laws' and biblical and talmudic exegesis authored by Orthodox rabbis and scholars have been published in Hebrew, although the current trend in the Orthodox community is to publish some of this literature in English.

The early 1900s saw the appearance, for one year periods, of a Hebrew monthly, *Hed heHinukh* (1915) for teachers, and a monthly, *Kuntros ha-Modiyin* (1916) for principals (*The Jewish Communal Register* 1918: 567). Thereafter, between 1919 and 1954, seven education quarterlies, each lasting for two years, were published. The quarterly *Shevilei Hahinukh*, sponsored by the National Council for Jewish Education appeared from 1940 through 1985. Reaching a peak readership of about 1,500 in the 1960's, *Shevilei Hahinukh* ceased publication for lack of subscribers, since U. S.-born Jewish school teachers found it difficult to read, while Israeli teachers in Jewish schools preferred Israeli educational publications.

Seven weekly Hebrew newspapers and one daily saw the light of day for short periods of time between 1889 and 1921. The first Hebrew newspaper in the United States – *haZofeh baArez haHadashah* [The Spectator in The New Land] – appeared weekly in New York before the onset of mass immigration from Eastern Europe, from 1871 through 1876.

In the early 1900's, there were several abortive attempts to publish juvenile Hebrew periodicals. These were followed by a more successful effort, *Hadoar Lanoar* (1930–1960) read by some 10,000 Jewish youth in New York during its peak subscription years in the 1940's, and *Musaf LaKorai HaZair* (1940–1950). After they ceased publication they were replaced by *Olam Hadash* (1961-) with a current circulation of 6,000 in North America and an estimated readership of 15,000 (Bloch 1994).

LaMishpahah (1963–), a family oriented monthly in simplified Hebrew, has about 6,500 subscribers in North America, the bulk of them in Greater New York, and an estimated readership of 25,000 (Galanter 1994). There are two ultra-Orthodox weeklies in Hebrew – *Hamahaneh HaHaredi* and *Panim Hadashot* – read by Ultra-Orthodox Jews who lived in Israel and sold in storefronts in Brooklyn, with an estimated combined readership of 6,000.

Challenging the current role of Hebrew reading and study of Hebrew texts in the United States is the increased number of English translations of Hebraic sources. During the last two decades much effort has been invested in translating classical Jewish texts into English. A veritable Judaic English language library of hundreds of books for children and adults has been developed. On the college campus, most Judaic studies courses utilize anthologies of texts translated into English. One can now study the Bible, the Talmud, most of their traditional commentaries, almost all the major post-biblical medieval contemporary Judaic sources, without needing to know one word of Hebrew (Mintz 1993).

5.3. The Impact of Israelis on Hebrew usage

Israelis in the United States may be classified into two general groupings: *yordim*, permanent residents who are in the United States for four or more years and plan to remain; and temporary residents including Israeli emissaries, students, business people and long term visitors. The demographic profile of the Israeli migrant population in New York and the rest of the country is a matter of much variability. Estimates vary from 20,000 to 300,000 in New York and from 89,000 to 500,000 nationally (Harel 1994; Ritterband 1986; Rosen 1993; Herman 1988). American born children of Israelis in the U. S. would make the total number of Israelis in the United States considerably larger.

In metropolitan New York, Israelis generally live in close proximity to each other, establishing their own sub-communities in several sections of the City – Riverdale, Rego Park, Forest Hills and Flatbush – where Hebrew is frequently heard in apartment houses, street corners, stores and restaurants. Their language is laced with terminology derived from the English language, for example: *svedder* for sweater; *televzziah* for television; *integratziah* for integration; and *correlatziah* for correlation. The latter terms and their like are used generally by Israeli academics who find them more convenient than Hebrew words to convey the same meaning.

Israeli adults, by and large, speak Hebrew among themselves and in their homes and are avid readers of the Israeli press and publications. While exact figures are not available, the number of weekend editions of *Ma'ariv* and *Yediot*, two of Israeli's most popular dailies sold in North America is about 22,000 with a readership of approximately 90,000 (Lazarov 1994). About one third of the circulation and readership is in New

York. In addition, Hebrew booksellers in New York import thousands of fiction and non-fiction books each month from Israel (Harel 1994). The most often read publication by Israelis, especially by *yordim* who have been in the United States for several years, is the Brooklyn-based weekly *Yisrael Shelanu* [Our Israel], founded in 1979 (Prawer 1994). Currently, 70,000 copies are sold each week in the Tri-State area, largely in New York City (*Yisrael Shelanu 1994*). In some communities, Israelis have established their own local Hebrew publications.

Among other kinds of Hebrew reading material available to Israelis in the United States and to other Americans in areas populated by Israelis are store-front posters, menus in eateries, and organizational and commercial mailings to Israeli homes. In 1991, *Yisrael Shelanu* published *ha-Madrich Shelanu* [Our Guide], a Hebrew telephone directory featuring lists of businesses and advertisements about New York and the United States to recently arrived Israelis. In addition, one hundred and fifty thousand copies of *Israel Yellow Pages* are distributed annually throughout the United States, seventy percent of which goes to the New York area (Israel Yellow Pages 1994). Other ways Israelis maintain their Hebrew connection are: Hebrew radio and television programs, a 900 telephone number that provides Hebrew language news bulletins from the Middle East, and frequent lengthy telephone conversations with friends and relatives in Israel. For some, regular flights to Israel are part of their way of life (Rosen 1993).

The Israelis in America are not a dominant force regarding the spread of Hebrew since they use Hebrew solely as their private language of communication among themselves (Caspi 1994). There is ample reason to believe that Israeli youths in New York and elsewhere in the United States are assimilating rapidly and do not constitute a major core of regular Hebrew speakers. Israeli children generally attend public schools and do not enroll in synagogue supplementary Hebrew studies programs since the overwhelming majority of *yordim* are secular. Only a small percentage of Israeli children attend Jewish day schools because these schools are almost always under religious auspices and Israelis are not accustomed to paying for Jewish and general education (Sheniak 1994). In New York there are less than 2,000 Israeli children of school age enrolled in Jewish day schools where they study Hebraic texts and speak Hebrew in their Judaic studies classes (Sheniak 1994, Prawer 1994).

Israelis in New York have organized several supplementary Hebrew studies programs – in Great Neck 1978, Forest Hills 1984, Canarsie 1985, Mid Island 1986, Woodmere 1990 – in which about 400 children were enrolled in 1993 for four to six hours per week (Silberstein 1994).

A branch of the Israeli scout movement was established in the 1980's in order to help Israeli youths retain their national identity and their Hebrew language proficiency and maintain Israeli cultural contact. In 1993 there were some three hundred Israeli youths in New York and a similar number in the rest of the United States in Israeli scout programs. Recent experience with the various Israeli scout groups in New York demonstrates that Israeli children of *yordim* do not speak Hebrew regularly. In several scout troops it has been difficult to conduct meetings in Hebrew (Sheniak 1994). United States born progeny, particularly second and third children tend to speak to their parents in English even when their parents address them in Hebrew, a situation not unlike the preceding Yiddish speaking immigrant generations. To address this problem, the *Noar Vehalutz Department* of the Joint Authority for Jewish Zionist Education in Jerusalem and its counterpart in New York, the American Zionist Youth Foundation, established, in 1992, the *Hetz Vakeshet* (Bow and Arrow) program which arranges Israel summer visits for 16–17 year old children of Israelis. About one hundred children of *yordim* in the New York area have participated in this program each summer since its founding (Prawer 1994, Silberstein 1994).

Many Jewish schools engage resident Israelis as teachers. However, their impact on Hebrew language instruction is minimal since the emphasis in the curricula is not on Hebrew language per se, but rather on Judaic subjects in the *day school* and on synagogue skills in the *supplementary congregational school*. In addition to the resident Israeli teachers there are some one hundred Israeli *shlihim* 'emissaries' to schools, youth organizations and communal institutions. While not a major factor in motivating greater use of Hebrew among Americans, the presence of the *shlihim* in Jewish communal institutions, youth organizations and schools has raised Jewish consciousness about Hebrew language and Hebraic culture. The Israeli Cultural Affairs officers in the larger Jewish communities do not directly attempt to impact the level of Hebrew language usage. Their main thrust is providing Israeli cultural enrichment through art, music, theater, film and special events (*Tarbut* 1994).

Despite the relationship between the American Jewish community and Israel, the Jewish State has not been able to contribute significantly to enhancing the role of Hebrew in the United States. To the contrary, it has been witness to the eclipse of Hebrew by English as the national – and the international – language of the Jewish people. The language of oral and written communication between Israeli officials, political leaders and academics and the American Jewish community is solely English. Meetings and conferences involving Israelis and American Jews are always conducted in English. At best, the overwhelming majority of American Jews can manage only a few Hebrew terms. The current Israeli use of English makes it unnecessary for Jews in New York to learn to communicate in Hebrew (Mintz 1993).

6. *Hebrew in New York: A summary*

When viewed in demographic perspective, there are significant differences between Hebrew language use in New York and the rest of the United States. Hebrew usage in New York is more widespread, more habitual, and more varied than elsewhere in the country. This is attributable to three conditions: the size of the Jewish population, the type of Jewish residents (their ideological and ethnic backgrounds), and the Jewish educational institutions in the community.

While the number of Jews in New York City – and even in the surrounding suburban counties – has declined annually since the onset of the 1970s because of low birth rates and population shifts to the Sunbelt and the West Coast, 1.8 million Jews, one third of the total United States Jewish population, resided in metropolitan New York in 1994. More significantly, about seventy-five percent of American Orthodox Jewry, approximately ninety percent of all Ultra Orthodox and Hasidic Jews, and the vast majority of Israeli immigrants and Sephardic Jews in the United States live in Greater New York. In addition, over one half of all American Jewish day school pupils and over three-quarters of all students in schools of higher Jewish learning are in Jewish educational institutions in New York.

Translated into Hebrew language usage, these demographic factors mean that, in New York, many more Jews pray in Hebrew and devote much more time to Hebrew prayer. Also in New York considerable more time is spent in Hebrew language learning and in Hebraic text study. Finally, Hebrew is spoken regularly by more adults in the New York area than elsewhere.

7. *Conclusion*

Hebrew, the language of the Bible and the voluminous post-biblical Judaic literature, is employed in New York City and elsewhere in the United States in a variety of ways. For most American Jews who have a relationship to this old-new language, it is a medium of prayer ranging in use from several hours per year to several hours per day. For less than ten percent of the adult Jews in the United States, particularly first generation Israelis, Hebrew is their mother tongue. Many of them regularly read Hebrew newspapers, periodicals and books printed in Israel and in this country.

Approximately seventy percent of Jewish children are enrolled in some type of Jewish school during their school-age years. They are exposed, in varying degrees, to the study of Hebrew language and Hebrew texts. Less than 20 percent of the Jewish youth population attends Jewish day schools at the elementary and secondary school level.

Hebrew was never a "dead language". Even though it was not used as a vernacular in the Diaspora since the destruction of the second Temple in Jerusalem almost two thousand years ago, it was employed regularly during the last two millennia by Jews wherever they resided as a language of prayer, study and ritual observance. Although it did not "die", it was revived during the last century as a vernacular. The revival of Hebrew as a daily vehicle of communication in Palestine/Israel boarded on the miraculous, given the many languages that Jews spoke during the last century. However, the effect of the linguistic renaissance of Hebrew on U. S. Jewry has been minimal.

In the early years (1654–1880) the small number of Jews living in the United States used Hebrew essentially for prayer, infrequently for study, and never as a vernacular. The revival of Hebrew in the last two decades of the nineteenth century and the first third of the twentieth century led to many attempts by devotees of modern Hebrew to promote its study and active use via instruction, public lectures and forums, and publications. However, with the exception of Israeli *yordim* and temporary Israeli residents, very few Jews in the United States – somewhat more in New York City – can read modern unvocalized Hebrew or speak Hebrew fluently. For the vast majority of Jewish residents in New York and the rest of the country who have an ongoing relationship with the Hebrew language, it remains a medium of prayer. For some, it is a matter of sacred text literacy.

Notes

1. In order to support the elimination of Hebrew in Reform congregations, Dr. David Einhorn (1809–1879), a major Reform religious leader, cited – out of context – the rabbinic dictum *shema bekhol lashon she-attah shomea.*

2. This kind of zeal is personified by the East European literary figure Y. L. Gordon (1831–1892) who proclaimed, "I am an eternal slave to the Hebrew language," and by Daniel Persky (1887–1962), popular New York Hebraist, educator, and writer who said in jest that he never married because he was wedded to the Hebrew language and stressed, "Above all, I am a Hebrew, a Hebrew speaker, a Hebrew reader and a Hebrew writer." His calling card bore the legend "I am a slave to Hebrew forever".
3. According to J. D. Eisenstein, *Otzar Zichronotai*, quoted in Grinstein 1945: 562, the first Hebrew book outside of prayer books and Bibles published in the U. S. was *Avnai Yehoshua*, a volume on Judaica, in 1860.
4. The information regarding Hebrew publishing was compiled from the world-wide listing of Hebrew newspapers and periodicals appearing since 1750 in *Encyclopedia Judaica*, Volume I. Jerusalem: Keter Publishing House, 1972, p. 193–219.

References

Alcosser, Edward
1994 Interview with Executive Vice President of the American Sephardi Federation, April 1, 1994.

Band, Arnold J.
1967 "Jewish studies in American Liberal Arts colleges and universities", in: O. Janowsky (ed.), *The education of American Jewish teachers*. Boston: Beacon Press, 255–264.

Bickerton, Derek
1990 Language and Species. Chicago: University of Chicago Press

Bloch, Sam
1994 Interview with Director of Publications, World Zionist Organization, March 15, 1994.

Caspi, Ben
1994 Communication from New York Bureau Chief of *Ma'ariv*, April 13, 1994.

Deuteronomy 6: 7.

Dushkin, Alexander M.
1970 *Comparative study of the Jewish teacher training schools in the Diaspora*. Jerusalem: The Hebrew University.

Fromer, Seymour
1969 "The Colonial period", in: *A History of Jewish education in the United States*. New York: The American Association for Jewish Education.

Galanter, Harold
1994 Communication from Histadruth Ivrith official, March 24, 1994.

Gates of Prayer – The New Union Prayer Book
1975 New York: The Central Conference of American Rabbis.

Glinert, Lewis
1991 "The 'Back to the Future' syndrome in language planning: The case of modern Hebrew", in: David Marshall (ed.), *Language planning*. Amsterdam: John Benjamins, 215 – 243.

Goldman, Shalom
1993 "Biblical Hebrew in Colonial America", in: Shalom Goldman (ed.), *Hebrew and the Bible in America – The First two centuries*. Hanover, New Hampshire and London: Brandeis University Press and Dartmouth College.

Grinstein, Hyman B.
1945 *The Rise of the Jewish Community of New York*, 1654–1860. Philadelphia: Jewish Publication Society.
1969 "In the course of the nineteenth century", in: J. Pilch (ed.), *A History of Jewish education in the United States*. New York: American Association for Jewish Education, 25–50.
Halkin, Abraham S.
1942 "Hebrew in Jewish culture", in: O. Janowsky (ed.), *The American Jew: A composite portrait*. New York: Harper and Brothers, 122–132.
Harel, Yehezkel
1994 Interview with Director of Student and Youth Leadership Department, Jewish National Fund, March 24, 1994.
Herman, Pini
1988 Jewish-Israeli migration to the United States since 1948. [Unpublished MS.] Cited in Sherry Rosen 1993.
Horowitz, Bethamie
1993 *The 1991 New York Jewish population study*. New York: United Jewish Appeal – Federation of Jewish Philanthropies of New York.
Horowitz, Edward
1960 *How the Hebrew language grew*. New York: Jewish Education Committee Press.
Israel Yellow Pages
1994 Communication from publisher, Flushing, New York, April 13, 1994.
Lazarov, Mali
1994 Communication from Advertising and Public Relations Coordinator, Ma'ariv American Office, New York.
Learsi, Rufus
1954 *The Jews in America: A History*. New York: The World Publishing Company.
Levy, Leon
1994 Interview with president of American Sephardi Federation, New York, April 5, 1994.
Lieberman, Zevulun
1994 Interview with Syrian Jewish Community Hacham, Brooklyn, New York. Maybaum Professor of Sephardic Studies and Sephardic Rosh haYeshiva, Yeshiva University, April 1, 1994.
Marcus, Jacob R.
1953 *Early American Jewry: The Jews of Pennsylvania and the South 1655–1790*. Philadelphia: Jewish Publication Society.
Midrash Rabbah Leviticus 32:5.
Mintz, Alan
1993 Hebrew in America. *Commentary*, July.
Morahg, Gilead
1993 "Hebrew on campus: Student motivations and expectation", *Bulletin of Higher Hebrew Education* 5–6, 21–34.
Patai, Raphael
1971 *Tents of Jacob: The Diaspora yesterday and today*. Englewood Cliffs, New Jersey: Prentice Hall.

Pinchuk, Miri
1994 Interview with Director, Ulpan Center, New York, May 5, 1994.
Prawer, Ehud
1994 Interview with senior Israeli emissary to Department of Education, American Zionist Youth Foundation, March 22, 1994.
Ritterband, Paul
1986 "Israelis in New York", in: Arnold Dashefsky (ed.), *Contemporary Jewry*, volume 7. New Brunswick, New Jersey: Transaction Books.
Rosen, Sherry
1993 *The Israeli corner of the American Jewish community*. New York: Institute on American Jewish – Israeli Relations, The American Jewish Committee.
Schiff, Alvin
1967 "The students of the Hebrew Teachers Colleges: Profile and career choice", in: O. Janowsky (ed.), *The Education of American Jewish teachers*, Boston: Beacon Press, 83–110.
1979 "Jewish education in light of peace", *Jewish Education* 47: 3.
1981 "The Significance of Hebrew language for Jewish education", *Jewish Education* 49: 2, 3 - 5.
1988 *The Jewish supplementary school: A system in need of change*. New York: Board of Jewish Education.
Sheniak, Rafi
1994 Interview with Director of the Department of Education and Culture, Joint Authority for Jewish Zionist Education, March 15, 1994.
Silberstein, Chana
1994 Interview with Director of Division of Informal Education, Board of Jewish Education of Greater New York, April 22, 1994.
Spolsky, Bernard – Robert Cooper
1991 *The Languages of Jerusalem*. Oxford: Oxford University Press.
Tarbut
1994 de Sola Mendes (ed.) New York: Consulate General of Israel.
The Jewish Communal Register of New York City 1917–1918
1918 New York: Kehillah of New York City.
The New Union Prayer Book
1975 New York: Central Conference of American Rabbis.
The Union Prayer Book
1922 New York: Central Conference of American Rabbis.
Urofsky, Melvin I.
1975 *American Zionism from Herzl to The Holocaust*. New York: Anchor Press/Doubleday.
Wassertzug, Marta
1993 *The Teaching of Hebrew at The Jewish Community Center*. Washington, D. C.: The Jewish Community Center of Greater Washington.
Wolowsky, Joel
1990 "Ivrit B'Ivrit", *Ten Da'at*, Spring.
1991 "Responsive Readers", *Ten Da'at*, Spring.
Yisrael Shelanu
1994 Communication with office manager, March 30, 1994.

IV THE LANGUAGES WITH THE NEWEST SOUNDS AND OF NEWEST FACES

Chinese in New York*

Shiwen Pan

1. Introduction

When speakers of different Chinese dialects communicate in either Mandarin or Cantonese in the city, they easily perceive "peculiarities" in the others' speech, such as strange tones and lexical items unheard of before. Some careful listeners may even notice semantic and syntactic differences in their interlocutors' utterances. However, during prolonged contact with others, their speech begins to show those linguistic features which they once thought peculiar.

How do Chinese dialects interact in Chinese communities in New York City? What strategies do speakers of mutually unintelligible Chinese dialects use for effective communication? What are the general linguistic behavioral patterns of these speakers? And how does Chinese heritage affect the present Chinese-American experience? These issues are the major concerns of this chapter.

2. Chinese in the United States

2.1. Chinese immigration history

It is generally known that the early Chinese immigrants came to the United States of their own accord as fortune seekers, although the true stories behind them were far less pleasant.

The arrival of Chinese in the United States dates back to the early 1800s. The U. S. Immigration Commission recorded the arrival of three Chinese between 1820 and 1830 (Marden–Meyer 1968: 180). However, the cheap-wage Chinese laborers did not come in large numbers until news of the gold rush spread in the 1840s (Kwong 1987: 11–20; Sandmeyer 1973: 13–24). In 1849, there were 325 Chinese among 100,000 gold miners in San Francisco. Subsequently, Chinese arrived in large numbers in California and elsewhere to take part in most labor markets.

By the time the Chinese Exclusion Act was passed by Congress in 1882, there were already 107,000 Chinese in the United States, about 0.2 percent of the total population of the country. In those days, more than 90 percent of the Chinese coolies came from a few counties along the coast of Guangdong. Taishan County alone provided 60 percent of them (Chen 1980: 3, 18–19).

Severe punishment once deterred Chinese from leaving their homeland. In the Qing Dynasty (1636–1911 A. D.), the legal punishment for emigration was death by decapitation and this law remained effective until 1860 (Chen 1980: 6–7). Qing emperors considered any channel of contact with the Western nations a potential threat to the empire and tried very hard to isolate their empire from the outside world. However, being severely weakened by repeated invasions by Western powers, the Qing government could hardly control its remotest coastal areas like the Provinces of Guangdong and Fujian.

By 1851, there were about 25,000 Chinese in California gold mines, as well as in restaurants, and in laundries. By 1860, the immigrants constituted 40 percent of the total population of 380,000. Among them were 35,000 Chinese who were outnumbered by immigrants from Ireland, England and Germany (Chen 1980: 46; Kwong 1987).

When the gold mines were exhausted in the 1860s, the railroad, in turn, became the biggest attraction. In 1858, the first fifty Chinese were hired to build the California Central Railroad from Sacramento to Marysville. The second wave of Chinese immigrants came to the West coast to complete the difficult sections of the transcontinental railroad going through the Rocky Mountains. About four-fifths of the work from Sacramento to Ogden was done by Chinese. In those years, there were 12,000 Chinese on the payroll of the Central Pacific Railway Company, out of a total 13,500 in the work force. The job was completed in May 1869 (Sandmeyer 1973: 15–16).

The completion of the first transcontinental railway was immediately followed by four more lines. Chinese were employed on all of them. On the Northern Pacific alone, there were about 15,000 recorded Chinese workers (Chen 1980: 76).

The completion of the railroads left a huge Chinese labor surplus that was later absorbed by other industries in the West: textile mills, cigarette factories, canneries, and garment factories.

In 1882, Congress passed the Chinese Exclusion Act, the first legislation to ban the immigration of a specific ethnic group to the United States. As a result, the Chinese population declined drastically because more departed for their homeland than arrived in the U. S. during the following years (Sandmeyer 1973). In the heyday of the gold rush, Chinese laborers in the West numbered approximately 260,000, constituting about a quarter of the male workers in California. At the turn of the century, the number was reduced to about 90,000 (Marden – Meyer 1968: 180; Kwong 1987: 14).

After the Chinese Exclusion Act, Chinese immigration to the United States came to a standstill for about sixty years. During this period, a limited number of Chinese succeeded in landing in the United States through illegal channels. This situation remained unchanged until 1943 when the Act was repealed by authorizing an annual visa quota of 103 persons for Chinese nationals (Kraly 1987; Kwong 1987).

The Immigration Act enacted in 1965 marked a shift of immigration policy. It replaced the more biased national origins quotas with a visa preference system. This law set an annual immigration quota of 20,000 for Chinese nationals from Taiwan and the People's Republic of China. An additional quota of 600 was provided for immigration from Hong Kong. Shortly after formal diplomatic relations were established between the United States and the People's Republic of China in 1979, a separate annual quota of 20,000 was set for immigration from the People's Republic of China, making the overall annual immigration quota for Chinese nationals exceed 40,000. The Immigration and Nationality Act of 1965 has significantly changed the size and composition of Chinese communities in the United States. The population of Chinese-Americans increased from 117,629 in 1950 to 431,583 in 1970, to 812,178 in 1980, to 1,079,400 in 1985 and to 1,648,696 in 1990. It is expected that the Chinese-American population in the United States will reach two million by the turn of the century (Kraly 1987; Kwong 1987: 22).

2.2. *Chinese-Americans today*

The rapid growth of the Chinese population in the United States has brought about changes in Chinese communities throughout the country. Immigrants from the People's Republic of China (P. R. C.), Taiwan (R. O. C.), Hong Kong and Malaysia remain a large pool of manual laborers who are vital to the traditional Chinese businesses, such as restaurants, garment making, grocery stores, and laundries. However there is an appreciable tendency toward new domains which require higher levels of training and professional know-how because of the availability of a great number of educated new immigrants and influx of foreign capital from Asian countries.

In 1949 when the Communists ousted the Nationalist government, about 5,000 Chinese elites were allowed to stay in the United States as refugees (Kwong 1987: 59–70). Among them were young scholars, generals, high-ranking government officials, diplomats and financial tycoons. Between 1960 and 1980, when the government in Taiwan lifted strict restrictions on emigration to foreign countries, about 150,000 students came to enroll at graduate schools in the United States. After their graduation more than 90 percent were employed and later became permanent residents in the U. S. (Kwong 1987: 60 – 62).

Chinese students and immigrants from the People's Republic of China began to come to the United States after 1979. Since then, the educated Chinese circle has been substantially enlarged as thousands of students from the People's Republic of China arrive to study at graduate schools in the United States.

After the crackdown against the student demonstrations in Beijing on June 4th 1989, the U. S. Congress succeeded in passing the Chinese Students Protection Act in 1992, according to which Chinese nationals from the People's Republic of China were eligible to apply for immigration status in a twelve month period. Up to September 1993, about 51,000 stranded students and visiting scholars, as well as some tourists, from the People's Republic of China had submitted applications to become permanent residents. In December 1993, about 45,000 of the applications were approved.

At present, the gap between the middle class and the lower class among American Chinese is increasing. With limited education and English, most non-student immigrants still have to work in garment factories and restaurants where they work long hours with poor salaries and little job security.

On the other hand, educated immigrants and the American-born Chinese who have had higher education have more potential to move into higher paid professions. Usually, they end up in corporations and government organizations where benefits and pay are better than those offered by the small businesses, in Chinatowns. The traditional businesses owned by Chinese have been in decline. Chinatowns are no longer the boundary for Chinese-Americans – as they used to be decades ago. Successful Chinese immigrants and second and third generation Chinese continue to move out of old Chinatowns or Chinese communities, leaving behind them new Chinese immigrants and the less fortunate.

Today, there is actually a back-flow of former Chinese immigrants to their country of origin. The economic boom in Taiwan, Hong Kong and Singapore has increased the need for well-trained scientists, professors and researchers. The governments and larger corporations are offering excellent conditions to attract them. Many professors and scientists who received advanced education in the United States are returning to resettle in that region.

3. *Chinese communities in New York City*

There are currently two Chinatowns in New York City: the Manhattan Chinatown, or the Old Chinatown, and the Flushing Chinatown, the New Chinatown. In recent years, another Chinese community is flourishing around Eighth Avenue in Brooklyn.

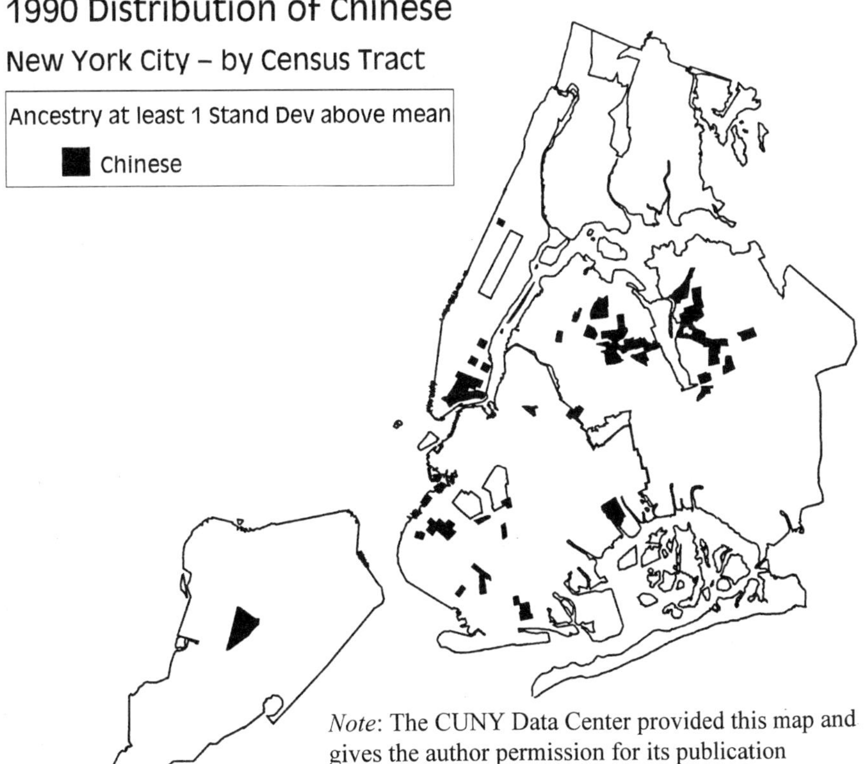

Note: The CUNY Data Center provided this map and gives the author permission for its publication

The New York Chinese community came into being in the 1870s when thousands of Chinese laborers came from riot-stricken small Chinatowns and Chinese communities in California, Nevada, Colorado, Wyoming and elsewhere. In this Chinatown, thousands of Chinese were employed by the Chinese-owned businesses. Benefiting from both Chinese heritage and favorable conditions provided by U. S. society, many Chinese succeeded in running their businesses despite economic slowdowns. New York's Manhattan Chinatown has witnessed a gradual expansion and covers an area between Bowery Street and Mulberry Street. It had a population of about 10,000 in the 1880s. Following the repeal of the Chinese Exclusion Act in 1943, the population increased to 11,700 (Chen 1980: 258).

The Manhattan Chinatown used to be dominated by a Cantonese-speaking population. It has constantly attracted Cantonese speakers from all over the world. After the Vietnam and the Cambodian Wars, Vietnamese, Laotian and Cambodian refugees of Cantonese descent came by thousands to settle. Now the largest in North America, New York's Manhattan Chinatown and its vicinity contains about 72,000 Chinese-Americans and Chinese immigrants (Zhou 1993). As compared with the Flushing Chinatown, this Chinese community still remains a self-contained ethnic enclave where minimal interaction with other ethnic communities occurs.

The Flushing Chinatown is a new Chinese community which emerged two decades ago in the center of the old Dutch colony established around 1628. The Flushing Chinatown began to take shape in the late 1960s when immigrants from Taiwan and Hong Kong came to the United States in large numbers after the removal of the 1924 national origin provision by the new Immigration Act of 1965 (Kwong 1987: 21). In the past ten years, the Flushing Chinatown has experienced a rapid development by expanding more than ten blocks from Northern Boulevard to Elder Street along Main Street and Kissena Boulevard. In the area there are three dozen Chinese restaurants, ten fish markets, numerous grocery stores and gift shops. The presence of a large number of banks in this area is a manifestation of the prosperous businesses operating there. They include branches of Citibank, Chemical Bank, Anchor Bank, Great Eastern Bank, Asian Bank, and AmerAsia Bank; the last three are owned by Chinese-Americans. Because Chinese speakers constitute the majority of the customers, each bank employs a considerable number of Chinese-Americans who speak, in addition to English, either or both of the two Chinese dialects – Mandarin and Cantonese. The proportion of Chinese employees in the non-Chinese banks range from a third to two-thirds, while in the Chinese-owned banks the Chinese-Americans comprise more than 90 percent. Regardless of their English ability and dialect backgrounds, new Chinese immigrants feel more comfortable and secure communicating with Chinese bankers in Chinese. This creates an incentive for Chinese-owned banks, which might otherwise have difficulty competing, to locate here. Flushing attracts new Asian immigrants for whom a convenient living is a priority. The 1990 Census shows that the Chinese population in Queens reached 86,000.

The third New York Chinatown began to emerge ten years ago at 8th Avenue near Brooklyn's Sunset Park, a formerly run-down Scandinavian neighborhood (Zhou 1993). Cantonese-speaking Chinese moved into the area between 50th Street and 61st Street, opening grocery stores and restaurants. This Chinese community currently has twenty Chinese restaurants, twelve grocery stores, ten super markets, five bakeries, five real estate offices and two banks. Although the real estate market has dropped to the lowest point in recent memory, prices of houses in the Brooklyn Chinatown keep rising steadily because the Chinese population continues to expand, bringing about enormous investment in the area.

4. Chinese languages and dialects

The word Chinese has been used to denote either the people of China or the language used by this group of people. When it is used to refer to the latter, it often causes confusion as it is too general to account for the heterogeneous mixture of languages and dialects. At the macro level, Chinese may refer to the language used within the Chinese territory with boundaries that have been roughly established since the Tang Dynasty (618–914 A.D.). At the micro level, however, the English word Chinese is equivalent to the Chinese word *Hanyu* which refers to the language spoken by the Han majority. *Hanyu* differs from the other languages used in Chinese territories, such as *Mongolian*, *Zhuang*, *Tibetan* and *Uiguric* Turkish. Some non-Chinese speakers, *Zhuang* speakers for example, often claim that their language is a dialect of Chinese, while a *Tibetan* or an *Uigur* is more likely to differentiate their language from the Chinese language.

4.1. Languages in the People's Republic of China and Taiwan

There are three major language families which encompass languages and dialects used in China as mother tongues: *Malayo-Polynesian*, *Ural-Altaic* and *Sino-Tibetan*.

Malayo-Polynesian includes a large number of languages and dialects in the Pacific area (Muller 1964). About 30,000 Taiwan aborigines speak languages belonging to this language family. *Paiwanic*, *Atayalic* and *Tsouic* are the principal sub-families of Taiwan Polynesian.[1]

Ural-Altaic includes languages and dialects spoken by people in North and Northeast China and is further divided into three subgroups: *Mongolic*, *Turkic* and *Tungusic* (Muller 1964; Miller 1980).

Finally, the *Sino-Tibetan* family embraces languages spreading over a large expanse of China proper, Southeast Asia and the Tibetan Plateau. It includes *Burmese-Tibetan*, *Thai,*[2] *Miao-Yao*,[3] and *Chinese* (Chao 1976; Summerfield 1991).

Chinese is spoken by about 1.1 billion people, who constitute 93 percent of the total population in the People's Republic of China. It is the language used by the most numerous population in the world. Chinese is used here in its narrow sense to denote Chinese dialects which have shared a common written system 漢字 *Hanzi* 'Han characters'. Chinese has a number of mutually-unintelligible variations, called 方言 *fangyan* 'dialect' in Chinese, which share the same written system. They are *Mandarin* (北方方言), *Wu* (吳方言), *Cantonese* (廣東話), *Min* (閩方言), and *Hakka* (客家話). The classification of the Chinese dialects is based chiefly on phonology, and, to the lesser extent, on lexicon and syntax. A text read by a Cantonese speaker is unintelligible to speakers of Mandarin, Min, Wu and Hakka, and vice versa. The Mandarin speaking population is estimated to reach 850 million, twice as large as the English speaking population in the world (DeFrancis 1984). Wu has the second biggest speaking population with 94 million. Cantonese is spoken by about 60 million. Min and Hakka have about 62 million and 41 million speakers respectively.[4]

4.2. Written Chinese

The Chinese written language was first developed based on the principle that each 字 *zi* (character) was used as a pictograph divorced from sound. Each 字 *zi* (character) carries a distinct meaning and one of the designated tones. The Chinese spelling system is simple: a spelled sound may be shared by several Chinese characters that are different in meaning. To distinguish them phonologically, a tonal system is added to the phonic system. In Chinese, a tone is semantically meaningful when assigned to a sound; this tonal meaning could be roughly analogous to the differentiation of English words 'present and pre'sent which mean "gift" and "give" respectively partially due to the different tonal values.

5. Chinese dialects in New York City

Since the gold rush in California, Cantonese has been the dominant dialect used by the Chinese-American population. The dominance of Cantonese was a direct outcome of the rather homogeneous linguistic background of the early Chinese immigrants. In order to communicate, speakers of other dialects within the Chinese community had to learn Cantonese.

For the past three decades, linguistic heterogeneity has increasingly become an obvious feature of the Chinese communities in New York City as a result of the influx of new immigrants from Taiwan and China's non-Cantonese speaking regions. Nearly all major Chinese dialects are spoken among Chinese in New York City, but the most commonly heard dialects are Mandarin and Cantonese. The other three Chinese dialects, Min, Hakka and Wu, are rarely heard on the street and are used chiefly among family members and hometown friends.

5.1. Mandarin

Mandarin speakers in New York City are those who are either immigrants from the Mandarin-speaking regions in the People's Republic of China and Taiwan, or their offspring born in the United States. These Mandarin speakers have little difficulty in understanding each other. *Taiwan Guoyu* and *Mainland Putonghua*, the two varieties of Northern Mandarin, are the most commonly spoken Mandarin in Chinese communities. It is rapidly becoming the *lingua franca* in Chinatown.

5.2. Cantonese

Cantonese is spoken by Chinese from Hong Kong, Singapore, Malaysia, Vietnam and two regions in the People's Republic of China – Guangdong Province and the Guangxi Autonomous Region. It is also the first language of many American-born Chinese. Spoken by more than 90 percent of the early Chinese immigrants, Cantonese was once the most popular Chinese dialect in Chinese communities in the United States. In recent years, its dominance in Chinese communities has been challenged by Mandarin.

5.3. Min

Speakers of Min as a *first* dialect (that is, language acquired first) constitute the biggest Chinese dialect group in New York City (36.6% in our survey which appears in section 6). Min is spoken by people who come from Taiwan and Fujian Province in East China. Based on both intelligibility and geographical location, Min is divided into *Minnan* 'Southern Min' and *Minbei* 'Northern Min'. In New York City, people commonly call *Minbei* by the name of *Fuzhouhua*, meaning 'Speech of Fuzhou City'. *Taiwanhua* (Taiwan Speech) is a direct descendant of Minnan.

5.4. *Wu (Shanghainese)*

The term *Shanghaihua* 'Shanghainese', a subgroup of Wu, is a more popular term used among Chinese-Americans when they refer to Wu. Wu speakers were originally from Zhejiang Province and Shanghai City.

5.5. *Hakka*

Hakka speakers constitute a small proportion of the Chinese-American population in New York City, only one percent of the Chinatown population in our survey. They are either first generation or descendants of immigrants who came from Fujian, Jiangxi, Hunan, Guangxi and Guangdong Provinces in Southern China, Sichuan Province in Midwest China, and Taiwan.

6. *A survey of Chinese dialect distribution in New York*

The U. S. census has never given a discerning account of dialect distribution among the Chinese speaking population in New York City. To estimate dialect distribution among the Chinese population, between December 1993 to March 1994 we drew a sample of 200 employed informants in the Manhattan Chinatown and the Flushing Chinatown.[5] The sample constitutes about 0.2 percent of the total and about 0.4 percent of the employed Chinese-Americans in these two communities. Of the 200 informants, 122 were from the Manhattan Chinatown and 78 were living in the Flushing Chinatown. This survey is based on the *first spoken dialect* of the informants regardless of their second or third dialects. The sample was taken from the two Chinatowns in New York City, and the findings are included to reflect the linguistic conditions specific to New York City, as well as to similar communities where the Chinese population is concentrated.

Table 1
First spoken Chinese dialects in New York Chinatowns

	Unskilled worker N	Skilled worker N	Professional N	Total Pop. N	%
Mandarin	5	6	10	21	10.4
T. Guoyu[a]	2	2	3	7	3.5
Putonghua	3	4	7	14	6.9
Min	62	4	8	74	36.6
Minnan[b]	9	3	6	18	8.9
Xiamenhua	5	0	3	8	4
Taiwanhua[c]	4	3	3	10	5
Minbei	53	1	2	56	27.7
Cantonese	48	9	5	62	31.7
Wu	25	6	10	41	20.3
Hakka	2	0	0	2	1
Overall	142 (71%)	25 (12.5%)	33 (16.5%)	200 (100%)	

[a] *T. Guoyu* stands for Taiwan Guoyu, and *Putonghua* for the standard Mandarin spoken in the People's Republic of China.

[b] *Minnan* (Southern Min) consists of *Xiamenhua* spoken in southern Fujian Province and *Taiwanhua* spoken in Taiwan. *Minbei* (Northern Min) is spoken by people from the northern Fujian Province.

[c] In this table, informants from Taiwan are divided into *Taiwan Guoyu* and *Taiwanhua* subgroups. The former are commonly referred as *Waishengren* (emigrants from the mainland) whose family came to Taiwan after the 1940s. The latter refers to those from a native Taiwanhua family.

Since the enactment of the Immigration and Nationality Act of 1965, there has been a rapid increase of non-Cantonese speakers in the United States. This group has altered the demographic composition of the Chinese population in New York City. Hence, the Chinatowns here are no longer dominated by Cantonese speakers, as has been the case for more than a century.

Table 1 shows that of all Chinese dialects – Min and Cantonese were spoken as *first dialect* by the largest number of people (36.6% and 31.7% respectively). Wu, Mandarin, and Hakka make up 20.3 percent, 10.4 percent and 1 percent respectively.

Min speakers consist of people of two migration sources: Taiwanese immigrants who came to the United States in the 1960s and after, and people from China's Fujian Province who came during the 1980s and 1990s. The latter group includes a considerable number of illegal immigrants who find New York's Chinatowns alluring places where they can make a living. Thus, it is estimated that the proportion of Min speakers in New York City is higher than elsewhere in the United States. Since they are dialects of low prestige in their home country, Min and Hakka are rarely learned by other dialect speakers. Nearly all Min and Hakka speakers, before coming to the United States, had already acquired near-native proficiency in Mandarin. Some can even speak Cantonese and Wu (Shanghainese).

Speakers of each Chinese dialect group are distributed among a variety of trades. We used three occupational categories in Table 1 and Table 2: unskilled worker, skilled worker, and professional. Unskilled workers include restaurant help, garment factory workers, and grocery store help; skilled workers include technicians, precision workers and office clerks; and professionals include managerial staff, medical practitioners and financiers. The figures in Table 1 show that the overall distribution of the sample in the three occupational categories is 71 percent for unskilled workers; 12.5 percent for skilled workers; and 16.5 percent for professionals. However, the occupational distribution in each dialect group or subgroup differs from the other to varying degrees. Interestingly, these differences indicate that there is a link between occupational stratification and dialect group.

As shown in Table 2, the Mandarin group has the highest percentage of professionals (47.6%), and the lowest proportion of unskilled workers (23.8%), while the Min group has the highest proportion of unskilled

Table 2
Occupational distribution within Chinese dialect groups*

	Unskilled worker	Skilled worker	Professional	SUM
	%	%	%	%
Mandarin	23.8	28.6	47.6	100
T. Guoyu	28.6	28.6	42.8	100
Putonghua	21.4	28.6	50	100
Min	83.8	5.4	10.8	100
Minnan	50	16.7	33.3	100
Xiamenhua	62.5	0	37.5	100
Taiwanhua	40	30	30	100
Minbei	94.6	1.7	3.7	100
Cantonese	77.4	14.5	8.1	100
Wu	61	14.6	24.4	100

* The Hakka group was excluded from this table because there were only two in our sample. For actual numbers refer to Table 1.

workers (83.8%). The Cantonese group ranks last in percentage of professionals (8.1%), and second in unskilled workers (77.4%); and the Wu group ranks second in percentage of professionals (24.4%) and third in unskilled workers (61%).

Many factors, such as education, professional attainment, length of stay in the U. S., economic background, and English proficiency affect the occupational status of the Chinese population. In our sample, unskilled employment in the Chinatowns is associated with low education and rural background while professional status correlates with higher degrees earned and professional training. But this generalization has exceptions. Many individuals who arrived with professional backgrounds and higher education are currently working as manual workers. They are mostly newcomers who have limited English proficiency and little knowledge of mainstream U. S. culture.

It is worth noting that, underlying this first dialect phenomenon, there is a rather complicated picture of Chinese bidialectism and multidialectism. With the exception of native Mandarin speakers who tend to be reluctant to learn other low prestige dialects, most other Chinese can speak, in addition to their first dialect, Mandarin, and to a lesser extent, Cantonese or Wu (Shanghainese). The widespread proficiency in Mandarin of the population has become a threat to the status of Cantonese as a *lingua franca*. Mandarin is well on its way to replacing Cantonese.

What has happened in New York's Chinatowns demonstrates that the selection of a shared code by a linguistically diverse community is not only linked to the number of speakers of a given code as the first dialect, but also to the multilingual background of the community. As compared with either Min or Cantonese, Mandarin has a rather small population of native speakers (10.4 percent in our survey), but as a second dialect, it has the greatest number of speakers who readily use it to communicate with others in the Chinese communities.

The importance of Mandarin in the United States Chinese community is a result of language policy and attitudes in the People's Republic of China and Taiwan, as well as support rendered by Chinese publications and broadcasts in the United States, as we will see later. Since Mandarin was decreed the national language in China in the 1910s, no other Chinese dialect has received as much support. Compulsory education in Mandarin has successfully turned millions of non-Mandarin speakers in both the People's Republic of China and Taiwan into Mandarin-speaking bilinguals. Whereas people from Mandarin-speaking provinces in the People's Republic of China can rarely speak Cantonese, or any of the other Chinese dialects, most new immigrants from areas of minor Chinese dialects already possessed proficiency in Mandarin before coming to the United States. Min and Cantonese have never had as high a status as Mandarin has, although recent economic achievements in regions of these dialects – Taiwan, Hong Kong, and China's Guangdong Province – have boosted their popularity.

It should be pointed out that Min is a dialect that is rarely learned by speakers of any other Chinese dialects. Although it has native speakers making up a third of the Chinese population in the Chinatowns, the highest of all, Min does not seem to have a chance to rise as the *lingua franca* because there are no Min speakers from other dialect groups.

7. Language interaction and language interference

In the Chinese community of New York City, speakers of different Chinese dialects are in constant contact through either Chinese or English. As mentioned previously, Chinese dialects are mutually unintelligible. Different dialect speakers choose either Mandarin or Cantonese to communicate with other Chinese speakers. Except for Hong Kong Cantonese immigrants, those speaking dialects other than Mandarin are also speakers of Mandarin which was learned as a second dialect through schooling in Taiwan, the People's Republic of China and Singapore.

The Chinese communities of New York City are experiencing a shift in *lingua franca* from Cantonese to Mandarin. Both are being used and Chinese speakers are faced with choosing the right code to communicate with another whose dialect he or she does not know. In the course of verbal interaction, code-selecting and code-switching are frequent among the Chinese.

Certain code-selecting strategies are employed by Chinese speakers to avoid embarrassment and breakdown of communication when they initiate talk with other Chinese speakers. The linguistic background of a Chinese community is important for determining the code used for a particular occasion. An English-Chinese bilingual who speaks Mandarin and Cantonese tends to use Cantonese in the Manhattan Chinatown and in the Brooklyn Chinese community, while using Mandarin in the Flushing Chinatown. However, beyond the boundary of the Chinese community, English is preferred to address other unknown Asians who could be either Chinese, Korean, Vietnamese or Japanese. Because few native Mandarin speakers speak another Chinese dialect, when a Mandarin-English bilingual is in Chinatown, he or she usually tries Mandarin on strangers, hoping that the interlocutor can speak Mandarin. If the interlocutor is a Cantonese speaker who cannot speak Mandarin, the former will usually switch to English.

Chinese monolinguals of a less prestigious dialect, mostly members of older generations, have limited linguistic choices. They usually stay within a small social circle in which their native dialect is spoken. One predictable result of this linguistic inability is insularity from speakers of other languages and dialects, as reported by Lum (1991) in his study of a monolingual family from Hong Kong.

For most Chinese-Americans, English is considered to be necessary for upward mobility. English language schools in Chinatowns enroll a large number of new Chinese immigrants throughout the year. Unlike old timers, younger adults have little incentive to learn other Chinese dialects. For those who make their living in Chinese communities, Cantonese and Mandarin remain useful linguistic tools for employment in Chinese-owned businesses.

Unintelligibility among Chinese dialects results in limited linguistic influence from one to the other. Yet, loan words from Cantonese, and especially from Mandarin, are present in other dialects. For example, words of Cantonese origin such as 開心 *kaixin* 'happy' and 多謝 *duoxie* 'thanks' are used frequently by Mandarin speakers from both the People's Republic of China and Taiwan. Many more Mandarin words have found their way into Cantonese. In Cantonese, a Mandarin loan word may be used side-by-side with a Cantonese counterpart, or may replace a Cantonese word altogether. For example, Mandarin words 省會 *shenghui* 'provincial capital', 護士 *hushi* 'nurse', and 合同 *hetong* 'contract' are used interchangeably with words of Cantonese origin 省城 *sangsan* 'provincial capital', 看護 *honwu* 'nurse', and 合約 *hubyok* 'contract'. Other words such as 消息 *xiusat* 'news' and 請假 *qinga* 'ask for leave' are widely used in place of those of Cantonese origin.

A noticeable amount of linguistic influence has been found between the two polarized versions of Mandarin: *Mainland Putonghua* and *Taiwan Guoyu*. Being mutually intelligible to each other, one is easily influenced by the other through language contact.

Based on my study of ninety-three Mandarin speakers (forty-seven from the Taiwan Guoyu group and forty-six from the Mainland Putonghua group), linguistic interference among the two groups is apparent in most linguistic domains. Phonological interference is the most obvious of all. For example, through language contact in New York City, some Taiwan Guoyu speakers acquired Mainland Putonghua retroflexed sounds /zh/, /ch/, /sh/ which are lacking in Taiwan Guoyu. On the other hand, some Mainland Putonghua speakers imitate Taiwan Guoyu by either reducing the frequency of the retroflexed or substituting them with alveolar sounds /dz/, /ts/ and /s/ (Pan 1994).

Language change could be motivated by various reasons. Socio-psychological factors may contribute significantly to the linguistic interference among the speakers of different Chinese dialects. Based on Giles' *accommodation theory*, people may intentionally draw close to others by shifting their language to their interlocutors' language which could be either a high vernacular or a low vernacular. Thus upward convergence and downward convergence may occur in the process of accommodation (Giles 1977).

The general speaker of Taiwan Guoyu only uses 你 *ni* to denote the second person singular 'you', while Mainland Putonghua has both the generic *ni* and honorific 您 *nin*. When using the honorific *nin* 'you', a Taiwan Guoyu speaker is making an effort to draw closer to a Putonghua listener. For Putonghua speakers, the use of Taiwan Guoyu lexical items 漢字 *S(h)uiz(h)un* 'standard', 錄音帶 *luyindai* 'video-tape' and 垃圾 *lese* 'garbage' indicates accommodation to Taiwan Guoyu speakers.

For some Mandarin speakers, lexical items from the two inventories are used interchangeably in accordance with changes of interlocutors, settings, and time. It is common to hear a speaker utter Taiwan Guoyu 垃圾 *lese* 'garbage' and 和 *han* 'and' to Taiwan Guoyu listeners, but the same speaker shifts to Putonghua 垃圾 *laji* 'garbage' and 和 *he* 'and' in the presence of Putonghua listeners. By doing so, the speaker initiates an intimate relationship with the interlocutors.

8. *Institutional support*

Although a minority language in the United States with a small population, Chinese is considered to have rather strong institutional support from various sources (Fishman et al. 1985: 15). These resources help foster linguistic and cultural awareness and maintenance among the Chinese-American population, and explain partially its ethnolinguistic vitality, which refers to what makes a group likely to behave as a "distinctive and active collective entity in intergroup situations" (Giles 1977: 307–324).

8.1. *Chinese publications*

Chinese publications in the United States are a vigorous source of language support. Because one-third of Chinese-Americans know little or no English, these publications have become indispensable to keep this monolingual population informed of events of the world. Like Chinese publications elsewhere in the world, articles in these Chinese publications follow the Mandarin style and syntax, rather than those of Cantonese or any other Chinese dialects. This rather biased linguistic choice has resulted from the New Cultural Movement of the 1910s, aimed at modernizing the Chinese language and culture. Prior to the Movement, Chinese was written in 文言文 *Wenyanwen*, a classical style with little similarity to any of the Chinese dialects.

In 1982, there were about forty-two Chinese newspapers and journals published daily or periodically in the United States (Fishman et al. 1985: 88). According to our recent survey[6], there are twenty-four Chinese language newspapers printed and sold in New York City, of which ten are published daily, twelve weekly, one biweekly, and one monthly.

Table 3
Chinese newspapers in New York City

		Frequency	Founded	Circulation*
World Journal	世界日報	daily	1967	75,000
Sing Tao Daily	星島日報	daily	1966	60,000
Sing Pao Daily News	成報	daily	1966	50,000
International Daily News	國際日報	daily	1982	40,000
The United Journal	聯合日報	daily	1951	30,000
The China Press	僑報	daily	1990	20,000
Overseas Chinese Economics Journal	信報	daily	1986	7,000
Ta-Kung-Pao	大公報	daily	1979	5,000
Wen Wei Po	文匯報	daily	1986	3,000
People's Daily	人民日報	daily	**	**
Amerasia News	紐約華報	weekly	1992	30,000
Real Estate & Business Times	地產工商時報	weekly	1989	30,000
Chinese Community News	華埠新聞	weekly	1989	**
Asian American Times	亞美時報	weekly	1986	20,000
China Times Weekly	中國時報周刊	weekly	**	20,000
Neo Asian American Times	新亞時報	weekly	1991	18,000
Asian Entertainment Weekly	歌影視周刊	weekly	1985	15,000
Chinese Commercial Journal	美華工商報	weekly	**	14,000
China Times Weekly News	新聞娛樂周刊	weekly	1980	13,000
China Journal, New York	紐約新聞報	weekly	1988	8,000
New York Chinese Business	紐約商報	weekly	1994	8,000
Pacific Journal	太平洋時報	weekly	1987	2,000
New Chinese Times	新天地	biweekly	1991	10,000
Herald	號角	monthly	1988	25,000

* These numbers were provided by publishers through telephone interview. The actual numbers may vary considerably.

** Data are not available.

The World Journal, *The China Press*, *Sing Tao Daily*, *The United Journal*, *People's Daily*, and *Sing Pao Daily News* have become the most influential daily papers which affect, to a certain extent, everyday life of the Chinese-American population. This lucrative business generates sizable revenue from advertisements and subscriptions. With the exception of *The World Journal* which is generally believed to be subsidized by the Taiwan Government, and *The China Press* and *People's Daily* which are funded by the People's Republic of China, these newspapers can all support themselves and claim to be politically unbiased towards Mainland China and Taiwan.

What makes these papers special is the sections that have detail coverage of news and events happening in Taiwan, the People's Republic of China, Hong Kong, and Singapore. In the entertainment section, pictures and anecdotes of Hong Kong and Taiwan celebrities dominate entire columns. The business sections closely trace the Taiwan and Hong Kong stock markets and record daily prices of all major stocks in these markets. The Chinese newspapers enrich the intellectual and social life of Chinese-Americans and facilitate Chinese business transactions.

In addition, there are about fifty-six Chinese periodicals sold on newsstands in New York Chinatowns. Except for nine published in New York, most are published in Hong Kong (about 30), Taiwan (10) and the People's Republic of China (7). These periodicals cover cooking, comics, fashion, health, sports, politics, literature and entertainment. They are available in the waiting areas of employment agencies, offices, clinics, restaurants, law firms, and real estate offices in Chinatowns. A more comprehensive array of periodicals from Taiwan and the People's Republic of China could be found in World Book Store and Orient Book Store in the Manhattan Chinatown.

Chinese publications are an indispensable source of information and entertainment for literate Chinese immigrants who remain deeply-rooted in Chinese culture and tradition. They are a significant factor in popularizing Mandarin among the Chinese-American population.

8.2. Chinese radio and television broadcasts in New York City

Two Chinese dialects, Mandarin and Cantonese, are used in radio and television programs targeted for Chinese audiences, while the other dialects stand virtually no chance of being on the air. There are currently four radio stations broadcasting round-the-clock: *Chung Wah Commercial Broadcasting*, *Sino Radio Broadcasts Corporation*, *Chinese American Voice*, and *China Radio Network*. Listeners must pay a one-time fee from $50 to $200 for a special radio receiver for each of the broadcasts.

No medium nowadays has a greater impact on the daily life of Chinese-Americans than television. In New York City alone, there are six television companies featuring Chinese programs with varied length of broadcasting time.

Table 4
Chinese radio and television broadcasts in New York City

		Hours	Founded	Language	Channel
RADIO					
Chinese American Voice	僑聲電台	24/day	1986	Mandarin	
Chung Wah Commercial-Broadcasting	中華商台	24/day	1968	Cantonese	
Sino Radio Broadcasting	華語廣播	24/day	1976	Cantonese	
Chinese Radio Network	中國廣播網	24/day	1992	Mandarin	
TELEVISION					
Sino Vision	中國中文電視	19/week	1991	Mandarin/Cantonese	26; 31
North American Satellite TV	北美衛星電視	12/week	1987	Cantonese/Mandarin	35; 69
Overseas TV Network	海外電視	5/week	1975	Mandarin/Cantonese	35
World Television	世界電視	2/week	1986	Mandarin	31
United Chinese TV	聯合華語電視	2/week	1982	Mandarin	25
Hong Shen Broadcasting	宏聲	2/week	1984	Mandarin	26; 31

Programs on these TV stations include world news, domestic news, and news of Taiwan, the People's Republic of China and Hong Kong, as well as business news, movies and shows. More than half of the broadcast time is filled with programs emanating from Hong Kong, Taiwan or the People's Republic of China, while the remainder are produced in the United States.

8.3. Chinese language schools and Chinese-English bilingual education

The earliest Chinese language schools began in 1886 in San Francisco to help Cantonese speakers learn written Chinese. In those schools, students were trained to read and write classical Chinese. Cantonese was the only dialect of instruction as the overwhelming majority of the students were from Cantonese speaking areas of China. Because they were excluded from mainstream U. S. society, the Chinese ran these schools as an act of patriotism toward China where they planned to return sooner or later (Wong 1988: 213). This tradition continues in Chinese communities in the United States although patriotism is no longer a motivation.

Contemporary Chinese language schools operate as a supplement to regular day schools during after school hours and weekends. Either Mandarin or Cantonese is used in classroom instruction depending on the needs of students. Classical Chinese is no longer taught. These Chinese schools satisfy the needs of Chinese parents for knowledge of the Chinese culture and language, rather than that of their children.

Currently, there are about twenty Chinese language schools in New York City. *The Chinese Overseas School of New York*, *The New York Ming Yuan Chinese School*, *The Zhishan School*, and *The Brooklyn Chinese Christian Church School* are the largest. More than 1,000 students are enrolled in Chinese, computer training, art, and Kung Fu classes at the first two. *The Zhishan School*, located in Elmhurst and Flushing, has an enrollment of a few hundred students, the number varying from season to season. These schools offer after-school classes.

Under regulations of New York State, public bilingual programs in Chinese and English are provided for school-age Chinese immigrants. These programs are aimed at the students whose English language deficiency prevents them from participating in the learning process in regular classes. In 1992–1993, 6,154 students of Chinese descent, about 44 percent of the total 14,069 LEP (Limited English Proficient) Chinese students were in bilingual education programs, and about 300 Chinese bilingual teachers were involved in teaching them (*Facts and Figures 1992–1993*, Published by New York City Public Schools, Division of Bilingual Education). Unlike Chinese language schools, these bilingual programs are designed to expedite the adaptation of Chinese immigrant children to the English language and U. S. culture.

8.4. Religious groups

Although houses of worship are not as important in the language maintenance of the Chinese community as they are in other ethnolinguistic communities, they do play a role. According to Fishman et al. (1985: 112–113), there were 353 Chinese churches and twenty-two Asian temples throughout the United States in 1985.

In New York City alone, there are about one hundred Chinese Christian churches, of which seventy-two are listed in the telephone directory, as well as seventeen Buddhist and Taoist temples. Each of the Chinese churches has members numbering from fifty to over one thousand. While language maintenance is not their primary objective, the functioning of these religious units depends, to a large extent, on their Chinese speaking population. Most of these churches use either Cantonese or Mandarin in their activities. A few employ both English and Chinese in accordance with the multilingual and multicultural nature of the congregation. There is a growing tendency to offer more bilingual services.

9. Conclusion

The Chinese communities in New York City experienced a long history of linguistic homogeneity, during which Cantonese remained unchallenged as the *lingua franca* for the Chinese population. Because of the impossibility of integration into mainstream U. S. society, the early Chinese never attempted to give up their cultural and language heritage.

This situation has been altered as a result of the recent changes in the composition of the Chinese-Americans, as well as the shift in the general attitudes towards minorities in the United States. For the past three decades, waves of Chinese immigrants of diverse dialectal background have arrived in the United States, bringing about more linguistic heterogeneity to the Chinatowns. Unlike the Chinese old-timers, new Chinese immigrants, as a whole, have a stronger demand for social justice and are more ready to compete in the larger society. For the educated newcomers and U. S.-born Chinese, English appears to be more useful than Chinese. The time-honored tradition of Chinese language maintenance is more threatened today.

Yet, the U. S. Chinese communities of today keep frequent contacts with Chinese-speaking regions and countries in the world, including Taiwan, Singapore, Hong Kong, and the People's Republic of China. The rapid development of science and technology has made Chinese media in those countries easily accessible. This international dynamics for language maintenance counterbalances those factors undermining Chinese language maintenance in today's Chinatowns.

The existence of institutional support for the Chinese language in New York City seems to offer a rather hopeful prospect for language maintenance. Chinese publications and Chinese broadcasts have contributed most significantly. It is worth noting that the linguistic role played by these institutions is interestingly in conformity with the language policies carried out in the Chinese-speaking countries, where Mandarin has been chosen as the national standard and given the greatest amount of attention. In the Chinese communities in New York City, except Mandarin and Cantonese, other Chinese dialects hardly benefit from these Chinese institutions. It is thus predictable that, because of the enormous support given to Mandarin, its status as the *lingua franca* will be further strengthened in New York's Chinese communities. It remains to be seen whether Mandarin, competing for the first time with English in the Chinese community, will be intergenerationally transmitted with more success than was Cantonese in the past.

It has been argued that the strength of Chinese language maintenance remains more "a function of continued immigration than an intergenerational transmission of the language" (Wong 1988: 217). With continuous influx of Chinese immigrants, Chinatown's symbol as an enclave of foreign culture still prevails. Conceivably, the efforts of Chinese language maintenance depend largely on these newcomers: Chinese institutions provide them services; Chinese languages schools enroll their children; publications rely on their readership; and Chinese businesses need their patronage. Although most U. S.-born Chinese inevitably move out, the Chinese population in New York's Chinese communities, as a whole, still possesses a high level of language vitality to resist full shift to English.

Notes

* The author wishes to thank Edward Bendix for his careful reading of this paper.

1. *Paiwanic* has the largest speaking population in the Taiwan's southeastern mountain regions, which is estimated to reach 20,000; *Atayalic* has about 8,000 speakers living in the northeastern mountains; and *Tsouic* is spoken by a few thousand people. In fact, many of the languages of the Taiwan aborigines have already become extinct (Kubler 1981: 20). With the popularization of *Guoyu* (see note 4) and compulsory education in Chinese, the new generation of Taiwan aboriginals have become bilingual and the number of Polynesian speakers is on the decline.
2. *Zhuang*, a subbranch of *Thai*, remains the second biggest language in the People's Republic of China. It has never been developed into a full-fledged system of writing and literature by its speakers, who instead learn and speak Chinese, the more prestigious language in the country.
3. *Miao-Yao* is spoken by about three million Miao people and one million Yao people who inhabit areas in the Southern Provinces of Hunan, Guangxi, Guangdong, Guizhou and Yunnan Province (Summerfield 1991; DeFrancis 1984). In addition, there are more than twenty-five nationalities in Yunnan and Guizhou Province who speak dialects belonging to either *Thai*, *Miao-Yao* or *Tibetan-Burmese*. A great proportion of *Thai* and *Miao-Yao* speakers have lived in mountainous regions where the unfavorable environment and harsh living conditions have never given them the luxury of developing their written languages.

4. *A. Mandarin* has three subgroups: *Northern Mandarin* (which is spoken in the Yellow River Basin and Northeast China), *Southern Mandarin* (which is spoken in the three southern provinces of the People's Republic of China: Jiangsu, Anhui and Jiangxi) and *Southwestern Mandarin* (which is spoken in the middle and upper Yangtze River basin, including the provinces of Sichuan, Guizhou, Guangxi, Yunnan, Hunan and Hubei). These subgroups are considered mutually intelligible as they share the same syntax structure, and a large part of their vocabulary remains identical. Within these Mandarin subgroups, linguistic differences remain mostly in deviation of tones and lexical items. However the English term *Mandarin*, an English translation of the Chinese word *Guanhua* (official language), usually refers to Northern Mandarin to which both *Mainland Putonghua* and *Taiwan Guoyu* belong (Li & Thompson 1979). *Mainland Putonghua* and *Taiwan Guoyu* were both decreed standard Mandarin based on the vernacular spoken by people in the vicinity of Beijing. The term *Guoyu* meaning 'National Language' was first used in the 1910s when the National Language Unification Movement swept throughout China (Chao 1968: 97–99). In the 1950s, the term *Putonghua* was coined by the newly-established Communist government. *Putonghua*, meaning 'Common Speech', has since replaced *Guoyu* on the Mainland, though this politically-oriented move hardly conceals the fact that *Putonghua* refers to the same linguistic entity as *Guoyu* used to.
The most deviant Mandarin is Southwestern Mandarin, which differs from the others chiefly in lexicon and phonology. A phonological feature of Southwestern Mandarin is the confusion of initial /l/ and /n/, that is, Southwestern Mandarin has two variants [l] and [n] for the initial nasal /n/. In Southwestern Mandarin, its second, third and fourth tone sound like the third (the first half), the fourth and the second tone respectively in Northern Mandarin.
Beijing Putonghua speakers clearly distinguish retroflexed /zh/, /ch/, /sh/ and /r/ from alveolar /dz/, /ts/ and/ s/. Influenced by Min which is the mother tongue of more than 80 percent of the Taiwanese (Kubler 1982), Taiwan Guoyu does not have retroflexed sounds, and the merging of /n/ and /ŋ/ is also common among its speakers.

B. Min has consonantal endings and nasal vowels which are lacking in most Chinese dialects. Min's consonantal system is comparatively simple as many sounds of other Chinese dialects are absent, such as /f/, /j/, /q/ and /x/, while its rich nasal sounds, /ã/, /ĩ/, /ũ/, /õ/ and /ẽ/, distinguish it from other dialects.

C. Cantonese is one of the three Chinese dialects which preserve the ancient consonantal endings of /p/, /t/, /k/ and /m/. A comparison of Cantonese and Mandarin indicates that, in addition to drastic differences in phonetics and vocabulary, Cantonese word order differs from that of Mandarin in many ways. In Mandarin, a direct object always follows an indirect object, while Cantonese commonly has a direct object followed by an indirect object. Certain adverbs in Mandarin, resultative adverbs for example, appear to come after the verb, but most other adverbs precede the verb, e. g. *ni xian zou* 'you first go'. However, Cantonese prefers the post-verbal position for the above adverb: *nei hang xin* 'you go first'. Cantonese can use "yau" (have) as an auxiliary preceding a verb, but Mandarin, except *Taiwan Guoyu*, does not have the auxiliary use of "yau" (have). To express the meaning "have you read the book?" Cantonese has *nei yau mou dok sy*? 'you have not read the book?', while Mandarin has *ni du le shu ma*? 'you read the book?'

D. The most prominent characteristic of *Wu* is its preservation of the ancient Chinese tripartite division of initial stops: voiceless unaspirated, voiceless aspirated, and voiced unaspirated like /b/, /d/, /g/, /v/ and /z/ (Chao 1976). Acoustically, Wu vowels are shorter than those in other dialects. A Wu speaker is likely to shorten a diphthong or substitute it with a monophthong when they speak Mandarin.

E. *Most Hakka* dialects keep the distinction of three nasal endings /m, n, ŋ/, while half the Chinese dialects do not have the /m/ ending. Another phonological feature of Hakka is the devoicing of all the ancient Chinese voiced obstruents. As a result, all obstruents become voiceless aspirated consonants in the dialect (Li & Thompson 1979; Hashimoto 1992).

5. Judgement sampling was employed to get data for the survey. The sample was constructed based on occupational distributions of the Chinese population provided by the 1990 Census. Liya Wang, a graduate student at the City College of New York, contributed significantly to the data collection for this survey.
6. This survey was undertaken from December 1993 to February 1994 in cooperative efforts with Hongbiao Zhao, a graduate student at the City College of New York. It covers subjects of Chinese newspapers, periodicals, and Chinese radio and television broadcasting.

References

Chao, Yuen Ren
1968 *Language and Symbolic system.* Cambridge: Cambridge University Press.
1976 *Aspect of Chinese sociolinguistics.* Stanford: Stanford University Press.

Chen, Jack
1980 *The Chinese of America.* San Francisco: Harper and Row Publishers.

DeFrancis, John
1984 *The Chinese language, fact and fantasy.* University of Hawaii Press: Honolulu.

Fishman, Joshua, A. – Michael Gertner – Esther Lowy
1985 *Ethnicity in action, the community resources of ethnic languages in the United States.* Binghamtom: Bilingual Press.

Giles, Howard
1977 *Language, ethnicity and intergroup relations.* New York: Academic Press.

Hashimoto, Mantaro J.
1992 "Hakka in Wellentheotie Perspective", *Journal of Chinese Linguistics* 20–21: 1–49.

Kraly, Ellen P.
1987 "U. S. immigrants and the immigrant populations of New York", in: Nancy Foner (ed.), *New Immigrants in New York.* New York: Columbia University Press.

Kubler, Cornelius C.
1981 The Development of Mandarin in Taiwan. [Ph. D. Dissertation, Cornell University.]

Kwong, Peter
1987 *The New Chinatown.* New York: The Noonday Press.

Li, Charles – Sandra Thompson
1979 "Chinese dialect variations and language reform", in: Timothy Shopen (ed.), *Languages and their Status.* Cambridge, Ma.: Winthrop Publishers 295–335.
[1987] [Reprinted Philadelphia: University of Pennsylvania Press]

Lum, Casey Man Kong
1991 "Communication and cultural insularity: The Chinese immigrant experience", *Critical Studies in Mass Communication*, 8: 91–101.
Marden, Charles – G. Meyer
1968 *Minorities in American society*. New York: American Book Company.
Miller, Roy Andrew
1980 *Origins of the Japanese language*. Seattle and London: University of Washington Press.
Muller, Siegfried H.
1964 *World's living languages*. New York: Frederick Ungar Publishing Co.
Pan, Shiwen
1994 A sociolinguistic study of Mainland Putonghua and Taiwan Guoyu in New York City. [Ph.D. Dissertation, CUNY Graduate School.]
Sandmeyer, Elmer C.
1973 *The Anti-Chinese movement in California*. Urbana: University of Illinois Press.
Summerfield, John
1991 *China*. New York: Random House Inc.
Wong, Sau-Ling Cynthia
1988 "The language situation of Chinese Americans", in: Sandra Lee McKay – Sau-ling Cynthia Wong (eds.), *Language diversity: Problem or resource?* New York: Newbury House Publishers.
Zhou, Yunzi
1993 "The Third Chinatown: A promising future", *World Journal Weekly*. No.492, Aug. 22, 1993.

The languages of India in New York*

Kamal K. Sridhar

1. Introduction

The Asian Indian immigrants in the U. S. are a group divided along several identities, e. g., regional (language); social (caste, occupation, income, etc.); religion (Hindu, Muslim, Christian, Buddhist, etc.). They come from a traditionally multilingual and pluricultural country. The 1981 census of India reported 107 mother tongues being spoken in India (Krishnamurti 1989). However, this figure is not reliable because in the 1961 census, 1,652 mother tongues were reported (Pattanayak 1971; Srivastava 1988). The figures vary for a number of reasons: a given language may be reported under as many as forty-seven different names reflecting the returnee's ethnic, professional, attitudinal and other affiliations; several varieties of the same language exist, some are mutually unintelligible, others are not. If only languages reported by more than 1,000 persons and excluding foreign mother tongues are counted, there are approximately 400 languages used in India. These belong to four different language families: Indo-Aryan, Dravidian, Sino-Tibetan, and Austro-Asiatic. Complicating the linguistic scene is the presence and use of more than 40 scripts, religious and caste dialects, diglossic variation (high and low varieties of the language), and code-mixed varieties (mixing of two languages, Sridhar 1989, ch. 1). Code-mixing is very common all over the country, and is significant for our purposes in discussing language maintenance among the members of this group, to be discussed later on in the chapter.

Historical reasons contributed to the linguistic reorganization of India, with 25 major states and other "union (federal) territories", most of which are identified by a distinct language being spoken by the majority of the people in the region. Apart from the dominant regional language, every region is inhabited by several types of minority language speakers, e. g., speakers of tribal languages, migrant language speakers, religious minorities, etc. The number of minority language speakers varies from one state to another, ranging between 5% in Kerala to 84.5% in Nagaland. The educational system also promotes multilingualism as is evidenced by the protection given to minority languages, and the active promotion of the 'Three Language Formula', according to which every school-going child learns to read and write in his *mother tongue* (or the regional language in the case of languages without scripts or literary traditions), *Hindi* (the official language of the country), and *English* (the associate official language of the country). In order to understand this community, it might be helpful at this point to identity the salient features of Asian Indian bilingualism (for more details, see Sridhar 1989). These include:

(a) the fluidity of language identity, leading to the under-reporting and variable reporting of the extent of bilingualism in the area (Khubchandani 1983);
(b) the high degree of societal bilingualism, not only in border areas and among the educated population, but also on a very widespread scale among the population in general;
(c) the widespread use of "mixed" language varieties;
(d) the phenomenon of linguistic convergence (i. e., the tendency for languages in contact to adopt one another's formal features, resulting in the formation of a South Asian "linguistic area" (Emeneau 1956; D'Souza 1987);
(e) the tendency on the part of minority language speakers to maintain their languages, despite a low level of literacy and inadequate formal language instruction.

As Pandit (1972) explains it, a Gujarati spice merchant settled in Bombay can simultaneously control five or six languages. Such a merchant will speak Gujarati in his family domain, Marathi in a vegetable market, Hindi with the milkman, Kacci and Konkani in trading circles, and even English on formal occasions. Such a person may be poorly rated in the area of explicit knowledge of linguistic rules of these languages, but in terms of verbal linguistic ability, he can easily be labelled a multilingual, fairly proficient in controlling different life situations with ease and skill. For this reason, in spite of mass illiteracy, a societal type of bilingualism/multilingualism (e. g., the case of the Gujarati spice merchant) has become the life blood of India's verbal repertoire. It is this type of bilingualism that has contributed to language maintenance rather than language shift.

Another distinctive feature of Indian bilingualism is its stability, i. e., speakers of Indian languages tend to maintain their languages over generations and centuries, even when they live away from the region where it is spoken (Agnihotri 1979; Bhatia 1981; CIIL 1994; Gambhir 1981; Ghuman 1994; Mesthrie 1992; Moag 1978; Mukherjee 1980; Rangila 1986; Satyanath 1982; Siegel 1987; to mention just a few). Although this claim has not gone unchallenged, especially with reference to the loss of some tribal and minority languages (Mohan 1989; Chakledar 1981; Ekka 1979; Mahapatra 1979; Srivastava 1988), there is enough evidence of long range maintenance to warrant a detailed study of this phenomenon. The migrant speech communities continue to speak their own language in the home domain. Through their mother tongues, they endeavor to maintain their ethnic identities. Since diversity in food habits, dress, rituals, and languages is expected, and both the migrant speech community and the host community agree on limited separation, this results in cultural pluralism. Thus, while the migrant speech community retains its native language as an effective device for ethnic separateness and survival, it may acquire the language of the host community as a job-select language. Such cases of partial shift rather than total assimilation are seen all over India (e. g., the Tamil-speaking Palghat Iyers settled in Malayalam-speaking Kerala (Subromoniam 1977); the Saurarashtri-speaking Gujaratis settled in Tamil-speaking Tamil Nadu (Sharma 1977); the 300+ year old Marathi community settled in Tamil Nadu (Sridhar, forthcoming); the Tamil speakers settled in Marathi-speaking Bombay (Ayyar – Murthy 1988); the Telugu-speaking merchants and other Andhra's from the neighboring Andhra Pradesh in Kannada-speaking Karnataka; the Bengalis settled in Hindi-speaking New Delhi (Mukherjee 1980); the Kannada speakers in Hindi-speaking New Delhi (Satyanath 1982); to mention just a few). Several explanations have been offered for this maintenance. In addition to "group internal" factors such as maintenance of social ties and kin relationships (a continuous link between the out-of-state community and the home-based community), Gumperz – Wilson (1971) have proposed "ethnic separateness of home life", that is, a strict separation between the public and private (intra-kin) spheres of activity, as the central variable. The crucial question, as Southworth – Apte (1974) rightly point out, is why "ethnic separateness" is so critical in South Asia as compared to other parts of the world. They also offer a partial answer by noting that the groups who have maintained their linguistic separateness are for the most part "rather small groups who could be said to have some particular reason for remaining separate", such as prestige (e. g., Brahmins), particular occupational identification (e. g., goldsmiths, tailors), or enforced separation (e. g., in the case of the so-called "untouchables").

2. *Asian Indians in the U. S.: A historical perspective*

A colonial diary from the year 1790 records the first arrival of an East Indian in North America, a man from Madras (South India) to Salem, Massachusetts. He had come to America with a colonial sea captain and with a desire to expand trade between New England, Britain, and South Asia (Helweg – Helweg 1990: 45–46). The numbers that followed him are not in any way substantial. Only six Asian Indians participated in Salem's Fourth of July celebrations in the year 1851. Most of the Asian Indians who came during this period were mostly merchants, who travelled to Chicago and San Francisco for trade purposes, but returned to India. A larger number of Asian Indians came to the U. S. through Vancouver, Canada. Hundreds of Asian Indians (mostly Sikhs, a religious group from the Punjab. The men keep their beards and grow long hair, tied in a bun, covered by a turban) were brought by the Canadian Pacific Railway Lines. They were followed by a substantial number of others. From Vancouver they spread south to the U. S., to Washington State, and to California. The first Asian Indians in the U. S., most of whom were farmers from the state of Punjab, probably never exceeded 6,000 during the period 1904–1923. They settled down in California, forming little communities in Yuba City. Due to their distinctive turbans, language, and food habits, they were noticeable. During the same period, a small group of educated Asian Indians also came to the United States. The increasing number of Asian Indians created a clamor among the local residents. Responding to this public clamor, the U. S. Supreme Court ruled in 1923 that East Asians were not eligible for citizenship because they were not white according to a 1790 naturalization law that restricted citizenship only to "free white" people. This law was successfully challenged by an Asian Indian lawyer, Sakaram Ganesh Pandit, who argued that East Asians are Aryans (hence white). In 1946 the U. S. Congress enacted laws allowing East Indians citizenship in the U. S., and allotted an annual immigration quota of 100 people. The 1965 immigration law that allowed every nationality equal immigration rights and gave preferential treatment to professionals increased immigration of Asian Indians to the U. S. (for a more detailed history of the Asian Indians in the U. S., readers are referred to Saran – Eames 1980, Helweg – Helweg 1990). Thus, almost the entire population of Asian Indians in the U. S. (except for the Sikh communities in Yuba City) are post-1960 arrivals.

According to the 1990 census, the total population of Asian Indians in the U. S. is 815,447. (The corresponding figure in the 1980 Census was

361,500.) They are spread all over the U. S., with varying degrees of concentration. The largest numbers of Asian Indians are in California (159,973), followed by New York (140,985). The rest of the figures for Asian Indians in the different states in the U. S.. is presented in Table 1 below.

Table 1
Distribution of Asian Indians in the U. S.*

Alabama	4,848	Montana	248
Alaska	472	Nebraska	1,218
Arizona	5,663	Nevada	1,825
Arkansas	1,329	New Hampshire	1,697
California	159,973	New Jersey	79,440
Colorado	3,836	New Mexico	5,193
Connecticut	11,755	New York	140,985
Delaware	2,183	North Carolina	9,847
Dist. of Columbia	1,601	North Dakota	482
Florida	31,456	Ohio	20,848
Georgia	13,926	Oklahoma	4,546
Hawaii	1,015	Oregon	3,508
Idaho	473	Pennsylvania	28,396
Illinois	64,200	Rhode Island	1,975
Indiana	7,095	South Carolina	3,900
Iowa	3,021	South Dakota	287
Kansas	3,956	Tennessee	5,911
Kentucky	3,922	Texas	55,795
Louisiana	5,083	Utah	1,557
Maine	607	Vermont	529
Maryland	28,330	Virginia	20,494
Massachusetts	19,719	Washington State	8,205
Michigan	23,845	West Virginia	1,981
Minnesota	8,234	Wisconsin	6,914
Mississippi	1,872	Wyoming	240
Missouri	6,111		

* **Source: The 1990 Census. Figures obtained on the phone from The Bureau of Census.**

In a recent report, *USA Today* (1993) uses the census data to rank the 50 most common languages spoken in the U. S. It also mentions the state which has the highest concentration of each of these language groups. Following is an extract of the most commonly spoken Asian Indian languages, based on the data in *USA Today* (1993) (Table 2, p. 262).

Asian Indians tend to live mostly in big cities and towns, a preference probably due to the fact that most of them lived in metropolitan cities in India prior to their migration (see the section below).

Table 2
The fifty most common languages of India spoken in the U. S.*

Rank	Language	TOTAL IN U. S.	HIGHEST CONCENTRATION
14.	Hindi	331,484	New Jersey
26.	Gujarati	102,418	New Jersey
39.	Panjabi	50,005	California
44.	Bengali	38,101	New York
48.	Malayalam	33,949	New York

*** Source: Census: Languages not foreign at home. *USA Today*, April 13, 1993.**

3. *Asian Indians in New York City*

According to the 1990 Census, a total of 140,985 Asian Indians live in New York state. Of these, 53,590 or 38% live in the five boroughs of New York City. The highest numbers are in Brooklyn. The figures for Asian Indians in the five boroughs are given in Table 3 below.

Table 3
Distribution of Asian Indians in the five boroughs

Borough	Total
Queens	15,601
Brooklyn	15,641
Bronx	11,051
Manhattan	7,395
Staten Island	3,902

*** Source: The 1990 Census.**

While language-wise breakdowns are not available for the five boroughs, impressionistically speaking, most of the Asian Indian languages are represented in each of the boroughs, though one does notice a heavy concentration of Bengali speakers in Brooklyn, Gujarati speakers in Queens, and Malayalam speakers on Long Island.

4. *Patterns of language use in the New York area*

Coming from a traditionally multilingual and pluricultural society where English serves as the most commonly used second language among the educated speakers at least, what patterns of language maintenance, if any, are being followed by the speakers of Asian Indian language groups? As post-1965, mainly professional, Asian Indian immigrants are sometimes referred to as the *new ethnics*:

> The new wave of Indian immigrants, which started in 1965, has brought mostly professional and middle class people from India .... Although no surveys are available, it is reasonable to assume that Indians are not considered "colored" in the United States today as they are in Britain. In England, Indians are a racial category; in the United States they are an ethnic group (Varma 1987: 30).

Compared to the earlier Asian Indian immigrants, the new generation of immigrants occupies mostly professional jobs (engineers, doctors, lawyers, professors, scientists, and so on). They also have the added advantage of extensive knowledge of and fluency in the English language, unlike many other immigrant groups. This allows them to take up well-paying white collar jobs and directly enter the American middle-class, economically speaking, without much hardship. In a recent bulletin posted on Internet, David Briscoe, an associated press writer, reported that Asian professionals from China, South Korea, and India have a higher income than the native-born Americans in several professions, with Black and Hispanic Americans getting the lowest paying jobs (Internet, Tuesday April 19, 1994). In another study, Singh (1991) compares the economic achievements of Asian Indians to Whites, Blacks and Hispanics. He concludes, "Asian Indians appear to outperform their 'comparable' white counterparts when it comes to converting their overall resources into economic achievement" (Singh 1991:1). However, due to liberalization of immigration laws (that allow children, parents, and siblings of naturalized citizens to immigrate to the U. S.), the Asian Indian community is no longer made of professionals only. It is now a little more diverse in levels of education and occupation.

The rankings and figures for the Asian Indian languages spoken in the State of New York are presented in Table 4, p. 264.

There are a few community organizations that serve the pan-Indian clientele. *The Association of Indians in America* (AIA) is an umbrella organization for the local and language-specific associations in New York, eg., the *Kannada Koota*, *Gujarati Samaj*, *Tamil Association*, *Kerala Samajam*, etc. Most of these organizations host cultural events such as picnics, celebrations of religious holidays, performances of dances/dramas/classical and pop music concerts, literary get-togethers, etc. The older generations tend to use the regional languages at these gatherings, the younger

Table 4
The languages of India in New York State*

Rank	Language	Totals in N.Y. State
1.	Hindi	56,070
2.	Bengali	11,960
3.	Malayalam	10,362
4.	Gujarati	9,910
5.	Tamil	3,518
6.	Telugu	2,322
7.	Punjabi	2,180
8.	Marathi	1,544
9.	Kannada	744

*** Source: The 1990 Census.**

generations use a code-mixed variety with English. The younger generations feel more comfortable with English. Keeping this in mind, all formal meetings use the regional language as well as English.

The AIA organizes several annual events, such as Indian Independence Day (August 15), Diwali (festival of lights, which according to the lunar calendar is usually celebrated in November). These are major events, and are attended by local dignitaries and thousands of Asian Indians living in the tri-state area. The Indian Independence Day parade has featured past New York City mayors as Grand Marshals. Usually one or two leading actors from Hindi films are also invited to lead the parade. In addition to the parade, there are usually cultural performances featuring invited film stars and local artists. Both Hindi, English, and the regional languages are used, but for the benefit of the younger generations, more English is used during these celebrations. The AIA also celebrates Diwali (the festival of lights, an important festival for all Hindus) at the South Street Seaport. It is almost like a village fair in India, a whole day event, where local merchants set up shops (jewelry, clothes, arts and crafts). Food stalls serve the different regional cuisines of India. More than 75,000 people attend these events. There are cultural programs that feature music and dances from different parts of India. Some local private organizations, owned and managed by Asian Indians, hold concerts featuring popular actors and actresses from Hindi films, in places such as Madison Square Garden and Nassau Coliseum. These events draw major crowds, as up to 100,000 people attend these concerts. The *Gujarati Samaj* holds week-long religious events in the summer. Gujaratis and other Indians from the tri-state area and from other states in the U. S. participate in these functions. Along with such events of potentially pan-Indian interest, each language group celebrates festivals important to their provenance in India, eg., the Bengalis celebrate Durga Puja (Durga, the female goddess who kills a demon) in the month of October, the Kannadigas celebrate the Gauri-Ganesha festival (Gauri is consort of the god Shiva, and Ganesha, her elephant-headed son and "trouble shooter" deity, is the most popular godhead in the Hindu pantheon) in the month of August. In all these events, as it is in India, the native language is mostly used and regional cuisines are featured. Since children are expected to participate in all social, religious, and cultural events (both formal and informal), they are exposed to the native language outside the home on a fairly regular basis. A fair amount of English is also used for the benefit of those youngsters who may not be very fluent in the ethnic tongue.

Since Asian Indians practice different religions, there are several Hindu temples, Muslim mosques, and Christian churches that cater primarily to Asian Indians, and there are also *Gurudwaras* for the Sikhs. Religious recitations and services in the Hindu temples are in Sanskrit, in the mosques they are in Arabic. The Christian services for the Malayalis are in Malayalam and English, and for the Sikhs the services and recitations are in Punjabi. Phillipose (1989) observes that religious services in churches for Malayali Christians are usually in Malayalam, though English is also used to accommodate the members of the younger generation who are not very fluent in Malayalam. The same can also be said about services in temples and *Gurudwaras*. Regional languages are primarily used for group singing of hymns. The Sanskrit recitations are often explained in English for the benefit of the younger generation. The houses of worship are the primary centers for the celebration of religious events, birth and death rites, and special offerings to celebrate birthdays, passage into adulthood (similar to bar-mitzvah), death anniversaries of the elders, and other religious events.

In New York City, there are several radio stations in the area that play regional language songs and songs from regional language films or from Hindi movies. There are three television stations that broadcast approximately one to two hour programs weekly. These programs are bilingual, in Hindi and in English. There are no broadcasts in other regional languages of India. A typical T. V. program includes news from the Indian subcontinent (in English), interviews with visiting artists and politicians (usually a code-mixed variety, featuring the native language plus English), South Asian versions of music videos (clips of Hindi films featuring popular Hindi songs and regional language film songs). The bulk of T. V. programming is in English. There are discussions about real estate and investments, about immigration laws and quotas, and reports about local events such as picnics, religious events, beauty pageants, etc. There are a few cable networks that primarily show two to three popular Hindi films daily. The local merchants and the travel and financial institutions advertise their goods and services on these programs. There are a few movie theaters in Queens that feature Hindi and other regional language films (e. g., Tamil, Kannada, Gujarati). These films are featured on an *ad hoc* basis, are very popular, and largely attended. Most Hindi and other regional language films (e. g., in Tamil, Telugu, Kannada, Malayalam, Bengali, Gujarati, Marathi, and smaller number of films in other regional languages) are available on a rental basis in the city, especially in Jackson Heights, and in several localities on Long Island (e. g., Selden, Smithtown, Hicksville). These videos are housed in video stores as well as in Indian grocery stores.

Many of these language communities publish newsletters, which are either in the native language or in English. Some of them even publish dailies and weekly newspapers. These dailies and weeklies discuss issues related to their community. In addition to the international and local news, these magazines and newspapers are popular for their matrimonial columns. There is great demand for magazines and newspapers from the South Asian sub-continent. These magazines and newspapers are sold by local merchants, and are available in English, Hindi, Punjabi (in Gurumukhi script, as well as the Urdu script), Bengali, Urdu, Gujarati, etc. In addition to the above publications, the stores in Jackson Heights also sell Indian magazines and newspapers published in other parts of the world, e. g., Canada and United Kingdom, and from other cities in the U. S., e. g., California, Illinois and Texas. Several magazines as well as weekly and fortnightly newspapers are published in New York. Most of these are in English, Bengali, and Gujarati. The language-wise breakdown of the magazines and newspapers, including their figures of circulation are given in Table 5 (most of the circulation figures include both regular subscribers and copies sold in newsstands).

There are several other weekly newspapers that are published elsewhere (e. g., Chicago, San Francisco, Canada, London) that have New York editions. Several of the weeklies listed above are distributed to other cities in the U. S., Canada, England, Bahrain, and the United Arab Emirates. Some of the weeklies in India and Bangladesh have news items sent through the satellite for their sister weeklies that are published in New

Table 5
Weeklies and magazines published in New York*

Magazines	*Language*	*Circulation*	*Published since*
Masala	English	10,000	1994
NRI Today	English	13,500	1994
India World-Wide	English	15,000–20,000	1994
Parichoy	Bengali	6,000	1989
Sambadik	Ben./Eng	500	1994
Newspapers (Weekly)			
News India	English	67,000	1975
Asia Online	English	150,000	1994
India Abroad	English	60,000	1975
Bangali	Bengali	7,000	1991
Thikana	Bengali	10,000	1990
Shombad	Bengali	3,000	1993
Naya Padakar	Guj./Eng.	8,000	1990
Gujarati Samachar	Gujarati	11,000	1984

* **Source: Compiled by the author.**

York. The *Gujarati Samachar* (published by *India Abroad*) and the *Shombad* (from Bangladesh) are examples of such weeklies.

Jackson Heights in Queens is the major shopping area for Asian Indians, followed by "Little India" on Lexington Avenue in Manhattan. There are several clothing and garment stores, jewelry stores, appliance stores that specialize in small appliances that can be used in India, grocery stores that sell grains, spices, vegetables, pickles, and other ingredients required for the regional cuisines of India. There are several Indian restaurants, some that are primarily vegetarian (approximately 60% of Indians are vegetarians), and some that serve both vegetarian and non-vegetarian dishes.

In terms of language use, be it Jackson Heights or Little India, the example of the Gujarati merchant cited above seems most relevant when describing language use in the Asian Indian community. The merchants carry on the Indian tradition of making every effort to speak the language of the customers. If they know the language, the exchange is primarily in the customer's language. The second choice is usually Hindi. This may be because the hired help (at check-out counters, the 'errand boys', and those assisting the customers) might not be highly educated, and thus not very comfortable in using English. The order of preference seems to be the regional language, Hindi, and lastly, English.

5. *A study of language maintenance and shift among three groups*

Given the diversity of the Asian Indian community and the salience of regional languages and cultures as rallying points, it is advisable to study language maintenance and/or shift with reference to specific regional groups, arriving at generalizations inductively. Between 1985 and 1989 I conducted a study of language maintenance and/or language shift with speakers of Kannada, referred to as Kannadigas, and expanded the scope of the study to include speakers of Gujarati, referred to as Gujaratis, and Malayalam, referred to as Malayalis (Sridhar 1988, 1993). The *Kannadigas* were chosen for two reasons: (1) my earlier studies of language use by Kannada speakers might help me to better interpret Kannada-English bilingualism, and (2) the existence of a systematic study of language maintenance and/or shift among Kannadigas in New Delhi permits a comparison between patterns of language maintenance within and outside India. The *Gujarati* community was chosen for several reasons, chief among them being: (1) It is one of the largest communities in the U. S. (it is the fourth largest community in New York state with a population of 9,910 speakers); (2) it has pioneered as a migratory community both within India, eg., the Saurashtri's in Tamil Nadu, South India, and outside of India, e. g., Kenya (Neale 1974), Britain (Clark – Peach – Vertovec 1990); and, (3) the members of this community are spread across a wide range of educational and socio-economic status more so than speakers of other Asian Indian languages. The *Malayalis* were chosen for purposes of comparison and contrast. A large percentage of Malayalis follow Christianity. This allows us to see if religion is an important variable in language maintenance. Both Hindus and Christians were included in the study. The majority (80%) were Syrian Orthodox Christians, 14.4% were Hindus and 4.7% were Catholics.

All the three language groups speak major regional languages in their respective geographical areas in India, e. g., Kannada in the state of Karnataka, Malayalam in Kerala, and Gujarati in the state of Gujarat. Each of these languages has a rich literary tradition, with Kannada dating back to the 9th century. The state of Kerala, in Southern India, has the highest rate of literacy, followed by Karnataka, also in South India. Gujarat, a state in the Northwestern part of India, is also a state with a relatively high level of literacy.

The primary data for this study comes from a fifty-five item questionnaire given to twenty-one Kannadiga families, twenty-one Malayali families, and ninety-one Gujarati families. Compared to their compatriots, the Kannadigas and the Malayalis, who are mostly professionals, the Gujaratis are spread across a wide range of professions and occupations. Keeping this factor in mind, the questionnaire for this group was written in Gujarati. While most of the Kannadiga and the Malayali respondents were from Queens and Manhattan, several of the Gujarati families were from New Jersey. The questionnaire elicited the following: (a) demographic details; (b) opportunities for use of their respective native language(s); (c) indicators of rootedness in the ethnic tradition; (d) parents' use of languages in different domains; (e) childrens' proficiency in their respective ethnic tongue; (f) children's use of and attitude toward their ethnic language; (g) parents' efforts toward language maintenance; and (h) parents' attitude toward the future of their ethnic tongue in the U. S. Data from the questionnaire was substantiated by (participant) observation in the home setting, in the community setting (during picnics, concerts, meetings, and religious celebrations), and in the school/playground setting.

5.1. Results of the study

The families included in the study represented a fairly young group, ranging in age between 31 to 50 years old. The average length of their stay in the U. S. for the groups ranged from 6.4 years to 16.3 years. The educational qualifications of the men and the women for the three groups were as follows:

Table 6
Educational qualifications of sample studied (in percentages)*

	Kannadigas		*Malayalis*		*Gujaratis*	
	Males	Females	Males	Females	Males	Females
Professional	76	33	76	43	35	17
BA/B. Sc.	24	62	24	43	41	36
High School	–	–	–	14	18	41
Grade Sch	–	–	–	–	6	–
No answer	–	5	–	–	–	6

*** Source: Sridhar 1993: 59.**

The level of education correlates with types of professions. Most of the males and the females among the Kannadigas and the Malayalis were engaged in some sort of professional job (doctors, lawyers, company and bank executives, etc.). Most of the respondents received their college education through the medium of English (Kannadigas 95%, Malayalis 95%). For the Gujaratis there was a substantial difference between the males and the females. Approximately 94% of the males and 30% of the females were educated through the medium of English at the college level. These figures are important in that they show the respondents' familiarity with English. Most of the respondents in the Malayali and the Kannadiga groups lived in metropolitan cities prior to their immigration. Compared to these groups, only 27% of the men and 37% of the women in the Gujarati group came from metropolitan cities. These data are significant in that they document the respondents' use of the ethnic language and their familiarity with English. In metropolitan cities, English often is the common medium of communication, the *lingua franca*.

In India as well as in the U. S., friendships are based on shared language. All three groups reported having several friends and relatives in the New York/New Jersey area, anywhere from twelve to thirty-four families speaking the same Indian language per family. Data on the presence of friends and relatives is complemented by information on the frequency of interaction among the families. The communities stay pretty much in touch with other members of their ethnic group. The families get together often on weekends and during Indian festivals. They attend social events organized by their respective cultural organizations. This indicates a high degree of social interaction which often results in the use of the ethnic tongue. All the respondents said that they visit India at least once a year. It is not uncommon for parents to take their children to India for the summer. Also, most of them said that they entertain relatives and friends visiting from India on a regular basis. Given the extended family structure of the Indian society, where all married sons live together, and hospitality is extended to even distant relatives, these visitors often stay as long as 3–6 months with them. The native language tends to be used more if the visiting relatives are of an older generation.

Regarding interaction with other ethnolinguistic groups in the United States, the three groups were asked about the frequency of get togethers, and whether they invited mixed groups of people or mostly members from their own regional language group. Most of the respondents indicated that they got together with friends and relatives at least once in two weeks. As to their patterns of socialization, the results are interesting and are summarized in Table 7.

Table 7
Interaction and socialization patterns (in percentages)*

Groups Invited	*Kannadigas*	*Malayalis*	*Gujaratis*
only ethnic group	43	74	77
ethnic+other Indians	57	26	23
mostly Americans	0	0	0

*** Source: Sridhar 1993: 60.**

This indicates that the groups are very much rooted in their ethnic culture and traditions, with the Gujaratis and the Malayalis being more traditional. There is very little interaction with Americans, which indicates that the groups are self-contained and insular to a certain extent. There are several neighborhoods in the borough of Queens, eg., Jackson Heights and Flushing, where there are ethnic enclaves of Punjabis, Gujaratis, etc. People tend to interact socially on a regular basis primarily with members of their own language groups. During these get-togethers, the language of conversations is usually the ethnic tongue. Hegde's (1991) study supports these findings. Her study explored the patterns of intra-ethnic (between members of the same language group) and inter-ethnic (between speakers of different Asian Indian languages) interactions of one hundred and thirty-three Asian Indian immigrant families in the New York/New Jersey area. She concludes that the immigrants in her study maintained two distinct interpersonal networks, intra-ethnic and inter-ethnic. Similar findings are reported in Alexander (1990) and Gibson (1988) about earlier settlements of Asian Indians in California.

This pattern of interaction is consistent with other data that show the lack of interest of Asian Indians in United States sports and neighborhood activities. Asian Indians are still heavily rooted in their home culture, as is evidenced by their preference for Indian food, especially for dinner and on weekends, although the younger generation shows interest in American fast food. Most of the Gujaratis in the study indicated that they were vegetarians, so their children ate mostly Indian vegetarian food.

While most people reported using their mother tongues in social get-togethers, in telephone conversations within groups, a pattern of code-mixing, or mixing of the home language and English within sentences was reported (Table 8).

Table 8
Language of phone conversations (in percentages)*

	Kannada	*Malayalam*	*Gujarati*
native language	43	40	57
native lg+English	57	60	43
only English	0	0	0

* **Source: Sridhar 1993: 61.**

While most parents were categorical in their support for maintaining their languages, the data under Table 9 presents a different story.

Table 9
Parents' use of language (in percentages)*

	Kannada	*Malayalam*	*Gujarati*
completely in native lg.	19	14	56
mostly in native lg.	24	38	16
native lg.+ English	57	48	28

* **Source: Sridhar 1993: 61.**

Most parents admitted that in conversing with their friends, they tended to use a somewhat code-mixed variety with English. The Gujarati community is the only exception, but even here, about 43% of the parents report using a code-mixed variety of the language. English is often used along with the native language in order to accommodate the younger generation who are sometimes not as fluent as their parents in the ethnic language. These findings are consistent with studies of Kannadigas in New Delhi (Satyanath 1982), and Gujaratis in England, Kenya and Uganda. This is pretty much the pattern in urban India, with most groups using a code-mixed variety and English slowly moving into the home domain (Mukherjee 1980). This is not surprising, as English is the most often used second language among the educated in India. This data is significant in that it indicates the use of English in the home domain for all the three groups. Considering the high level of education and the fact that they tend to use mostly English in their job-related conversations, this intrusion of English into the home domain is not surprising.

The answers to a number of questions relating to efforts made by parents to maintain the ethnic language at home provided insights into the commitment the parents feel towards the maintenance and use of the ethnic tongue. The efforts range from "insisting on children speaking only the native language at home" to "driving children to the local temple(s) and church(es) for native language instruction". These classes in local temples/churches are mostly run by concerned parents. Instruction is offered in Hindi, Bengali, Gujarati, and Kannada. Most parents do make an effort to keep the language alive by indicating that they read stories to the children in their native language, and that the children are familiar with nursery rhymes, religious verses/hymns, and popular folk songs from their language area.

Against this background of parental use of the native language and English, it is interesting to compare the patterns of language use among the children. It is important to keep in mind that the data reported is based on the parents' report rather than actual samples of children's language use. The validity of parents' reports was confirmed by the researcher in informal observations, though a more direct study is certainly needed.

First of all, parents were asked whether their children understood the variety of native language spoken in everyday conversations (eg., when discussing foods, friends, holidays). The parents were unanimous in pointing out that their children can understand a conversation about these topics in the ethnic tongue. Asked about the language the children choose when responding to the parents, the majority indicated that a code-mixed variety with English was the preferred language (see Table 10 below).

Table 10
Childrens' competency in the native language (in percentages)*

	Kannadigas	*Malayalis*	*Gujaratis*
can read	24	0	66
can write	14	0	90
can recite poem	48	5	58

*** Source: Sridhar 1993: 3: 62.**

The only respectable figures for *use* of the native language is from the Gujarati parents. This may be because the mothers in this language group tended to be less educated than the mothers in the other two groups and might not have been fluent in English.

The next set of data indicates that when visiting India, the children tend to use a mixed variety (with English) and not the native language. In a subsequent question, when asked if the children seem to be using the ethnic language more with grandparents than with parents, the Kannadiga responses indicate that this is indeed the case with their children. For the Malayali children, it is not an important variable. The responses from the Gujarati parents was surprising. Only 45 percent of the parents claimed this to be the case, while 35 percent claimed that the children use the same amount of Gujarati with the grandparents as they do with the parents.

The true measure of maintenance is, of course, the use of the ethnic tongue by younger generations among themselves. There were a few questions that attempted to explore the children's attitude to the ethnic tongue. As a background for this, the parents were asked if the children got together with other children from their language/cultural group on their own. Not surprisingly, the children's pattern of socialization is much more assimilatory than that of their parents. As expected, the children get together with children from different language and cultural backgrounds. Asked about the language used when they get together with children from their native language backgrounds, the Gujarati children tended to use more Gujarati. In the case of the Malayali children, the use of Malayalam was non-existent. English seems to be the preferred language among the second generation. The use of more English by Kannada children is consistent with the findings in Satyanath's study (1982), where Kannada children growing up in New Delhi tend to use the language of the majority (in this case, Hindi). The Gujarati children use more Gujarati, which is supported in the studies of this community by Mercer – Edwards (1978); Neale (1974); Desai (1963); and others who have looked at the Gujarati community in different parts of the world. The children do have a positive attitude about being spoken to in the native language. Asked how the children feel about being spoken to in the native language, "they don't mind" was chosen by the majority of parents (Kannadigas 95%, Malayalis 48%, Gujaratis 66%). The observed pattern of children asking their parents to speak to them in English did not receive a high rating for the Kannadigas (5%) or the Gujaratis (11%), but it did so in the case of the Malayalis (78%).

Asked about the future of their language in the United States, "it will be maintained by a small number of people" was chosen by 86% of Gujarati parents and 100% of Kannada parents. The Malayali parents, on the other hand, were more pessimistic and opted strongly in favor of "it will disappear in the next generation".

When probed in a subsequent question about the possibility of their language not surviving after the present generation, few agreed with this fatalistic proposition. They wished that their children would learn the language and use it for inter-ethnic communication. "Children would be better off with English" was opted for by 80% of the Malayali parents, 36% of the Kannadiga parents, and only 19% of the Gujarati parents. The parents are realistic. They realize that complete maintenance is not feasible.

In the final section of the questionnaire the parents were asked to share their thoughts on the topic of language maintenance. Most parents wrote a sentence or two about their efforts and their commitment to maintain their mother tongue. About 70% of the Gujarati parents and 64% of the Kannada parents pointed out that while they did not expect their children to be fluent in the native language, they hoped that the second generation would be aware of their roots, and make an effort to maintain the culture, if not the language.

6. *Conclusion*

As we continue to observe the interaction between the two generations, and the interaction between the second generation Asian Indian children and youths among themselves, there are several differences that we need to keep in mind. *First*, while the older generation still professes loyalty to their native language, the younger generation does not identify with language groups. The children from all the three groups tended to identify themselves as Indian-Americans, and not as Gujaratis, Kannadigas, or Malayalis. In fact, in the Malayali group, a separate question relating to the children's self-labelling was requested. Forty percent of the Malayali children claimed themselves to be Asian Indians, thirty percent claimed themselves to be Americans, ten percent identified themselves as Malayalis, and twenty percent did not respond to this question.

Second, the children of Asian Indian immigrants may not be *bilingual* in the sense that their parents are; nevertheless, they are not completely monolingual either. Informal observations also indicate that they are bicultural, aware of the cultural norms that have to be observed in the presence of other Asian Indians. They show the same enthusiasm for American pop music as their Anglo-American counterparts, but they are equally enthusiastic about attending Asian Indian pop music concerts, especially the Hindi music concerts organized at Madison Square Garden and Nassau Coliseum. The younger generation attends these concerts in large numbers. "Selective adaptation" or "accommodation without assimilation" seem to be more appropriate terms for describing these communities. Gibson's (1988) claim regarding the second and third generation Punjabi-Americans in Valleyside, California, seems to be appropriate here. In Gibson's words, "[P]arents firmly instruct their young to add what is good from majority ways to their own but not to lose what is significant abut their [ethnic] heritage. Young people, for their part, adopt more of the majority group's values than their parents would like, but still they resist assimilation..." (1988: 198).

Third, code-mixing and code-switching are a way of life in India. In previous case studies, code-mixing and switching have been used to support claims of language shift, and sometimes even attrition. But, in the Indian context, code-mixing with English may account for the survival of not only minority languages, but also majority languages. The mixing is so pervasive that one finds code-mixed languages in newspapers, popular magazines, books of fiction, and sometimes even in published documents from state governments. In oral speech, mixed language is used by everyone, from politicians and film stars to the low-level shopkeepers and household servants (for a detailed discussion, readers are referred to Dubey (1991); Kachru (1990); Sridhar – Sridhar (1980); to mention just a few).

Finally, the Asian Indians in the United States seem to be a fairly distinctive group in terms of their patterns of language use. They are not the type of maintenance communities, as complete maintenance does not exist even in India. Most members of bilingual/multilingual communities are not literate in either of their languages, neither do they use all the languages in their repertoire in all the domains. Like the case of the Gujarati merchant, cited earlier in this chapter, most Asian Indians are multilingual. They have partial competence in each of the languages in their verbal repertoire. It is precisely this kind of bilingualism/multilingualism that needs to be studied, and the terms "maintenance" and "shift" need to be defined within these parameters for the Asian Indian community.

Note

* I would like to thank Tony Polson and Soma Phillipose for help in collecting the Malayali data and to Ms. Hema Shah for her help in collecting the Gujarati data. I would also like to thank Professors Ofelia García, Joshua Fishman, Braj Kachru, Yamuna Kachru, and S. N. Sridhar for their comments on an earlier draft of this paper. They are, of course, blameless, for the opinions expressed here.

References

Agnihotri, Rama Kant
1979 Process of assimilation: a sociolinguistic study of Sikh children in Leeds. [Unpublished doctoral dissertation, England: York University.]

Alexander, George P.
1990 Asian Indians in the San Francisco Valley. [Unpublished doctoral dissertation, San Francisco: Fuller Theological Seminary.]

Annamalai, E. (ed.)
1979 *Language movements in India.* Mysore: Central Institute of Indian Languages.

Ayyar, Indira – Lakshmi Murthy
1988 Maintenance of Tamil in Bombay. [Unpublished MS. State University of New York, Stony Brook.]

Bhatia, Tej Kishan
1981 "Trinidad Hindi: three generations of a transplanted variety", *Studies in the Linguistic Sciences* 11 (2); 135–150.

Central Institute of Indian Languages (CILL)
1994 Proceedings from the International Conference on the maintenance of Indian languages and culture abroad. [Unpublished MS.]

Chakledar, Snehamoy
1981 *Linguistic Minority as a Cohesive Force in Indian Federal Process.* Delhi: Associated Publishing House.

Clark, C. – C. Peach – S. Vertovec (eds.)
1990 *South Asians overseas: Migration and ethnicity.* Cambridge: Cambridge University Press.

Desai, Rajni
1963 *Indian Migrants in Britain.* London: Oxford University Press.

D'Souza, Jean
1987 South Asia as a sociolinguistic area. [Unpublished doctoral dissertation, Urbana-Champaign: University of Illinois.]

Dubey, Vinod S.
1991 "The lexical style of Indian English newspapers", *World Englishes* 10 (1): 19–32.

Ekka, Francis
1979 "Language loyalty and maintenance among the Kuruxs", in: E. Annamalai (ed.), 99–106.

Emeneau, Murray B.
1956 "India as a linguistic area", *Language* 29: 339–353.

Fisher, Maxine
1980 *The Immigrants of New York City.* Columbia, Missouri: South Asia Books.

Fishman, Joshua A. (eds.)
1966 *Language Loyalty in the United States.* The Hague: Mouton.

Gambhir, Surendra
1981 The East Indian speech community in Guyana: A sociolinguistic study with special reference to Koine formation. [Unpublished doctoral dissertation, Philadelphia: University of Pennsylvania.]

Ghuman, Paul A. Singh
1994 *Coping With two cultures: British Asian and Indo-Canadian adolescents.* Clevedon: Multilingual Matters.

Gibson, Margaret A.
1988 *Accommodation without assimilation: Sikh immigrants in an American High School.* Ithaca: Cornell University Press.
Gumperz, John J. – Robert Wilson
1971 "Convergence and creolization: a case from Indo-Aryan Dravidian border", in: D. Hymes (ed.). *Pidginization and creolization of languages*, Cambridge: Cambridge University Press, 151–167.
Hegde, Radha Sarma
1991 Adaptation and the interpersonal experience: A Study of Asian Indians in the United States. [Unpublished doctoral dissertation, Columbus: Ohio State University.]
Helweg, Arthur W. – Helweg, Usha M.
1990 *An Immigrant success story.* Philadelphia: University of Pennsylvania Press.
Kachru, Braj B.
1990 *The Alchemy of English: The spread, functions, and models of non-native Englishes.* Urbana: University of Illinois Press.
Khubchandani, Lakshman M.
1983 *Plural languages, plural cultures.* Hawaii: East-West Center.
Krishnamurti, Bhadriraju
1989 A profile of illiteracy in India: problems and prospects. [Unpublished MS.]
Mahapatra, B. P.
1979 "Santali language movement in the context of many dominant languages", in: E. Annamalai (ed.), 107–117.
Mercer, N. – D. Edwards
1978 *Communication and Context.* Open University Press, Milton Keynes.
Mesthrie, Rajendra
1992 *Language in indenture: A sociolinguistic history of Bhojpuri-Hindi in South Africa.* London and New York: Routledge.
Moag, Rodney F.
1978 "Linguistic adaptations of the Fiji Indians", in: V. Mishra (ed.) *Rama's banishment: a centenary volume on the Fiji Indians.* Heinemann: Australia.
Mohan [Bhatt], Rakesh
1989 "Language planning and language conflict: the case of Kashmiri", *International Journal of the Sociology of Language* 75: 73–86.
Mukherjee, Aditi
1980 Language maintenance and language shift among Panjabis and Bengalis in Delhi: A sociolinguistic perspective. [Unpublished doctoral dissertation, Delhi: University of Delhi.]
Neale, Barbara
1974 "Language use among the Asian communities", in: W. H. Whiteley (ed.) *Language in Kenya.* Nairobi: Oxford University Press, 263–318.
Pandit, Pradodh B.
1972 *India as a sociolinguistic area.* Ganesh Khind: Poona University Press.
Pattanayak, Debi Prasanna
1971 *Distribution of languages in India, in states and union territories.* Mysore: Central Institute of Indian Languages.
Phillipose, Soma
1989 Language maintenance among the Asian Indians in the U. S.: Malayalis in the New York area. [Unpublished manuscript.]

Rangila, Ranjit Singh

1986 *Maintenance of Panjabi language in Delhi: A sociolinguistic study.* Mysore: Central Institute of Indian Languages.

Saran, Paramatma – Edwin Eames

1980 *The new ethnics: the Asian Indians in the U. S.*. New York: Praeger.

Satyanath, T. S.

1982 Kannadigas in Delhi: a sociolinguistic study. [Unpublished doctoral dissertation, Delhi: University of Delhi.]

Sharma, Bal Govind

1977 "Indian bilingualism", in: Bal Govinda Sharma and Suresh Kumar (eds.), 3–16.

Sharma, Bal Govind – Suresh Kumar (eds.)

1977 *Indian bilingualism.* Agra: Central Hindi Institute.

Siegel, Jeff

1987 *Language contact in a plantation environment.* Cambridge: Cambridge University Press.

Singh, Gopal Krishna

1991 Immigration, nativity, and socioeconomic assimilation of Asian Indians in the U. S. [Unpublished doctoral dissertation, Columbus: Ohio State University.]

Southworth, Franklin C. – Mahadev L. Apte

1974 "Introduction", in: F. C. Southworth and M. L. Apte (eds.), *Contact and convergence in South Asian languages. International Journal of Dravidian Linguistics* 3.1: 1–20

Sridhar, Kamal K.

1989 *English in Indian bilingualism.* Delhi: Manohar.

1993 "Meaning, means and maintenance", in: J. E. Alatis (ed.), *Language, communication, and social meaning.* Georgetown: Georgetown University Press.

forthcoming Three centuries of language maintenance: Marathi in Tamil Nadu.

Sridhar, Shikaripur N. – Kamal K. Sridhar

1980 "The syntax and psycholinguistics of bilingual code-mixing", *Canadian Journal of Psychology* 34 (4): 409–418.

Srivastava, Ravindra Nath

1988 "Societal bilingualism and bilingual education: a study of the Indian situation", in: C. B. Paulston (ed.), *International handbook of bilingualism and bilingual education*, Connecticut: Greenwood Press, 247–274.

Subramoniam, V. I.

1977 "A note on the preservation of the mother tongue in Kerala", in: Bal Govinda Sharma – Suresh Kumar (eds), 21–38.

USA Today

1993 "Census: languages not foreign at home", April 13, 1993.

Varma, Baidya Nath

1987 "Indians as new ethnics: A theoretical note", in: P. Saran and E. Eames (eds.), 29–41.

Haitian Creole in New York

Carole M. Berotte Joseph

1. Introduction

Haiti, once known as the Pearl of the Antilles, is one of the countries of the four Greater Antilles sharing the island formerly known as Hispaniola with the Dominican Republic. It is only a few hundred miles south of Miami, Florida and is roughly the size of the state of Rhode Island. The word *Ayiti* in Arawak means mountainous land.

Haitians are one of the newest immigrant groups to arrive in the United States during this last decade. Wherever they go, they have carved a reputation as being industrious and staunch believers of the work ethic. In New York City, they have established themselves in almost every job, career and profession. They are factory workers, housekeepers, nannies, doctors, nurses, college professors, engineers, school teachers, cab drivers, police officers, social workers, and entrepreneurs. Many social scientists cite Haitian welfare use as being among the lowest (Miller 1994). In New York City they have organized themselves in a number of significant ways, thereby responding to the needs of the community in the media, in the economy, in the schools, as well as in the community at large. Yet, in spite of these positive characteristics and behaviors, they are often stereotyped and perceived as problems. They are probably the most misunderstood of the more recently arrived ethnolinguistic groups in the United States.

2. Haitian arrival and settlement in the United States

Of Haiti's estimated seven million peoples, more than one-seventh has emigrated. They have settled in other Caribbean and South American countries, in Canada (primarily in Québec City & Montreal), in France, in several French-speaking African nations (former colonies of France and Belgium), but mostly in the United States. Although the 1990 census figures report that only 289,521 Haitians live in the United States, in the Haitian community the figure is estimated to be about a million. New

York counts about 500,000 Haitians; Florida 300,000, and smaller numbers live in Washington, D. C., Massachusetts, New Jersey, and Illinois.

As early as 1526 immigrants from Hispaniola lived in North America. And in the late 1700's a contingent of Haitian soldiers fought in the American Revolutionary War.

Haitian immigration to the United States can be divided into four major waves. The first group of Haitians was composed of colonists who were fleeing the Haitian revolution of 1791, free mulattoes and slaves who had escaped or who came along with their masters.

The second major wave of immigration came during and after the United States occupation of Haiti between 1915 and 1934. After months of turbulence and instability, the United States invoked the Monroe Doctrine and United States marines occupied Haiti for nineteen years. The second wave, according to Laguerre (1984), settled mostly in Harlem and integrated into the mainstream of U. S. society. They were mostly businessmen, professionals and politicians. They participated actively in the cultural and political activities of the Harlem Renaissance and Marcus Garvey's Universal Negro Improvement Association (UNIA) Back-to-Africa movement. Since they tended to be better educated than the majority of Harlem Blacks and were generally more leftist than their American neighbors (Reid 1939: 96), they were able to obtain white collar jobs. It was also during this period that Haitians began sending their children to universities in the United States. Several attended Teachers' College of Columbia University since scholarships were given to the Haitian government for that purpose (Reid 1939: 97). Several Haitians held key positions in the UNIA, including Napoléon Francis, Eli García and Théodore Stephens. Other Haitians shunned the Back-to-Africa movement in favor of the Communist Party. Jacques Roumain became one of the most outspoken Communists of the early 1930's (Laguerre 1984: 168).

Immediately after François Duvalier's (Papa Doc) ascendance to power in 1957, a large number of Haitians left for the United States. This third wave, initially, were mostly the elite or political rivals of Duvalier. Soon after, members of the middle class followed. Their main motive was fear of political reprisals and economic instability. Most of them settled in the New York metropolitan area, followed by Miami, Chicago, Boston, and Philadelphia. By 1964, Dr. François Duvalier had named himself "President for Life". After six or seven more years of the Duvalier regime, many middle class Haitians and professionals also emigrated to the United States.

The fourth and largest wave of Haitians came after the death of "Papa Doc" Duvalier when his young son, Jean-Claude, was named "President for Life." Many of the new arrivals to the United States included working class Haitians disgruntled by their economic situation under the new regime (Dreyfuss 1993). Most were unskilled or had limited skills (Laguerre 1979) and suffered a kind of double invisibility (Brice-Laporte 1972). They could not work readily because of their undocumented immigrant status, their lack of English language proficiency, and their blackness. Many risked their lives on small boats to reach the United States shores – thus the name "Boat People". Others died at sea and never reached the United States. The great majority of the boat people, as many as 35,000, settled in or near Miami (Dewind 1991). About 10,000 to 15,000 moved to the greater New York area, and the rest settled elsewhere in cities in New Jersey such as East Orange, Irvington, and Newark, and also in Stamford, Connecticut. Since the 1991 coup against President Aristide, a new wave of Haitian refugees have begun to leave Haiti again, although Haitian immigration to New York City has decreased since Aristide was restored to the Presidency in 1994.

As mentioned previously, before 1971, the majority of Haitians who came to the United States were from distinguished families, but in New York City they were just blacks who did menial jobs for middle class white families, drove cabs or worked in the garment district. They were concentrated mostly on the West side of Manhattan around 86th Street (Dreyfuss 1993). They integrated into the mainstream, but most of them still clung to their Haitian identity and regularly kept in touch with their old Haitian friends.

As the Haitian population increased, there was a tendency towards greater social stratification. Middle-class Haitians always differentiated themselves from the poorer Haitians who were the majority.

3. Settlements in New York City: Demographic, social and economic characteristics

Sixty-five percent of all Haitian immigrants reside in New York City (Schiller et al. 1986). New York City is the second-largest Haitian Creole-speaking city in the world after Port-au-Prince, the capital of Haiti. In 1990 Haiti ranked fifth among the top twenty source countries to New York City although by 1997, Haiti had dropped to ninth (Department of City Planning 1992, 1997). Between 1982 and 1989, New York City received 40,819 Haitians, which represents roughly 6% of the legal immigrant population to New York City during those years (NYC Dept of

City Planning 1992: 29, 32). This was also about 40% of the total Haitian population of more than 100,000 legally admitted to the United States between 1982 and 1989. Most community leaders agree that this figure can be easily quintupled, given the high numbers who enter illegally by overstaying their tourist or student visas or who arrive as refugees/entrants, temporary workers or business people.

A more realistic number of Haitians residing in New York City is approximately 500,000, although only 86,000 claimed to be of Haitian ancestry in the 1990 census. It is obvious that there are problems with these census figures since so many of these immigrants are non-English speaking and undocumented and may not have even completed a census survey form. It is also interesting to note that Haitian Creole does not appear in the census as a language spoken in the home.

Haitians make their homes in significant numbers in the boroughs of Brooklyn, Queens, and Manhattan. Brooklyn, by far the borough most heavily populated by Haitians (about 60% of Haitians in Brooklyn), is so well-known in Haiti that a slum area in Port-au-Prince has been renamed *Bwouklin*. Haitians can be found in the following Brooklyn neighborhoods: Flatbush, Canarsie, Park Slope, Crown Heights, Bushwick, Brownsville, Bedford-Stuyvesant, and East New York. Queens, where 30% of Haitians in NYC live, concentrates Haitians in South Jamaica, Jamaica Hills, Jamaica Estates, Hollis, Queens Village, Laurelton, Rosedale, Richmond Hill, Cambria Heights, Corona, Elmhurst, East Elmhurst, Woodside, and Jackson Heights. Manhattan, third in density, has Haitians on the Upper Westside, but under pressure from gentrification, more and more Haitians are moving further North into West Harlem, Washington Heights and Inwood. According to the Department of City Planning (1992), only some 2,000 Haitians live in the Bronx. Even fewer live in Staten Island. Many hope for economic betterment so that they can improve their status and add to the growing enclaves in the nearby suburbs of Nassau, Suffolk, Westchester, and Rockland counties. In spite of the fact that second and third generation Haitians have grown up in the United States, the dream of the majority of Haitians is still to go back to their native country. Many refuse to become homeowners or U. S. citizens for fear of becoming tied permanently to this country. The popular song *"Ayiti Cheri"* attests to that. It says, "… I had to leave you to realize how great you are".

Haitian society, as many others in the Caribbean, is stratified by class and color. Haitians in New York City have settled on the basis of class, color and culture (Buchanan 1983). In addition to the social divisions of the old country, they are further divided in the United States by different legal status, occupations, and income levels (Schiller 1977). As Ti Manno (now deceased, whose real name was Antoine Rossini Jean-Baptiste), a popular Haitian singer put it, "Haitians living in Queens feel superior to those who live in Brooklyn, as Haitians in Port-au-Prince despise those who live in the provinces" (translation from a song entitled *"Nèg kont Nèg"* [Blacks against Blacks]). Status in Haiti is defined by family history and circumstance rather than by the simple racial definitions used in the United States. And so the Haitian elite consists not only of Europeans, Lebanese, Syrians, Jews, Asians, but also of non-mixed Haitians of pure African descent as well as mulattoes. The difference is that in the U. S. all are considered Blacks, whether mulatto or black.

The Haitian presence is also reflected in New York City's school systems, both in public and Catholic parochial schools. It is estimated that Haitian children number more than 30,000 in the New York City public schools. Exact figures have been difficult to obtain because those who are not English language learners (ELL's) are counted simply as Blacks. Presently, Haitians are the fourth-largest non-English speaking ethnolinguistic group in the New York City public schools, numbering about 8,000, after Latinos, Russians, and Asians. Haitians are the majority in many Brooklyn and Queens Catholic parochial schools. In the United States, Haitians continue their traditional regard for education as the key to upward mobility, especially the poor and working class. Many parents make great sacrifices often working two jobs in order to send their children to parochial schools, continuing the preferred Haitian pattern of private schooling.

4. The sociolinguistic situation in Haiti

Presently, Haiti has two official languages: French which was declared official in 1918, and Haitian Creole[1] more recently adopted as a co-official language in 1987, thus granting it official status. Some intellectuals, especially in the United States, have begun to use the term "Haitian" to refer to their language in order to distinguish it from the generic term "creole" (for more on creole, see Winer and Jack, this volume) and to present it as a symbol of national identity and prestige. Because this debate has not been resolved, the term Haitian Creole will continue to be used in this chapter.

The relationship between French and Haitian Creole in Haiti has been referred to as an example of diglossia (Ferguson 1959). But as has been pointed out by Dejean (1983), Haiti is not a bilingual diglossic country. In fact, only about ten percent of the Haitian population can be said to be functionally proficient in French (Dejean 1983; Joseph 1984; and Valdman 1982). On the other hand, all Haitians are proficient in Haitian Creole. According to Buchanan (1987), "the ability to speak Creole is believed to be practically a genetic trait: it is part and parcel of being Haitian" (1987: 212). Haitian Creole, therefore, is the only means of communication and expression for the majority. According to Valdman (1982), "Haiti is the leading creolophone country in the world: its entire population, estimated at more than five million, speaks the vernacular language, Haitian Creole."

Cornevin (1982) dates the origin of Haiti's Creole to the seventeenth century, when the vocabulary of the French buccaneers and of the inhabitants of Hispaniola coexisted. There is enough evidence to suggest that Haiti's Creole resulted from the languages in contact during the seventeenth century (Adler 1977; Ans 1968; Sylvain-Comhaire 1936; Cornevin 1982; Faine 1937).

This historical process produced a *pidgin*, an adaptive form of language that is used primarily for "out-group" communication processes. Through the years it has evolved into a *creole* which is used by Haitians for "in-group" communication. It has therefore been spoken by Haitians for many generations. It has achieved autonomy and partial official status, and has an official orthography. Recently, there has been more writing in Haitian Creole, and the language lags only in the area of prestige.

Because of the fact that "official" literacy has been based on a knowledge of French alone, Haiti suffers from one of the world's highest "official" illiteracy rates, even though the first schools were established in 1805, shortly after independence. About 80% of the people are still illiterate. Although the constitution states that public education is free, only fifty percent of children between the ages of three and thirteen go to school in the cities. The rate is even lower in the rural areas. Seventy percent of the schools are private, whereas only thirty percent are public. Only ten percent of secondary school graduates go on to college. One of the salient reasons cited for the creation of a new private university in Haiti, *Université Quisqueya* (Uni Q), in 1988 was precisely the inability of the State University of Haiti to accommodate secondary school graduates who wished to continue their education. Many Haitians are forced to go abroad to continue their tertiary studies (Tardieu 1989).

In French, literacy is limited to those who have been schooled, i. e. about twenty percent of the population. Even among these, competence in French varies depending upon the number of years spent in school, the amount of time spent studying abroad – in France, Belgium or Canada – as well as the use of French at home.

Haiti won its independence from France in 1804, and although it has the distinction of being the first black nation to become independent in the New World, it had to face its colonial heritage. The linguistic situation today is clearly interwoven to this past history. French became the language of the learned ruling class which kept close contact with the ancient French metropolis in Europe, even though French was not yet made an official language by the Haitian elite.

More than a century later, from 1915–1934, when Haiti was occupied by the United States, French became Haiti's official language. A United States-drafted constitution, which Franklin D. Roosevelt himself claimed to have written in 1918 (Trouillot 1990), made two noteworthy changes: (1) foreigners "whites", who since 1805 had been prohibited by the Haitian constitution from owning land, were allowed to do so; and (2) French was declared the official language of Haiti. The French Embassy, the French missionaries, and the Haitian elite were elated. These actions understandably pleased France, and the United States, as a result, strengthened its friendship with France.

Haitian Creole continued to evolve through the years in spite of the fact that the same attitudes about the prestige of French and low status of Haitian Creole continued. The colonialist attitude and ambivalence toward Haitian Creole that plagued Haitians in Haiti have been transplanted to the diaspora. French is still the language of promotion and prestige in Haiti (Adler 1977; Dejean 1975; Joseph 1986; Lofficial 1979; Valdman –Highfield 1980; and Zephir 1990). It is used by all official institutions, whereas the overwhelming majority of the population (90%), who are poor and illiterate in French, speak and understand only *Kreyòl* (as it is written in the language). For most, Haitian Creole is still the only means of communication, and yet for too many it still has the sociopolitical connotation of a "second class language" inherited over three centuries ago from slave ancestors.

Although attempts to write the Haitian language date back to the early 1900's, it is only recently that serious efforts have been made to establish an official orthography. In the 1940's, the first systematic orthography was developed by an Irish Methodist Minister, Ormande McConnell, and a North American literacy expert, Frank Laubach. This writing system was based on the International Phonetic Alphabet but was criticized for being too "Anglo". In the 1950's, another effort was made by two Haitians, Charles-Fernand Pressoir, a philologist, and Lelio Faublas, an educator. Their changes modified the writing system moving it closer to French. The Faublas-Pressoir orthography was used until 1975, at which time it was also revised by the *Institut Pédagogique National* (IPN) and a research and study group called GREKA (*Gwoup Rechèch pou Etidye Kreyòl Ayisyen* 'Research Group for the Study of Haitan Creole'). This was done in preparation for the reform program that was to introduce Haitian Creole in the schools as a medium of instruction. The IPN version included elements of both systems and was given official status in September 1979 as the official orthography, when the Haitian government, through the Ministry of Education, authorized and encouraged the use of Haitian Creole as a medium of instruction, as well as an object of study in schools.

La Réforme Bernard (1978–1979) refers to efforts by Minister of Education Bernard to introduce Haitian Creole in the school curriculum, at least in the first four years of schooling, as a tool for teaching children reading and writing. The Ministry of Education began to disseminate information on the orthography to be used. Some schools began to implement this policy, but to date it remains primarily a recommendation. It has not been implemented on a significant scale by any of the subsequent Haitian Ministers of Education, in spite of the 1979 decree.

Interestingly, some monolingual Haitian Creole speakers, most of whom are among the poorest, opposed these reforms as one more ploy to restrict their access to social mobility (Devonish 1986). In the United States many Haitians in the diaspora still do not know of this government move and even today refer to Haitian Creole as "broken French" or as a "patois." They still see Haitian Creole as a language to be used in the home, but that is not appropriate for formal contexts.

Despite resistance, changes in policy and in attitudes toward the use of Haitian Creole for instructional purposes have been observed (Joseph 1992; Valdman 1982) both in Haiti and in the United States. In 1987, the new Constitution was written in both French and Creole, thus further recognizing the official status of Creole by the government.

The change in language policy also became most apparent in churches both in Haiti and in the diaspora. Buchanan (1987) reports that the churches were the first institutions to use Haitian Creole to reach their faithful. Haitian Creole is also widely used in radio and television in Haiti as well as in the United States, especially for advertising.

According to Valdman (1982), since the 1940's the vernacular has evidenced steady progress toward attaining the status of a national language. Yet it is known that legal recognition alone is not sufficient. The

Haitian Creole discussion is not just a linguistic one, it is social and political, as well (Adler 1977; Dejean 1975; Joseph 1986, 1992; Lofficial 1979). The ambivalence with which the Haitian language question is faced reveals the tension between the dominant bilingual minority and the oppressed monolingual Creole-speaking majority.

5. Haitian Creole in New York: Attitudes

The superficial linguistic attitudes of Haitians living in the United States are probably not very different from those of Haitians living in Haiti. In Haiti, French and Haitian Creole enjoy varying degrees of prestige and are used in various settings to perform different functions. For many immigrant Haitians, French is still the preferred status language. Those who did not have a chance to learn French in Haiti very often try to learn it in the United States because French is considered an asset (Buchanan 1987; Foster 1981). In fact, mere knowledge of French gives differential access to power and prestige (Trouillot 1990). French language and culture become markers of status differences, especially for upper class Haitians who have suffered downward economic and social mobility in New York City. Fluent speakers of French can continue to maintain social distance by excluding from their social circles Haitians of lower social standing who speak French poorly or not at all.

Dejean (1975) and Joseph (1984) have shown that in the United States it is widely believed that all Haitians speak French. Until the 1970's, Haitians who came to the United States were either professionals or had a fair level of education in Haiti which enabled them to communicate in French. In recent years, however, most of the immigrants fleeing from the military dictatorships and the worsening economic conditions are from rural areas and never had the opportunity to attend schools. For the most part, they are illiterate since they have not had the opportunity to be formally schooled in either French or Creole and are monolingual Creole speakers.

Service providers, including school personnel dealing with the Haitian community in the United States, have now realized that these recent immigrants speak only Haitian Creole, which is a distinct language from French. Haitian Creole has finally been recognized for what it is and not as "Haitian French," as it used to be called. Though this difference has come to light, and despite the fact that Haitian Creole has become an official language in Haiti, Haitian Creole is still seen by many as a lower status language.

My 1992 sociolinguistic study of the language use, proficiency and attitudes of Haitians in New York (Joseph 1992) found that Haitian Creole is still predominantly an oral language and is the language of choice in the personal domains of family, friends, intimate relations and religious observances among a mostly young, first generation immigrant community. In the more formal domains of school, work, neighborhood and with professionals, English was the language that was most often used. The Haitian community is already beginning to experience vernacular language loss as it gains proficiency in English. French was not used as a primary language in any domain. It was also clear that if attitudes towards Haitian Creole were to become more positive, then the language would have to be used not only orally, but also in writing.

A follow-up study (Joseph et al. 1994), surveyed eighty-two persons using the same sociolinguistic questionnaire. One of the most salient findings was that English was the dominant language of all respondents. There was also increased evidence of code-switching between Haitian Creole and English. After English, however, Haitian Creole was used most among female respondents, while French was used most among males. French was not the language of preference in either group nor was it the language of day-to-day interactions for any of the respondents. Positive changes in use and in mastery of Haitian Creole are taking place in the United States. As more non-Haitians begin to study the Haitian language, Haitians are enrolling in reading and writing classes in Haitian Creole in unprecedented numbers.

6. *Haitian Creole in publications, media and church: Haiti and New York*

Parts of the Bible were translated into Haitian Creole in the 1920's. The New Testament and the Psalms were completed in 1960. In 1985, the complete Creole version of the Christian Holy Bible was published by the Haitian Bible Society. Since the early 1980's three monthly periodicals: *Bon Nouvèl*, *Boukan* and *Bwa Chandèl* have been published completely in Creole in Haiti. Their circulation reached more than 50,000 (Valdman, 1982: 139). In the late 1980's, *Edikatèl/l'Educateur*, a promising bilingual Haitian Creole and French monthly educational magazine, was published in Haiti, but it is no longer in print. Today, *Jounal Libète*, a weekly newspaper, is published completely in Creole in Haiti.

In New York, several periodicals have also been published totally in Haitian Creole: *Sèl*, *Lyezon*, and *Ayiti Ekran*, to name a few. In the United States, the Haitian press produces four regularly published weekly newspapers which range in cost from 75¢ to $1.00 per paper: *Haiti Observateur*, *Haiti Progrès*, *Haiti en Marche* and *Haiti-Lutte*. *Haiti Observateur* is the largest Haitian paper in the United States as well as the first to be published in New York. It began publication in July 1971 and boasts a circulation of about 32,000. It is written in French with some Haitian Creole and English pages. *Haiti Progrès*, which has been published in New York since April 1983 is written in French and Haitian Creole. It has played an important role in the development and use of the Haitian Creole language by regularly publishing news articles, vocabulary analyses, poetry, and reflections on the language itself. It does not publish in English at all. *Haiti en Marche*, which has been published in Miami, Florida since 1986, also publishes mostly in French and in Haitian Creole, although since 1991 it has published some articles in English. The most recent is *Haiti-Lutte* which began publishing in January 1992 in both French and Haitian Creole. It is clear that the New York press targets first generation literate Haitians who were educated in French since most of them publish 75–80% in French. A few other newspapers have been published sporadically, e. g. *Haiti Ekran*, *Haiti Tribune* and *Haiti Demain-Hebdo* (Hebdo is an abbreviation for the French word "hebdomadaire" which means weekly) but they are no longer in circulation. All of the weekly papers are available throughout the diaspora in the United States, in Canada, in Europe, as well as in Haiti.

The New York Haitian community has more than a dozen radio programs on various local A. M. and F. M. stations. Among them "L'Heure Haitienne" on WKCR (89.9 F. M. on Sundays from 6–8 A. M.) and "Moment Créole" on WLIB (1190 A. M. on Sundays from 10 A. M. to 4 P. M.) are the most popular. During the last five years, two Haitian-owned sub-carriers have been functioning. They are *Radyo Solèy* in Brooklyn and *Radyo Tropical* in Hempstead which broadcast 24 hours a day. Special receivers are needed to tune in to them but because these are relatively cheap (between $75 – $125 per unit), jointly they have about 70,000 subscribers. *Radyo Tropical* is heard throughout the United States from New York to California, as well as in Haiti. *Radyo Solèy* is heard in the tri-state area.

Over a dozen television programs are also available through cable TV channels 25, 34, 38, 44, 47 and 54 on various days and at various times during the week. Their programs focus on community affairs, health and educational issues, politics/news of Haiti and videos of Haitian artists/performers.

Almost all radio and television programs use Haitian Creole as their primary language of communication and they report having a wide audience – well over a half million – in all five New York City boroughs and in the neighboring counties of Nassau, Suffolk, Westchester and Rockland, and various areas of New Jersey and Connecticut. Some radio shows use French, and audience participation is therefore very limited on such programs. Over 90% of the commercials on both radio and TV are in Haitian Creole.

Buchanan (1980) found that the language issue in the church seems to be the same in Brooklyn as in Haiti. Some priests and their supporters wanted to conduct masses in Haitian Creole because "the use of French, which few Haitians speak or understand, contradicts the idea that the message of Christ is for everyone" (p. 209). The pro-French group claimed that "Creole was not suitable and appropriate in the formal, sacred setting of the Catholic Church" (p. 208–209).

The Catholic Church took the lead in providing church services in Haitian Creole, but today many Catholic churches offer a bilingual liturgy in French and Haitian Creole. In most Baptist, Adventist, and Jehovah Witnesses services, French is used as the primary language, even though members use Haitian Creole in most of their social interactions. The Pentecostals, on the other hand, use more Creole in their services. A Pentecostal Pastor explained the wider use of Creole by this group:

> The Pentecostals use Creole as the primary language because historically that denomination has always recruited its faithful and its pastors from the economically deprived sectors of Haitian society; those with the least education and so the formal academic and religious preparatory studies that are required of the pastors of the other denominations are not exigencies for us. ... That is not to say that all the storefront churches have less prepared pastors (Joseph et al. 1994: 4).

7. *The use of Haitian Creole in education, health and government services, and community organizations in New York*

The New York City public schools offer bilingual Haitian Creole/English classes in at least three boroughs, Manhattan, Brooklyn, and Queens. However, to date there are no full bilingual programs utilizing Haitian Creole.

In June 1984, at the First Symposium on Haitian Creole held in New York City, the resolutions passed underscored the reality that children of Haitian background are primarily Creole speakers and that "true bilingual education for Haitians residing in the United States requires the use of both English and Haitian Creole." *Anmwe* – a Creole word which means "help", really a desperate call for help – is the name of a New York City based educational advocacy organization, known as the Haitian Educators League for Progress. It has been a strong advocate for bilingual Haitian Creole/English education since it was founded in 1988.

At the Board of Education in New York City, many of the most important documents and letters to parents and forms for students have been translated into Haitian Creole. Several New York state exams are now available in Haitian Creole, including many of the rigorous Regents High School examinations.

A Haitian Bilingual/ESL Technical Assistance Center (HABETAC), funded by the New York State Education Department, is presently housed at The City College of New York. This center organizes services, activities and programs, as well as develops resource materials and other publications in Haitian Creole and English. Instructional materials and software are also being developed in Haitian Creole. For the past two years, the Haitian BETAC has offered, twice a year, a Haitian Language Academy consisting of Haitian Creole language immersion classes for non-native educators and Advanced Haitian Creole classes for native speakers which focus on the reading, writing, and teaching of Haitian Creole Native Language Arts.

In the New York metropolitan area, all the major hospitals have Haitian Creole-speaking volunteers to help as translators or to talk to the patients' families or to read to them. Some efforts have also been made to hire regular staff members who are bilingual in Haitian Creole and English to better serve/communicate with the Haitian patients.

Other institutions such as the Department of Aging, the Department of Agriculture, the Immigration and Naturalization Service, the Department of Health, the Housing Department, the Commission on Human Rights, all have advertised their services, in writing, in Haitian Creole.

Haitians have overcome some of the odds of being black, undocumented, unskilled and non-English speaking through the help, in part, of organizations like the National Coalition for Haitian Rights (NCHR) and the Haitian Centers Council, (HCC). Both organizations were established in 1982. The National Coalition for Haitian Refugees as it was known in 1982, was established to advocate on behalf of Haitian refugees who were seeking asylum in the United States. It has evolved into a full-fledged human rights organization and has broadened its scope to the entire community. Thus, since 1995 its name has changed to the National Coalition for Haitian Rights. The Haitian Centers Council is a consortium of eight community centers, mostly located in the borough of Brooklyn. Some of the member centers of the consortium have been in existence for over 25 years and have provided a variety of services for thousands of Haitian immigrants. The services include basic adult education, English as a Second Language (ESL) classes, immigration assistance (advocacy, counseling, referrals), job training, employment referrals, youth, family, health, and housing services. The Haitian Centers Council has also played a very important role in the education and prevention of AIDS and the HIV virus in New York City through its component program, Haitian Coalition on AIDS.

HCC, through funding of the NYC United Way, is also collaborating with the New York City Public Schools on a number of projects at Erasmus Hall and Prospect Heights High Schools to help Haitian students achieve in school through attendance and dropout prevention, enhancing youths' self-esteem and self-worth, teaching and disseminating cultural values, as well as fostering academic success.

Two important women's groups have been established in recent years in the community. They are the Haitian Women for Haitian Refugees (HWHR), and HAWANET, the Haitian-American Women's Advocacy Network, founded in 1991. Both are doing advocacy as well as service delivery with little outside funding. Volunteerism is very high in the Haitian community.

Several geographically-based clubs, *Solidarité Jacmelienne* (*Jacmel*) and *Association des Petit-Goaviens* (*Petit Goave*), to name just two, have also been established during the last decade. People from these regional organizations have organized themselves to send goods, medicine and also sponsor local educational and social projects in various Haitian cities and towns. They are financed through donations and fund-raisers, and some towns have had hospitals and schools built through this kind of support.

One of Haiti's most vivid and unique cultural expressions has been the visual arts. Haiti's paintings are recognized around the world. A group of Haitian artists formed the *Haitian Artists Association of New York* in 1993 in an effort to promote themselves and inform the public about the breadth and wealth of their artistic expression. One can easily attend a Haitian art exhibit, as often as once a month, throughout the city.

In Rockland County, a group of Haitian painters from Cap-Haitien formed the *Ecole du Nord* 'Northern School' and organized themselves as the Hudson Valley Haitian painters. There are now seven painters in this group who paint Rockland County subjects in a Haitian style.

Since 1986 and President Aristide's election in 1991, there has been revival of nationalism among Haitians in the diaspora. An example of this vibrant and dynamic nationalism was demonstrated by the "Great March", on the Brooklyn Bridge in April 1990, when Haitians demanded that they be removed from the Center for Disease Control (CDC) list of high-risk AIDS carriers and that the blood ban be lifted. Many believe that this successful rally raised the community's political consciousness to organize themselves around other issues.

In cultural/social organizations Creole, French and English are used. If members of the organizations are made up of people who grew up or were educated in the United States, they tend to speak English. If they consist of people who were educated in Haiti and it is a cultural organization, they tend to speak French. In the educational, political and sports-based organizations, Haitian Creole is the primary language while English is sometimes used.

Some secondary school teachers have observed that Haitian adolescents are not only at least bilingual, but are also becoming bidialectal. Haitian adolescents can often speak Black English among their African-American peers and English Creole among their West Indian peers. This apparent linguistic flexibility has developed as both a self-defense strategy and as a tool to gain acceptance because same young English proficient Haitians very often do not want to be identified as Haitians. They present themselves as African Americans or West Indians, depending upon the sociopolitical climate of their school and community environment.

8. Conclusion

During the last five years, Haitian Creole has been valued and legitimatized in Haiti. But for Haitian Creole to gain full prestige, it would need to be widely used in oral and written form by everybody, including those who are bilingual, both in Haiti and in the diaspora.

With the official orthography in place, a certain degree of standardization has occurred, but ambivalence and negative attitudes still persist. The promotion of Haitian Creole must take place not just in schools, but also in political and social contexts. In order for Haitian Creole to be equal to French, it has to serve functions similar to French in all the domains of interaction in Haitian society. Only then would Haitian Creole acquire socioeconomic value for the entire population.

Although it is believed that the future status of Haitian Creole must derive from developments in Haiti, it is clear that Haitians living in the United States have been instrumental in pushing for change in the role that Haitian Creole plays in society. It has been in the United States, and particularly in New York City, where Haitian Creole has slowly come to be accepted and used in official domains as the *bona fide* language of Haitians. A popular Haitian proverb *dèyè mòn, gen mòn* 'beyond mountains, there are mountains' taps the innermost complexity of being Haitian. There is more to a Haitian than meets the eye.

Note

1. Caribbean countries where African languages came into contact with the French language developed creoles that are French-based. And so in addition to Haiti, St. Lucie, Dominica, Martinique and Guadeloupe also speak a local creole derived from French. Although a Martinican Creole speaker can understand a Haitian Creole speaker and vice versa, the languages are not the same.
   The grammar or syntax of Haitian Creole is derived from that of the West African languages: Fon and Ewe. The verbs maintain their infinitive form. They do not vary with tense, person or number. For example, the verb to have, *genyen* is conjugated as follows:

Mwen genyen	I have
Ou genyen	You have
Li genyen	He/She has
Nou genyen	We have
Yo genyen	They have

   The verb *to be* has two forms in *Kreyòl*: *se*, *ye*.
   The time of the action (tense) is shown by the markers past, *te*; conditional, *ta*; past progressive, *tap*; future, *pral*, *apral*, *ava*; recent past, *fèk*; imperfect, *konn*.
   Although Haitian Creole is primarily a French-based creole, it has been enriched with words from Amerindian, African and European languages.
   Every word is pronounced as it is spelled. Every letter has only one sound and every sound is delineated by one sign. There are no silent letters in Haitian Creole.

References

Adler, M. K.
1977 *Pidgins, creole and lingua franca.* Hamburg: Helmut Buske Verlag.

Ans, A. Marcel d'
1968 *Le créole français d'Haïti.* The Hague: Mouton.

Brice-Laporte, Robert Jr.
1972 "Black immigrants: the experience of invisibility and inequality", *Journal of Black Studies* 3 (1): 29–56, September.

Buchanan, Susan Stafford
1980 Scattered seeds: the meaning of migration for Haitians in New York City. [Unpublished Ph.D. dissertation, New York University.]
1983 "The cultural meaning of social class for Haitians in New York City", *Ethnic Groups* 5: 7–30.
1987 "Language and identity: Haitians in New York City", in: Constance R. Sutton – Elsa M. Chaney (eds.), 202–217.

Cornevin, Robert
1982 *Haïti*. Paris: Presses Universitaires de France.

Dejean, Yves.
1975 *Dilemme en Haïti: Français en peril ou peril français?* New York: Connaissances d'Haïti, Inc.
1983 "Diglossia revisited: French and Creole in Haiti", *Word* 34, 189–213.

Department of City Planning
1992 *The Newest New Yorkers: An Analysis of immigration into New York City during the 1980's*. New York: City of New York.
1997 *The Newest New Yorkers*. New York: City of New York.

Devonish, Hubert
1986 *Language and liberation: Creole language politics in the Caribbean*. London: Karia Press.

Dewind, Josh
1991 "Haitian boat people in the United States: Background for social service providers," in: D. Drachman (ed.), *Social work practice with refugees*. Washington, D. C.: Institute of Mental Health.

Dreyfuss, Joel
1993 "The invisible immigrants", *New York Times Magazine*, May 23, 1993.

Faine, Jules
1937 *Philologie créole*. Port-au-Prince: Imprimerie de L'Etat.

Ferguson, Charles
1959 "Diglossia", *Word* 15, 325–340.

Foner, Nancy
1987 *New Immigrants in New York City*. New York: Columbia University Press.

Foster, Charles
1981 "L'enseignement bilingue pour les enfants haïtiens aux Etats Unis", *Enfants de migrants en Amérique du Nord*. Université de Montreal, Centre de Récherches Caraibes.

"Hidden exiles no more: the changing face of the Haitian diaspora in New York, Miami, and the Dominican Republic"
1990 Special 32 page supplement. *The City Sun*, June 6–12, 1990, A1 – A32.

Jean-Charles, H. L.
1987 Attitudes of teachers and parents toward French and Creole in Haiti. [Unpublished Ph.D.dissertation, Stanford University.]

Joseph, Carole Berotte
1984 "The child, the family and the school in English-Haitian education", in: Charles Foster and Albert Valdman (eds.), *Haiti today and tomorrow: An Interdisciplinary study*. Lanham, MD.: University Press of America, 351–358.
1986 "Bilingual education and Creole languages", *Bulletin, Journal of the Council on Interracial Books for Children* 17: 13–14.

1992 A Survey of self-reports of language use, self-reports of English, Haitian and French language proficiencies and self-reports of language attitudes among Haitians in New York. [Unpublished Ph.D. dissertation, New York University].

Joseph, Carole Berotte – Patrick Charles – Jocelyne Daniels
1994 Haitian Bilingual education in the New York City Public Schools. [Unpublished MS.]

Laguerre, Michel S.
1979 "The Haitian Niche in New York City", *Migration Today*, September, 12–18.
1984 *American Odyssey: Haitians in New York City*. New York: Cornell University Press.

Lofficial, F.
1979 *Créole-Français: une fausse querelle*. Québec, Canada: Collectif Paroles.

Miller, John J.
1994 "One answer to Haitians' crisis: Let them in", *Wall Street Journal*, August 2, 1994, A14.

Pressoir, C. F.
1947 *Débat sur le créole et le folklore*. Port-au-Prince, Imprimerie de l'Etat.

Reid, Ira de A.
1939 *The Negro immigrant: His background, characteristics, and social adjustment, 1899–1937*. New York: Columbia University Press.

Schiller, Nina Glick et al.
1986 Home ties: The Relationship of Caribbean migrants in New York City to their countries of origin. Columbia University, Center for Social Sciences.
1987 "All in the same boat? Unity and diversity in Haitian organizing in New York", in: Constance R. Sutton – Elsa M. Chaney (eds.), 182–201.

Schiller, Nina Glick
1972 The Formation of a Haitian ethnic group. [Unpublished Ph.D. dissertation, Columbia University.]
1977 "Ethnic groups are made, not born: The Haitian immigrant and American politics", in: George L. Hick and Philip E. Leis (eds.), *Ethnic encounters: Identities and context*. Massachusetts: Duxbury Press.

Sylvain-Comhaire, Suzanne
1936 *Le Créole Haïtien. Morphologie et syntaxe*. Belgium and Port-au-Prince: De Meester.

Sutton, Constance R. – Elsa M. Chaney (eds.)
1987 *Caribbean life in New York City: Sociocultural dimensions*. New York: Center for Migration Studies of New York.

Tardieu, Charles
1989 *L'éducation en Haiti*. Port-au-Prince, Haiti. Imprimerie Henri Deschamps.

Trouillot, Michel-Rolph
1990 *Haiti, state against nation: The Origins and legacy of Duvalierism*. New York: Monthly Review Press.

Université Quisqueya
1988 Plans to establish a new University: A Report. Port-au-Prince, Haiti.

U. S. Bureau of the Census
1990 United States Census of Population and Housing, 1990: Census Tracts: New York City and Ancestry. Washington, D. C.: U. S. Government Printing Office.

Valdman, Albert
1982 "Education reform and instrumentation of the vernacular in Haiti", in: B. Hartford – A. Valdman – C. Foster (eds.) *Issues in international bilingual education: The Role of the vernacular.* New York: Plenum Press, 139–170.
Valdman, Albert – Highfield A.
1980 *Theoretical orientations in Creole studies.* New York: Academic Press.
Zéphir, Flore
1990 Language choice, language use, language attitudes of the Haitian bilingual community. [Unpublished Ph.D. dissertation, Indiana University.]

Caribbean English Creole in New York

Lise Winer and Lona Jack

1. Introduction

A striking feature of discussing the English Caribbean in New York is confusion of identification, description and definition – of both people and language: "Black" but not "Black American," "Caribbean" but not "Black," "English" but not "American English," "Creole" but not "Haitian." Because there is so much overlap, both physical and cultural, differences are often difficult to perceive correctly. And the Caribbean is not monolithic; even within the "Anglophone" or "English" Caribbean, there are tremendous differences in language and culture.

Over the last decade or so, there have been notable shifts in attitudes towards Caribbean English and English Creole language, from more negative to more positive. Increasing public usage in New York City, and increasing awareness of language factors in education, social services, and daily communications are related both to changes in the home countries, and to the perception of Caribbean culture and language by non-Caribbean people.

2. Language in the English Caribbean

The English Caribbean region is generally considered to include all the islands of the Caribbean Sea, as well as parts of coastal South and Central America, thus including Antigua-Barbuda, Barbados, the Bahamas, Belize, Dominica, Grenada, Guyana, Jamaica, Montserrat, Nevis, St. Kitts, St. Lucia, St. Vincent and the Grenadines, Trinidad & Tobago and the Virgin Islands. (Hispanic DoMINicans, from the Dominican Republic, should not be confused with Dominicans ["DomiNEEkans"] from Dominica.) The term "Anglophone" or "English Caribbean" applied to these countries, which have English as an official language, is a "convenient inexactitude" (Carrington 1983: 15). The larger proportion of these populations habitually use a vernacular medium of communication, usually a variety of Caribbean English Creole; several have a large number of people who are bilingual, often in another creole language. Creole languages are typically defined by the process in which they were formed, rather than solely by linguistic characteristics; they developed,

> as communication systems between Europeans and West Africans during the period of European colonial expansion, the trade in enslaved Africans, and the plantation phase of Caribbean economy. Initially, the early versions of these languages were purely compromise cross-linguistic communication systems. The duration of the circumstances that created them and of the social settings which demanded their use was sufficient that they stabilised as indispensable languages (Carrington 1988: 6).

In most of the Caribbean, there is still a very strong oral tradition in which language is commonly and characteristically *performed*, and in which full play and respect are given to the wisdom of eloquence, and the excitement of improvisation (Abrahams 1983). Many speech styles are highly ritualized, from carnival performances to argument. The proper attitudes and behavior of speakers are of course important – who speaks, who is silent, what kinds of reply are acceptable or admired. For example, a well-brought up child receiving a scolding from an adult looks at the ground, not at the person speaking, and does not offer any explanation or excuse. There is a large element of entertainment and competition in speech styles; this carries over into traditional oral speech forms such as calypso lyrics, to dialogue in novels, emcee chat at entertainment shows, and everyday conversations.

The standard English spoken in the English Caribbean differs slightly from standard British English (BrE) and American English (AmE), in some features of word stress, intonation, pronunciation, and vocabulary. More different are the varieties of Caribbean English Creole (CEC). (See Cassidy 1961, and the Appendix on pp. 332–334 for more detailed description of language features.)

Although the sound systems of varieties of CEC differ considerably throughout the region, there are some widespread features, including the use of the stop sounds [t] and [d] where English would have the voiceless and voiced fricatives of *th* (e. g. *tick/thick* and *dis/this*); and the "reduction" of some final consonant clusters as in *stan* 'stand'. The most noticeable vowel is the [ɑ], found in AmE in e. g. *father, log*, in contrast to the AmE [ae] sound, e. g. *man, bath*. In Caribbean English and Creole, as in

BrE, there is no [ae] sound, and the same vowel [ɑ] appears in *father* and *man*. AmE speakers typically interpret this as the AmE sound [aw] as in *lawn*, and then "imitate" a Caribbean accent by saying, for instance, *mawn/mon* for 'man'. Such imitations can be regarded by Caribbeans as friendly, ridiculous, irritating, condescending or belittling. Differences in intonation and stress can lead to misunderstandings, virtually never identified as linguistic in origin; e. g. the sentence *Take it* said in Creole with a non-falling intonation could indicate emphasis, but might be interpreted as angry by an English speaker.

The most salient grammatical features of CEC to English speakers are the common use of unmarked verbs in the past, e. g. *I go there plenty times*; the use of subject and adjective without the *be* required in English, e. g. *She sweet*; forms of pronouns that differ from English, e. g. *Him gone already, I tell he so*; the base verb form for all persons, e. g. *She have plenty money*; and the plural unmarked or with *-dem/and them*, e. g. *Take the book dem off the table*.

Many lexical items are found over a wide area, e. g. *cut-eye* 'a hostile glance', *study your head* 'think hard', *hard-ears* 'stubborn, disobedient', *next* 'next, another, the other'. Other words, such as Jamaican *bammy* (a kind of fried cassava bread), or Trinidad & Tobago *macocious* 'nosy', are found primarily in one country. Some referents have several different names, e. g. the person selling along roadsides or in markets is a *huckster* in Guyana, Montserrat and Antigua, a *trafficker* in Grenada and St. Vincent, a *marchand* in St. Lucia, a *hawker* in Barbados, a *tun han* in St. Kitts, a *higgler* in Jamaica, a *vendor* in Trinidad and the Bahamas. Many "false friends" exist between Creole and English; for example, *miserable* in Creole means 'badly behaved' but in English 'very unhappy'; *fresh* in Creole can mean 'smelling slightly rotten' (as in "That fish too fresh"). Telling students *mind you bring your books with you* means you want the books to be brought by the students in English, but left behind in Jamaican. These allow a good deal of misunderstanding to develop without anyone suspecting that the same word might have quite different meanings in the two languages.

2.1. *The Creole continuum and Creole space*

Linguists do not agree on whether to call Creole a separate language or a dialect/variety of English; certainly, CEC varieties at points quite distant from standard English have grammatical structures and vocabulary items quite different from those of the related standard, despite the overwhelming shared overlap. Superficial similarities between Creole and English hide real and fundamental differences in language. For example, in Trinidadian Creole, the *does* in *he does go* indicates a habitual aspect marker for the verb, as in English *he goes (every day)*. In English, however, the same *does* would indicate emphasis: "He doesn't go." "Oh yes, he *does* go. I've seen him."

The relationship between English and Creole varieties in the Caribbean has often been described as a *creole continuum*: the *basilect* – the "broadest" or "most conservative" forms of the creole, furthest from the standard; the *acrolect* – the local internationally acceptable variety of the European lexifier language (in this case English); and the *mesolect*, intermediate varieties. However, Carrington (1992) has argued that linear representations of the continuum model give the mistaken impression that the acrolect/English is always the speaker's target. He considers more realistic images like the chocolate-and-vanilla marble cake which "allows the kinds of blends and swirls that could depict the variable penetration of the upper, middle, and lower layers into their neighbors" – having strata but no obligatory directionality.

Variation is not simply related to socio-economic status, but includes a "complex interaction of motivation and attitude, interpersonal relationships and [ɑ] whole host of other 'extralinguistic' variables ... [for example,] heavy use of creole ... is understood by the community to symbolize local loyalty" (Winford 1988: 101). The ability to span widely different varieties of Creole and English is quite widespread, although receptive competence tends to be greater than productive competence. Monolingual Creole speakers in particular may suffer from the lack of mutual intelligibility between speakers of Creole and standard; this can be crucial in situations such as court cases (Devonish 1986: 89–91).

Even widely travelled and educated speakers may often find it difficult to determine the boundaries between Creole and English, and between these and other varieties of English. Word lists of "local slangs" and native speaker judgments commonly characterize informal or colloquial standard English as local only, e. g. *bamboozle, jack up prices*. Speakers familiar only with formal or book standard English may refuse to recognize colloquial words or phrases as "real, proper English". Sometimes AmE variants are considered *slangs* compared with "proper English" (i. e., British), e. g. *pick up* vs. *take up*. Journalists and other writers are often uncertain about the local nature and acceptability of many words, seen for example in inconsistent use of italics or quotation marks, and by difficulties in deciding which words need to be glossed for foreign readers. The use of individual Creole lexical items is, however, generally regarded with less stigma and more affection, in a wider variety of types of speech, than often stigmatized phonological or grammatical features. People frequently passionately – if sometimes apologetically – state categorically that there is simply no word in English which conveys the exact meaning, or emotional connotation, as the Creole word. As Donna Yawching said in the *Sunday Express* (Trinidad) (16 Dec. 1990,2: 9): "How do I explain the utter kick I get out of the special language of Trinidad, so unlike any other? Where else do you find words as rich in nuance as *mamaguy, basodee*, and – my personal favourite – *wajang*? *Flatter*, *confused* and *guttersnipe* don't even come close."

Thus, within a creole speech community, it is not a single grammatical or other linguistic marker which unifies or identifies a group of speakers, but a complex set of linguistic and social judgments and interactions. As Winford (1988: 102) points out, "These evaluations of the respective roles of creole and standard in creole continua are fairly uniform at all social levels and are an important key to understanding the subtle ambiguity of sociocultural values that characterizes such communities."

2.2. Attitudes towards Creole

The attitude towards language in the Caribbean is a multifaceted one. Like all nonstandard languages, Creole has had to fight against the twin stigmata of scorn for its "bastardization" and of romanticization for its "colorful charm". Recognition of creoles as legitimate languages has been slow, because of the negative values arising from their associations with slavery and degradation. These languages have been seen as "broken", "bad", "corrupt" and "degenerate" forms of their European lexifier languages, a relic of slavery and colonialism to be discarded as people learned to express themselves in, for example, "proper English". This is clearly one part of the formerly widespread and even now frequent deprecation of local culture as inferior to that of the metropolis, and is still an attitude found today, as in a "Letter to the Editor" complaining about low standards of English: "We are too lazy to pronounce and enunciate correctly. We want short cuts to everything. For example, "th" in "the" is never heard. It takes too much effort." (*Express [Trinidad & Tobago]*, 19 Oct. 1986: 10). Such perceptions have discouraged both popular and scholarly attention to the language.

Individual Creole speakers – like native speakers of *any* language – rarely have a linguistically accurate perception of their own speech, that is, what they actually say, under what circumstances, and how that language may be analyzed, e. g. as "good Creole". It is not uncommon for people to deny what they speak while they are speaking it, e. g. *I doesn't speak dialect.*

Until the 1940s the primary English influence in most of the English Caribbean was the standard BrE of British and British-educated speakers, both local and foreign-born. This was clearly the model for public figures such as school teachers and government officials, and radio and television newscasters. However, the sudden influx of thousands of American service personnel to military bases in Trinidad during World War II, and increasing opportunities for education throughout the 1950s, marked the beginning of a shift to a multiple metropolitan standard including the U. S. and Canada. The allure of the United States led some speakers to imitate an American accent after brief – or even nonexistent – visits, earning them the name of *saltwater* or *freshwater Yankees* (Ho 1991).

Within the Caribbean, television programs are still mainly imported – from England, the U. S. and Australia; for financial and other reasons, the proportion of locally produced programs remains small. With the exception of some local cultural and public service programs, the language of newscasters and program hosts is overwhelmingly in the local standard English. (A major exception is a distinctive American-like accent used by many radio disk jockeys.) Since the 1980s, however, many local advertisements – both commercial and public service – have been broadcast in Creole.

In the last two decades, there has been a real change in public attitudes towards Caribbean creoles. Mostly negative attitudes have been giving way to positive identification with the vernacular; the rising political nationalism of the post-colonial, post-independence era has powerfully affected views of language as part of national cultural identity – something that is *we ting* 'our own culture,' worthy of nurture and respect:

> The evolution of socio-political self determination has resulted in rejection of some aspects of foreign culture in the region. In the wake (or possibly the vanguard) of this rejection, moves a revaluation of the creole as the vehicle of protest, the badge of Antillean identity and consequently a positive social force (Carrington 1979: 10).

This has led to the concept of "nation language" (Brathwaite 1984, Devonish 1986), a term mostly used in Jamaica, but spreading, to indicate that the Creole variety is just as valid a language as that of any independent country. Some people may thus object to the blanket use of "Creole":

> This term is problematic as it doesn't truly identify the language. Although there is a movement away from the designation of "patois" to "creole" ... considering that we're in a postcolonial context and not a colonial one, we need to abandon some of these terms .... While ... there are different levels of consciousness about language on the different islands, it's more accurate to describe languages as close to their social reality as possible, such as Jamaican, Vincentian, etcetera, as in the case of Bajan. We need to look at linguistic developments on our sister island of Haiti. What was known as Haitian Creole is increasingly referred to as Haitian (Folkes 1994).

Popular usage in the Caribbean includes "dialect," "vernacular," and "patois/patwa." Note also that "Creole" to most people now means "Haitian", encouraging the use of country-specific names as well. Carrington (1988: 11–12) lists several additional factors which have contributed towards more positive attitudes towards Caribbean creoles: the attainment of political independence; changes in the routes to social acceptability and in the social structure of Caribbean societies; the erosion of the power of the traditional land-owning classes; the emergence of recognized literary and artistic figures who use the vernacular in their works; and the accumulation of a body of scholarship associated with the creole languages.

The use of Creole is now acceptable within wider circumstances than before, such as in newspaper reports and in writing dialogue in formal school-leaving examinations. Despite increasing public acceptance of Creole, formal occasions such as public meetings, Parliamentary sessions, formal interviews, and classroom instruction are generally considered to call for use of formal English. (See below for discussion of language in Caribbean schools.)

Although Creole is increasingly written in newspapers and other public writing, there is considerable variation in spelling. The most common writing system for those literate in English uses English, with a few obviously non-English items spelled in an English manner, and often marked by underlining, italics, or quotation marks. A more negative judgmental version of this system is often used for English dialects. It uses, for example, apostrophes to indicate "missing" parts, e. g., *mus'* 'must', *an'* 'and', marking them as "deviations" from English. While most readers of English Caribbean material (particularly newspapers) are native Creole speakers, many writers (especially novelists), are also concerned with a large potential audience of non-Creole speakers of standard international

English. All these writers are literate in English, and their orientation to the writing system is largely English-based. However, with a few notable exceptions (e. g. Jamaican author Olive Senior and some newspaper columns), Creole inclusions are generally single words or dialogue embedded in a basically English text.

3. *Migration and population*

New York City is both historically and currently an integral part of the Caribbean context of operation; movements to and from the region are a long-standing pattern. English West Indian migration to the U. S. has come in three distinct waves (Kasinitz 1992: 23–24). A large group came in the first three decades of this century. A much smaller and somewhat more middle-class group came between the waning of the Depression and the changes in U. S. immigration policy of the mid 1960s. The largest wave began in 1966 and continues to the present; continued hardships in rural areas led to increased numbers of Indo-Guyanese immigrants.

Many people note 1965 as a turning point in the number and nature of recent immigration. In contrast to previously more "exclusionary, selective, and racist" legislation (Bryce-Laporte 1987: 57), the Immigration and Nationality Act Amendments of 1965 (INS 1993 App. 1, A14–15) replaced the national quota system with hemispheric ones, facilitating immigrants from non-North American colonies in the Western hemisphere, especially the reunification of families. At around the same time, immigration restrictions into England were severely tightened.

The causes of Caribbean migration are multiple, including the poverty of plantation economies, population pressures, local class, ethnic and political conflicts, household structure, family, kinship and gender roles, and the pull of foreign travel and experience (Chaney 1987: 11). Migration is a long-standing process, "part of the interlocking relationships that form a single regional economic system" (Basch 1983: 142, quoted in Chaney 1987: 11). The proportion of Caribbean immigration is large, both as percentages of the donor populations, as well as of total international migration.

> Between 1950 and 1980, about 4 million persons left the Caribbean to establish permanent residence elsewhere, principally in Europe and North America .... This number represents 5 to 10 percent of the total population of nearly every Caribbean society, a higher proportion than for any other world area .... [I]n the mid-1970s ... 16 percent of the total population of Jamaica was living abroad (Chaney 1987: 8).

Free West Indians were present in New York City "even during the early period of slavery and some individuals among them were active in the city during the War of Independence .... [By] 1930, New York City already was the place of settlement of 60 percent of the country's foreign black population" (Bryce-Laporte 1987: 60), with West Indians constituting between a fifth to a quarter of New York's Black population (Sutton 1987: 17). There are substantial populations of Caribbean immigrants and their descendants in other metropolitan areas in North America, most notably in Toronto, Miami, Fort Lauderdale, Los Angeles, Chicago, and Hartford. However, New York City remains

> the leading target and ... port of entry ... for Caribbean peoples to the United States .... [T]here is no other metropolitan area in which one would find a greater number of West Indians of any country .... Long before even thinking of migrating or visiting the United States, most people of the Caribbean region would at least know of New York City (Bryce-Laporte 1987: 55).

Not surprisingly, Ramcharitar (1993: 7) says: "For most Trinidadians, I know, New York exists solely on television and in Queens and Brooklyn."

In 1992, immigration from the English Caribbean was 32,351, (not including a large number of temporary workers) (INS 1993 Table 2, 28), over half from Jamaica, and almost entirely from the agricultural sector (INS 1993 Table 41, 111). In that same year, there were 590,958 visitors for pleasure, 117,520 visitors for business, and 5,186 students from the Caribbean (INS 1993, Table 39, 105).

New York was the first choice of intended state of residence for immigrants from the English Caribbean, followed by New Jersey, Florida, New Jersey, and Connecticut (INS 1993 Table 17, 60–61). New York City was the metropolitan area of intended residence for 6,265 Guyanese (69%) and 7,904 Jamaicans (42%) (INS 1993 Table 19, 64).

While it is clear that New York City has the largest number of people of Caribbean birth and descent, totally accurate figures are not available. This is partly because of the presence of non-legal immigrants, permanent or transient. It is also because most reports, including the U. S. census, divide people into groups of "White," "Black/African-American," and "Hispanic." Thus it is usually impossible to separate English speaking from Spanish or French Creole speaking Caribbeans, or from African-Americans; people of Indian descent are not separated within country of origin. Nonetheless, some estimate of the size of the population can be made (Table 1, p. 310).

Table 1
Caribbean immigrants to New York City 1982–1992*

Country of origin	Number of immigrants
Antigua-Barbuda	13,536
Bahamas	8,465
Barbados	17,639
Dominica	7,514
Grenada	11,286
Guyana	109,361
Jamaica	232,979
St. Kitts & Nevis	11,198
St. Lucia	6,797
St. Vincent & Grenadines	8,249
Trinidad & Tobago	50,349

*** Source: INS 1993 Table 3, 31.**

In the mid-1980s, the estimated number of West Indians – English-speaking and Haitian-Creole speaking – was about 1 million (half of whom were Jamaicans). "West Indians, referred to as 'Afro-Caribbean', and Puerto Ricans and Dominicans, referred to as 'Hispanic-Caribbeans' ... now number over 2 million of New York City's 7 million people" (Sutton 1987: 15).

Table 2
Caribbean immigrants resident in New York City in 1980, by Origin*

Country	Population
Jamaica	37,336
Trinidad & Tobago	17,035
Guyana	14,813
Barbados	9,168
Other Commonwealth Caribbean Islands	6,738

*** Source: Bryce-Laporte 1987:76.**

Such figures are not entirely accurate. For example, recent counts "identify some 2,700 Vincentians and 5,000 Grenadians living in New York City .... [I]nclusion of the undocumented would probably extend the combined number to over 15,000" (Basch 1987: 161).

Residence patterns both hide and highlight the presence of Caribbeans in New York City (Conway – Bigby 1987):

> Crown Heights, Bedford Stuyvesant, and East New York in Brooklyn emerge as a Commonwealth Caribbean "core district" where many of the English-speaking West Indian nationalities are highly concentrated. Elsewhere in South Queens in the neighborhoods of Jamaica, South Jamaica, Hillside, and Cambria Heights, other concentrations of English-speaking immigrants are observed .... Relatively few English-speaking West Indians live in Manhattan; few live in the northern part of Queens, and although the Bronx is another area where English-speaking West Indians reside, there is little evidence of large concentrations in any one of its neighborhoods (Bryce-Laporte 1987: 77).

Some changes in attitudes are related to greater numbers. Prior to 1965,

> ... there was a tendency for people to want to hide their Caribbean accent, and even to hide their Caribbean identity and to blend into the African-American fabric, because they were few in numbers. They didn't want to stick out like a sore thumb .... [After 1965] you now had *numbers* coming. And there is confidence in numbers. As more Caribbean people came, you began to see more Caribbean stores ... more Caribbean restaurants ... more Caribbean record shops, you began to hear Caribbean music playing loud on Nostrand, at church. Before 1965, you weren't going to get that. You weren't going to have people wearing their dreadlocks, and wearing their Caribbean costumes and outfits, and talking (Irish 1994).

Along with the greater population, some people have identified shifts in the backgrounds of immigrants who came before and after 1965:

> The people who came prior to 1965 were in many ways a select population ... with a solid educational base, people who came from very good civil service jobs. Many of them were teachers, many of them were public servants in the post office, in the treasury, and so on, so that they came here with a level of academic preparation and social status that allowed them to move into the society at a certain level, and even if they had to come and adjust to certain – what people might call menial – jobs, in the initial stages, they had a certain concept of themselves and their knowledge, especially when they were put in situations where they were compared with other people .... And they saw their advantages, their writing skills, their speaking skills, their reading skills, their broad general knowledge, because of the type of education they had .... So, the whole discrimination issue really didn't impact on their psyche in the same way that it impacted on people who were less confident about themselves (Irish 1994).

Unlike most other immigrants, Caribbean immigration is often marked by long periods of separation between family members. Typically, one parent, often the mother, goes to the U. S. first to work, leaving children with relatives or guardians until they are financially able to be reunited, after periods of one to several years. Reunification after separation may lead to severe family and individual stresses (Coelho 1988: 57–67).

Children act "not only [as] ... agents of cultural change but as critical actors in maintaining cultural links between home and host societies .... [Parents] try to travel back to the Caribbean with their children in an attempt to keep these links active .... [T]he relative ease of travel between countries, and the constant influx of new immigrants ... continue to feed this system of interaction between the two ends of the migration continuum" (Soto 1987: 132–133, 141). Thus, adults and children in the same family may have rather different ranges of linguistic varieties that they use, depending on where they have lived, gone to school or worked, and the extent to which they have had both motivation and opportunity to learn them.

3.1. Employment and language

"Of the approximately 91,000 West Indian legal emigrants to the United States between 1962 and 1971 who were listed as workers, about 15 percent were classified as professional, technical and kindred workers and about 12 percent as clerical and kindred workers" (Foner 1987: 123). Caribbean self-employment is mostly found within the "ethnic economy" (Kasinitz 1992: 101–102), including bakeries, restaurants, shipping companies, travel agencies and entertainment services. In such businesses, the majority of clients tend to be other West Indians, and to a certain extent, African-Americans (Foner 1987: 125). The crowd at a popular bakery on Flatbush Avenue is "at home" to the extent that in addition to feeding the body, there is talking, joking, and arguing in their most comfortable and expressive language.

Caribbean immigrants are well represented in the service sector in the city in general (Kasinitz 1992: 103–104), particularly in such jobs as messengers, secretaries, data entry personnel, maintenance workers, office clerks, restaurant workers, crafts people, taxi drivers, private security guards, nurses, nursing aides, domestic servants, cleaners, maids, housekeepers, bookkeepers, welfare service workers, sewing machine operator, cashiers, machine operators, welders, auto mechanics, carpenters, and production supervisors. Their ability to fit into this growing but generally low wage sector is "no doubt partially attributable to immigrant drive and to the versatility that is engendered by the very small societies of the Caribbean. Their success is also explained by *a mastery of the English language that, to the ears of many New Yorkers, is superior not only to that of other immigrants but also to that of many natives*, and by the high rate of female labor force participation in an economy that increasingly relies on low-wage female labor" (Kasinitz 1992: 103–4, emphasis added). In the city's economy, the labor power of people from the entire Caribbean region has been crucial.

The effect of all this immigration on New York has been not only economic but cultural:

> [The] Caribbeanization of New York City is also manifest in the richness introduced into the city's life styles: new languages and public speech forms (e.g. ... West Indian creoles in public places and plays); new Afro-Caribbean religious practices; new community and city-wide organizational activities ...; new programs and content in schools, museums, and public theatres; new popular arts, foods, music and dance; and finally, the new political struggles and issues being addressed – concerning bilingualism, community control of resources, educational content of school curricula .... Most of Caribbean social life is played out in public, not private, arenas ... from Reggae and Salsa concerts, Rastas and domino street players, graffiti and politicized street mural arts, to productions of the Caribbean Cultural Center ... dance and theatre groups (Sutton 1987: 18).

4. *Community*

4.1. *Identification*

Identification in the Caribbean community has been increasingly moving from an overall one of race to one of ethnicity and nationalism. Generally speaking, Caribbean immigrants have been placed

> within one or the other of the city's two principal minority status categories – 'Blacks' and 'Hispanics' – there are few incentives to become Americanized into either of these low-status categories .... [On the other hand] they also know that they have benefitted from the political struggles carried out by these two peoples whose insistent claims to equality and justice have strongly influenced, and sometimes radicalized, Caribbean immigrants (Sutton 1987: 19).

The areas in which Caribbean immigrants have been most influential, apart from economic ones, are both political and cultural. Basch 1987: 172 explains:

> The 'corner soap-box or ladder street meeting' in Harlem [was] a pungent West Indian type of oral journalism that emerged in the 1930s in response to the informational needs of the mostly illiterate southern Blacks and West

> Indians who had come to New York City .... After the 1930s ... it was the more educated West Indians who moved into leadership roles" (Basch 1987: 171). By the 1950s and 1960s, Stokely Carmichael, Roy Innis, Malcolm X and others of West Indian origin were politically important, their identity derived "from their emphasis on their 'Blackness', not their West Indianness .... Since the mid-1960s the Black American/West Indian political equation has undergone significant change.

The "exclusion West Indians experience from the dominant institutions of U.S. society by virtue of being Black strengthens the already existing cultural bond between West Indians and Black Americans" (Basch 1987: 171). There are, however, forces pushing apart the African-American and Afro-Caribbean populations. They may "feel in competition for the scarce resources allocated them" (Basch 1987: 170). Many African-Americans resent the attitude exhibited by some Afro-Caribbeans, e. g., "[Some people say] 'now, you been in America this long, and you don't have no businesses, nothing to show for it. When *we* come here, we come here and we get together and we build up something. We have our business and whatnot, we get our homes and whatnot, American people just want to live in apartment house, and pay the Man the money, instead of saving it to get some house or something'" (Sanders 1994).

> In terms of their relations with Black American women it seems to me from what I observed as a child that the West Indian woman considered herself both different and somehow superior .... [M]y mother and her friends perceived themselves as being more ambitious than Black Americans, more hard working, and in terms of the racial question, more militant and unafraid in their dealings with White people .... [T]he society itself ... often praised them for being more reliable, trustworthy and hard-working .... With this kind of insidious divide and rule encouragement it is no wonder that even in the face of the racism they inevitably encountered, these West Indian women sought to escape identification with those who were considered the pariahs of the society. *"If only we had had our own language", my mother used to lament – meaning by that something which would have clearly established that they were different, foreign, and therefore, perhaps more acceptable* (Marshall 1987: 90, emphasis added).

One explanation for the relative success of Caribbean immigrants stresses heritage: "[T]hey bring their ethos of hard work, saving, and investment with them when they emigrate .... [They] come from societies where Blacks are a majority .... They have not been subject to such a large 'blast of inferiority complex pressure' or ... debilitating effects of segregation .... [They] bring with them an emphasis on education ... traditions that accord status to academic success" (Foner 1987: 118). Another reason given for their success is that "West Indians [are] … more often willing to scrimp and save in low-status jobs to advance themselves" (Foner 1987: 118).

4.2. Identity and language

The relationship between a person's language and a person's self and group identity is one of the closest and most complex. Despite continuing problems in understanding and dealing with Caribbean language both in the region and elsewhere, there has clearly been a massive shift in attitude from the overwhelmingly negative to one more positive.

> The primary identification of a person, apart from the color of his skin, is the language he speaks …. [T]he moment he opens his mouth, you can start formulating perceptions about his level of education, about his social background, about his national identity, his regional origin – his language becomes one of the primary factors determining his identity.
>
> Prior to '65, people used to try to mimic the American accent, it was the fashionable thing to do. Everybody who came on a vacation, and stayed three weeks here, went back home with an accent …. The sixties [was] a period of nationalism for the Caribbean. Independence for Trinidad & Tobago and Jamaica in 1962, Barbados and Guyana coming up in 1966, and the other islands, progressively, right up to 1981. So there's a greater sense of national identity, that also feeds into the attitudes of youth, and the perception of the value of their language, their speech style, their dress style, their food.
>
> Once people have developed a sense of nationhood, and they have understood that the colonial legacy in many ways has become irrelevant to their true identity, they're going to be searching for those forms that are authentic to their self-expression. In their art, in their music, in their speech, in their dress …. Young people use language as one of the primary assertive elements of their culture …. In London, it is the fashionable thing to talk Jamaican! … Now you have the white youngsters trying to wear dreadlocks! you have the white youngsters trying to speak Jamaican …. It is part of the youth culture that came with the Bob Marley popularity at the international level.
>
> A lot of them have not yet come to the point yet either where they recognize the value of the standard in its international marketability. To them, power is the I-talk, the youth-talk, the gesticulations. That is one of the reasons why they hold onto the language in the way that they do. When youngsters now come from the Caribbean and they go into a public school, and the teacher says to them, "Well, you can't talk like that anymore," the kids will tell them straight, "I don't want to talk your language" (Irish 1994).

A particularly interesting phenomenon occurs among the overlapping "Rasta"/"Dread"/"posse" sub-groups. True Rastafarians are very religiously observant, do not eat meat or salt, use *ganja* 'marijuana' as a sacrament, do not cut their hair, and follow non-violence. They have also developed a reconfigured and highly metaphorical speech, known as "dread talk," e. g. *Babylon* 'modern world', 'police', *downpress* 'oppress', *I-man* 'I', reflecting their world view (Pollard 1994). Some of these words, and some aspects of lifestyle such as hair in *dreadlocks*, are also used by both Jamaicans and non-Jamaicans who are not, strictly speaking, Rastas. The highly publicized Jamaican-based gangs known as *posses*, deeply involved in drug trafficking and crime, use some of this speech, as well as their own jargon, such as *beast* 'police'.

4.3. Organizations

Kasinitz (1992) describes West Indian organizations:

> West Indian voluntary associations, particularly benevolent societies and sports clubs, were established in fairly large numbers ... during the first decades of the century; at least thirty such organizations ... existed prior to World War II .... Several of these early groups, such as the Grenada Benevolent Association [and] the Sons and Daughters of Barbados ... survive to this day .... [T]hese organizations held regular meetings, heard political speakers, and organized charitable activities as well as social events, outings, and sporting activities" (Kasinitz 1992: 112).

Since the 1960s, the total number of associations has increased, though most of the older associations have lost members. More common are charitable groups raising funds for specific projects in the now independent home countries. Cultural and subcultural identities are highly differentiated; the benefits of belonging to such groups are social, cultural, economic and political.

> Barbadian nurses, former Vincentian teachers, former Jamaican [firemen], folk dance enthusiasts from Carriacou, and other West Indian subgroups of various ages, social classes, tastes, and political persuasions all have their own associations (Kasinitz 1992: 117).

The fastest growing organizations in the community are the predominantly Trinidadian fraternal groups.

> Like the old benevolent societies these groups bring recent immigrants together for camaraderie, but they also *provide forums for alternative status hierarchies, where the good talker, the skilled dancer, the outstanding disk jockey (not necessarily the professional or the entrepreneur) are the "natural" leaders* (Kasinitz 1992: 117–118, emphasis added).

There are also, however, movements towards an ethnic pan-Caribbean identity. Perhaps the most established, and certainly the most publically visible expression of this pan-Caribbean identity occurs around the West Indian Carnival. After independence in 1962, Carnival became "a source of the symbols of nation-building" (Kasinitz – Freidenberg-Herbstein 1987: 337), and the street carnivals held in Harlem since 1947 moved to Brooklyn in 1969. The Carnival draws up to a million people:

> Held during the Labor Day weekend, the festival consists of four nights of concerts, steel band contests and children's pageants on the ground of the Brooklyn Museum. On Labor Day, it climaxes with the huge Carnival procession on Eastern Parkway ... accompanied by dozens of dances, concerts and parties in West Indian neighborhoods around the city (Kasinitz – Freidenberg-Herbstein 1987: 337).

There are large West Indian carnival festivals and parades in other North American metropolitan centers – *Carifesta* in Toronto and *Caribana* in Montreal – but the New York one has a certain pre-eminence. Originally the parade was dominated by Trinidadians, but seems to have always been "self-consciously pan-West Indian," providing new songs, fashions and entertainers, reflecting "the larger pattern of linkage between home and host societies that is a distinctive feature of the Caribbean diaspora" (Kasinitz – Freidenberg-Herbstein 1987: 338). Carnival is mostly privately organized, with no real centralized structure; groups are organized by *mas* (masquerade bands), not by voluntary associations. "As a dramatic event, Carnival is strikingly leaderless. There are themes, a certain ebb and flow to the activity, but no particular center or head" (Kasinitz – Freidenberg-Herbstein 1987: 341).

There are other institutionalized attempts to merge the interests of the pan-Caribbean – or at least the pan-Anglophone Caribbean – community.

> One such effort is the newly created Caribbean Research Center at Medgar Evers College in Brooklyn which caters primarily to West Indian students. It aims to develop research on the West Indian immigrant experience and "problems and issues facing the Caribbean-American community" .... The other effort is the Caribbean Action Lobby (CAL) ... dedicated to the "economic, social, and cultural development of the Caribbean and its people both at home and in the U. S." .... [It] has conducted citizenship information drives ... [and] created an institute to further Caribbean interests with the U. S. government and to foster trade from the Caribbean to the U. S. (Basch 1987: 167–168).

As Sutton (1987: 19) has put it, "New York City has become the Caribbean cross-roads of the world .... [I]t is in New York that the different islanders … build social bridges and alliances …. [P]articular island identities become fused into broader ethnic identities; West Indian, pan-Caribbean, Third World, Hispanic and Afro-American."

Participation in religious activities and organizations within the Caribbean is relatively high, and may be high as well in New York, although no information on this was found. There are Shango and Baptist churches in some areas of the city; some Caribbeans attend African-American Baptist, or mixed-race Catholic churches.

Sports activities are clearly important to the community, and though mostly played by men, may involve women in social aspects. The pan-Anglo Caribbean passion for cricket is reflected not only in regular radio and newspaper reports on the international cricket scene, but in the large number of cricket clubs and leagues, usually based on nationality/social clubs, which involve not only local play but travel for matches. Dominos is a very popular Jamaican game, played casually outside or in large halls; Trinidadians will always establish regular all-fours card games, often for a group of friends who meet regularly.

4.4. Language in the media

In some neighborhoods, Caribbean language is often seen in writing, from flyers for carnival fetes to restaurant menus. Most local Caribbean restaurants and bakeries offer both Caribbean and "American" dishes, but of course it is the former that are most cherished by local Caribbeans and most striking to outsiders. For example, the menu of the Crispy Crust Caribbean Bakery & Restaurant in Brooklyn includes: Breads – Hard Bread, Buns, Bulla; patties; Breakfast: Ackee & Codfish, Mackerel & Bananas, Liver, Kidney, Callaloo, Fried Dumplings. The Caribbean Pavillion Restaurant in Brooklyn offers Steam Fish w/Bammy, Ram Soup, Fish Tea, Cow Foot Soup, Jerk Pork, Sorrel, Ginger Beer, Mauby, Sea Moss, Roti, Festival – some items are anglicized, e. g. "codfish cakes". Sybil's offers fried rice, cook-up rice, stewed ox-tail, souse, black pudding; the choice of pepper pot indicates Guyanese background, the inclusion of dhall-puri, bus-up shut, and phoulorie indicate an Indian background. Sybil's Bakery offers cassava pone, sweet bread and coconut drops, as well as Indian mitai.

In addition to newspapers imported from all Caribbean countries, there are newspapers produced in New York and including both local and home news – *Caribbean Life*, *Carib News* and *Carib Beat*, and specialized papers such as the Indo-Guyanese *Daylight* and *The Indo-Caribbean Review.*

The entertainment scene is rich. There are many carnival and calypso shows; programs by popular comedians such as Trinidadian Sullivan Walker, and Jamaican Oliver Samuel; frequent comedy and drama theater performances. For most such activities, audiences are mostly Caribbean, sometimes mostly from one country, sometimes mixed. Language may vary depending on the audience; sometimes non-Jamaicans may find it difficult to understand some Jamaican performers. However, Sullivan Walker in the ABC television series "Where I Live", is comprehensible to anyone, Caribbean or not. Some television channels carry "The Desmonds," a British Caribbean comedy program. Jamaican films such as *The Harder They Come* (now a general "cult classic"), *Rockers* and *Smile Orange* are popular; some American movies – *Cool Runnings*, *Water*, *The Mighty Quinn* – are set partly or entirely in the Caribbean, portraying life and language with varying degrees of success and reliability.

Caribbean language is heard with increasing frequency in New York City – in public, in offices, in homes, in schools. Some radio shows play Caribbean music – WLIB has all-Caribbean programming; individual programs on other stations, such as WNYE, carry commercial or university-sponsored music programs, mostly reggae. In addition to music, there is some limited radio advertising, e. g. for a bakery, in modified Jamaican.

In fact, the world-wide popularity of reggae (and to a lesser extent soca) has made Bob Marley, Peter Tosh, and many other stars household names in "world beat" music, across racial and national boundaries (Davis – Simon 1982). The perceived message of reggae – revolution, freedom, justice, marijuana – has been very positively received in many segments of non-Caribbean society, from inner-city African American youth to white college students. Even non-Caribbeans may use Creole words (mostly Jamaican).

> They was a time … because it was a new dance step, and they liked the beat of the music, they wanted to sound like them, the younger people … young American blacks … and they even start to speak exactly like [them] … And the Hispanic boys will start doing that now (Sanders 1994).

5. *Inter-community communication*

Communication problems between Caribbean English/Creole and American/African-American English speakers are often not recognized, or are incorrectly identified.

> I'll be able to understand what they say, if they just slow it down a little bit. But I've noticed, when Caribbean people are together, they can understand each other better than I can (Sanders 1994).

Lack of comprehension can lead to suspicion:

> I don't think too many of the Afro-Americans understand what [Caribbean people] are saying. They believe that the Caribbean people are talking about them. They would say something, things like I heard them say, "blood clot" .... [A]n Afro-American dude ... he's saying, "He got to be talking about me, or he talking about somebody in my family" (Sanders 1994).

When asked to specify components of a "different accent", Americans typically produce the exaggerated "no problem, mon" described above, or imitate, often unconsciously, shifts of tones of voice and intonation. Non-verbal behavior, such as who looks at whom, and when, can be particularly troublesome.

> And the way they carry theyself, they act in a different way. Some will walk with their head up, and some will walk ordinary, just look straight, they won't look at you ...; if I'm speaking to a fellow like that, I will be asking him questions like, what we gonna do, where we gonna go, they'll turn their head away like they're trying to figure it out. But I been looking at it like, maybe they don't want to look me directly into the [eyes] (Sanders 1994).

Attitudes are influenced by a general lack of understanding of the nature of "English," variation in English, and "correct English", especially vis-a-vis the African-American population. Some Caribbeans maintain, and some Americans/immigrants agree, that the English they speak is superior:

> The first time I heard them speak, in a shop to me, and I laughed, I laughed, I laughed. I think it was someone from the Virgin Islands. This was in the fifties. I laughed .... I were looking at them and saying like, "Where do you come from?" I'm black and they black, but ... they were speaking correctly, you know, so proper ... I mean, I believe they speak better English than I does (Sanders 1994).

But others point out that many Caribbeans, particularly younger ones, control only a narrow range of linguistic varieties:

> In England people know when it is appropriate to speak Standard English, for example, with teachers. Caribbeans in New York unfortunately don't have a sense of formal and informal use of language. This is disturbing. There is no need to compromise their heritage, but they *must* have a sense of standard English. The lack of this sense puts people at a disadvantage in America (Samuels 1994).

5.1. Communication in the health care system

There is a great deal of variation both within and among Caribbean countries in regard to traditional and current terminology and approaches to health problems.

> The client who has recently arrived from the West Indies may not be familiar with the roles and functions of various health care personnel in Canada. Explanations of the resources available to him or her may be helpful .... [However, m]any ... are fully cognizant of medical procedures and well able to communicate their health problems to professionals (Glasgow – Adaskin 1990: 229).

Problems with health services are both socio-cultural and linguistic-cultural. In some cases, for example, some immigrants "will not usually choose a West Indian physician for fear that their personal information will get back to the community or that they will have to face the professional at the next social event" (Glasgow – Adaskin 1990: 229). And, as for many others, finding their way to and through the health care system – and the city setting itself – may be overwhelming. Such difficulties are exacerbated by difficulties in linguistic communication – both terminology, and social patterns of discourse.

> Someone walks into the hospital. The first person they encounter is the security guard, who can be quite intimidating and doesn't speak their language. Next, the registration window is intimidating – lots of forms, questions about things people are not familiar with, such as insurance and special types of coverage. Health care workers are insensitive. They often ask why didn't the patient come with an interpreter if they are having difficulty communicating. Often the interpreters are children. That's fine if the patient's problem is a backache, chest pain or headache. How does one explain to their child that they have a sexually transmitted disease, in order for them to interpret? Most patients prefer to go untreated than face the intimidation of the health care system (Graham 1994).

> Most West Indians, especially men, do not like going to doctors or hospitals .... In emergency departments where busy nurses collect data to assess the potential severity of the problem, the information gathered will at times be insufficient or incorrect. This may be due to communication barriers such as the patient's accent or his ignorance of the terminology used for his ailments (Glasgow – Adaskin 1990: 229).

> West Indian people may use indirect methods of refusing invitations or requests. They may agree to attend or comply, and then fail to do so. This pattern may make it difficult for the health care worker who thinks that "yes" means agreement about the proposed plan of care when in fact, the person is only avoiding offensiveness. The ... health care worker may find it helpful to confirm an arrangement with a last-minute call, just to be sure.

> In such cases, polite greetings are in order first, prior to re-emphasizing the importance of the appointment. It is common to engage in preliminary social chatter before getting down to the business at hand (Glasgow – Adaskin 1990: 228–229).

Health terminology, nuances, bodily and cultural expressions are barriers to access. Take for example the word *foot.*

> For a Jamaican, for example, this means the entire appendage below the waist. A person can go to the doctor with a pain in the thigh or calf and complain of a pain in the foot. An American or Pakistani doctor who is not aware of this would x-ray the foot, and most likely prescribe medication for the foot. Lots of foreign doctors work in New York, and they don't understand. In the meantime, the person goes away without having their problems addressed. A Jamaican doctor would ask what *part* of your foot is giving you problems (Graham 1994).

The practitioner unfamiliar with Caribbean language may be faced with what appears to be unique characteristics of the population. For example, *gas pains* commonly cause aches, tenderness, pressure, or tingling pain – not in the stomach, but in muscles, teeth, and joints, especially in the shoulders, back or neck. This can be diagnosed by a doctor as a variety of illnesses, including neuralgia, muscle strain, or allergic sensitivity, but will be understood by the patient as caused by gas or wind travelling throughout the body. Problems may result from adults' persistent popular diagnosis of allergic symptoms in children as *the cold*, and the avoidance of the word *asthma* in favor of *bronchitis* or even *pneumonia.* When the practitioner is unfamiliar with such terminology, as often occurs in the U. S., disastrous miscommunication can result. For example, such common Creole descriptions as *mi belly wukkin mi* 'cramps', 'diarrhoea' or *I get gas pain in mi hand, it travel from mi head* are often mistakenly ascribed to psychosis, even in New York hospitals with a large West Indian clientele (Miriam Azaunce, pers. comm.).

Mental illnesses are particularly susceptible to social and cultural values. For example, strong differences have been noted (Matthews 1993: 131) in the ways that Indo-Caribbean and Afro-Caribbean families handle agression and frustration; in Indian families, suicide and unusual behavior may be seen as spiritual concerns, rather than medical. Generally, Caribbean immigrants are reluctant to tell problems to strangers. Traditional cultural value and practice may come into conflict with American systems, e. g. around issues of disciplining children, and parent-child relationships.

The large presence of Caribbean health care workers in the system,

> has affected the situation both positively and negatively. On the one hand, health care workers can immediately connect with the patients, and help them to express and articulate their problem; it is easier for them to understand in order to diagnose and treat problems. On the other hand, some Caribbean health care workers are very insensitive to and impatient with their patients, could be an issue of class and education (Graham 1994).

Although local practitioners may be frustrated or exasperated with what they perceive to be incorrect patient ideas about diagnosis and treatment, they are still often more or less familiar with them. This raises questions, both ethical and practical, about the nature of accommodation of belief systems. Of course, diagnosis or treatment considered to be actively harmful to the patient cannot be considered acceptable. However, a doctor who, for example, diagnoses a patient's *fips* 'convulsions' as epilepsy, but who dismisses the patient's assertion that this illness is caused by *maljo* 'evil eye', may simply lose access to the patient. Some doctors are willing to admit both systems, and recommend that the patient take a particular medication *and* get appropriate cultural treatment. Such treatment will not harm patients, and may contribute to their psychological well-being. Certainly, an attitude of non-challenge to the patient's belief system, and understanding – if not use – of patient terminology, can only help in the process of communication. However, it is probably true that sincere, patient, and sympathetic talking and listening, and establishing a relationship of rapport and trust with patients is more important than the use of any particular terminology.

> It is important for the health professional, when encountering difficulties in understanding, to ask the person to speak more slowly or to point to the affected area of the body. It will also be helpful if the person taking a medical or social history explains the purpose of routine questions which the patient may not easily relate to his condition (Glasgow & Adaskin 1990: 229).

The Caribbean Women's Health Association also carries out many workshops and cultural sensitivity training sessions for health workers.

5.2. Communication in police/legal services

Oftentimes police officers become very frustrated because they find Caribbean people difficult to understand. Sometimes a complainant may feel frustrated that the officer doesn't understand. Translation, in police stations and courts, is not provided; even if "you have a real deep accent you are supposed to speak English so this service is not provided" (Harding 1994). Here again, the assumption that everybody is speaking English actually prevents the police officers from viewing this language as anything but sloppy or bad English. Sometimes the complainant just leaves rather than pursue a problem. Someone who has been brought in or arrested as a criminal is really not in a position to react negatively to the use or non-use of any particular language by an officer. Confrontations can escalate quickly when language or tone, e. g. degree of anger, are misinterpreted. As one Jamaican-born police officer explained,

> Something that typically takes 10–15 minutes can take an hour. There is definitely a barrier. Because I'm Jamaican, I can see what's happening clearly. Sometimes if we pull over some people and they start getting hot and anxious sometimes I can say something in the language. Right away they see that I am someone they can relate to and it calms them down (Harding 1994).

If an officer uses some kind of Caribbean language, people may feel more comfortable, or may be really offended:

> I have seen a few white officers try to really get tuned into the language if they worked in a large Caribbean community. They would familiarize themselves with certain terms and really get accustomed to the way the people talk, for example, the Rastas. But that's one in five thousand .... Sometimes white detectives will use Jamaican language. One uses real Rasta language, but he's really respectful, it's kind of a personal exploration for him. But some other officers are indiscriminate about using expressions like "Hey man" with everybody they perceive as speaking with a Caribbean accent (Harding 1994).

African-American officers are also more sensitive now than before to the language differences of English speaking Caribbean people:

> There is something happening with the language now that's different from when I was growing up. The first thing you did back then was to change your accent or you might get beat up. Now everyone wants to talk this language. The implication of this is that the African American and Caribbean communities are more in harmony now than years ago (Harding 1994).

There are not many Caribbean officers, but depending on where they are posted it can really make a difference to the community. Most of the Caribbean police officers are not first generation, but second or third generation.

6. Language and education

The majority of West Indian children arriving in the United States are in the 10- to 19-age range at a time when New York City's public and private school enrollment has been steadily declining. Black student enrollment in secondary schools, public and private, has increased … attributed in part to the presence of children of West Indian immigrants (Soto 1987: 140). From 1989 to 1992 about 25,000 children from the English-speaking Caribbean enrolled in New York City schools (Sontag 1992).

> In the schools, teachers used to grab the West Indian students, because usually the West Indian student who came here at that time was a grade or two above his age peer, and they were ahead of the class. They were seen as geniuses! And most teachers rushed to get them –'Oh, give me that new kid!' (Irish 1994)

Not all students from the Caribbean countries where English is the official language will speak only Creole; those who have had access to more education will tend to have greater competence in a Caribbean standard English which varies from other standard varieties only minimally in pronunciation, vocabulary and grammar. Nonetheless, because these immigrants are classified as "English speakers" by teachers, by educational and psychological assessors, and often by the Caribbean parents and students themselves, they are generally placed in mainstream English classes. Sometimes Caribbean students who are perceived as having "language problems" – i. e., usually because teachers find their language difficult to understand – are placed in English as a Second Language classes, or speech therapy classes, neither of which is appropriate. "Truly there is no official policy and if there is any policy it is to regard Caribbean students, particularly those of African ancestry, as African-Americans. In essence, English speaking Caribbean kids get lost in a sea of Black kids" (Folkes 1994).

Caribbean immigrant students usually face for the first time a situation in which many teachers do not understand them. Although Caribbean teachers may disapprove of Creole, they do generally understand it. Too frequently in North American schools, however, neither students nor teachers recognize problems for what they are. Teachers commonly report Caribbean students as "behavioral problems," "deaf" or "slow learners" –because of linguistic and paralinguistic differences in communication patterns. For example, a well brought up Caribbean child receiving a reprimand for not having done an assignment is expected to remain silent and look at the ground – certainly not to be *bold-face* 'rude, aggressively challenging' by looking directly at the teacher (for a good account of one kind of traditional Caribbean schooling, see Hodge 1970). However, this behavior is often interpreted in North American schools as sullen, sneaky, insubordinate, stupid, or dishonest ("he didn't even look the teacher in the eye"). Teachers often lump all students together as "Jamaicans" or do not pronounce names of countries correctly, e. g. "British Gee-yana" for "Guy-ana."

North America is also the first place that most immigrant Caribbean students have found themselves in a situation where they are a racial minority and the object of extensive overt racism. Although racism exists in the Caribbean, the kind shown in North America, particularly from teachers and school administrators, is unexpected and very hurtful. General ignorance of the students' backgrounds is linked to the general foreign perception of the Caribbean as "paradise", but uncivilized. Students are often made to feel that they have nothing to offer except tourist beaches, good times, sexy calypsos, and "drug-ridden" reggae. This makes inclusion of Caribbean content in curriculum areas such as literature especially crucial for *all* students.

Lack of respect for the culture and language of West Indian children has devastating effects on students:

> A man's language is part of him. It is his only vehicle for expressing his thoughts and feelings. To say that his language and that of his entire family and culture is second rate, is to accuse him of *being* second rate (Coard 1971: 29).

In the Caribbean, "Bad English" is certainly not acceptable in schools, although Creole is often used by students and sometimes by teachers. The vernacular has not been considered a "real" language, i. e. with standardized grammar and spelling, and it did not, like a "real" language, have a "proper" dictionary or grammar reference book. The greater accessibility of public education, particularly after political independence, has not led to all students attaining full competence in standard English. In 1975, the Ministry of Education in Trinidad & Tobago officially recognized that the majority of children in the school system had a first, primary, and sometimes sole competence in their first language, the "vernacular" or "dialect". The Ministry's 1975 syllabus called for the recognition of the vernacular as a real language and as a legitimate vehicle for oral and written expression; the English language sections of the Caribbean Examinations Council 'O' level tests would now include questions which allowed or explicitly elicited writing "in dialect". Educators were called on to use teaching strategies based on the differences between the two language varieties, and to incorporate spoken and written "dialect" in schoolwork and formal examinations.

At the time, the syllabus drew a barrage of protest from parents and the general public. Many objections were based on the fear that acknowledging – much less using – an "inferior" and "useless" kind of speech would undercut the learning of "proper" English, thus limiting a child's opportunities for successful education and employment. Local situations vary. Although few in Trinidad & Tobago would advocate the use of Creole as the main educational medium, even in primary education, many teachers and community people now accept a need for its use in education, although still as complementary, basic and transitional to an added language, standard English. In Guyana and Jamaica, however, stronger cases are made for a more global recognition and use of Creole (Devonish 1986).

All this has given the vernacular some official educational legitimacy. Nonetheless, both educators and the public are concerned over the extent to which acceptance of the vernacular might negatively affect students' becoming competent in standard ("proper") English. Even those who are supportive of Creole often cite the lack of an arbiter of spelling, for example, as a reason they have difficulty carrying out the Ministry of Education's requirement that the curriculum include writing in dialect. The effort to increase use of written Creole in schools has indeed been hampered by, for example, the lack of a standardized orthography and the lack of conventional references such as dictionaries and grammars (but see Allsopp 1996). Despite this, however, it should be noted that there is in fact a great deal written in Creole, consistent or not, mostly in the realm of literature and newspaper commentary.

Since creoles have traditionally had very low prestige, both inside and outside the countries where they are spoken, many creole speakers, especially those resident in North America for many years, will identify themselves as speaking only English. As Carrington has pointed out (1983), students may then have very little motivation to learn English because they already perceive themselves as speaking it. When pressed, they may admit to speaking "slangs," "broken English," or "patois," none of which they consider to be a "real" language with grammatical rules. To escape such negative perceptions, many people in the Caribbean call their language "dialect," this term implying that their language is really just another legitimate version of "real" English.

The low self-esteem which results from considering oneself not a competent speaker of any real language is a significant problem even within the Caribbean. In North America, where ignorance about the Caribbean as a whole reigns, the effect on a student trying to learn language arts skills *and* other subjects *through* standard English only can be devastating.

The superficial similarities between Creole and English yield positive results for Creole speakers learning standard English very quickly in the beginning. Immigrant Caribbean students generally have and develop recognition and productive skills more quickly than true ESL students, for example. But the Creole speaker will reach crucial "humps" or plateaus at particular points and often be more frustrated and resentful than a typical ESL student. For example, years may pass without a Creole speaker realizing that in North America, "good night" is said only on leaving, not entering; it is difficult to judge the disconcerting effect this can have on monolingual English speakers.

Both students and teachers are aware of frustrations in the school setting, as shown in these quotations from students (Pratt-Johnson 1994):

> Before I had to go trough a lot with my peer's because they would tease mi of the way I use to speak in class, let alone read in class.
>
> I felt stupid talking in class. At that time I can't speak like the Americans can do. So sometimes I stayed home and didn't come to school. Sometimes when I did go to school, I would put my head on the desk and pretend I wasn't interested. But I really was. At least the teacher didn't call on me and [the students] didn't laugh at me and make me feel small.
>
> I was scared in class. One day in my math class, my teacher asked me to read a paragraph. I came across the number '338'. Because of my accent, I said 'tree-tree-hate'. My classmates laughed at me and I felt so embarrassed, you see? My hands started to shake, and got sweaty and my heart started racing then my mouth started trembling. I tried to finish my paragraph but because I was nervous, I made even more mistakes. The teacher stopped me from reading.

and teachers (Pratt-Johnson 1994):

> It is difficult for me to understand my Jamaican students who have a heavy accent, and many of them write as they speak.
>
> I feel bad that I can't offer them [Jamaican students] help in overcoming their language problems as I can with other students, but, honestly, I don't know where to begin.
>
> I wish I could give my Jamaican students confidence. The most difficult part is that you are trying to change something that has been the only way they've known for so long.

As Raymond (1994) points out: "Teachers don't realize what the linguistic problems are. They first of all assume that these students are English speaking. When their expectations are not met they assume it's because something is wrong with the students."

In one school, for example, though 75% of the children are of Caribbean origin, the majority from English speaking countries, "there is no official policy to address their language needs. The children often cannot make the adjustment, no one understands the child. The child is therefore rejected; no one bridges the gap. There is no program to address their needs, so they're usually placed in 'at-risk' classes" (Mirvil 1994).

> A study called "Perform or Perish" has identified schools and districts where students are failing. These communities are typically low socio-economic areas with high immigrant populations – communities where many English speaking Caribbean people live .... [S]ome local initiatives such as Project Omega and activities of the Caribbean Research Center ... have addressed the cultural issues, approaching it from a multicultural perspective .... The "Schools Under Registration Review" study ... examines all aspects of the school environment including large populations of language and ethnic minorities. However, Caribbean students are not acknowledged. They continue to be lumped with African Americans. In some districts, Caribbean students make up the majority of the student population, yet they remain invisible .... For example, the system requires that all students be given a Home Language Identification Survey. There are several versions, including English only, English/Spanish, English/Haitian Creole .... Depending on how students respond they will be placed in classes or first administered a Language Assessment Battery (LAB) in the appropriate language. So if a Haitian child or parent indicates that Haitian is spoken at home the child will be given a Haitian LAB and then placed. However, if a Jamaican child indicates that it's Jamaican Creole that is spoken at home, the system will choose to completely ignore this and place the child in mainstream English classes. In essence, the [English] Caribbean population is ignored completely, as it is also clear that any other response will affect the disbursement of funds (Folkes 1994).

There is, however, a growing recognition of the need to move towards an overt consideration of language issues with a vast majority of Caribbean school-age immigrants (State Education Department 1994). One public medium of communication is a series on "Issues on Education" on WNYE-TV, run by Karl Folkes, begun in the spring of 1994, addressing issues affecting Caribbean students.

In P. S. 147, the issue is addressed by having: a) an Orientation group for children, to introduce them to the school, and to the school and classroom culture, b) a Foreign Language Month, in which the English speaking Caribbean is also highlighted and students native to these countries share their culture and experiences, and c) Caribbean teachers who help facilitate the transition for students (Mirvil 1994).

Project Omega (Karp 1994) was designed five years ago to address the special language needs of high-school aged children coming from the English-speaking Caribbean. This was not funded under Limited English Proficiency legislation, and was earmarked to enroll only a certain number of students. Criteria for selection were: reading below the fifth grade level; difficulty using standard English; and newly arrived, usually in the country for less than one year. The program is currently based in three high schools: Wingate, Tilden, and Prospect Heights. Students remain in the program for one year. The focus of the curriculum is literacy, language acquisition, learning about the new country and culture and the school system. There are about 150 students in the program. In addition, there is a transition program for the second year that serves about 80 students. The transition class focuses on literacy and provides support for the students. Some teachers are Caribbean and some are not. They teach language and literacy and a content area. Unfortunately, the staff turnover is high. It is difficult to get people to remain with the program; although the students are very polite and very respectful of the teacher, and attendance is good. Parents are pleased.

Any approach to the teaching of students whose first language is Creole, recognized or not, must include overt knowledge about and acceptance of the language and its culture, contrasted specifically with English language and culture varieties. Without the basic recognition of the validity of creoles and an understanding of their relationship to English, the students' progress will be continually short-circuited. Native Creole speakers can be in the classroom or school as resources, but both community resources and audio and video recordings, as well as print sources, can be used within a context of teaching about language variation.

> We will never get our youngsters to understand the value of learning foreign languages – *including* English – until we show an appreciation for the language that they appreciate .... People have to understand that there is a fundamental difference between bad English and good Creole .... If education is going to have any meaning, and any success, it makes more sense to start off with people's strengths, start off with the experiences that they have, and then from the particular and personal experiences, you branch up to the universal, you teach them everything else about the world. People must start out knowing themselves first (Irish 1994).

There is, indeed and at last, some concerted movement in this direction:

> Although the [New York City] Board [of Education] has not seen the need for a policy, the issue has been getting a lot of attention from a lot of educators, including Chancellor Cortines. In fact the National Association

of Bilingual Education [NABE] put forth a resolution this past February that special attention should be given to English-based Creole-speaking Caribbean students. NABE's taking of the leadership in this matter has promoted a number of responses by legislatures. The New York State Education Department is now developing legislation around this area (Folkes 1994).

Appropriate classroom materials, whether purchased or student-produced, are essential in any teaching situation, and particularly in this one. Excellent classroom-specific resources include Coelho (1988, 1991) and Pollard (1994). However, it is often too easy for educators not only to fail to take advantage of existing materials, but to realize that it is attitude, more than any specific knowledge or materials, that is crucial to understanding and helping Caribbean students. Teachers do not have to become fluent in Creole, although the teachers' own varieties of English can be a valuable resource in classroom discussion (Winer 1993). Teachers should work with their students to figure out the linguistic – or other – bases of difficulties and differences, to formalize and revise hypotheses about Creole and English. The two guiding principles throughout should be: (1) *respect* the student, the student's culture, and the student's language; and (2) *suspect* language to be involved in apparent nonlinguistic problems.

Some errors in English produced by Creole speakers can be useful starting points for discussion. Samples of Caribbean students' written English work, taken from (Coelho 1991: 54–56), show influences of Creole as a first language, plus language developmental patterns typical of any learner of English.

> *Rohan mother send for her son because she miss him a lot and she want him to have a better opportunity in Canada.* (< Creole, nouns not marked for possession, verbs not marked for past tense)
>
> *Rohan mother didn't realized her son was big. She shouldn't treated him like a child. He didn't appreciated all that stuff and that why he couldn't stayed with her no more.* (Student is aware of need to mark past, leading to several instances of hypercorrection, a common developmental error)
>
> *In other word, I think the Government should stop wasting so much money on outer-space projeck and warfear material and spend it on Welfear to help the homeless people instead.* (< Creole pronunciation on *projeck, warfear, welfear*)
>
> *Creole is a language which speak in the West Indies. When the African bring to the West Indies and separate because the owner didn't wanted them to communicted together, a new language were create.* (Difficulty with passives, not used in Creole as in English. Includes two verbs as active, as in Creole, one with auxiliary verb *were* but not subject-verb agreement; past participle unmarked; and hypercorrection in *didn't wanted*)

> *When we leave the park we went to MacDonalds for lunch and we order two can of pop and two apple pie and two cup of coffe and two hambuer.* (< Creole rule for plurals, no marker if number indicated in some other way; past tense sometimes marked on strong verbs *went*, sometimes not *leave*; non-English subject-verb agreement; developmental, non-Creole errors in spelling)

The use of pictures and the discussion of topics familiar to the students are helpful, particularly at early stages, so that the student is not struggling with both language and content at the same time, and so that students have an opportunity to show some of their own knowledge. Given the significant differences in pronunciation, standard phonics-based approaches to reading are not very helpful, except in a limited way such as the recognition of consistent consonant sounds: "Students need to associate spelling with the sounds that *they* make" (Coelho 1991: 55). It is important not to attack or change the Creole speaker's speech at first if one is attempting to establish validity of both creole and standard. Later, contextualized discussions of intelligibility and appropriateness can help students decide what they want to do in their own speech and writing. Any successful approach must combine affective, academic, and linguistic factors.

APPENDIX: Language Features

Phonology. Although the sound systems of varieties of CEC differ considerably throughout the region, there are some widespread features, including the use of the stop sounds [t] and [d] where English would have the voiceless and voiced fricatives of *th* (*tick/thick* and *dis/this*), and the "reduction" of some final consonant clusters as in *stan* 'stand'. In Barbados, Guyana and Trinidad & Tobago, a sequence resembling *ong* replaces *own* in words like *down*. Some varieties have a *y* sound following *k* and *g* sounds before some vowels, e. g., *gyaaden* 'garden' and *kyan* 'can'.

The *r* sound is very variable. It is pronounced in all positions in Barbados; in the Leewards and Trinidad & Tobago, however, *r* is not present before consonants, e. g. *hard* [ha:d], or at the end of a word, e. g., *star* [sta:], although the vowel sound is lengthened, hence leading to spellings such as *haad* 'hard'. Jamaica and Guyana have no *r* sound before consonants, but do have it at the end of a word.

The vowels of words such as *lady* and *boat* are "pure vowels" in Barbados, Guyana, Trinidad, and elsewhere, i. e. [e] and [o] as opposed to AmE diphthongs [eɪ] and [oʊ]. However, in some varieties of Jamaican and

Leewards speech, they have developed preceding glides, sounding like *lyady* and *bwoat*.

Perhaps the least understood aspects of the Caribbean "accent" for outsiders are intonation – often described as "lilting" or "singsong" – and a tendency towards syllable timing, that is, giving each syllable an equal amount of time and stress, as opposed to standard English, in which many syllables are reduced in sound and length. Differences in intonation and stress can lead to confusion and misunderstanding, virtually never identified as linguistic in origin. For example, the sentence *Take it* said in Creole with a non-falling intonation could indicate emphasis, but might be interpreted as angry by an English speaker.

Grammar. The verb systems of Creole are characterized by particles used to mark the verb, including *did* and *bin*; once a time reference is established, the tense in focus is usually unmarked, e. g. *Yesterday I call him*. Aspect, such as continuous or habitual action, is almost always marked, e. g. *me a go* or *I goin* 'I am going', *me a go* or *I does go* 'I [usually] go'. Particles, including modals, can be combined, as in *me bin da go* 'I was going/often went (a long time ago)'; *she musi eh uses to go* 'she must not have used to go'. Verbs are not marked for third person singular, e. g. *He have plenty money today*.

The verb *be* is usually included in some form in sentences such as *She is a teacher*; *be* is also expressed for place by *be* or *de*, e. g. *im de de in di yaad* 'S/he is there in the yard'. No *be* is necessary in the present tense before an adjective, e. g. *she sweet, that good*. Verbs and adjectives often behave differently than in English, e. g. *It eat nice; I did tired*.

Possession is usually indicated by juxtaposition, e. g. *mi uncle house* 'my uncle's house', or by the particle *fi* (mostly in Jamaica and Guyana) e. g. *dat a fi mi truck* 'that is my truck'. (*Fi* has a number of other functions, as in *a wan fi go* 'I want to go'.) Pronouns do not usually change case endings, e. g. Jamaican *im a look* 'she/he is looking' and Trinidadian *I eh like she* 'I don't like her.' In most places, a distinction is made between second person singular, e. g. *you*, *yuh*, and plural, e. g., *unu*, *allyuh*, *yinna*.

Plurals are usually unmarked, but may be marked with *dem* or *an-dem*, e. g. *di boy-dem*, *di boy and them*. Comparative constructions often follow the form *mi brother more big than he* 'my brother is bigger than him'. There are several widespread emphatic sentence patterns, e. g. *Is tired I tired*; *A how you coulda say dat*? 'How could you say that?'

Vocabulary. A number of African languages, particularly the Niger-Congo family – including Yoruba, Twi, and Mandingo, and the Bantu languages – have contributed to CEC vocabulary, sound system and grammar. Proximity to areas where other languages are spoken, widespread bilingualism, or the presence of speakers of other languages, have influenced the creole, particularly in vocabulary; e. g. French Creole in Dominica, St. Lucia, and Trinidad; Spanish in Trinidad; Bhojpuri-Hindi in Guyana and Trinidad. However, most CEC vocabulary is English or derived from English; in Trinidad, for example, a car has an AmE *trunk* and a BrE *bonnet*. However, thousands of words in CEC are not part of standard English, from names of plants and animals, to occupational jargons and descriptions of appearance and behavior. Words have come from many different sources in addition to English, e. g. Bhojpuri-Hindi *roti* 'a flat bread folded over a filling', *jab-jab* 'devil' from French *diable*, *susu* 'cooperative savings plan' from Yoruba *esusu* and African-English translations such as *eye-water* 'tears'.

References

Abrahams, Roger
1983 *The Man-of-words in the West Indies: Performance and the emergence of creole culture.* Baltimore, Md.: The Johns Hopkins University Press.

Allsopp, Richard
1996 *Dictionary of Caribbean English usage*. Oxford: University Press.

Basch, Linda G.
1987 "The politics of Caribbeanization: Vincentians and Grenadians in New York", in: C. R. Sutton – E. M. Chaney (eds.), 160–181.

Brathwaite, E. K.
1984 *History of the Voice*. London: New Beacon.

Bryce-Laporte, Roy Simón
1987 "New York City and the new Caribbean immigration: A contextual statement", in: C. R. Sutton – E. M. Chaney (eds.), 54–73.

Carrington, Lawrence D.
1979 "Linguistic conflict in Caribbean education". Paper presented at the International Congress of Psychology of the Child. Paris, July.
1983 "The challenge of Caribbean language in the Canadian classroom", *TESL Talk*, 14, 4: 15–28.
1988 *Creole discourse and social development*. Ottawa, Canada: International Development Research Centre.
1992 "Images of Creole space", *Journal of Pidgin and Creole Languages* 7, 1: 93–99.

Cassidy, Frederic G.
1961 *Jamaica talk: Three hundred years of the English language in Jamaica*. London: Macmillan.

Chaney, Elsa M.
1987 "The context of Caribbean migration", in: C. R. Sutton – E. M. Chaney (eds.), 3–14.

Coard, Bernard
1971 *How the West Indian Child is made educationally subnormal in the British school system.* London: New Beacon Books.

Coelho, Elizabeth
1988 *Caribbean students in Canadian schools, Book 1.* Toronto: Carib-Can Publishers.
1991 *Caribbean students in Canadian schools, Book 2.* Agincourt, Ontario: Pippin Publishing.

Conway, Dennis – Ualthan Bigby
1987 "Where Caribbean peoples live in New York City", in: C. R. Sutton – E. M. Chaney (eds.), 74–83.

Creole must be a factor in U. S. education system
1994 *Caribbean Life* (Brooklyn Edition), March 29.

Davis, Stephen – Peter Simon
1982 *Reggae International.* New York: Random House.

Devonish, Hubert
1986 *Language and liberation.* London: Karia Press.

Folkes, Karl
1994 Interview with Lona Jack. Bilingual Research Analyst, Division of Bilingual Education, NYC, March.

Foner, Nancy
1987 "West Indians in New York City and London: A comparative analysis", in: C. R. Sutton – E. M. Chaney (eds.), 117–130.

Glasgow, Joseph H. – Eleanor J. Adaskin
1990 "The West Indians", in: N. Waxler-Morrison – J. M. Anderson – E. Richardson (eds.), *Cross-cultural caring: A handbook for health professionals in Western Canada.* Vancouver: University of British Columbia Press, 214 – 244.

Graham, Yvonne
1994 Interview with Lona Jack. Executive Director, Caribbean Women's Health Association.

Harding, Clive
1994 Interview with Lona Jack, March. Crime Prevention Officer, 81st Precinct, Brooklyn.

Ho, Christine
1991 *Salt-Water Trinnies: Afro-Trinidadian immigrant networks and non-assimilation in Los Angeles.* New York: AMS Press.

Hodge, Merle
1970 *Crick crack, monkey.* London: André Deutsch.

Hodge, Merle
1993 *For the life of Letitia.* New York: Farrar, Straus & Giroux.

Immigration and Naturalization Service, United States
1993 *Statistical Yearbook of the Immigration and Naturalization Service*, 1992. Washington D. C.: U. S. Government Printing Office.

Irish, George
1994 Interview with Lona Jack. Director, Caribbean Research Center, Medgar Evers College-CUNY, Brooklyn.

Karp, Wendy
1994 Interview with Lona Jack. Supervisor of Funded Programs, Brooklyn High School Office, Board of Education, Brooklyn.

Kasinitz, Philip
1992 *Caribbean New York: Black immigrants and the politics of race*. Ithaca: Cornell University Press.

Kasinitz, Philip – Judith Freidenberg-Herbstein
1987 "The Puerto Rican parade and West Indian carnival: Public celebrations in New York City", in: C. R. Sutton – E. M. Chaney (eds.), 327–349.

Marshall, Paule
1987 "Black immigrant women in *Brown Girl, Brownstones*", in: C. R. Sutton – E. M. Chaney (eds.), 87–91.

Matthews, Lear
1993 "Mental health problems among Caribbean immigrants in New York: Implications for intervention with East Indians", in: Tilokie Depoo (ed.), *The East Indian diaspora: 150 years of survival, contributions and achievements*. Flushing, NY: Asian/American Center at Queens College-CUNY, 129–135.

Mirvil, Jean
1994 Interview with Lona Jack, March. Assistant Principal, P. S. 147, Cambria Heights, Queens.

Pollard, Velma
1983 "The social history of Dread Talk", in: Lawrence Carrington (ed.), *Studies in Caribbean language*. St. Augustine, Trinidad: Society for Caribbean Linguistics, 46–62.
1994 *From Jamaican Creole to Standard English: A Handbook for teachers*. Brooklyn: Caribbean Research Center, Medgar Evers College-CUNY.

Pratt-Johnson, Yvonne
1994 "The use of Jamaican Creole in the Jamaican classroom and its implications for the New York City classroom". Paper presented at the International Linguistic Association, Annual Conference on Linguistics, Borough of Manhattan Community College of the City University of New York, April 17.

Ramcharitar, Raymond
1993 "The city that offers no foreplay", *Sunday Guardian Magazine* (Trinidad & Tobago), August 22, p. 7.

Raymond, Yves
1994 Interview with Lona Jack, March. Assistant Principal, Bilingual Studies, Erasmus Hall High School, Brooklyn.

Samuels, Jasmine
1994 Interview with Lona Jack. GED Counselor, Lehman College, Brooklyn.

Sanders, Lamar
1994 Interview with Lona Jack. Adult literacy GED student, Lehman College, Brooklyn.

Sontag, Deborah
1992 "Caribbean pupils' English seems barrier, not bridge", *New York Times*, Nov. 28.

Soto, Isa María
1987 "West Indian child fostering: Its role in migrant exchanges", in: C. R. Sutton – E. M. Chaney (eds.), 131–149.

State Education Department, The University of the State of New York
1994 Memorandum in support of "An Act to amend the Education Law, in relation to aid for educational services for immigrant students from English-speaking nations and territories of the Caribbean and Western Atlantic Region and making an appropriation therefor." EMS 7(A), April.

Sutton, Constance R.
1987 "The Caribbeanization of New York City and the emergence of a transnational socio-cultural system", in: C. R. Sutton – E. M. Chaney (eds.), 15–30.

Sutton, Constance R. – Elsa M. Chaney (eds.)
1987 *Caribbean life in New York City: Sociocultural dimensions*. Staten Island, New York: Center for Migration Studies of New York.

Winer, Lise
1993 "Teaching speakers of Caribbean English Creoles in North American classrooms", in: A. Wayne Glowka – Donald M. Lance (eds.), *Language variation in North American English: Research and teaching*. New York: The Modern Language Association of America, 191–198.

Winford, Donald
1988 "The creole continuum and the notion of the community as locus of language", *International Journal of the Sociology of Language* 71: 91–105.

Yawching, Donna
1990 "Sweet T&T ... is my country", *Sunday Express* (Trinidad), 16 Dec 1990, 2: 9.

V CONCLUDING OBSERVATIONS TO THE MULTILINGUAL APPLE

Do ethnics have culture? And what's so special about New York anyway?

Joshua A. Fishman

1. What DO we (and what DON'T we) know about ethnolinguistic minorities in New York City?

One of the "things" that common wisdom "knows" about New York City is that it is full of "ethnics" who are simultaneously poor, mainstream-discrepant, contentious and, sometimes (which is both good and bad), aspiring. A visiting missionary in 1643, who may well have been among Manhattan's earliest lay observers, reported that the city's 500 settlers spoke 18 languages (Tierney 1994), a sign of an incredible diversity which never seems to have disappeared. However, that same early observer did not claim – as do many more modern ones – that this diversity was associated with poverty, contentiousness, distance from the mainstream or unpredictable and not entirely welcome mobility strivings. On the other hand, more modern observers, lay or professional, seem to overlook the linguistic dimension of New York City rather completely, except, of course, for the few sociolinguists who have done fieldwork in New York. Thus Gans, in his justly famous study of an Italo-American neighborhood on the West-Side of New York (1962 [1982]), quite predictably said next to nothing about the linguistic component of being Italo-American in New York City (and neither "language", "mother tongue" nor "linguistic" appear in the index). The little he did say, in passing, about this component indicated that he believed Italian to be vestigial as early as in the first generation of immigrants and doubly so thereafter. If this was so in the 1960's, when the ethnic revival in the USA was already getting underway, how much more invisible must non-English languages appear to be to mainstream academics now, when a new exclusionary stage in American economic and immigration policy appears to be in the offing?

All of the above calls to mind the cautionary observation of an established scholar in the field of urban ethnicity in the United States, namely, that "ethnocentrism in place or time of observation haunts our [sociological] theory, and thinking about ethnicity seems a serious case of this habit" (Scott Greer's preface to Maldonado – Moore 1985). Such ethnocentrism manifests itself on many fronts. Scholars, having themselves "arrived" at mainstream temples of knowledge and having often re-identified themselves ethnoculturally in the process, share the common misperception that ethnicity is wholly a sidestream phenomenon (see, e. g. Cohen 1974 and the explicit rejection of this view by Hannerz 1974) and that the mainstream itself is, by definition, non-ethnic, i. e. universalistic rather than parochial (see Zukin 1995, for a welcomed exception). Because ethnicity is, from this perspective, marginal to core-society, it is also viewed as ephemeral (rather than as an evolving manifestation of a potentially long-term cultural [co-]identity). Accordingly, ethnicity is simply considered as something that is merely exploited (politically, economically, and, above all, conflictually), rather than as something "formally institutionalized" (Cohen 1974), or something that might be valued in itself and lived as an expression of daily life in its various pursuits. Although all social researchers do not necessarily share the Marxist view that ethnicity, like other societal phenomena, is best recognized only in conflict and competition (Southall 1985), its widely assumed tie to contentiousness, to peripherality and to poverty means that ethnicity is recurringly viewed as one of many non-constructive behaviors of underdogs (Cohen 1969, 1974), i. e., in the context of (or as contributory to) social disorganization. Those ethnic individuals and networks who succeed in breaking out of poverty, marginality and social dislocation, inevitably join the mainstream and leave their ethnicity behind (Glazer 1975). This entire stance represents the continuation of a very ancient pejorative and invidious moralistic distinction in which ethnicity is viewed as the more negative pole of cultural belongingness and cultural behavior (Fishman 1985).

The foregoing "monocular" characterizations of ethnicity also leads to unrealistically clear and rigid boundary distinctions between that which is ethnic and that which is non-ethnic, not only as between different individuals but even as within the same individuals at different times, thereby failing to recognize the truly subtle situationality, contextuality and fluidity of post-modern life (Waltzer 1994). New York itself is the perfect example of the fact that we are ethnics and strangers all of us, some of us more often, some less; some in more rounds of life, some in fewer. Where more than in New York can one so truly say, "we have met the ethnics and they are us"? If ethnic is side stream, then what exactly is left of daily life in a city in which expressions of ethnicity are encountered in virtually every food-market, at every newspaper kiosk, in every videostore, in every subway ride, at every house of worship? Where else in the

USA can one be an ethnic in so public, laid back and natural a fashion? It has been remarked that "to be young may not mean the same in Detroit as in San Francisco, to be a woman, not the same in Sao Paulo as in Rio de Janeiro" (Hannerz 1980). To be an ethnic (in the popular non-WASP sense of the word) is definitely not the same thing in New York as in Raleigh, or anywhere else in the USA, for that matter.

Unfortunately, much of American thinking about ethnicity derives from pre-sixties realities. That itself does not invalidate such thinking – indeed, much of it is still informative, as our discussion here will repeatedly reveal – but it does make it even more likely that newer realities will be interpreted away or be essentially overlooked, rather than brought into full view. Newer (post-sixties) immigrants to the USA are significantly less often white, less frequently European or Christian, and, therefore, also far less acceptable to mainstream fraternity on the former bases of propinquity, familiarity and upward mobility than were their immigrant predecessors. Furthermore, the U. S. economy as a whole, and the New York economy in particular, is far different now and the kinds of contributions that immigrants can commonly make to it are, correspondingly, quite different from those that were mythologized and anthologized during the period of the United States most intensive industrialization, unionization and growing governmental interposition between, and regulation of both, capital and labor. Immigration as a whole is less desirable now – when manufacturing is being relocated in areas around the globe where labor is less expensive and where raw materials are often present *in situ* – than it was then. The result is that newcomers to the cities must compete either for the lowest service (including civil service) positions, or for the highest academic, programming, financing, law, multinational commerce and arts-media-publishing positions. In either case, they are tied into global and extra-regional market developments, i. e., into developments that make urban life everywhere different than it used to be in the era before high-tech and cyberspace came into prominence both in the worksphere and in the economy as a whole. Under such circumstances, it is manifestly impossible to understand significant aspects of the cultural identities and of the functions of non-Anglo culture in the lives of Hispanics or Orientals, Blacks or Hasidim, Arabs or Pacific Islanders in our cities. Popular and social science notions of assimilation and social mobility, of reethnification and relinguification, that were developed and admired during the period of mass European immigration to the USA, either before the First World War or soon after the Second, are of even lesser validity than they used to be. And, if all of the foregoing is true with respect to language in ethnicity and urban life in general, it is all the more true vis-à-vis language in ethnicity and New York City life in particular. For nowhere else in urban America is multivaried and multilingual ethnicity as much at home as it is in New York. This is so whether we examine the New York of the poor or the New York of the rich or the interactive post-industrial city where the two meet (Mollenkopf – Castells 1991), often on a daily basis.

It is saddening to note that what is widely "known" about New York is only what makes it appear to be a veritable Rome-Carthage-Babylon of the 20th century, a huge public arena and an epitome of *Gesselschaft*, a den of strangers if not of thieves, in which only the hardiest of gladiators can survive and even they must bid farewell to intimacy and affection, to kinship and to neighborliness, in order to stay alive. The suspected impoverishment of life in New York City has led to (or has derived from) a similar impoverishment in fresh thinking about what life there is really like. At best, we think about it as if it were a city like any other American city, "only more so". We marvel at its size, its morphology in terms of commercial, financial, entertainment and residential districts, its social complexity. Kingsley Davis has taught us well (Davis 1965, Eames – Granish Goode 1977); indeed, too well. We see it quickly and only as a vortex of modernization and urbanization. But there are many more things about New York City that this undifferentiated and outdated perspective fails to reveal and ever so many questions that it does not prompt us to ask. Many of these perspectives and questions pertain to language and ethnicity in New York City, i. e., to the very focus to which this volume is dedicated.

2. *On race, religion, ethnicity and language, in New York City and in American urban life more generally*

Ever since my *Language Loyalty in the United States* (1966) it has been clear to me that, insofar as language maintenance was concerned, one could posit an implicational scale. Those groups whose languages were also accompanied by racial differences vis-à-vis the White American mainstream maintained their non-English mother tongues for more generations than did those whose languages were accompanied only by religious distance from the Protestant mainstream. Ethnic difference alone was the weakest guarantor of intergenerational mother-tongue maintenance. Of course, social mobility was, and is, a powerful moderator of the above three factors, but even social mobility has tended to be most delayed by race, on the whole, and least delayed by ethnicity. However, provocative though the above implicational scale may be, it still leaves unexplained the fragility and ephemerality of language, relative to most other markers of sociocultural group-membership. Race (wherever differences considered to be "racial" are recognized by the mainstream – as they very definitely are in New York), religion, ethnicity and language are, generally speaking, co-occurrences. They are clustered together experientially, whether viewed by insiders or by outsiders. This co-occurrence, this total "ball of wax", when taken together is commonly referred to as "culture". However, when the ball of wax begins to unravel, as it does for minorities that are dislocated by overpowering disadvantages (not to mention overt discrimination) vis-à-vis stronger competitors who demand accommodation as the price of even partial acceptance, it is recurringly language that unwinds fastest and is recouped, if at all, last. One cannot read Gans' revised edition and not ask oneself, why Italian foods have not only hung on into the second generation (and even into the still more commonly intermarried subsequent ones) –indeed, why Italian foods have impacted the mainstream (as have Jewish, Chinese, Hispanic and other ethnic foods) – whereas ethnic languages have classically evaporated a scarce generation after the cessation of immigration (Douglas 1984).

This is not the place to speculate at length about the successes of ethnic foods. Others have done so already (Robinson 1980, e. g.) and they are mentioned here only in order to sharpen our focus on language. When the "ball of wax" begins to unravel under the joint impact of dislocation and aspiration, language is often the first to go. Why a second language may become a necessity for disadvantaged minorities is rather obvious, but why a diglossic defense and protection of the first (traditionally associated "own") language is so difficult to arrive at is less obvious and, frankly, often unrecognized. Ethnicity is apparently easier to compartmentalize ("more or less") in the interactive city and the byproduct of such compartmentalization is biculturism. America's urban minorities are quite commonly bicultural and their ethnicity is, rather than fleeting, both intergenerational and situational, i. e., defined by time (occasion), place and "interactioners" (i. e., differentially, depending on whom they are interacting with). Religion is also easier to compartmentalize ("more or less"). It has its own very definite times, places and interactioners and it too is commonly intergenerationally transmitted, at least for several generations, even by relatively small groups on the American urban landscape. But language has long seemed to be hardest of all to hang on to in the interactive, multicultural American city. It is as if it were implicationally last, i. e., that it required the largest number of prior compartmentalizing social arrangements within any overarching interactive framework, without itself being a prerequisite for any of them.

Obviously, language compartmentalizes human aggregates that do *not* share a *lingua franca*, but once a *lingua franca is* widely utilized, then other kinds of compartmentalization are apparently quite a bit more enduring than the linguistic one. Nearly a third of a century ago, Glazer and Moynihan argued convincingly that "ethnicity is at the basis of extensive role summations, so that economic, political and religious alignments overlap with it" (1963: 18). Note, however, that ethnicity functions in the above inter-group and intergenerational arenas only if a *lingua franca* with the mainstream has become operational. The "own-ethnic" language, on the other hand, is an *intra-group medium* and, in an interactive context marked by considerable social mobility expectations, it is apparently easily dislodged by an intergroup medium, particularly by one that long leaves the greater compartmentalization of ethnicity and religion substantially unchallenged. This was already a problem for Dutch and for French speakers in the interactive New York of the late premelting pot colonial period (Goodfriend 1991).

All of which merely brings us to ask whether the intergenerational fate of non-English languages will be different in a deteriorating New York City with much diminished social-mobility possibilities? When the mainstream is less rewarding, will it be accorded less interactional deference? It is sometimes facetiously said that the personal computer has killed the American lower middle class. If this is true anywhere, it is true in New York City. And when the bifurcation in social-mobility that this remark alludes to is also associated with perceived racial-and-religious distance from the mainstream – as is the case for most Hispanics, Caribbean Blacks, Orientals, South and South East Asians and Pacific Islanders in New York City – do the intergroup rewards of English become even more minimized for those who are doubly distanced in this fashion? And, for the Euroethnics, new and old, what does a New York without rapid social mobility now mean for them? If it leads them to more easily and more frequently remembering the New York City of their grandfathers, will that rebirth of memory bring with it linguistic consequences as well? As (great-) grandfather-tongue courses, "circles" and "nooks" proliferate, what changes in functional language use will be noted among grandchildren and great-grandchildren? And if it is too late for more than "linguistic amateurism" among those Euroethnics who have roots in New York that are a century or more old, will they at least arrive at an intellectual and emotional appreciation of the great attainments in the realms of linguistically specific literatures, journalisms, school networks, choruses and theaters, not to mention the equally language suffused realms of political activity, union mobilization and social and cultural welfare pioneering, that their (great-) grandfathers created and supported as expressions of their visions of not only what New York City *meant* to them but of what *they had to bequest* to their own and subsequent generations within it? Will the post-sixties ethnics in New York City – with access to public multicultural funding (meager though it be, but historically unprecedented nevertheless) for their own museums, theaters and other cultural efforts and interests (such as "ethnic studies" in tertiary level institutions) – learn from earlier immigration waves that the time to begin reinforcing integenerational mother tongue continuity and mother tongue recognition is when the mother tongue is still vibrant, not when it has to be revived? Are such dreams more easily realized – rather than just more easily dreamt of – in New York City, precisely because of its multi- and omni-ethnic nature, precisely because of the real historical depth that many groups can find within it, precisely because of the endless renewals of worldwide ethnic immigration into it and precisely because of its very changed economic base? Our chapters may prompt such questions more than they answer them, but raising questions that have long been overlooked or suppressed is an indispensable first step toward searching for answers and achieving catharsis.

3. *Language in the Big Apple, or the overlooked elephant at the zoo*

The foregoing chapters underscore how erroneous it is to equate urbanization and the breakdown of culture, if not of all of human society, as even such giants as Robert Redfield (1956) and Louis Wirth (1964) unfortunately assumed in their classic studies of immigrants and rural migrants. Rather, a mix of continuity, adaptation and adoption seem to characterize the lion's share of the urban experience (Friedl – Chrisman 1975). The stress on urban dislocation posits an underlying romantic or pastoral view of a perfect past and a demonization of the present. Neither of these perspectives comes close at all to the reality of New York City life. Our chapters reveal a New York City that is not a welter of forlorn slums and battling ghettos but, rather, congeries of urban villages that have retained a substantial amount of traditional culture and have integrated it with an equal or even greater dose of *in situ* innovation and culture contact. (Where else would Hispanics acquire knowledge of Orthodox Jewish customs, or, for that matter, where else would Jews ask Irish neighbors why Good Friday is considered "good"?) Our chapters remind us that the ethnic revival was (like all ethnic revivals are) an urban phenomenon. Yes, traditionalization (more correctly: re-traditionalization) and the reinvention of *Gemeinschaft* are urban phenomena, but neither of them are true returns to the past but, rather, the byproducts or interactions of both continuity and culture change. "Folk" vs. "urban" and "orthogenic" vs. "heterogenic" (Redfield – Singer 1954) are dichotomous concepts that lend themselves to exaggeration. The continuum that lies between these poles better reflects real life because it represents its real variability.

Ethnic life in New York City continues to include thousands upon thousands of voluntary associations for self-help and for socializing, for religion and for child-care, for adult education and edification as well as for childhood indoctrination, socialization and enculturation, for entertainment and for cultural creativity, and all of the above involve places, times and interlocutors in which and with whom the "own language" is used, heard, understood and valued ("more or less"). The same is true for the ethnic food stores, record shops and sports teams, street fairs and celebrations, media broadcasts (including frequent rebroadcasts from "the old country") and film shows. All of these go on, notwithstanding neighborhood change and occupational change and exposure to as well as participation in the life of the "other New York City", the New York City that goes on outside of the "own ethnic" community per se. The co-occurrence of both of these "New York Cities" within the life-spaces of most New Yorkers results in a broadening of ethnic identity as well as in an enrichment of total culture. However, just as the gargantuan *perpetuum-mobile* and inevitably heightened friction of a megalopolis strengthens the need for and the benefits from ethnic islands within it, so these islands in turn render their members "better able to cope with the wider society" (Little 1965). It is the two processes together that overcome any tendencies toward disorganization and breakdown in New York City life. The use of non-English languages in New York City today, probably at a level not previously attained since the early thirties, helps the city itself function as such, whether in the realm of health care or of business, of government operations or of private enterprise. Just as non-mainstream ethnicity has changed and enriched New York City, making it what it is today, so the New York's non-English languages have simultaneously changed, enriched and preserved the "Big Apple". And what is more, the areas in the world from which its newcomers are increasingly attracted are such as to guarantee that New York City will be even more multilingual in the future than it is now or than it has been for many, many years. The Pakistani businessman who resettles in New York City arrives already knowing English, but he and his family may also keep their non-English mother tongue much longer than did Euroethnics arriving without any English at all in the mid-twenties.

4. Peering into the future: Can less and less become more and more?

If one compares 1956 with 1996 one cannot but recognize that a sea-change has occurred with respect to the language-and-ethnicity *Zeitgeist* in the USA. The country has not been re-ethnicized, of course, but it may be well along a path headed roughly in that direction and the elections of 1994 and 1996 may be viewed as revolts of the predominantly White middle class also against the manifold ethnocultural changes that has engulfed it. However, the flow of immigrants from non-European countries of origin cannot really be stopped or even controlled. New York City in particular is in for more and more immigrants and they may well be less and less welcome, not only or so much for where they are from, but also because of the increasingly problematic economic nature of New York City itself. Above and beyond economics, however, is the sense of legitimacy that non-Anglo ethnicity has attained, not only among the Blacks and the Hispanics and the Orthodox Jews but even among the relatively small White Protestant enclaves that New York still possesses. Being ethnic – and talking ethnic – is not only chic in New York City but it is natural and comfortable, precisely because it expresses and creates a sense of belonging to New York (Yancey et al. 1976).

When Gans revised his 1962 classic in 1982, the particular Italo-American neighborhood that he had studied was literally no longer there, but several other old ones were still in operation (e. g., in the North-East Bronx, surrounding the Orthodox Jewish affiliated Albert Einstein College of Medicine) and several new Italian neighborhoods had come into being. Originally an uncompromising champion of the so-called "straight line theory" which predicted the continued diminution and final disappearance of non-mainstream ethnicity in American life (as was also Glazer and, indeed, as were most other major American sociologists), Gans significantly soft-pedaled that view by 1982. He noted the rise of "symbolic ethnicity", a somewhat frivolous involvement in ethnic events and organizations without interrupting one's mainstream affiliations, but acknowledged that (as a result) it was taking longer than he had expected for side-stream ethnicity to die out. "It is possible to find 6th, 7th or 8th generation descendants of the Germans, Scandinavians and Hollanders who arrived in the first half of the 19th century [and] who still retain an ethnic identity" (Gans 1982: 237). As if that were not enough of a departure from prior predictions derived from "straight line theory", Gans finally conceded that intergroup and economic developments could still prompt "symbolic ethnicity" to "give way suddenly to a genuine ethnic revival"(p. 237). A theory with so much elasticity as to be able to cover all bases simultaneously (decrease, continuity and increase) may or may not be scientifically admirable (after all, even sociological theories should be capable of discomfirmation). Others too have had to modify their "three generations and out" views. Steinberg (1981), e. g., has suggested that the fourth generation was critical insofar as the future of ethnicity is concerned. But even four generations is close to a century and neither of the foregoing authors was thinking specifically about New York City. In New York City we are even further away, indeed, much further away, from the last of the Mohicans than we are elsewhere in the USA.

Some thirty years ago my sociolinguistic research led me to conclude that we often confused the continuity of identity with the continuity of culture (Nahirny – Fishman 1965). Identity is perspectival and, accordingly, can be experienced as continuous even while the underlying ethnic practices (customs, rituals and observations) undergo remarkable changes. In neither case are these "useless ascriptive barriers for the new urban man [and woman], but... important channels through which the new urban resident finds his [and her] place within the city" (Fox 1977). Language is crucial both to ethnic identity and to ethnic culture. The actual use of the perspectively "own-ethnic language" may vary considerably over and within generations, but it is always there ("more or less"), both as a sign and as a symbol, as a component of patrimony. Whenever I note the Chinese and Spanish options on my neighborhood bank's ATM machine, I think how lucky I am to be living in a once Jewish, but now vibrantly Irish, neighborhood of a city that enables and encourages all of its citizens to opt for their own ethnic identities if and whenever they are of a mind to do so. In such a city, the link to language is latent for some, halting for others and blatant for yet others, but it is always there. A post-structural sociology of urban life, one that more fully recognizes the importance of diverse human motives, goals, efforts and interests, including among them the reluctance to being submerged in the nondescript mainstream (Flanagan 1993, Yinger 1994 [the latter, alone among major American sociologists, even entertains the possibility of stable bilingualism in America's urban future]), is now beginning to emerge. Perhaps such a post-structural sociology of America's cities, and of New York in particular, will not trivialize the very linkages and options which cities in general, and New York in particular, invigorate.

But something more than conceptual clarification and empirical documentation are called for on the part of a volume such as this. What, after all, is the difference between the moral claim that Black disadvantage makes vis-à-vis the White mainstream and the moral claim that ethnocultural disadvantage makes vis-à-vis public attention and appreciation? The difference is a substantial one, because the Black plight is (or was, prior to recent attacks on "affirmative action") recognized as being at least substantially of White making, and, therefore, morally requiring and justifying White restitution. The handicap faced by ethnocultural disadvantage, even in New York City, is that it is considered private, if not exactly parochial. It is not yet recognized as making a valid moral claim on public life or as pertaining to a sphere that makes a positive and constructive contribution to the public weal via the family, neighborhood and institutional avenues of expression and social organization on which it depends and to which it contributes. In New York City and in the USA as a whole, but above all in New York City, it is high time that the ethnocultural and ethnolinguistic fabric of human life were publicly recognized. Then the answer to the first question posed in the title to these comments will be a loud and clear affirmative. And such an affirmative answer, followed up by concrete expressions of regard and recognition, will also provide the only suitable answer to the second question which our title poses. It will be yet another sign that New York City is not only special, but that it is ethnoculturally and ethnolinguistically special in a very positive, constructive and concrete way as well. May this volume help to foster such a sign.

References

Cohen, Abner
1969 *Customs and politics in urban Africa*. London: Routledge and Kegan Paul.

Cohen, Abner (ed.)
1974 "Introduction: The lesson of ethnicity", in his *Urban Ethnicity*. London: Tavistock, ix–xxiii.

Davis, Kingsley
1965 "The urbanization of the human population", *Scientific American* XX: 41–53.

Douglas, Mary (ed.)
1984 *Food in the social order.* New York: Russell Sage.
Eames, Edwin – Judith Granish Goode
1977 "What is urban anthropology?", in: their *Anthropology of the city: An introduction to urban anthropology.* Englewood Cliffs: Prentice Hall.
Fishman, Joshua A.
1966 *Language loyalty in the United States.* The Hague: Mouton.
1985 "*Am* and *goy* as designations for ethnicity in selected books of the Old Testament", in his *The Rise and fall of the ethnic revival: Perspectives on language and ethnicity.* Berlin: Mouton de Gruyter, 15–38.
Flanagan, William G.
1993 *Contemporary urban sociology.* Cambridge: Cambridge University Press.
Fox, Richard G.
1977 *Urban Anthropology: Cities in their cultural settings.* Englewood Cliffs: Prentice-Hall.
Friedl, John – Noel J. Chrisman
1975 "Continuity and adaptation as themes in urban anthropology," in: Friedl, John – Noel J. Chrisman (eds.), 4–23.
Friedl, John – Noel J. Chrisman (eds.)
1975 *City Ways: A selective reader in urban anthropology.* New York: Crowell.
Gans, Herbert J.
1962 *The Urban villagers: Group and class in the life of Italian-Americans.* New York: Free Press.
[1982] [Updated and expanded edition]
Glazer, Nathan – Moynihan, Daniel Patrick
1963 *Beyond the melting pot.* Cambridge: MIT Press.
Glazer, Nathan
1975 "The culture of poverty: The view from New York City", in: John Friedl and Noel J. Chrisman (eds.), 402–415.
Goodfriend, Joyce D.
1991 *Before the melting pot: Society and culture in colonial New York City, 1664 - 1730.* Princeton: Princeton University Press.
Greer, Scott
1985 "Prefatory note", in: Lionel Maldonado – Joan Moore (eds.).
Hannerz, Ulf
1974 "Ethnicity and opportunity in America", in: Abner Cohen (ed.), 37–76.
1980 *Exploring the city: Inquiries toward an urban anthropology.* New York: Columbia University Press.
Little, Kenneth
1965 *West African urbanization: A study of voluntary associations in social change.* New York: Cambridge University Press.
Maldonado, Lionel – Joan Moore (eds.)
1985 *Urban ethnicity in the United States: New immigrants and old minorities.* Beverly Hills: Sage.
Mollenkopf, John Hull – Manuel Castells (eds.)
1991 *Dual City: Restructuring New York.* New York, Russell Sage.
Nahirny, Vladimir – Joshua A. Fishman
1965 "American immigrant groups: ethnic identification and the problem of generations", *Sociological Review* 13: 311–326.

Redfield, Robert
1956 *Peasant society and culture.* Chicago: University of Chicago Press.

Redfield, Robert – Milton B. Singer
1954 "The cultural role of cities", *Economic development and cultural change* 3: 53–73.

Robinson, John (ed.)
1980 *Food, ecology and culture: Readings in the anthropology of dietary practices.* New York: Gordon and Breach.

Southall, Aidan
1985 "Introduction", in: Aidan Southall – Peter J. M. Nas – Ghaus Ansari (eds.) *City and Society.* Leiden: Institute of Cultural and Social Sciences, 3–28.

Steinberg, Stephen
1981 *The Ethnic myth: Race, ethnicity and class in America.* New York: Atheneum.

Tierney, John
1994 "What's New York the capital of now?" *New York Times Magazine.* November 20, 1994, 47–53, 96, 109–110 and 112.

Waltzer, Michael
1994 "The politics of difference: statehood and toleration in a multi-cultural world", in: Fons Strijbosch – Paul van Tongeren, eds. *Grensverkenningen: Over Groepsvorming, Minderheden en Tolerantie.* Nijmegen: Catholic University of Nijmegen Press, 151–160.

Wirth, Louis
1964 *On Cities and social life.* Chicago: University of Chicago Press.

Yancey, W. – E. Eriksen – R. Juliani
1976 "Emergent ethnicity: A review and reformulation", *American Sociological Review* 41: 391–403.

Yinger, J. Milton
1994 *Ethnicity: Source of strength ? Source of conflict?* Albany: State University of New York Press.

Zukin, Sharon
1995 *The Culture of cities.* Cambridge, Ma.: Blackwell.

Contributors

John Costello
New York University
Department of Linguistics

Chrysie Costantakos
Brooklyn College, CUNY
Department of Health,
Nutrition and Services, Emeritus

Joshua A. Fishman
Yeshiva University, Emeritus
Ferkauf Graduate School of
Psychology and
Stanford University
Linguistics and Language
School of Education

Ofelia García
City College of New York, CUNY
School of Education

Hermann Haller
Queens College, CUNY
Romance Languages

Lona Jack
Adult Learning Center
Institute for Literacy Studies
Lehman College, CUNY

Carole M. Berotte Joseph
City College of New York, CUNY
School of Education

Hannah Kliger
University of Massachusetts at
Amherst
Department of Communication
Studies

Kenneth Nilsen
St. Francis Xaver University
Gaelic Studies
Antigonish, Nova Scotia

Shi Wen Pan
Hong Kong Institute of
Education

Rakhmiel Peltz
Columbia University
Yiddish Program
Department of Germanic
Languages

Alvin Schiff
Yeshiva University
Azraili Graduate Institute

John Spiridakis
St. John's University
Department of Human Services

Kamal K. Sridhar
SUNY Stonybrook
Department of Linguistics

Lise Winer
Southern Illinois University at
Carbondale
Department of Linguistics

Ana Celia Zentella
Hunter College, CUNY
Department of Black and
Puerto Rican Studies

Index